An Introduction to African Politics

The fourth edition of *An Introduction to African Politics* is an ideal textbook for those new to the study of this fascinating continent. It gets to the heart of the politics of this part of the world. How is modern Africa still influenced by its colonial past? How do strong ethnic and religious identities on the continent affect government? Why has the military been so influential? How does African democracy differ from democracy in the West? These are the sorts of question tackled by the book. The result is a textbook that identifies the essential features of African politics, allowing students to grasp the recurring political patterns that have dominated this continent since independence.

Key features include:

- Thematically organised, with individual chapters exploring issues such as colonialism, ethnicity, nationalism, religion, social class, ideology, legitimacy, authority, sovereignty and democracy.
- Identifies key recurrent themes such as the competitive relationships between the African state, its civil society and external interests.
- Contains useful boxed case studies at the end of each chapter, including: Kenya, Tanzania, Nigeria, Botswana, Côte d'Ivoire, Uganda, Somalia, Ghana, Democratic Republic of the Congo and Zimbabwe.
- Each chapter concludes with key terms and definitions, as well as questions and advice on further reading.

This textbook is essential reading for students seeking an accessible introduction to the complex social relationships and events that characterise the politics of post-colonial Africa.

Alex Thomson is a Principal Lecturer of Politics at Coventry University in the United Kingdom. He has taught and published in the area of African politics for over twenty years.

An Introduction to African Politics

Fourth edition

Alex Thomson

Routledge
Taylor & Francis Group

LONDON AND NEW YORK

Fourth edition published 2016
by Routledge
2 Park Square, Milton Park, Abingdon, Oxon OX14 4RN

and by Routledge
711 Third Avenue, New York, NY 10017

Routledge is an imprint of the Taylor & Francis Group, an informa business

First edition published by Routledge 2000
Third edition published by Routledge 2010

British Library Cataloguing in Publication Data
A catalogue record for this book is available from the British Library

Library of Congress Cataloging in Publication Data

Names: Thomson, Alex, 1966- author.
Title: An introduction to African politics / Alex Thomson.
Description: Fourth edition.
New York : Routledge, 2016.
Includes bibliographical references and index.
Identifiers: LCCN 2015039192
ISBN 9781138782839 (hardback)
ISBN 9781138782846 (pbk.)
ISBN 9781315767420 (ebook)
Subjects: LCSH: Africa–Politics and government.
Classification: LCC DT31 .T5157 2016
DDC 320.96–dc23
LC record available at http://lccn.loc.gov/2015039192

ISBN: 978-1-138-78283-9 (hbk)
ISBN: 978-1-138-78284-6 (pbk)
ISBN: 978-1-315-76742-0 (ebk)

Typeset in Garamond
by Cenveo Publisher Services

MIX
Paper from
responsible sources
FSC
www.fsc.org   FSC® C013056

Printed and bound in Great Britain by
TJ International Ltd, Padstow, Cornwall

Contents

List of tables vii
List of maps viii
List of plates ix

1 Introduction: state, civil society and external interests 1

2 History: Africa's pre-colonial and colonial inheritance 7

Case study: Kenya's historical inheritance 22

3 Ideology: nationalism, socialism, populism and state capitalism 31

Case study: socialism and ujamaa in Tanzania 49

4 Ethnicity and religion: 'tribes', gods and political identity 59

Case study: ethnicity, religion and the nation-state in Nigeria 74

5 Social class: the search for class politics in Africa 84

Case study: social class in Botswana 100

6 Legitimacy: neo-patrimonialism, personal rule and the centralisation of the African state 108

Case study: personal rule in Côte d'Ivoire 122

7 Coercion: military intervention in African politics 130

Case study: Uganda's 1971 military coup 143

8 Sovereignty I: external influences on African politics 151

Case study: Somalia's international relations 173

9 Sovereignty II: neo-colonialism, structural adjustment and
   Africa's political economy   183

   Case study: Ghana's structural adjustment 203

10 Authority: the crises of accumulation, governance and state collapse 213

   Case study: Zaire – Mobutu's vampire state 229

11 Democracy: re-legitimising the African state?   240

   Case study: Zimbabwe's fall from democratic grace 259

12 Conclusions: the changing relationship between state, civil society
   and external interests in the post-colonial era   272

   Index   285

Tables

2.1	Chapter summary: potential problems created by the colonial inheritance	20
3.1	Decolonisation in Africa	33
3.2	Chapter summary: Africa's nationalist ideologies	44
4.1	Chapter summary: ethnicity and religion in African politics	72
5.1	Chapter summary: African social groups	97
6.1	Chapter summary: characteristics of a centralised state, personal rule and clientelism	120
7.1	African military coups since independence	132
7.2	Chapter summary: a typology of military coups	142
8.1	Chapter summary: characteristics of Africa's external relations since independence	171
9.1	Per-capita gross domestic product (US dollars), 1960–2013	184
9.2	African export concentration, 1982–86	187
9.3	Index of international trade, 1960–2000	188
9.4	Debt service payments of African HIPC countries, 2001–14	197
9.5	Chapter summary: Africa's recent political economy	201
10.1	Chapter summary: the crisis of political authority in Africa	228
11.1	Comparative African political systems, 1988 and 1999	241
11.2	Chapter summary: obstacles to democratic consolidation in Africa	257
11.3	Results of House of Assembly elections, Zimbabwe, 1980–2008	260
12.1	African economic indicators, 2000–13	276
12.2	African social indicators, 1990 and 2012	277
12.3	Freedom House's categorisation of political rights and civil liberties in sub-Saharan Africa, 1989–2015	282

Maps

Africa today   x
2.1   Selected pre-colonial African states   9
2.2   Africa at the outbreak of the First World War   12

Plates

2.1 Two colonists examine the rubber collected by the workers on a plantation in French Equatorial Africa   17

2.2 President Jomo Kenyatta of Kenya celebrating his country's independence, 1963   26

3.1 The British royal standard is lowered, and the flag of Ghana raised, during Ghana's independence ceremony, Accra, 3 June 1957   35

3.2 MPLA leader, Agostino Neto, addresses a political rally in Luanda, Angola, 1975   40

3.3 Portrait of Julius K. Nyerere, president of Tanzania and leading African socialist thinker, 1979   50

4.1 More than one million Zairian Christians gather for Pope John Paul II's mass at the Palace of the People, Kinshasa, Zaire, 5 April 1980   67

4.2 Muslims praying, Al-Ubayyid, Sudan   68

6.1 Portrait of Felix Houphouët-Boigny, president of Côte d'Ivoire and skilled manager of patronage, 1976   122

7.1 Sudanese troops relax in Khartoum following the 1969 coup that installed General Gaafar al Numeiry as president   134

7.2 President Idi Amin Dada of Uganda addressing his troops, 1978   146

8.1 Mobutu at the White House, Washington DC, meeting J.F. Kennedy, 1963   157

8.2 Mobutu at the White House, Washington DC, meeting Ronald Reagan, 1983   157

8.3 Arrest of rebel suspect during French military intervention in Kolwezi, Zaire, 1978   160

9.1 Zimbabwean school children, Mahwanke, Zimbabwe, 1994   194

10.1 Militias competing for power in Mogadishu, Somalia, 1993   223

10.2 Refugees returning to Rwanda having earlier been displaced by genocide, 1996   223

11.1 Voting in South Africa's first non-racial elections, De Aar, 1994   243

11.2 Robert Mugabe addressing journalists prior to becoming Zimbabwe's first president, 1979   261

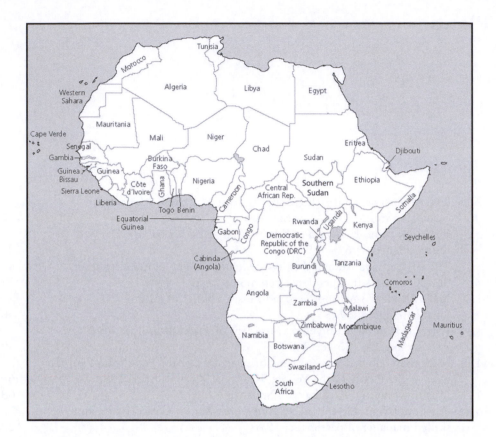

Africa today

1 Introduction

State, civil society and external interests

Chapter outline

- Why study African politics?
- The multiple political systems of Africa
- The book's thematic approach
- State, civil society and external interests
- Glossary of key terms
- Notes and references

Africa has a lot to offer the student of politics. Autocrats vie with democrats; governments espousing socialism neighbour those bound by liberal constitutions; some states are a model of stability, while others are near the point of collapse; multi-party systems jostle with one-party states; and social divisions based on ethnicity, religion, class and race all challenge political leaders in their attempts to maintain order. The politics that these realities create make Africa a stimulating and rewarding subject to study.

Why study African politics?

Yet, it could be asked, why should Westerners spend valuable time analysing the politics of Africa? Should they not concentrate on countries closer to home? Indeed, what is it precisely that this continent has to offer? Well, apart from the reward of investigating Africa's fascinating political nuances for their own sake, the continent is also invaluable for the study of comparative politics. Africa's variety of political ideas, processes and institutions provides an abundance of alternative case studies for the student of politics to investigate. After all, studying political phenomena outside familiar (Western) settings can add a new dimension of understanding. As many travellers have learnt, experiencing foreign cultures not only helps with an appreciation of the country visited, but also forces the traveller to view their own country in a different light. The method of comparative politics has a similar aim.

To benefit from what Africa has to offer, however, new scholars of this continent first need to abandon unhelpful preconceptions. Average Western views of Africa tend to be rather selective and not always accurate. The most common exposure the continent receives in the West is via broadcast journalism, and if individuals rely solely on this source, then Africa is a continent of corruption, famines, disasters and civil war. All these factors do exist on the continent from time to time, but to see such phenomena as the sum of African politics is to be profoundly misled. Media selectivity and ignorance, based on the images of Tarzan, mud huts and warring tribes, all have to be left behind before the real essence of Africa can be grasped. Newcomers to the continent should approach this part of the world with an open mind.

George Alagiah, a former Africa correspondent for the BBC, highlights this problem of perception. Assessing his stint on the continent, he was well aware of the 'bad press' that this part of the world received during his watch. Despite his efforts to inform, he conceded that Western television pictures painted Africa as 'a faraway place where good people go hungry, bad people run government, and chaos and anarchy are the norm'. He regretted that rarely do viewers get to see Africa 'in full flower'. Illustrating this point, Alagiah recounts an instance towards the end of his stint. While covering a famine in southern Sudan, he filed two reports. These were broadcast on the BBC's national news on consecutive nights. The first described the situation on the ground, and the second made a conscious effort to explain why this famine had occurred. It was the first film that had most impact. Letters from viewers reflected people's feeling of genuine sorrow 'for the poor souls of southern Sudan', but few recalled being told why this tragedy had actually happened. As Alagiah puts it, 'To get people in British living rooms to identify with the frazzled aid worker as she tries to cope with a humanitarian disaster is easy. To get people to see that the crisis is part of the convulsive process of post-colonial political realignment is more difficult'.[1]

This is precisely the problem that new students of Africa have to overcome. The difficulty is that many Westerners, when it comes to African politics, simply see cause and effect as the same thing. Why is there a civil war in the Democratic Republic of Congo? Why was there genocide in Rwanda? Why has the Somali state collapsed? All these questions are satisfactorily dealt with in people's minds by the answer 'because these countries are in Africa': these things happen 'naturally' on the continent; it is an inherently unstable region. This is the central myth that *An Introduction to African Politics* aims to counter.

Africans are innately no more violent, no more corrupt, no more greedy, and no more stupid than any other human beings who populate the planet. They are no less capable of governing themselves. Not to believe this is to revive the racism that underpinned the ethos of slavery and colonialism. In this sense, African political structures are as rational as any other systems of government. If there have been more military coups in Africa than in the United States, then there has to be a *reason* for this. An explanation also exists for why the continent's political systems are more susceptible to corruption than those of the United Kingdom. By applying reason, the worst excesses of African politics (the dictators and the civil wars) can be accounted for, as can the more common, more mundane, day-to-day features of conflict resolution on the continent. This book uncovers the genuine underlying post-colonial political processes that have been at work, and, as such, asks its readers to abandon any preconceived explanations they may harbour which involve Africans being seen as inferior, irrational, volatile or artless victims of their own political environment.

The multiple political systems of Africa

A second preliminary piece of advice that this book offers is for newcomers not to regard Africa as homogeneous. It is an extensive landmass, home to many different cultures and societies. There is no such thing as a typical African polity. There are 54 separate independent states. Each is unique, and each has its own system of politics. The Gambia is a tiny country of just 11,000 square kilometres, while Algeria's territory is 210 times larger than this; Nigeria has a population approaching 174 million, while Lesotho has just two million inhabitants; Botswana is largely an arid state, but Congo-Kinshasa is lush in vegetation; Ethiopia is racially homogeneous, while South Africa is home to several races. The north of the continent is predominantly Muslim and the south Christian, not to mention the mixture of indigenous spiritual traditions found throughout. No single political system would be capable of serving all these states, as local demands necessarily produce different and individual polities.

To cope with this diversity, there is certainly no substitute for studying every African country on its own terms. Each state deserves to be examined in as much detail as possible. A vast literature on the politics of the continent exists in an attempt to do just this. Yet apprentice Africanists often find it difficult to digest this detailed and sometimes complex body of work without investing first in some more general preparatory reading. The present book was written with this fact in mind. It is a stepping stone to the more specialised literature.

An Introduction to African Politics offers a comparative approach to the whole of Africa. The book will make a general sweep across the continent, identifying common elements within these societies. The grounding that such an approach gives with respect to the basics, the first principles, of African politics, makes up for what is lost in the detail by this broad survey. It allows newcomers to ease themselves into the politics of the continent, identifying the essentials, rather than grappling with the minute detail found in the literature addressing individual states. The book thus acts as a starting point for those interested in the politics of post-colonial Africa.

The book's thematic approach

Having established that the politics of Africa are rational and worthy of study, and that the continent is not homogeneous, it would be wise now to outline the book's methodology. As indicated earlier, the practice of politics on the African continent is not so different from political processes found elsewhere in the world. It is still about power, ideas, resource distribution and conflict resolution, as well as the governments that oversee these processes. In this sense, Africa may be a unique stage on which political transactions are carried out, but the actual processes themselves have more similarities to, than differences from, those on other continents. Note, for example, how ideology (the Soviet Union, for instance), issues of ethnicity and class (Belgium and Britain, respectively), military *coups d'état* (Portugal), state collapse (Yugoslavia), newly formed democracies (Spain) and one-party states (East Germany) have all been features within European politics during the same post-colonial period under scrutiny.

In this respect, new scholars to African politics should not be unduly daunted. The knowledge readers already have of (Western) political processes and concepts can be readily applied to the African continent.

And this, indeed, is how the book will be structured. Each chapter takes a familiar political concept, and then examines how this concept relates specifically to the African environment. Chapters tackle issues such as ideology, nationalism, social class, legitimacy, coercion, sovereignty, authority and democracy, among others. How have each of these concepts influenced the politics of post-colonial Africa? Not only does this thematic approach introduce the nature of the African polity, giving knowledge of what has actually happened since independence, but it also helps students to reinforce their understanding of these important basic political concepts.

In addition to the main discussion of the chosen concept, to avoid the book descending into a morass of theoretical assumptions and continent-wide generalisations, a short boxed case study is provided at the end of each chapter, focusing on just one state. The ideology chapter, for example, concludes with a case study on Tanzania's implementation of community socialism, while the democracy chapter focuses on Zimbabwe's struggle with multi-party politics. These ten case studies provide a practical demonstration of how abstract political concepts help to explain the reality of African politics on the ground.

State, civil society and external interests

As this book deconstructs the 'whole' of African politics chapter by chapter, dividing it into various thematic component parts and case studies, there is a need to provide some conceptual 'glue' to help the reader reconstruct all the separate parts. This glue comes in the form of a political relationship between three actors: the state, civil society and external interests. Each twist in the path of Africa's political development since independence can be traced back to a realignment of power among these three groups. As such, a commentary examining this relationship will run through all the chapters.

Given that state, civil society and external interests are to be recurring themes of the book, it is worth spending the rest of this introduction briefly discussing these terms. The state should be a familiar concept. A minimalist definition would identify *a set of political institutions that govern within a delimited sovereign territory*. A modern state, however, cannot be seen just as a geographic entity and a body of institutions. A more useful definition of the state also has to take into account the political authority that these structures generate. After all, it is the institutions and officials of the state to which citizens look for leadership and government, as well as being the sovereign body with which foreign states interact. In this respect, the state has immense power. Max Weber, in his definition of the state, pointed to the fact that deference of citizens is generated by the reality that the state claims a monopoly of legal violence within a territory.[2] Given that the state is the only authority able to establish and upkeep a society's laws, it starts from a position of strength, and clearly has a commanding influence over a territory's political development.

This is not to say that all politics happens as 'high politics' within the state. Conflict resolution is not confined to competition within parliaments, presidential palaces and bureaucracies. Political (and, indeed, economic and social) exchange can be found throughout society, at a 'deeper' level than that of the state. This is why the idea of *civil society* is so important to explaining African politics.

In the context of this book, civil society can be defined as *the organisations that arise out of voluntary association within society, found between the extended family and the state*. Examples of these include professional organisations, labour unions, trade associations, women's groups, church assemblies, businesses, special interest campaigns, community groups, and so on, right down to sports and social clubs. In this respect, any group organised beyond the family, but not part of the state apparatus, can be defined as part of civil society.

Political activity within civil society is diverse. Groups representing numerous different interests are, naturally enough, not united in their demands. Politics within civil society is competitive, just as it is in the 'high politics' of the state. These different interests also influence how civic associations relate to the state. Some groups will co-operate with the government; others will voice their opposition. In any case, each group will attempt to influence state decision making, with varying results. If, however, a large gap develops between the interests of civil society and the state, with the state unresponsive to civil society demands, this may lead to citizens actually challenging the authority of the state.

The third party within this competitive relationship is that of 'external interests'. African countries are identical to others around the world in that their fates are not decided totally within the domestic political arena. International relations are also influential. Historic and economic factors have conspired to ensure that the states of Africa are influenced by external events perhaps even more than their neighbours on other continents. Indeed, many Africanists have cited imperialism and 'neo-colonialism' as the major governing force behind Africa's poor economic and political performance. This is a debate taken up in the main text of this book, but whether they have had a negative or positive impact, there is no denying that foreign governments, international organisations and transnational companies have played a major part in Africa's post-colonial political development.

An Introduction to African Politics, in addition to applying conceptual themes to the continent's politics, is about exploring the competition between the above three actors. On the whole, it is a story of how states, civil societies and external interests have failed one another. The state, starved of resources (partially due to the influence of external interests), became somewhat introverted after independence, excluding civil society from the political process. This resulted in the under-representation of African citizens by their governments. Indeed, it was often the case that state actors deliberately muddled their public duties and their private interests. Consequently, most services or resources passed down to ordinary citizens were channelled through inefficient patronage networks. Civil society, for its part, never really engaged the state. Where it was possible, and advantageous, to do so, citizens bypassed state authority. Taxes were not paid, for example, and crops were not sold to state marketing boards. In many instances, this avoidance became a survival strategy of necessity against a predatory state. Consequently, state and civil society drifted apart during the first few decades of African independence.

All, however, is not lost. A wave of multi-party elections swept the continent from the late 1980s onwards, and initiated a process whereby state and civil society have built a more profitable relationship in recent times. This relationship falls short of Western democratic norms, and is far removed from Weber's model state, where politicians and bureaucrats clearly separate their private and public interests, and the 'national good' is served through neutral legal/rational institutions, but a new relationship has been brokered nonetheless. The question remains, however, whether this recalibrated balance of state, civil society and external interests will perform better than in the past. Post-colonial Africa has experienced long periods of poor, or no, economic development alongside limited political representation. Will this new, more democratic, political dispensation change things for the better?

The above analysis, however, is getting ahead of itself. Readers new to the continent first need a grounding in the fundamental building blocks of post-colonial African politics, alongside such commentary on state, civil society and external interests. The latter makes more sense after a discussion of the former. It is thus time to turn to the core text of this book, where basic thematic concepts and case studies are presented chapter by chapter. In this manner the intricate mechanisms that drive African politics will be revealed.

Glossary of key terms

Civil society	The organisations that arise out of voluntary association within society, found between the extended family and the state.
External interests	Foreign governments, international institutions and non-governmental organisations (including transnational corporations) that interact with African states and civic associations.
The state	A set of political institutions that govern within a delimited sovereign territory.

Notes and references

1 Alagiah, George. New light on the dark continent. *The Guardian* (London). 3 May 1999. Media section. 4–5.
2 Weber, Max. The profession and vocation of politics. In: Peter Lassman and Ronald Speirs, eds. *Weber: Political Writings*. Cambridge: Cambridge University Press, 1994. 310–11.

2 History

Africa's pre-colonial and colonial inheritance

Chapter outline

- The pre-colonial inheritance

    - Non-hegemonic states
    - Lineage

- The colonial inheritance

    - Modern states
    - Arbitrary boundaries
    - Reinforcing the non-hegemonic state
    - Weak links between state and civil society
    - The formation of state elites
    - The economic inheritance
    - Weak political institutions

- State and civil society
- Case study: Kenya's historical inheritance
- Questions raised by this chapter
- Glossary of key terms
- Further reading
- Notes and references

The world does not radically reinvent itself on a continuous basis. It evolves. There are no total revolutions where all that has gone before is laid to rest, and a new polity is born enjoying a completely clean slate. Traditions, customs, institutions and social relationships will survive and adapt from one era to another.

This is why the study of history is so useful to the political scientist. A scholar who wishes to understand the present must know something of the past. Some would say, for example, that modern French politics are still steeped in a republican tradition that stretches all the way back to the revolution of 1789. Similarly, those interested in the contemporary politics of the United States would be wise to familiarise themselves with the ideas of that country's 'founding fathers'. The same goes for Africa. As will be seen, there are lines of continuity that run from the pre-colonial period, through the colonial era, right into the modern age.

This chapter searches out the continent's historical trajectories. What in Africa's past still has an impact on the politics of the continent today? Although this chapter cannot do full justice to Africa's rich history, it is possible to highlight certain prominent trends that help to explain the politics of the present. First, influences that have their roots in the pre-colonial era will be acknowledged. Issues of 'porous' non-hegemonic states and lineage are identified. The chapter then goes on to explore Africa's colonial inheritance. An investigation of this later historical period highlights influences such as arbitrary boundaries, detached political institutions, and externally facing economies. Whether pre-colonial or colonial in origin, all these factors are legacies that modern African states and actors have to accommodate. They thus provide an excellent introduction to contemporary African politics.

The pre-colonial inheritance

The majority of historians studying Africa have concentrated on the colonial era. They concern themselves with the 'European' impact on Africa. These scholars have produced invaluable work, but their collective yield falls far short of revealing the continent's full history. This is bound to be the case given that formal European rule, for most states, usually represented just 70 or 80 years, comprising a tiny proportion of African history. Humanity, after all, originated in Africa, some two to three million years ago. Before investigating the colonial legacy, therefore, it would be wise first to consider what modern Africa has inherited from this earlier, pre-colonial period.

Pre-colonial Africa was as varied as the continent itself. Different circumstances produced different societies with different traditions, customs and politics, and these societies rose, fell and adapted as the centuries passed. Despite this variety, it is possible to divide political organisation among these communities into two broad categories: states and stateless societies.

Low population densities, and the production of relatively small economic surpluses, hindered the formation of states in many parts of pre-colonial Africa. This was particularly the case in central and southern regions of the continent. These stateless societies, however, did not lack political organisation. Westerners, steeped as they are in state traditions, often regard the lack of state institutions as a sign of backwardness. This simply was not the case. The political systems that these stateless societies developed were well adapted to the environment they served. Considerable evidence of sophisticated forms of representation, justice and accountability among these communities has been unearthed. In many cases, loose confederations of villages provided security and a community for many thousands of Africans.

Several of these larger stateless societies developed institutions and hierarchies that evolved, over time, into states (see Map 2.1). This occurred most commonly, though certainly not exclusively, in West Africa. The stimulus for state formation was often the production of an economic surplus. This wealth enabled communities to sustain leadership groups, as well as administrative structures to support these governors. The states of Ghana and Mali, for example, were built on the profits from trans-Saharan trade. Further east, it was agricultural surpluses, from the fertile lands of the Nile River and the central Great Lakes, which helped to establish ancient Egypt and the kingdom of Buganda. Elsewhere, the empires of Ashanti and Benin were founded on mining and metalwork skills. States could also be built around monarchical authority, religious affiliation or, in the case of the Zulu nation, military prowess.

Some of these grand civilisations were in advance, technically and socially, of their European contemporaries, but the fascinating details of these states, given the particular

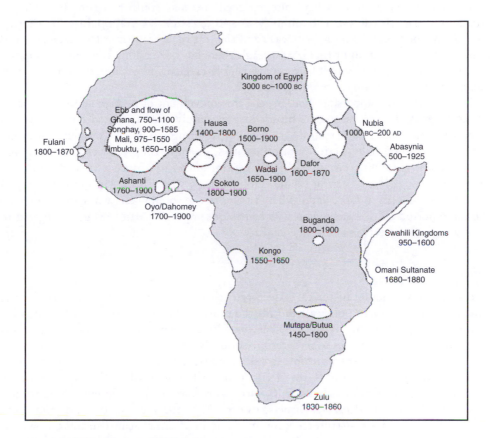

Map 2.1 Selected pre-colonial African states

focus of this book, will have to be left to the historians. The task of this chapter is to extract relevant aspects of history that help to explain African politics today. The factors of continuity that stand out from this pre-colonial era, in this respect, are the issues of non-hegemonic states and lineage.

Non-hegemonic states

Even when state formation did take place in pre-colonial Africa, the result was very different from what defines a state today. Permanent, precisely delineated boundaries were rare. Power broadcast from the centre of a kingdom would increasingly dissipate the further a village was from the capital, and would ebb and flow according to the fortunes of the central administration. Indeed, there could even be an overlapping of authority, with a community owing degrees of allegiance to more than one political leader. This was very different from the European states of the same time, where governments sought to be the sole source of political authority within rigidly defined sovereign territories. Consequently, European wars have largely been about securing or expanding borders. By contrast, inter-community conflict in Africa, given the abundance of land, was not about borders. It was more often about winning booty: gold, slaves and cattle.

The ready availability of land also reduced internal conflict within pre-colonial African societies. If parts of a community wished to escape a certain political authority, they simply occupied land further away from the centre. It was easier to escape political opponents rather than fight them. As a result there has been a long tradition of population movement in Africa, with groups of people creating new polities, moving their community, or choosing to join other states.[1]

The absence of defined state borders, the free movement of people, and the fact that pre-colonial African governments broadcast power only over a limited range, have led some scholars to label these states 'non-hegemonic'. Simply put, pre-colonial states were not designed to be all-powerful political entities, monopolising politics within a given region. Local autonomy coexisted with a central authority. Indeed, this idea of non-hegemonic states is a recurring theme throughout this book. The current chapter will explore this concept in more detail when it turns to the colonial era, while in Chapter 10 the same notion is used to explain why some contemporary African states collapsed in the 1990s and the early twenty-first century.

Lineage

The second pre-colonial historical trajectory is that of 'kinship'. This is the idea of the extended family which, politically, forms the basis of clans and 'tribes'. A lineage kinship group can theoretically trace its past back to the same ancestor, and these bonds of origin bind communities together. Consequently, ancestor worship is at the heart of many African spiritualist traditions. In reality, actual genealogical links are sometimes tenuous, with membership of the group usually being flexible. Outsiders may be brought into a clan, individuals will marry into families of different lineages, and groups as a whole interlink and disperse over time (commonly as a result of migration or war). Even the most instrumental (or 'manufactured') lineage associations, however, construct powerful social bonds. As a member of the group, individuals will obey life-determining customs regarding marriage, inheritance, justice and the allocation of land. This gives the leader of a clan, 'tribe' or ethnic group a great deal of political power. Lineage groups, in return, provide solidarity, offering security and welfare to their members. There is thus a reciprocal relationship between those who respect the authority of ethnic leaders and the chiefs who are obliged to look after their followers. Even today this results in Africans seeing themselves more as members of a community, rather than adopting the degrees of individuality that are widespread in the West.

Chapter 3, tracing the historical trajectory of these pre-colonial lineages, explores how this sense of community influenced the state ideologies of post-colonial Africa (notably 'African socialism'). Following this, Chapter 4 investigates just how these powerful 'tribal' or ethnic ties help to shape political exchange in the modern era.

The colonial inheritance

Africa did not evolve in isolation prior to European colonisation. The continent, like other parts of the world, adapted to invasions and imperial rule as history unfolded. Just as Britain experienced eras dominated by Roman and Norman occupation, North Africa played host to Persian, Greek, Roman and Ottoman empires over time. Africa was also subject to religious influences. Islam spread across the North, reaching the Atlantic Ocean in the first years of the eighth century, while Christianity had gained a permanent foothold in Ethiopia in the fourth century. Further south, to some extent, the barrier of the Sahara desert limited cultural exchange between the rest of the world and tropical Africa, but sub-Saharan Africans, by the fifteenth century, had built strong land and maritime trading links with both Arabs and Europeans. The whole continent, in this respect, participated in the international economy prior to European colonialism.

In 1415, the Portuguese established a garrison on Africa's Mediterranean coast at Ceuta. They then went on to build a number of trading posts on both the west and east coasts of the continent. Later, in 1652, the Dutch established Cape Town on the southern tip of Africa, which under British control developed into modern-day South Africa. By the eighteenth and nineteenth centuries, numerous trading settlements could be found along Africa's coastline, with Europeans busy acquiring gold, ivory and slaves, among other products. Christian missionaries were also establishing themselves on the continent by this time. All this was achieved without formal colonisation. This situation was to change dramatically, however, in the second half of the nineteenth century.

Again, it is best to leave the details and motivations behind the 'scramble for Africa' to the historians, but the results of this imperial competition are obvious.[2] Whether it was for economic, strategic or cultural reasons, agreements ratified at the 1884–85 Berlin Conference (and after) saw Africa carved up between the European powers. Only the empire of Ethiopia and the territory of Liberia (a country established for freed slaves) escaped this partition.

France favoured North, West and Central Africa; Britain claimed great chunks of West, East, Central and Southern Africa; Portugal took the territories of Angola, Mozambique and Guinea–Bissau; King Léopold of Belgium was awarded the Congo; Italy established control in Libya, Eritrea and part of Somalia; Spain did likewise in north Morocco, the Spanish Sahara and Spanish Guinea; Germany gained areas in the south-west and the east of the continent, as well as the Cameroons and Togoland. Germany, however, was to lose these possessions as a consequence of its defeat in the First World War, with the League of Nations distributing the mandate to govern these territories among the victorious colonial powers (see Map 2.2).

This colonial era may have been relatively short in duration (in most cases from the 1880s or 1890s through to the 1960s), but its impact on the subsequent political environment was considerable. Once more, lines of continuity can be traced between the past and the present. Seven elements within this colonial inheritance are of particular importance (summarised in Table 2.1). These are as follows: the incorporation of Africa into the international modern state structure; the imposition of arbitrary boundaries; the reinforcement of the non-hegemonic state; the weak link between state and civil society; the promotion of an African state elite; the building of specialist export economies; and the absence of strong political institutions. Each of these elements will now be examined in turn.

Modern states

The most obvious legacy of colonial rule was the division of Africa into modern states. European rule resulted in Africa being fully integrated within the international jigsaw puzzle of sovereign territories. This meant that, worldwide (Antarctica excepted), states now accounted for the entire land surface of the globe. All of these had clearly delineated and fixed boundaries, and all legal political interaction was now channelled through, or at least held accountable to, state institutions.

As already indicated, pre-colonial Africa hosted many stateless societies, and even where there were states, these were considerably less well defined than their modern descendants.

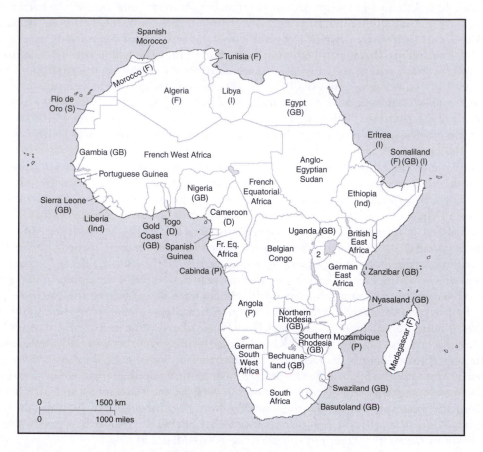

Map 2.2 Africa at the outbreak of the First World War

Notes

D = Germany; F = France; GB = Britain; I = Italy; Ind = Independent; P = Portugal; S = Spain

Changes after the First World War:

1 German South-West Africa: to Britain
2 German East Africa: to Britain (Tanganyika), except Ruanda Urundi to Belgium
3 Cameroon: part to France, part to Britain
4 Togo: part to France, part to Britain
5 Jubaland: ceded from Britain to Italy (joins Italian Somaliland)

In this respect, few Africans had previously experienced the reality of the modern state. The post-colonial consequences of being incorporated into such political structures and the international political system feature prominently in all the chapters of this book.

Arbitrary boundaries

The imperial powers' imposition of state borders on African territory had major ramifications. The problem lies with the fact that, when they were delineated, these state boundaries rarely matched existing pre-colonial political, social or economic divisions.

They were 'arbitrary', not in the sense of being random, but because they reflected the short-term strategic and economic interests of the imperial powers, and not the interests of the Africans they housed.[3] In short, these borders paid little heed to local realities.

A quick glance at the contemporary map of Africa, for example, clearly shows an external, rather than internal, logic to the units chosen. Many of the boundaries are ruler-straight, conveniently following lines of longitude and latitude. Historically determined political divisions, such as the state borders of Europe, do not do this. Other oddities also stick out. Why was German South-West Africa (Namibia), for example, awarded a narrow tract of land (the Caprivi Strip) to its north-east, and why does West Africa host the tiny state of The Gambia? In the first instance, Namibia's odd shape was created by the strategic requirements of Germany's foreign minister, Count von Caprivi. He insisted that this territory should have access to the Zambezi River, in order to deploy a gunboat. The second case arose because British commercial interests had established a trading post at the mouth of the River Gambia. Despite French cajoling, the British government refused to give up this territory. Consequently, The Gambia is a micro-state, no more than 50 kilometres wide at any one point, and entirely engulfed by francophone Senegal (except for its short coastline).

Then there is the curiosity of Cabinda. This oil-rich enclave is part of Angola. Yet the Democratic Republic of the Congo separates it from greater Angola. This is because King Léopold of Belgium insisted that his African kingdom should adjoin the Atlantic Ocean. Again, it is important to stress that if African state borders had reflected 'natural' local social and economic divisions, rather than having been imposed arbitrarily and virtually overnight, then these and other anomalies would not have become a reality on the modern map of Africa. As the British Prime Minister of the day, Lord Salisbury, quipped at an 1890 Anglo-French conference: 'we have been engaged in drawing lines upon maps where no white man's foot ever trod; we have been giving away mountains and rivers and lakes to each other, only hindered by the small impediment that we never knew exactly where the mountains and rivers and lakes were'.[4] Salisbury's after-dinner joke loses some of its humour when put into the context of the problems that these 'arbitrary' borders created for post-colonial governments.

Many of these borders, for example, do not make economic sense. As well as the initial disruption to existing lines of local communication and trade, colonial boundaries also created longer-term problems for African states. Decisions made in the capitals of Europe in the late eighteenth century, for example, have resulted in 14 African countries being landlocked. In terms of trade, this puts a state at a significant disadvantage. They have to rely on their neighbours' willingness and ability to transport the bulk of their imports and exports. No other continent is home to so many landlocked states.

Imperially imposed borders also left several states without significant resources from which to build their economies. Whether it is held back by a shortage of agricultural land, minerals, other raw materials or people, no country can secure its future without an economic foundation. Polities that grow into states 'organically' do this precisely because they can command such resources. There was no such imperative in the formation of African states. Niger, for example, has little land within its borders suitable for agriculture, and only minor mineral deposits. Consequently, this state, like many others on the continent, struggled to prosper after independence. Borders agreed at the Berlin conference simply ignored economic imperatives. It is only belatedly that the discovery of oil deposits within the Sahara region has made Niger, Chad and the Sudan more rational states in terms of their economies.

Alongside economic obstacles, the externally imposed artificial boundaries also ran through existing political and social units, resulting in many communities finding themselves split between different states. Some pre-colonial political entities did survive. Rwanda, Burundi, Lesotho and Swaziland have boundaries acknowledging pre-colonial realities, but such an acknowledgement was rare. Imperial partition scattered the Somali people, for example, among five sovereign states. Fellow Somalis were now to be found in British Somaliland, Italian Somaliland, French Somaliland, Ethiopia and Kenya. Similarly, the present-day borders of Burkina Faso cut across the traditional territory of 21 cultural and linguistic groups.[5] In this sense, colonial rule 'dehumanised' Africa's borders.[6]

This failure of the imposed boundaries to recognise existing social and political divisions was at the root of two major problems for post-colonial governments. First, there was the possibility of irredentism. Irredentism is *the desire to unite under one flag a community that is currently divided*. If a pre-colonial political unit found itself split between two states, then there was always a danger that, after independence, violence would be used in an attempt to reunite this community. Somalia unsuccessfully went to war with Ethiopia in the 1970s, for example, to try to win the Ogaden, an area populated by ethnic Somalis. The government in Mogadishu wanted to house all the Somali people within the boundaries of just one sovereign state.

The second potential problem is the possibility of internal ethnic conflict within a state. Imperial boundaries not only split social groups, but also caged them together within these new nation states. There are over 200 ethnic groups residing within the boundaries of Tanzania, for instance. Post-colonial states were thus forced to find institutions and political procedures that ensured that any conflict among their socially divided populations could be resolved peacefully. Just how successful governments have been at managing the legacies of these arbitrary boundaries is the focus of Chapters 3 and 4, which respectively examine nationalism and ethnicity in post-colonial Africa.

Reinforcing the non-hegemonic state

As well as producing arbitrary boundaries, European colonialism also reinforced the non-hegemonic nature of the African state. Only in South Africa, Southern Rhodesia, Kenya, South-West Africa and Algeria were there pretensions of building a modern state during the period of imperial rule, with each of these territories hosting significant numbers of white settlers. In the rest of the continent the imperial powers had only limited goals. There was no desire to invest resources to ensure the state could project its authority into every corner of the new colonies. Instead, colonial governments only concentrated on economically productive or strategically important regions. Less valuable land and more distant communities were lightly governed. A minimal infrastructure was built, backed by a 'thin white line' of administrators and troops. This was colonialism on the cheap. No wholesale economic or political development was planned for the colonies. As such, despite the massive impact that this period of European colonialism would have on African political development, the actual penetrative capacity of the state was relatively weak. This lack of state capacity, as will be seen in Chapters 6 and 10, was a significant legacy that post-colonial governments had difficulty overcoming.

Weak links between state and civil society

A natural consequence of this lack of state penetration was that independent Africa also inherited weak links between state and society. Colonial political authority had been gained on the continent through conquest, and political institutions imposed. Coercion acted as a substitute for legitimacy. The state, in this sense, did not rely on a social contract between government and people. Indeed, colonial administrators were not even accountable to the Africans they ruled. Instead, they obeyed orders emanating from their superiors back in the capitals of Europe. Government was therefore about maintaining order, balancing budgets and overseeing the extraction of raw materials for export. It was never about the provision of public services for citizens. This is why Crawford Young describes the African colonial state as 'alien to its core'.[7]

By comparison, stronger links between state and society developed more organically within the modern European state. Here the state had both grown out of, and been shaped by, its own society. Over centuries, elements of civil society had competed with monarchs and emperors, resulting in first the middle class and then the working class gaining empowerment. Each group eventually succeeded in shaping state institutions to reflect their demands. Today, notions of democracy underpin this relationship between state and society, and a complex provision of public services has resulted.

This contrasts strongly with Africa, where the modern state arrived almost overnight, and its nature owed little to existing indigenous civil society. Africans were simply left out of any representative relationship between government and people. Consequently, trust and shared political values never developed between the rulers and the ruled. State institutions never sought or gained the respect of the people.

This was a situation that did not bode well for a successful interaction between the state and society in post-colonial Africa. Chapter 6 will show how the independent governments followed the example of their imperial forebears, also restricting political activity within civil society. Legitimacy continued to be substituted by coercion. Chapter 10 examines this state/civil society relationship from a different angle. It explores how, during the 1980s and 1990s, civil society took its 'revenge' by disengaging from these authoritarian and exploitative states.

The formation of state elites

Although, by and large, colonial states were content to distance themselves from their African subjects, some contact was needed. After all, the 'thin white line' of imperial administrators could not keep the state going all by themselves.[8] A number of Africans were required to sustain the imperial administration's authority over the masses. This led to the creation of small indigenous elites within the colonies. These elites, having benefited from their access to state institutions, would then go on to fight the liberation campaigns, and form the first governments after independence.

Initially, colonial administrators selected traditional leaders to be the intermediaries of imperialism. Chiefs or monarchs, who already commanded authority among their people, were charged with raising taxes, supplying labour and ensuring that colonial laws and regulations were respected. In return, these intermediaries could expect the power of the state to back their leadership, with considerable benefits in terms of 'tribute'. Administrators, for example, fully expected chiefs to take for themselves a percentage of the tax revenue they raised or the fines they imposed. These traditional leaders were also left to run their jurisdiction largely as they saw fit, as long as colonial interests were not compromised. This method of 'indirect rule' was, again, colonialism on the cheap.

The state elite was not just composed of traditional leaders, however. As time progressed, a younger African elite began to emerge. These individuals also gained their position from their proximity to state power, but their source of social mobility was not necessarily traditional authority. The main currency was education. Access to an education (usually from a mission school) brought access to the state. This 'proto-elite' was often employed in the lower ranks of the government, as clerks, teachers or court interpreters, or became professionals such as lawyers and doctors. As such, they received relative prosperity from their salary, and they engaged in the 'Western' society of the towns and cities. Towards the end of colonial rule, most colonial governments attempted to 'Africanise' their civil service. As a consequence, the numbers of this bureaucratic class swelled, as did the numbers of professionals employed by the state.

In effect, imperial rule had created its own executioners. By the 1950s, forces of nationalism were challenging nearly all the colonial states, and these movements were led by those who had prospered most under colonial rule. Nationalist politics flourished among the educated urban elite. To take the example of the Uganda National Congress, its Central Committee consisted in 1952 of five shopkeepers, four journalists, three full-time politicians, two clerks, two lawyers, two schoolteachers, and a student studying abroad.[9]

Nationalism certainly had considerable support among the peasantry in the countryside, but it was not a case of society, as a whole, demanding independence. Instead, it was about the colonial governments handing over power to African educated elites. The very element of African society that had been most closely associated with the colonial state ousted its former employers. The clerks, teachers and lawyers captured state institutions for themselves. Chapter 5, investigating social class within African politics, assesses the consequences of this indigenous elite inheriting the state.

The economic inheritance

Of all the elements of Africa's colonial inheritance, it has been the economic legacy that has been most widely debated among Africanists. This is because of the continent's poor economic performance. Ignoring widely supported contemporary predictions, economies simply failed to 'take off' after independence. In several cases, despite economic development being the priority of governments, African states were worse off at the end of the twentieth century than they had been at decolonisation.

A dominant school of thought, at its height in the 1970s and early 1980s, directly blamed the colonial inheritance for this lack of development. Its followers maintained that the continent had been systematically *under*developed by imperial interests, and this now left the new independent states in a highly vulnerable 'dependent' position. As such, colonial administrators had failed to provide Africa with the basic economic foundations that governments now needed if their countries were to flourish.

Central to this idea of underdevelopment is the premise that all states operate in a single, global system. This has increasingly been the case over the last four centuries, with capitalism gradually coming to influence all societies around the world as the dominant method of economic exchange and production. Not all states are equal within this single international system, however. They are divided into two groups. There are those developed states at the centre or core (Western countries), and the less developed countries on the periphery (largely the Third World).

The differences in wealth between core and periphery have not resulted from the West and the Third World embarking on two historically different economic paths. They are

Plate 2.1 Two colonists examine the rubber collected by the workers on a plantation in French Equatorial Africa, unknown date.

the product of the same process, with the core developing at the periphery's expense. The prosperity the West enjoys today has been founded on exploitation of the periphery's resources. Development and underdevelopment, therefore, are two sides of the same coin. Economic activity, which could have helped African economies, has instead advanced the position of the West. Imperial rule was the formal political authority that underwrote this process of exploitation.

Numerous examples of underdevelopment have been put forward in support of this thesis. The more convincing of these included the exploitation of labour, the drain of capital from the periphery to the core states, and the failure of colonial states to diversify local economies. These three processes are discussed below.

Examining the issue of labour exploitation first, the West began to take advantage of African workers even before formal colonial rule was established. The Atlantic slave trade transported up to 15 million people from Africa to work on the plantations of the Caribbean and the Americas, and more died in the process of capture, or during transit. Portuguese and Arab merchants organised a similar trade in human beings from the east coast of the continent. The results were far reaching. Populations in parts of Africa were devastated. Also destroyed were local political and social formations. People whose labour could have advanced the development of African economies and societies were, instead, forced to contribute to capital accumulation elsewhere. Europeans (and Arabs) had underdeveloped Africa by literally stealing its labour force.

Exploitation of labour also continued into the formal colonial era. Once imperial authorities realised that the bulk of Africa (South Africa excluded) was not going to be a new Eldorado, as gold-rich South America had been for the Spanish empire, they set about exploiting other resources that could be found on the continent. African labour was an obvious target. Colonial laws and tax systems were devised to force peasants from their subsistence farming, pushing them into employment in mines, on commercial plantations, or growing cash crops to be exported to the West. The colonial authorities, however, did not pay African labour the wages enjoyed by European workers. Even taking into account the vast gap in standards of living, a worker on the African continent was still paid below the level of his or her subsistence needs. This forced workers to supplement their cash income from sources elsewhere (usually additional subsistence farming).

Indeed, in parts of Africa, if a labour force could not be raised voluntarily, forced labour was introduced. Africans in the Congo and Mozambique, for example, were legally compelled to work for the state for part of the year, or face prosecution. Had African workers been paid more for their labour during the colonial era, enough capital might have been accumulated and reinvested locally to ensure that post-colonial governments inherited a much healthier economic situation. Instead it was Western economies that benefited from the fruits of this labour.

Underdevelopment also resulted from the 'export of surplus'. Instead of African economies benefiting from new economic activity on the continent, raw materials extracted and profits raised by African labour were simply whisked away from the periphery in order to develop the economies of the West. For economic advancement to occur anywhere in the world not only does a surplus have to be produced, but also it has to be invested productively. Reinvestment of profits into the economies of Africa could have stimulated growth locally. Instead, the West expropriated this surplus for its own use. It is no coincidence that the economies of the core expanded at a previously unprecedented rate during the years of colonialism.

Underdevelopment also stunted African advancement by only developing primary production (mining and agriculture) on the continent, as opposed to secondary industries (manufacturing and services). Colonial rule ensured that peripheral economies became predominantly export economies (minerals, coffee, tea, cocoa, vegetable oil, groundnuts, cotton, sisal, etc.). As a result, at independence, many African states were faced with the problem of a 'monocrop' economy. In Zambia, for example, the economy is overwhelmingly dominated by copper extraction, while in Ghana it is dominated by cocoa production. If the price of this commodity falls on the world market, then there is no other economic sector that the country can fall back on. A balance of payments crisis ensues. If the colonial authorities had developed economic sectors such as food production and secondary manufacturing industry, then post-colonial African economies would have been less specialised, and consequently less vulnerable. Imperial administrators, however, were only concerned about the needs of Western industry (the demand for raw materials). They had no interest in building strong integrated economies in the periphery.

The external imperatives of African economies are also very apparent with respect to investments that the colonial authorities did make in their territories. Transport infrastructure, for instance, only revolved around moving goods from the point of extraction to a port, permitting export to the West. By comparison, few lines of communication were built to enhance internal or regional trading links. Again, Africa's development was being governed by an external, rather than a locally beneficial, logic. This is why African commerce today remains more engaged with Western, rather than local, markets. The Côte d'Ivoire (Ivory Coast), for example, trades more with France than it does with its neighbour, Ghana.

Similarly, little investment was made in African human resources. As David Lamb observes, after 300 years of Portuguese rule in Guinea–Bissau, imperialism left just 14 university graduates, an illiteracy rate of 97 per cent, only 265 miles of paved road, and a single factory (a brewery that served the Portuguese troops).[10] A greater proportion of the profits generated in Africa reinvested locally would have produced a much healthier economic inheritance for post-colonial African governments.

More recent academic thought, however, considers the underdevelopment thesis too polemic. Although most scholars agree that exploitation and expropriation held back potential African development to a considerable degree, they argue that the colonial economic experience was not entirely negative for Third World countries. The African continent prior to imperial rule, for example, was not on the brink of economic 'take-off'. Population densities were relatively stable, and there were no imminent major technological breakthroughs. The plough and the wheel were not utilised, wind and water power remained largely absent, and irrigation was limited. Indeed, Bill Warren argues that colonialism, as the pioneer of capitalism, was necessary to close the development gap between the West and the Third World.[11] Imperial rule may have brought great hardship to Africa, but it also brought improved economic techniques, better health and wider experience of education to the continent. Warren contends that, in this respect, there is no better indicator of development than infant mortality rates and life expectancy. Both of these improved dramatically under colonialism. Smallpox, diphtheria and tuberculosis were reduced considerably with Western medicines, and better health enhanced productive forces across the entire continent.

Similarly, it could be argued that although the imperial authorities only really concentrated on developing the primary sector within their colonies, at least this was one area of the economy that had the potential to provide a platform for later diversification. Zimbabwe, for example, was left with modern coal mines to produce power for any post-independence industrial development, while Algeria had a small steel industry to build upon.

How, then, should one judge Africa's economic inheritance? Did colonial exploitation destroy Africa's potential, or did minor (self-interested) investments leave these territories with at least the substructure of a modern economy? Well, there is no doubt that the imperial powers extracted a great deal of wealth from their colonial possessions via labour exploitation, and raw material and profit export. This capital could have been used to benefit Africa rather than the West, and might have resulted in a more prosperous continent today. The colonial era did, however, leave Africa with economic foundations based on the primary sector. These economies may not have been particularly diverse, but nor were they condemned to permanent poverty as some underdevelopment theorists have suggested. Political independence brought at least the potential for more rapid economic growth. The flow of profit export to the core could now be stemmed by political means, and the capital reinvested locally. The successful diversification of several ex-colonial economies in the Far East (the Asian 'Tiger' economies) would seem to support this view. The book returns to this issue of economic underdevelopment in Chapter 8, where attempts of post-independence African governments to overcome these colonial economic obstacles are examined, alongside charges of continued exploitation by Western interests.

Weak political institutions

The final element of Africa's colonial inheritance to be examined consists of the weak political institutions left by the imperial powers. As decolonisation approached, nationalist movements began to mobilise, leading the colonial authorities to look for means of transferring power to indigenous governments. In the majority of cases, negotiation proved to be the key to independence.[12] Most often the eventual result was multi-party elections, with the victor of this poll taking up the reins of power under a new independence constitution. These new constitutions guaranteed pluralist democracy and the rule of law.

This was the ultimate irony of colonial rule. Imperial powers sought to leave a legacy of constitutional liberal democracy. These were the liberties and the political representation that imperial administrators had consciously withheld from Africans during their own time in power. Colonial structures were about control and expropriation at the lowest possible cost. Imperialism did not have as its goal the creation of legal-rational institutions on foreign soil. In this respect, colonial states had been highly bureaucratic

Table 2.1 Chapter summary: potential problems created by the colonial inheritance

Arbitrary boundaries	*Potential problems*:
	• Illogical territorial units
	• Divided communities
	• Irredentist movements
	• Internal ethnic competition
	• Inappropriate economic units (landlocked, under-resourced)
Non-hegemonic states	*Potential problems*:
	• Inability to project state power into hinterland
	• State power concentrated only on strategic and profitable regions
Weak links between state and society	*Potential problems*:
	• No shared political culture between state and society
	• A deficit of legitimacy
	• Unaccountable states
	• Distant civil societies
	• Society disengaging from the state
Formation of a state elite	*Potential problems*:
	• Strong links between political office and personal wealth
	• Social mobility dominated by access to the state
	• Corruption
	• An exploitative 'bureaucratic bourgeoisie'
The economic inheritance	*Potential problems*:
	• Disadvantage in the international economy
	• Underdevelopment of human resources
	• Lack of public services
	• Economies over-reliant on primary sector
	• Over-reliance on exports
	• Bias towards European, not local or regional, markets
Weak political institutions	*Potential problems*:
	• Fragile liberal democratic institutions without historical moorings
	• Return to colonial-style authoritarian and bureaucratic state

and authoritarian. They never sought legitimacy from their subjects, they were highly interventionist, they had few pretensions about representing local interests, and they ruled through domination, supported by coercion. The political culture that these realities underpinned was hardly an appropriate midwife to oversee the birth of new liberal democratic states. Not surprisingly, despite the last-minute installation of democratic trappings, many of the elements of the colonial authoritarianism listed above would simply resurface in the post-colonial era. Bureaucratic authoritarianism would be the true institutional legacy to the former colonies, not liberal democracy, as will be seen in Chapters 6 and 10.

State and civil society

Having identified the most relevant elements of Africa's past which would have an influence on post-colonial politics, this chapter can now conclude by briefly considering this historical inheritance in the light of the book's underlying theme: the relationship between state, civil society and external interests.

There were certainly major obstacles to be overcome if Africa was to achieve economic and political development after independence. The new states were in a vulnerable position. Post-colonial governments had to manage divided communities created by arbitrary colonial boundaries. Institutional mechanisms and ideologies of solidarity, for example, would have to be found to reduce ethnic tensions, while 'good neighbourliness' would also have to emerge to prevent the threat of irredentism. Similarly, the newly independent economies had to be diversified and expanded. This was the only way to reduce their monocrop insecurity and provide the capital for previously absent basic public services (such as health and education).

Civil society also had to overcome major challenges in the post-colonial era. The danger was that these voluntary associations would become dominated by the state. This would damage opportunities for pluralist competition, and thus limit society's influence over state policies. After all, modern states in Africa had no track record of either representation or accountability. The colonial example had been one of bureaucratic authoritarianism, silencing the voice of civil society. It was now possible that the educated elite that had inherited these states would simply adopt the same style of rule that had been practised by their imperial predecessors. If state domination returned it would be civil society that would suffer.

This is not to say, however, that the pre-colonial and colonial inheritance predestined independent Africa to fail economically and politically. It was never inevitable that this legacy would get the better of the continent's politicians. Independence had been won. The nationalists who took over the state had gained the trust and support of civil society through their liberation leadership and independence election campaigns. Consequently, a degree of legitimacy had been generated between the governors and the governed. There was also an economic base to work on, however fragile this was. And, what is more, democracy had been proven to work once, with multi-party elections successfully selecting the successors to colonial governments. Indeed, at the time, there was great hope in Africa, as well as abroad, that the continent was poised to enter a prosperous new epoch.

Building on the historical trajectories explored in this chapter, the rest of the book will seek to explain why, at the start of the twenty-first century, Africa is still yet to enter into this more affluent era.

Case study: Kenya's historical inheritance

Kenya straddles the Equator on the east coast of Africa, and has a number of climatic zones. Much of the country is arid or semi-arid, only supporting low-density subsistence farming. Other areas, however, are suitable for intensive agriculture. The coastal strip along the Indian Ocean is one such region, but it is the highlands on either side of the Great Rift Valley, and the shores of Lake Victoria, that have proved to be especially productive. Kenya can also boast the bustling cities of Nairobi, Mombasa and Kisumu.

Archaeological evidence shows present-day Kenya to have been one of the first hosts to human life. Human remains have been found near Lake Turkana dating back two to three million years. An equally significant event in the peopling of Africa was the Bantu migrations. These Bantu people, originating from West Africa, over centuries would in time inhabit all of Tropical Africa, eventually pushing down into what is now South Africa itself. As they travelled south and east, they colonised many of the societies they came across. The Kikuyu, Embu, Mbere, Kamba, Tharaka, Luhya and Gusii of present-day Kenya are the descendants of these Bantu migrants. Their ancestors reached the Rift Valley approximately 1,000 years ago.

Another significant migration arrived later, in the fifteenth century. Niolitic and Cushitic groups came from the north, and produced lines of descent that formed today's Masai, Kalenjin, Luo and Somali ethnic groups. In addition to these African peoples, Arab traders have also been visiting Kenya since the seventh century, while Europeans settled here from the end of the nineteenth century onwards. Adding to this diverse population, Asians originating from the Indian subcontinent have been a significant part of Kenya's society since the twentieth century.

Political organisation in pre-colonial Kenya rested largely on stateless societies. The most sophisticated of these could be found in the highlands, and westwards towards Lake Victoria. Although each of the African groups mentioned in the previous paragraph had its own identity, social, economic and cultural boundaries were permeable, and there was coexistence (as well as war) between these various parties. The 'Lords of the Rift' (the Masai), for example, were the 'bankers of the highlands'.[13] They were a purely pastoral people, but benefited from residing close to other, mixed farming, ethnic groups. This was so that they could profit from providing cattle to their neighbours, cattle being the primary form of currency and exchange among these communities (used for trade and paying social debts, such as the marriage bride-price).

This region was also well connected with both the rest of Africa and the wider world. Coastal trade existed from early times, while Arab caravans entered the interior regularly throughout the nineteenth century. Largely trading for ivory and slaves, these caravans operated between Mombasa (on the Indian Ocean coast) and Lake Victoria. This commercial activity was controlled from the island of Zanzibar, from where Omani Arabs exerted authority over the whole region.

The British gained influence in this part of Africa towards the end of the nineteenth century. In 1888, a royal charter for what would become Kenya was granted to the commercial Imperial British East Africa Company. Company rule, however, proved something of a disaster. London had to take direct control itself when the company became bankrupt. The British government established its East African Protectorate in 1895. Kenya became a formal crown colony 25 years later, by which time white settlement was firmly entrenched. In the space of these 25 years, Kenya had been transformed from a region that provided a home for numerous stateless societies into a single modern colonial state. The territory now had powerful central administrative structures, defined borders and a significant white settler community.

Kenya reflects the rest of Africa in that it inherited arbitrary state boundaries from its colonial past. To the south, for example, Kenya's ruler-straight border with Tanzania suddenly changes course at Moshi. It is as if a mistake has been made, and the map-maker's pen has slipped temporarily, before continuing its geometrically correct journey to the Indian Ocean. Queen Victoria wished to make a gift of Mount Kilimanjaro to her grandson, the future Kaiser Wilhelm II. The border between German and British East Africa was thus moved accordingly. In this respect, and illustrating the irrational nature of African borders, the reality of whether thousands of Africans are today citizens of Kenya or Tanzania was decided by the bestowing of a birthday present.

Although this is an extreme case, it is obvious that African states and their borders were not created with local necessities in mind. Instead, they were shaped to meet the demands and interests of imperialism and its managers. This is a fact also reflected in Kenya's western border with Uganda. This boundary, despite being moved in 1926, still cuts across the territory of ten cultural groups.[14]

It is Kenya's north-eastern boundary, however, that has created most problems in the post-colonial era. As discussed above, the Somali people were divided among five colonial states as a result of imperial partition. Consequently, north-eastern Kenya has a large ethnic Somali population, many of whom identify more with their ethnic origins than with the Kenyan state. Across the border, the Somali Republic itself, before its collapse in the 1990s, certainly wished to see this part of Kenya become Somali sovereign territory.

During the First World War, the British government partially addressed this situation. It came to a secret agreement with Italy to transfer 94,050 square kilometres of its East African protectorate to Italian Somaliland. This was Italy's reward for allying with Britain against Germany. The treaty was honoured, and Jubaland was ceded in 1924. Many ethnic Somalis, however, were still left living on Kenyan territory, even after this boundary change. The issue was thus revisited just before independence, in 1963. Britain negotiated with Somalia, and was apparently willing to give up further territory. Somalia, however, demanded the whole of Kenya's Northern Province for itself. This was much more than Britain would cede, and the talks ended in stalemate. Consequently, Kenya's independent government inherited this boundary dispute and an irredentist guerrilla war. Relations did improve between Kenya and Somalia from 1967, however, and the war faded out. The fact remains, though, that there are still many Somalis living in Kenya who owe their political loyalties more to kin across the border than to the Kenyan government.

Kenya's economic inheritance from its colonial rulers was equally problematic. Evidence supporting the underdevelopment thesis can certainly be found. Land was alienated in the most fertile areas (the 'white highlands') from Africans and used to settle European farmers instead; labour was also exploited, with Africans being taxed, forcing them into the cash economy; and economic development concentrated largely on cash crops (tea and coffee), denying the Kenyan economy the chance to diversify. Even today, after 40 years of 'independence', relatively industrialised Kenya is still buying the vast bulk of its imported goods from the old metropolitan state of Britain, rather than from neighbouring, local markets in East Africa.

The result of this 'underdevelopment' would be that post-colonial administrations would inherit a land problem: how should the land owned by European settlers be returned to the farmers it was taken from? There was also the difficulty of producing development from an economy based primarily on agricultural exports. The Kenyan economy would indeed suffer each time the price of coffee or tea fell.

The economy was not completely underdeveloped, however. Kenya inherited a good communications infrastructure from the colonial state, a basic health service and an education system. What is more, by comparison with the rest of Africa, Kenya had a significant industrial sector. Based on a nucleus that developed to serve white settlers, manufacturing grew during the post-colonial period. Kenya has consequently profited from sales to the rest of East Africa and beyond. Although it still relies heavily on its cash-crop farming, the Kenyan economy is also active in the chemical industry, in producing cement, manufacturing consumer goods, and is particularly successful in refining petroleum products (from imported oil). Tourism also attracts considerable sums of foreign exchange each year. Although Kenyan labour and resources had been exploited by imperial interests before independence, and it had inherited an economy seriously skewed towards the export of primary produce, it would seem that the economy was not 'underdeveloped' beyond hope. The present-day economy still has massive obstacles to overcome, but it has reaped limited successes through diversification.

Organised opposition to colonial rule in Kenya, especially among the Kikuyu, can be traced back to the 1920s. It was the so-called Mau Mau uprisings, however, that finally forced the British into the negotiations that led to Kenya's independence. Some 13,000 Africans and 1,000 Europeans died in this unrest that centred on land rights in the highlands. The Kikuyu wanted access to their ancestral land, and threatened to take this by force. Over 80,000 Africans were detained in 're-education' camps by the colonial authorities. When the level of violence rose sharply in 1952, a state of emergency was declared. Nationalist leaders were imprisoned (including future president Jomo Kenyatta), and British troop reinforcements were deployed to quell the rebellion. Once this had been achieved, the colonial authorities sought to foster a political class with which it could build a collaborative partnership of government.

The nationalist leaders that the imperial authorities sought to engage certainly did not represent a cross-section of Kenyan society. They were an urban educated elite, who often already had close associations with the state (as employees or business partners). When, for example, Africans were allowed to sit alongside European representatives in the Legislative Council for the first time in 1957, the employment of the candidates standing was revealing. Most were teachers; others included veterinarians, journalists, businessmen, civil service union leaders, an army warrant officer, a social worker and a lawyer. The vast majority of these had a secondary school education, a sizeable proportion were university graduates, and several had studied or worked abroad.[15] They shared few social characteristics with the peasants who sustained the Mau Mau rebellion. It would be this elite that would inherit the Kenyan state from the imperial authorities at decolonisation. As will be shown later in the book, it can be argued that this elite subsequently formed an exploitative 'bureaucratic bourgeoisie'.

Kenya's independence came in 1963, rather more quickly than Britain had planned. Nationalists were looking for complete independence and self-rule, rather than just a junior partnership within the imperial administration. Power-sharing formulae were swept aside, and with this, colonial rule perished. Before departing, however, the British government did leave Kenya with a liberal democratic constitution, drawn up during pre-independence negotiations.

With the benefit of hindsight, it was obvious that the political institutions created by this constitution would be incredibly weak. Like the colonial state itself, these institutions were imposed. They had not grown organically, over time, out of society, but had been ushered in overnight. The new constitution enshrined multi-party democracy for Kenya, but such pluralism had no roots in this country. There had not been a single African national political party established prior to the Second World War; and after the war, organisations of this nature were often banned. Nor had there been a representative parliament in Kenya under colonial rule. In short, liberal democracy had no historical foundations in Africa. Yet this was the legacy that imperial rule left. Kenya was expected instantly to create a political culture that could support and sustain these pluralist political institutions.

The Westminster constitutional model of politics soon broke down in postcolonial Kenya. Within a year of decolonisation, the smaller of two parties that had contested the independence elections, the Kenya African Democratic Union, merged with the victor, the ruling Kenya African National Union (KANU). KANU governed Kenya without an opposition from this point in 1964 right

Plate 2.2   President Jomo Kenyatta of Kenya celebrating his country's independence, 1963.
Photographer: Harry Benson.

through until electoral reforms were forced upon the state, and it lost elections in 2002. The most serious challenge to the ruling party came in 1966, when the Kenya People's Union was formed. President Kenyatta promptly banned this organisation.

Other moves to centralise state power were also undertaken by KANU. In 1964, for example, the Office of the Prime Minister was abolished, with a more powerful and centralised presidential office being established instead. Similarly, in 1966, Kenya's second chamber was dissolved, creating a unicameral system, further centralising the state. Also in that year, the Preventative Detention Act became law, bypassing the independence constitution's Bill of Rights (by permitting detention without trial in the interests of 'public security'). Power was systematically being taken away from Parliament, and given to Kenyatta's Office of the President, and his allies in the civil service and army. Kenya was reverting to a style of bureaucratic authoritarianism familiar in the colonial era.

The accession to the presidency of Daniel arap Moi in 1978, following Kenyatta's death, promised a programme of political liberalisation. Moi did indeed release a number of political prisoners and start to tackle issues of corruption, but this did not last. Moi's rule proved more authoritarian than Kenyatta's. The new head of state, consolidating his own position of power after an attempted air force coup in 1982, introduced a formal one-party state. The last vestiges of liberal democracy were thus removed. The independence constitution that had tried to usher in pluralist, multi-party competition, but had been built on the shaky historical foundations of colonial bureaucratic autocracy, was now itself history.

It was only in the 1990s that Moi came under serious pressure to reform his government. Multi-party politics returned to Kenya during this decade (events which will be examined in Chapter 11). The president himself managed to deploy his wily and brutal political skills to survive two competitive general elections, eventually retiring in 2002. His party, KANU, was finally removed from office in December of that year, defeated in multi-party elections by an opposition coalition. Yet, despite this political watershed, and an outpouring of optimism at the start of the new millennium, Kenya has still to live up to the standards demanded by the independence constitution of 40 years previously. The 2008 power-sharing arrangement agreed between the two leading political parties, in the wake of serious post-electoral violence, effectively ignored the will of the voting public. Meanwhile, corruption among state officials of all political allegiances remains endemic. These events would suggest that a colonial inheritance of 'bureaucratic authoritarianism' still has more influence on Kenyan political culture than do ideals of liberal democracy.

Kenya[16]

Territory:	580,367 sq. km.	Population:	44.4 million
Colonial power:	Britain	Independence:	1963
Major cities:	Nairobi (capital)	Major ethnic groups:	Kikuyu
	Mombasa		Luhya
	Kisumu		Luo
Urban population:	25 per cent		Kamba
Languages:	Kiswahili		Kalenijin
	English		Masai
Currency:	Kenyan Shilling	Life expectancy:	62 years
Infant mortality:	48 deaths/1,000 live births	Adult literacy:	72 per cent
Religions:	Traditional	Major exports:	Tea
	Christian		Vegetables
	Hindu		Oil
	Islam	GDP per capita:	US$943

Questions raised by this chapter

1. Which elements of pre-colonial African society continue to influence African politics today?
2. How have Africa's imperially imposed borders affected the continent politically, economically and socially?
3. To what extent did the state and civil society engage in colonial Africa?
4. What role did the African educated elite play in colonial rule and national liberation?
5. Does the evidence from Africa support the thesis of underdevelopment?
6. How appropriate were the political institutions left to Africa at independence?

7.   Did Africa's colonial inheritance make political authoritarianism and economic poverty inevitable in the post-independence period?

Glossary of key terms

Arbitrary borders	State boundaries reflecting imperial interests, rather than local economic, social or political realities.
Bureaucratic autocracy	A system of government that relies on coercion rather than legitimacy, and seeks to administer a territory avoiding public representation and accountability.
Cash crop	Agricultural produce grown for export (e.g. coffee, tea, cocoa, sisal and other commodities), not produce for personal or domestic consumption (e.g. food staples).
Core and peripheral states	The notion that the international system consists of wealthy states (the West), which have enhanced their economic position by exploiting and 'underdeveloping' those territories on the periphery of the international system (the Third World).
Export of surplus	The export of profits denying local investment opportunities in the country of origin.
Indirect rule	A system of colonial administration favouring the use of local intermediaries, rather than full-scale central government intervention.
Irredentism	The desire to unite under one flag a community that is currently divided between separate states.
Lineage and kinship ties	Social bonds based on ties of family, clan, origin and descent.
Monocrop economy	An economy that is over-reliant on one commodity.
Primary sector	Economic activity (e.g. mining and agriculture) other than secondary manufacturing industry or the service sector.
Scramble for Africa	The late nineteenth- and early twentieth-century partition of Africa among European imperial powers.
State elite	An educated and urban class which owes its privilege to its access to state institutions.
Stateless society	A society whose political organisation does not rely on strictly defined territory or centralised political institutions.
Underdevelopment	The systematic holding back of a state's economic potential in order to serve instead an imperial power's interests.

Further reading

Basil Davidson's book provides an excellent place to start learning about pre-colonial Africa, while Molefi Kete Asante's historical survey covers more of the continent, over a wider time span. These works could be combined with Colin McEvedy's collection of maps giving a different perspective of African history, stretching from 175 million years ago to the present day.

For a more specialist text on the state, Crawford Young's look at colonial Africa is invaluable. For those interested in Africa's boundary politics, Saadia Touval's book, although dated, is still the best introduction to this subject. Similarly, Jeffrey Herbst provides an excellent account of Africa's 'non-hegemonic' states through time.

Underdevelopment theory commands a vast literature. For an introduction to this school of thought from one of its strongest advocates, it is well worth reading Andre Gunder Frank's *Capitalism and Underdevelopment*. To see how this thesis was applied specifically to Africa, a combination of Samir Amin's article and Walter Rodney's book will prove useful. These should be balanced by criticisms of underdevelopment theory, of which Bill Warren's *Imperialism: the Pioneer of Capitalism* stands out.

Ieuan Griffiths has written a particularly profitable and accessible book that covers many of the issues tackled in this chapter, while those interested in developing their understanding of Kenya's post-colonial political relationship with authoritarianism, and its historical roots, would find Susanne Mueller's article a good starting point for their research.

Amin, Samir. Underdevelopment and dependency in Black Africa. *Journal of Modern African Studies*. 1972, 10(4), 503–24.

Asante, Molefi Kete. *The History of Africa: the Quest for Eternal Harmony*. New York: Routledge, 2007.

Davidson, Basil. *West Africa Before the Colonial Era: A History to 1850*. London: Longman, 1998.

Frank, Andre Gunder. *Capitalism and Underdevelopment in Latin America*. London: Penguin, 1971.

Griffiths, Ieuan Ll. *The African Inheritance*. London: Routledge, 1995.

Herbst, Jeffrey. *States and Power in Africa: Comparative Lessons in Authority and Control*. Princeton, NJ: Princeton University Press, 2000.

McEvedy, Colin. *The Penguin Atlas of African History*. London: Penguin, 1995.

Mueller, Susanne D. The resilience of the past: government and opposition in Kenya. *Canadian Journal of African Studies*. 2014, 48(2), 333–52. Available online at www.tandfonline.com/doi/pdf/10.1080/00083968.2014.971835 (accessed 13 January 2015).

Rodney, Walter. *How Europe Underdeveloped Africa*. Nairobi: East African Educational Publishers, 1989.

Touval, Saadia. *The Boundary Politics of Independent Africa*. Cambridge, MA: Harvard University Press, 1972.

Warren, Bill. *Imperialism: The Pioneer of Capitalism*. London: Verso, 1980.

Young, Crawford. *The African Colonial State in Comparative Perspective*. New Haven, CT: Yale University Press, 1994.

Notes and references

1 See Herbst, Jeffrey. *States and Power in Africa: Comparative Lessons in Authority and Control*. Princeton, NJ: Princeton University Press, 2000. *Passim*.

2 See, for example, Robinson, Ronald and John Gallagher (with Alice Denny). *Africa and the Victorians: The Official Mind of Imperialism*. Basingstoke: Macmillan, 1981.

3 See Nugent, Paul and Anthony I. Asiwaju. Introduction: The paradox of African boundaries. In: Paul Nugent and Anthony I. Asiwaju, eds. *African Boundaries: Barriers, Conduits and Opportunities*. London: Pinter, 1996. 1–14.

4 See Wilson, Henry S. *The Imperial Experience in Sub-Saharan Africa since 1870*. Minneapolis, MN: University of Minnesota Press, 1977. 95.

5 Griffiths, Ieuan Ll. *The African Inheritance*. London: Routledge, 1995. 91.

6 *Ibid.* 84–98.
7 Young, Crawford. The African colonial state and its political legacy. In: Donald Rothchild and Naomi Chazan, eds. *The Precarious Balance: State and Society in Africa.* Boulder, CO: Westview, 1988. 37.
8 Hodder-Williams, Richard. *An Introduction to the Politics of Tropical Africa.* London: George Allen & Unwin, 1984. 32.
9 Mamdani, Mahmood. *Politics and Class Formation in Uganda.* New York: Monthly Review Press, 1976. 208.
10 Lamb, David. *The Africans.* New York: Random House, 1984. 5.
11 Warren, Bill. *Imperialism: The Pioneer of Capitalism.* London: Verso, 1980.
12 The Portuguese territories of Angola, Mozambique and Guinea–Bissau were exceptions to this relatively peaceful transfer of power, as were the white settler states of Algeria, Southern Rhodesia (Zimbabwe), South-West Africa (Namibia) and South Africa. Guerrilla war was required to force independence in each of these cases. Kenya, with its Mau Mau uprising, could be added to this list, but the intensity of this guerrilla war was not as widespread as in the other settler states listed. See the case study at the end of the chapter.
13 Berman, Bruce and John Lonsdale. *Unhappy Valley: Conflict in Kenya and Africa.* London: James Currey, 1992. 19–20.
14 Griffiths. *The African Inheritance.* 91.
15 See Ogot, Bethwell A. The decisive years 1956–63. In: Bethwell A. Ogot and William R. Ochieng, eds. *Decolonization and Independence in Kenya, 1940–93.* London: James Currey, 1995. 54–7.
16 Statistics taken from United Nations Conference on Trade and Development. *UNCTAD Handbook of Statistics 2014.* New York: United Nations, 2014. Tables 8.1, 8.4 and 3.2.D; World Bank data http://data.worldbank.org/indicator/SP.DYN.LE00.IN (accessed 24 July 2015) and http://data.worldbank.org/indicator/SP.DYN.IMRT.IN (accessed 24 July 2015); and UNESCO data www.uis.unesco.org/DataCentre/Pages/regions.aspx (accessed 24 July 2015).

3 Ideology

Nationalism, socialism, populism and state capitalism

Chapter outline

- Decolonisation in Africa
- Nationalism
- African nationalism
- The differing ideological shades of African nationalism

  - African socialism
  - Scientific socialism
  - Populism
  - State capitalism

- State and civil society
- Case study: socialism and *ujamaa* in Tanzania
- Questions raised by this chapter
- Glossary of key terms
- Further reading
- Notes and references

Robert Putnam describes an ideology as *a lifeguiding system of beliefs, values and goals affecting political style and action.*[1] In this sense, individuals use ideologies to help them understand and explain the world. They provide a way for human beings to synthesise the mass of information around them into something more logical and meaningful, giving them a 'world view'. Socialism, liberalism and anarchism, for example, all serve as guides to their disciples, as do Catholicism, Islam and even capitalism, if looser definitions of ideology are used. Ideologies provide interpretations of history, and explanations of present events, as well as supplying an accompanying set of values to which followers can adhere.

The study of politics is furthered by analysing the key characteristics of these ideologies, as well as by examining their impact upon the process of governing. Ideology, in this respect, acts as a socialising force. People with similar world views will cooperate to further mutual interests and defend this lifestyle against competitors. Consequently, most societies have a dominant ideology that provides the basis of social order. Liberal democracy, for example, prospers in Western Europe and North America, permeating right through society. It is an ideology that binds state and civil society together, and it provides governments with their mission, coherence and, most importantly, their legitimacy.

If the study of ideology helps political scientists to understand the politics of the West, then the same should also be true for post-colonial Africa. Any book seeking to explain the politics of this continent therefore needs to identify and explore the dominant ideologies that are at work in this environment. This is precisely the task of the current chapter. The ideologies investigated will reveal the very foundations of African political systems.

As the following paragraphs will show, it has been nationalism that has dominated modern African politics. This can be explained by the shared struggle against imperialism, and the desire to build cohesive nation-states after independence. This is not to say, however, that all African countries share a common ideology. Numerous, distinct shades of nationalism have emerged. The chapter groups these different nuances into four general categories: African socialism, scientific socialism, populism and state capitalism. Each of these ideologies is examined in turn, followed by some concluding thoughts on how nationalism has helped shape the relationship between state and civil society in the post-colonial period.

Decolonisation in Africa

Nationalism was the mobilising force that saw Africans liberate themselves from imperial rule. Libya (1951), Morocco (1956), the Sudan (1956), Tunisia (1956), Ghana (1957) and Guinea (1958) were the first countries to expel their colonial masters. Most African states, however, gained their independence during the 1960s (see Table 3.1).

The majority of francophone colonies in sub-Saharan Africa secured their political sovereignty, more or less en masse, in 1960. Three other French territories had to wait longer. Algeria won its independence in 1962; the Indian Ocean state of the Comoros (minus one of its islands) did likewise in 1975; Djibouti, a tiny state on the Red Sea coast, completed France's mainland decolonisation in 1977. Algeria proved to be the most problematic case of French withdrawal. Only a bitter war of independence, and the collapse of the Fourth Republic back in France itself, secured this country its political freedom.

By contrast, Britain opted for a steadier programme of decolonisation. Pressures from within Africa ensured that there were regular Union Jack flag-lowering ceremonies throughout the 1960s. All but the Seychelles (decolonised in 1976) and Zimbabwe (Rhodesia) had become independent by the end of this decade. Britain only formally relinquished control of Zimbabwe in 1980. The delay was created by Ian Smith's rebel minority white settler government, which had unilaterally declared independence from London in 1965. Smith's administration only submitted to negotiations, and majority rule, after a protracted war of insurgency.

Portugal put up most resistance to the 'winds of change' sweeping through Africa. Lisbon held on desperately to its colonies of Angola, Mozambique and Guinea–Bissau until the mid-1970s. It was at this point that strains created by the guerrilla wars fought in these territories precipitated a military coup in Portugal itself. On taking power, Lisbon's new military government withdrew its forces from Africa, and independence followed for the three colonies in 1975.

Since Zimbabwe's independence in 1980, two remaining loose ends of imperialism have been tidied up. Namibia gained its independence from South African occupation in 1990, while majority rule came to South Africa itself in 1994. This leaves just two externally governed territories remaining on the African mainland (Spain's pair of Mediterranean enclaves at Ceuta and Melilla). There are also several sets of islands in both the Atlantic and Indian Oceans still under European sovereignty.

Table 3.1 Decolonisation in Africa

Country (former name)	Imperial power	Independence
Algeria	France	1962
Angola	Portugal	1975
Benin (Dahomey)	France	1960
Botswana (Bechuanaland)	Britain	1966
Burkina Faso (Upper Volta)	France	1960
Burundi (Urundi)	Germany, then Belgium from 1916	1962
Cameroon	Germany, then Britain/ France from 1918	1960
Cape Verde	Portugal	1975
Central African Republic (Ubangi Chari)	France	1960
Chad	France	1960
The Comoros	France	1975 (except Mayotte Island)
Congo, Republic of (French Congo, Congo-Brazzaville)	France	1960
Congo, Democratic Republic of the (DRC) (Belgian Congo, Congo-Kinshasa)	Belgium	1960
Côte d'Ivoire (Ivory Coast)	France	1960
Djibouti (French Somaliland, Afars and Issas)	France	1977
Egypt	Britain	1922
Equatorial Guinea (Fernando Po and Rio Muni)	Spain	1968
Eritrea	Italy	Federated within Ethiopia 1952, seceded 1993
Ethiopia	None	—
Gabon	France	1960
The Gambia	Britain	1965
Ghana (Gold Coast)	Britain	1957
Guinea	France	1958
Guinea–Bissau	Portugal	1974
Kenya	Britain	1963
Lesotho (Basutoland)	Britain	1966
Liberia	None	1847
Libya	Italy	1951
Madagascar	France	1960
Malawi (Nyasaland)	Britain	1964
Mali (Soudan)	France	1960
Mauritania	France	1960
Mauritius	Britain	1968
Morocco	Spain and France	1956
Mozambique	Portugal	1975
Namibia (South-West Africa)	Germany, then South African mandate from 1920	1990
Niger	France	1960
Nigeria	Britain	1960

(Continued)

Table 3.1 Decolonisation in Africa (Continued)

Country (former name)	Imperial power	Independence
Rwanda (Ruanda)	Germany, then Belgium from 1916	1962
Sahrawi Arab Republic (Western Sahara)	Spain	Occupied on Spanish withdrawal by Morocco in 1976
São Tomé and Principe	Portugal	1975
Senegal	France	1960
Seychelles	Britain	1976
Sierra Leone	Britain	1961
Somalia	Britain and Italy	1960
South Africa	Union of British colonies and Boer republics	1910, (majority rule 1994)
South Sudan	Britain (Anglo-Egyptian Condominium)	Within Sudan 1956, seceded 2011
Sudan	Britain (Anglo-Egyptian Condominium)	1956
Swaziland	Britain	1968
Tanzania: union of Tanganyika and Zanzibar		Unified in 1964
(Tanganyika)	(Germany, then Britain from 1919)	(1961)
(Zanzibar)	(Britain)	(1964)
Togo	Germany, then Britain and France from 1919	1960
Tunisia	France	1956
Uganda	Britain	1962
Zambia (Northern Rhodesia)	Britain	1964
Zimbabwe (Southern Rhodesia)	Britain	1980 (UDI 1965*)

*The white-settler-led government of Southern Rhodesia claimed political autonomy in 1965, issuing a unilateral declaration of independence (UDI). The territory's colonial power, the United Kingdom, alongside the wider international community, did not recognise this new state of Rhodesia. Legal independence came in 1980, after non-racial democratic elections led to the formation of Zimbabwe.

A number of factors combined to produce this tidal wave of decolonisation. In most cases, the imperial powers recognised that (eventually) they would have to grant all peoples the self-determination and democracy that they had demanded for themselves during the Second World War. Arguments that only civilised (for 'civilised', read 'white') human beings could cope with liberty and political autonomy were beginning to wear thin. The United States, in particular, was pushing for its version of liberalism and capitalism to spread across the globe. Also there was the issue of cost. Empire, now that it involved responsibilities and not just exploitation, proved to be a heavy burden on the metropolitan powers' treasuries. In this respect, there were financial, as well as moral, motivations for political withdrawal. Above all, however, it was pressures created from within the colonies themselves that secured independence. 'Africa for the Africans' was now the demand. African nationalism had come of age, and, indeed, would remain at the centre of the nation-building project during the post-colonial period.

Plate 3.1 The British royal standard is lowered, and the flag of Ghana raised, during Ghana's independence ceremony, Accra, 3 June 1957.

Nationalism

Nationalism is relatively simple to define. It is *the desire that the nation should be housed in its own sovereign state*. The problem with this definition is that the inquirer first has to know what a nation is.

A nation is not so much a physical entity as a sentiment. It is *a collection of people bound together by common values and traditions, often sharing the same language, history and an affiliation to a geographical area*. Individuals within the group will identify with fellow members of the nation, and define themselves in contrast to outsiders belonging to other nations. Benedict Anderson talks of nations as 'imagined communities'. This is because the members of even 'the smallest nation will never know most of their fellow-members, meet them, or even hear of them, yet in the minds of each lives the image of their communion'.[2] Using interpretations of the past and symbols such as flags, anthems and ceremonies, the people of the nation generate social cohesion based on their shared national values and way of life. In this sense, individuals gain psychological and material protection from a sense of belonging. What is more, this security can be greatly enhanced if the nation is united with political power. This is where the idea of nationalism comes to the fore.

Nationalism occurs when members of a nation desire to be united as one political unit. This gives the nation political organisation and power. Only then is it likely that a nation can enjoy self-determination, with tailor-made state institutions serving its interests and controlling its destiny. State power can protect the nation from the unwanted influences of other nations, as well as guarding national values internally.[3]

A classic example of nationalism giving birth to a new state can be found with the formation of Italy in the mid-nineteenth century. Prior to 1861, the Italian people were divided among several territories. However, diplomatic activity and a guerrilla war assisted these previously divided people to unite and form the single sovereign state of Italy. The Italian nation had secured itself the prize of statehood, which in turn brought self-government and dedicated political institutions to serve the Italian people. Germany emerged from a similar process ten years later, in 1871. In both cases, a nation demanded a state, and then it was up to the new state to sustain and develop the nation that had created it.

African nationalism

The nature of African nationalism is slightly different to its European cousin. In terms of origins, for example, modern African states were not created by the demands of indigenous social forces. They were not the product of local nationalist appeals. Instead, African states were externally imposed. As was seen in the previous chapter, imperial powers drew political boundaries that meant very little to the Africans they enclosed. This meant that groups with diverse, or even conflicting, identities were gathered together within these 'alien' states. A lack of unity or common culture meant these communities could not be described as nations. Instead, Africans retained and developed ideas of community at a more local, sub-state level (lineage groups, clans and 'tribes'). Imperial administrators encouraged these divisions, contributing to the absence of a national identity within the colonial states. In short, modern states arrived in Africa well before any nation considered these states their own. Unlike the example of Italy or Germany, the state existed before the nation, not vice versa. It was not until the mid-twentieth century that political activists began successfully to arouse widespread nationalist sentiments on the continent.

African nationalism began seriously to challenge imperial rule in the 1950s. It emerged as a reaction to colonialism, and its immediate aim was to rid the continent of foreign rule. In this respect, African nationalism was a classic expression of the demand for self-determination. The leaders of these liberation movements, however, only rejected imperial rule. Unlike the European nationalists before them, they were not seeking to establish a new state to house their nation. Instead, they aimed to capture the existing colonial states for Africans themselves to govern. As such, the retention of the 'alien' state would be wholesale, including the recognition of its associated 'arbitrary' boundaries. The mission was to build new African nations within the prefabricated structures of the already existing colonial states. This, the nationalists argued, would bring Africans into the modern era of nation-states.

National unity was at the heart of African nationalism. The objective was to transform multi-ethnic, multicultural, multi-religious and even multiracial societies into single unitary nations. A new nation would be built to fill the political space delineated by the borders of the already existing (colonial) state. In this respect, cultural pluralism was frowned upon by nationalist leaders. Where previously Africans had rooted their identities in descent and ethnicity, rather than territory, now they were called upon to join the community of the nation-state. As President Hastings Banda of Malawi declared, 'So far as I am concerned, there is no Yao in this country; no Lomwe; no Sena; no Chewa; no Ngoni; no Nyakyusa; no Tonga; there are only "Malawians". That is all'.[4] President Samora Machel of Mozambique was more succinct. He stated that 'For the nation to live, the tribe must die'.[5]

In striving to build nations such as Malawi and Mozambique, nationalists (politicians and academics alike) regarded Africa's complex ethnic relationships as a hindrance. 'Tribes' were the antithesis of a nation. They were portrayed as retrogressive, part of the past, and an obstacle to progress. In this respect, 'tribalism' was regarded as a sin against the post-colonial state, and the freedoms that had been won. The nation was now the priority, not outdated 'tribal' associations, and state power would be used to promote this process of nation building.

For these reasons, nationalism lost none of its urgency after the winning of self-determination and independence. It became the dominant component within the ideologies of all Africa's new states. Added to this theme of unity was the related goal of economic growth. These words of President Julius Nyerere, written just after Tanganyika's independence in 1961, captured the mood of nationalist thinking at this time. He described his state's work as:

> a patriotic struggle that leaves no room for differences and unites all elements of the country; the nationalists who led them to freedom must inevitably form the first governments of the new States. Once the first free government is formed, its supreme task lies in building up the economy…. This, no less than the struggle against colonialism, calls for the maximum united effort by the whole country if it is to succeed. There can be no room for difference or division.[6]

As a consequence, after independence, political activity was often channelled through just one state-sanctioned party, with opposition groups banned. Similarly, organisations that had previously been active within civil society, such as trade unions, youth movements and women's groups, were co-opted by the state, restricting their autonomy. Ethnic associations were also often banned, and even the numerous indigenous languages spoken within each African state were disregarded. Usually just one official 'national' language was chosen, generally that of the departing colonial power. In short, pluralist competition was sacrificed to the higher goal of nation building. Preaching the necessity for unity and economic development, nationalism, fostered by the state, became the dominant ideology in the post-colonial era.

The differing ideological shades of African nationalism

Although all the newly independent African states were clearly anti-imperial and nationalist in outlook, this did not result in these countries adopting identical ideologies. Each state followed its own unique ideological path in its attempt to secure national unity and economic development. Indeed, most nationalist leaders had their own personal political philosophies, which were often placed at the heart of all state activity. Senghor, for example, preached *négritude*; Kaunda advocated *humanism*; Nyerere promoted *ujamaa*; and Mobutu fashioned *Mobutism*. Despite this diversity, however, it is possible to gather these nationalist ideologies into four general categories (African socialism, scientific socialism, populism and state capitalism; summarised in Table 3.2).

By looking at each of these categories in turn, it is possible to analyse in more detail the ideological foundations underpinning Africa's post-colonial political systems.

African socialism

It is not surprising that most states on the continent adopted a socialist outlook after independence. Having rid their countries of colonial rule, the task now was to reduce dependence on the West, and to restructure economies to ensure that local development needs were prioritised. Only in this manner could poverty be reduced and social welfare provided for all.

Few African leaders considered capitalism and liberalism appropriate methods to achieve these goals. These, after all, had been the ideologies of their former colonial oppressors, and remained the philosophy behind the international system that continued to disadvantage African economies. Instead, the more egalitarian approach of socialism was adopted. Socialism represented a 'political amulet' that many thought could bring progress and material gains to the continent.[7] As Aristide Zolberg wrote at the time, 'for those who are faced with the overwhelming burdens of government in Africa, socialism is more than a scientific method. It is a modern gnosis which promises to unveil to its initiates the secrets of economic development'.[8]

This is not to say that African leaders adopted socialism as prescribed by the Soviet Union. Although fraternal links were extended, African states were careful to keep their distance. As Ahmed Sékou Touré, the President of Guinea, warned, 'trying to "Westernise" or Easternise" Africa leads to denying the African personality'.[9] Instead, true to their nationalist roots, politicians on the continent promoted their own specific version of socialism, that of *African socialism*.

The new President of Senegal, Léopold Senghor, outlined the problem of adopting orthodox European socialism. He argued, 'It is evident that African socialism can no longer be that of Marx and Engels, which was designed in the nineteenth century according to European scientific methods and realities. Now it must take into consideration African realities'.[10] Classical theories of socialism, for example, saw the proletariat as the revolutionary class that would defeat the bourgeoisie. In Africa, with its small industrial base, there was no real working class to talk of, nor were there societies marked by massive inequalities. African states needed guiding ideologies more relevant to their own experiences.

This is why African socialism stressed the continent's traditional values. African leaders portrayed their communities as having been classless, communal and egalitarian prior to colonial rule. There had been no landowners in these societies, it was argued, and the interests of the community had always been put above those of the individual. In this respect, Senghor believed Africans had 'already realized socialism before the coming of the Europeans'.[11]

African socialism was therefore an attempt to recover these traditional values, and to marry them with new technology and the nation-state. More specifically, it was about combining the equality, co-operation and humanism of the village community with the wealth and organisation potential that could be generated by modern production methods and state institutions. African socialism, in this manner, sought to skip the capitalist stage of development outlined in classical Marxist analysis. Neither would an alternative Soviet-style 'dictatorship of the proletariat' have to be constructed. African leaders believed this self-reliant, non-capitalist path to socialism would create a new social order where poverty could be reduced, welfare improved and human dignity maximised.

This pursuit of African socialism cast the state in a central role not only politically, but also economically and socially. The state would be the engine of development. Public enterprise came to dominate these centrally planned economies; large elements of the private sector were nationalised (including foreign capital); and the state itself embarked on grand development projects of infrastructure and industrialisation. Similarly, harvests were bought by state marketing board monopolies; consumer goods were sold largely in state-run shops; prices were set by government agencies; and imports and exports were controlled centrally. In short, the free market was curtailed, with the state itself commanding both production and distribution.

The state, in a similar vein, also came to dominate politically (as will be seen in Chapter 6). Most African countries became one-party states led from the centre, with little leeway given to opposition movements or local politics. This curtailment of pluralism was justified in the name of national unity and the need for the government to deliver a coherent and consistent development strategy.

Whether political or economic in nature, these practical characteristics of African socialism dovetailed neatly into those aims of nationalism already mentioned (anti-imperialism, self-reliance, national unity and the promotion of economic development). African leaders were convinced they had found a non-capitalist path to future prosperity.

All African states struggled in their nationalist ambitions, however, and those espousing African socialism proved to be no exception. Like other ideologies, this particular strain of socialism was hampered by a number of realities: the nature of the international economy (explored in more detail in Chapter 9); an inability to mobilise the peasantry (see the case study at the end of this chapter); internal social division (see Chapter 4); and the tendency of state elites to serve their own, and not the wider community's, interests (see Chapters 5 and 10). Consequently, many of these experiments perished with the onset of military coups from the mid-1960s onwards (see Chapter 7).

African socialism also came under attack intellectually. Many regarded it as merely a convenient justification for the repression of alternative viewpoints and the suppression of civil liberties. Others, on the Left, criticised these states for not following a classical (European) Marxist–Leninist path to socialism. They judged the radical rhetoric of Africa's nationalist leaders not to be matched by their public policy. The Soviet Union itself, in this respect, regarded many of these governments as merely 'reformist'. They saw fault in the independent nature of African socialism, with its strong traditional and humanist, rather than scientific socialist, values.

Scientific socialism

'Our socialism cannot be called Somali socialism, African socialism, or Islamic socialism….Our socialism is scientific socialism founded by the great Marx and Engels'.[12] These words of President Mohamed Siad Barré acknowledged a change in the ideological approach undertaken by Somalia and several other African states from 1969 onwards. Marien Ngouabi's military regime in Congo-Brazzaville was the first government to declare its allegiance to scientific socialism. Somalia followed suit a year later, and the mid-1970s brought a further wave of ideological change. The Portuguese coup of April 1974 saw Marxist–Leninist-inspired guerrilla movements take power in both Mozambique and Angola; in September of that year Emperor Haile Selassie of Ethiopia was deposed, making way for a regime advocating scientific socialism; two months later, Lieutenant Colonel Mathieu Kérékou launched a 'revolution within a revolution' in

Benin; while Madagascar's military government moved to Marxism–Leninism in June 1975. Given that the liberation movements fighting in Zimbabwe, Namibia and South Africa also expressed sympathies with this ideology, events had provided scientific socialism with a firm foothold on the African continent by the late 1970s.

Marxism–Leninism began to prosper on the continent after the first wave of (African) socialism began to be criticised. African socialism had failed to break the shackles of economic dependence, and many of the governments it inspired soon degenerated into corrupt dictatorships vulnerable to military coups. Marxist–Leninists considered this inevitable. They thought African socialism was too amorphous and shapeless. Romantic notions of inherent African communalism masked the reality of underlying class antagonisms. Indeed, in many cases it was argued that a petty-bourgeois state elite was simply disguising its exploitation of the masses with a disingenuous socialist rhetoric. In this respect, the Marxist–Leninists declared there to be only one true socialism, that based on the science of class analysis. This demanded that petty-bourgeois state elites should immediately commit class suicide, and in their place working class governments should be established. These would then rule, allied to the peasant masses. Only after these revolutionary changes were undertaken could a true socialist society be built.

Ethiopia provides an excellent case study of what actually happened to an African state after a Marxist–Leninist regime came to power. In 1975, Colonel Mariam Mengistu's

Plate 3.2 MPLA leader, Agostino Neto, addresses a political rally in Luanda, Angola, 1975. Photographer: Francoise de Mulder.

new government nationalised all major domestic industrial, financial and commercial enterprises without compensation. The role of private capital was severely restricted, as decreed by the 'Government Ownership and Control of the Means of Production Proclamation'. The state itself was now to command the economy. Similarly, the small amount of foreign investment present in Ethiopia was also nationalised (with compensation). Land ownership, too, came directly under government control (previously, Ethiopian society was unique in Africa in hosting a landlord class). In terms of economic development, the government concentrated its efforts on industrialisation, promoting state factories, and the socialisation of agriculture with the establishment of state farms. The working class and peasantry, after all, were to be the leaders of the revolution. The regime also eventually established the Workers' Party of Ethiopia to act as the vanguard of the revolution.[13]

In terms of public policy, it is often difficult to distinguish between these Marxist–Leninist governments and their African socialist neighbours. Scientific socialist states may have been more systematic about their socialism, and may have avoided the personalisation of this ideology, yet it cannot be said that scientific socialist regimes were any less nationalistic than their African socialist predecessors. There was no 'proletarian internationalisation', for example, with African states joining the global ideological block led by the Soviet Union. Just as President Samora Machel of Mozambique declared 'We do not intend to become another Bulgaria', Moscow reciprocated by only regarding these Afro-Marxist regimes as 'socialist in orientation'.[14]

Indeed, the Afro-Marxist regimes took a very pragmatic approach to Marxism–Leninism. Tell tale signs, such as the absence of antagonism towards organised religion and government co-operation with transnational corporations, were obvious. Indeed, Africa's Marxist–Leninist regimes consistently traded more with the West than they did with the Soviet Union or Eastern Europe. This independent interpretation of scientific socialism led Kenneth Jowitt to conclude that 'The most striking feature [of Afro-Marxist regimes] is the absence of ideological commitments, developmental strategies, and institutional developments consistent with their identity'.[15] Nationalist demands of unity and development, more often than not, gained priority over considerations of the class struggle.

Despite the rhetoric, the reality remained that there was an absence in Africa of the material conditions that Marx himself predicted would bring about a socialist revolution. In Barry Munslow's words, there was no 'strong, self-conscious working class which could lead the revolutionary take-over and construct socialism on a strong technological base, a socialism with such high levels of production and productivity that the power of the world capitalist economy would be incapable of bringing it to heel'.[16] Even the Soviet Union, with its strong foundation of heavy industry, technological innovation, military might and an abundance of natural resources, failed to do this. African states whose security forces had difficulty subduing internal conflict (most Afro-Marxist states had to contend with ongoing civil wars), and whose economies remained dependent on the capitalist international economy for their very survival, were never going to make the transition to scientific socialism. However committed to Marxism–Leninism these states' leaders were, post-colonial Africa was not to be a utopia of worker and peasant power.

Compromised by the harsh economic realities of the 1980s, scientific socialist regimes, along with all other African states, began to liberalise their public policy. Governments had little choice but to accept structural adjustment programmes imposed by the international financial institutions (IFIs) of the World Bank and the International Monetary Fund (see Chapter 9). The continent's socialist experiments were now at an end. Ironically, it was the IFIs, found at the very heart of the international capitalist economy, which had succeeded in reeling in both African socialist and Marxist–Leninist states.

Populism

A third group of states sharing a similar nuance of nationalism can be termed populist regimes. Although populism is not usually considered a true ideology, given that it is found right across the political spectrum (as indeed is nationalism), these governments did have similar belief systems influencing their decision making.

Populism involves putting the 'ordinary person' in society to the fore. It is the idea that individuals should be involved in the political process, and that state institutions should be more responsive to their needs. Populist movements often evolve where existing governments have become too self-interested, and advocates of populism have as their goal the return of power to the masses.

On the African continent, populism is often associated with military governments. Officers instigate a *coup d'état*, removing the previous dictatorial and corrupt regime. The military government then attempts to consolidate its legitimacy by reconstructing or building new public institutions that close the gap between the state and civil society. Ideas of morality, probity and accountability are stressed, and new levels of democracy and participation are encouraged within the political process.

The governments of Captain Thomas Sankara and Flight Lieutenant Jerry Rawlings, in Burkina Faso and Ghana, respectively, provide two excellent examples of African populist regimes. Sankara's leadership lasted from 1983 to 1987, while Rawlings governed Ghana from New Year's Eve 1981 until he retired after multi-party elections in 2000. Other candidates to be included in this populist category include Colonel Muammar Gaddafi's Libya (1969–2011), and possibly the government of Yoweri Museveni in Uganda (which since the rebellion of 1986 has sought to build a 'no-party state'). Many other African regimes have been described as populist, given that welfare issues are often prominent within African public policy. Yet it is the institutions introduced by the governments mentioned above that set these states apart as a separate populist category.

In Ghana, for example, the Rawlings regime established Peoples' Defence Committees (PDCs) after the 'revolution'. These were designed to bring the masses directly into the governmental process. These committees oversaw the work of state officials, and PDC members theoretically had the power to hire and fire administrators at the local level, as well as to overrule any decisions they made. As the *Worker's Banner* newspaper read, 'power will not be concentrated at the top anymore'.[17]

In Burkina Faso, Sankara's government built 'revolutionary committees' in villages, urban areas and workplaces right across the country. This was combined with anti-corruption drives and a tighter control of state salaries. In Libya, Colonel Gaddafi's brand of populism attempted to blend Islam with notions of Greek direct democracy. Changing the name of his country to the Socialist People's Libyan Arab Jamahiriyya (state of the masses), workers took over businesses, students replaced diplomats, and non-professionals moved in to run government departments in Tripoli.

All these populist governments, however, faced an identical problem. Those commanding the state's core executive were reluctant to devolve too much power to local committees. They feared the consequences of losing control. In reality, nationalist demands of building tight central authority, in order to maintain national unity and coherent economic development, overruled populist demands of letting the masses truly administer themselves. Devolution would only go so far. This is why Pearl Robinson talks of the state trying to 'overcontrol' politics in Burkina Faso, while she suggested that there was only a 'façade of quasi-democratic institutions'. Robinson concluded that 'the objective function of grassroots participation was subversive of the rulers' intent'.[18] The state president and members of the core executive, as in all other African political systems, remained very much in control. In reality, the African populist experiment proved to be more useful as a method for the state to penetrate civil society than it was for civil society to penetrate the state.

State capitalism

The final ideological category that this chapter seeks to highlight is that of 'state capitalism'. Although most African countries followed socialist paths of political and economic development after independence, a number adopted a more liberal approach. Countries such as Côte d'Ivoire, Kenya, Malawi, Nigeria, Cameroon, Morocco and Gabon all left their economies, to varying degrees, open to free market activity.

Instead of presiding over a command economy, where the state directly controls economic production, distribution and exchange, state capitalist regimes encouraged private enterprise. Indigenous activity of this nature occurred most frequently in the agricultural, transport and trading sectors of these countries' economies. As such, independent commercial farmers and import/export entrepreneurs, for example, could go about their business.

There was also a more benign attitude towards foreign investment forthcoming from these state capitalist regimes. Notions of 'self-reliance' were relatively absent, as long as the transnational corporation concerned was not perceived as exploitative. Nationalist sentiments, however, still determined that joint ventures (involving a mixture of local and foreign capital) were the most popular form of investment, rather than wholly foreign-owned enterprises.

Even the most liberal of these state capitalist regimes, however, could not be regarded as truly laissez-faire in outlook. The state, rather than civil society, was still very much the senior partner in any economic or political activity. Crawford Young, in this respect, considered these regimes to practise 'a highly nationalist version of capitalism'. The development and unity goals of African nationalism were still paramount, making it impossible, in leaders' minds, for the economy to be left entirely to 'the beneficent workings of the invisible hand' of the free market.[19]

This resulted in heavy state intervention in the economy. State enterprises competed with smaller private concerns; prices, imports and exports were still largely controlled centrally; the government dominated the marketing of cash crops; and there was considerable public spending on welfare programmes. This intervention, however, can be regarded as more pragmatic, rather than ideologically motivated. The state considered itself as acting in the interest of strategic economic development, rather than following the principles of socialism or populism.

Similarly, the (tempered) liberalism found within these economies rarely spread to their countries' political systems. State capitalist countries were not necessarily more democratic than their neighbours, nor were they any less exempt from being dominated

Table 3.2 Chapter summary: Africa's nationalist ideologies

African nationalism	*Characteristics*: • Anti-imperialist – initial goal of decolonisation • Autonomy – eliminating state's economic and political dependency on the West • Unity – the desire to build a nation within inherited boundaries • Economic development – restructured economies to serve Africans • State led – nation-building project defined and controlled by government • Against 'tribalism' – state discourages sub-national identities • Strong executive – controlling activity within civil society *Examples*: All African states
African socialism	*Characteristics*: • Independent – building upon, not the dogmatic reproduction of, Marxism • Importance of tradition – emphasising African traditions of community, classlessness and co-operation • Modern – combining tradition with technology and modern production methods • Skipping the capitalist stage of development – non-capitalist path to socialism • Nationalisation – private capital taken into state control • State marketing monopolies – farmers have to sell cash crops to state agencies • State distribution – goods sold in state shops, at state-determined prices • State control of imports and exports • State control of banking and finance • Curtailment of political pluralism – legally, only one party allowed to mobilise *Examples*: Senghor's Senegal, Nyerere's Tanzania, Kaunda's Zambia and Touré's Guinea
Scientific socialism	*Characteristics*: • Marxist–Leninist – following the class analysis of orthodox Marxism • Importance of working-class/peasant alliance • At its height in the 1970s and early 1980s • Fraternal links with the Soviet Union – but still independent • Still an African version of socialism – tolerant of religion, economic links with the West • Nationalisation – private capital taken into state control • State marketing monopolies – farmers have to sell cash crops to state agencies • State distribution – goods sold in state shops, at state-determined prices • State control of imports and exports • State control of banking and finance • Curtailment of political pluralism – only one legal party *Examples*: Machels's Mozambique, Neto's Angola and Mengistu's Ethiopia
Populism	*Characteristics*: • Advocates people's representation/participation – formation of people's committees • Probity – anti-corruption drives • Often formed in the wake of military coups – regimes seeking legitimacy *Examples*: Sankara's Burkina Faso, (earlier) Rawlings' Ghana and Gaddafi's Libya

Table 3.2 Chapter summary: Africa's nationalist ideologies (Continued)

State capitalism	*Characteristics*: • Tolerant of private capital – both domestic and foreign • Lively small-scale capitalism – farmers, transport and export/import entrepreneurs • Still heavy state intervention – marketing monopolies, price setting, large parastatals • State still the largest producer and distributor within economy • Curtailment of political pluralism – often only one legal party permitted *Examples*: Houphouët-Boigny's Côte d'Ivoire, Kenyatta's Kenya, and Nigeria

by a self-interested political elite. And in terms of economic performance, despite better records in the first two decades after independence, capitalist-oriented countries still floundered, like the others, in the 1980s. Consequently, just like their neighbours, they were forced to succumb to the demands of international financial institutions. Structural adjustment programmes, for example, required state capitalist regimes to sell many of their public enterprises to the private sector.

State and civil society

The final section of this chapter looks at the impact of ideology on the relationship between the state and civil society in post-colonial Africa. The ideologies adopted, particularly dominant sentiments of nationalism, have in some respects been a positive force on the continent; they have contributed to the maintenance of a basic nation-state system. Without this mutual respect for international borders, political instability in Africa could have been far worse than it actually was during this period. This stability, however, came at a price. The ideologies adopted tended to favour the interests of state elites, hampering political and economic expression in civil society. Nationalism, in all its guises, may have brought stability internationally but, in the long run, the myopic crusade for unity (or perhaps, more accurately, state conformity) generated conflict internally.

Despite the problems of 'non-organic' states and international borders cutting across cultural boundaries, there have only been three occasions when the map of Africa has been radically redrawn during the post-colonial period. This was to accommodate Tanganyika and Zanzibar unifying soon after independence in 1964 to form the new state of Tanzania, and to recognise Eritrea's and South Sudan's secession from Ethiopia and Sudan in 1993 and 2011, respectively. In all other cases, colonial boundaries have endured. This reflects a remarkable victory for African nationalism and its ability to protect the concept of the inherited nation-state.

When the Organisation of African Unity (OAU) was established in 1963, its members soon agreed that colonial boundaries should be regarded as inviolable. Although Africans certainly considered these borders to be problematic, there was general agreement that alterations to the colonial frontiers would only create even greater conflict. Only Morocco and Somalia refused to agree to this principle. As a result of this OAU doctrine, post-colonial Africa has avoided a scale of international warfare found elsewhere in the world during periods of nation building. The examples of Europe's Hundred Years War or the Third Reich have not been repeated in Africa.

Indeed, the only instance of full-scale international conflict (where one state totally defeats another) came in 1979, when the Tanzanian army occupied Uganda. Even here, there was no annexation. Tanzania withdrew its forces once the irritant of Idi Amin had been removed from power. The OAU agreement has thus resulted in even Africa's weakest states surviving the post-colonial period intact.

This is not to say that international clashes have been entirely absent on the continent. South Africa in the 1980s persistently destabilised its neighbours in its attempts to defend apartheid; Morocco continues to occupy Western Sahara, claiming it (and parts of Algeria and Mauritania) as part of the historic Moroccan empire; while Libya and Chad have battled over the Aouzou Strip. It is the irredentist state of Somalia, and the separatist movements in Katanga, Biafra, Eritrea and South Sudan, however, that have proved to be the greatest threats to Africa's nation-state boundaries. It is worth investigating these four conflicts briefly, as they prove to be exceptions to the rule, and show what could happen in Africa should political support for the inherited boundaries disappear.

Irredentism is a desire to unite a cultural community under one flag that is currently located in more than one state. Donald Horowitz defines it as a 'movement by members of an ethnic group in one state to retrieve ethnically kindred people and their territory across borders'.[20] Of all the African states, it is Somalia which has pursued irredentism to the greatest extent. The Somali people were divided among five separate states during the era of colonialism: French Somaliland (Djibouti), British Somaliland, Italian Somaliland, Ethiopia and Kenya. At independence in 1960, only British Somaliland and Italian Somaliland were reunited. This left ethnic Somalis living across international boundaries in the three remaining states.

By refusing to agree to the OAU principle of inviolable boundaries, Somalia served notice that it wished to provide a nation-state for all the Somali people. Soon after independence, the Mogadishu government supplied rebels in north-east Kenya with arms to fight the irredentist cause. Support was also given to Somali groups in the Ogaden region of Ethiopia. This latter conflict escalated, and the Somali national army eventually invaded the Ogaden in 1977. Only foreign intervention by the Soviet Union ensured that this Somali invasion was unsuccessful (see the case study in Chapter 8).

Nationalism has also triumphed in defending Africa's new nations from separatist threats. Only two such movements, the Eritrean People's Liberation Front (EPLF) and the Sudan People's Liberation Army, have secured their demands in post-colonial Africa. The motivation for separatism usually stems from the sentiment that a community is suffering internal colonialism; the government at the centre, and the state in general, are not serving the interests of the local community. As a reaction, rather than trying to establish a more favourable balance of power through central state institutions, the oppressed community demands territory for itself, and independence.

In Congo-Kinshasa (later Zaire, and then the Democratic Republic of the Congo (DRC)), the region of Katanga tried to gain autonomy when the Belgian imperial authorities withdrew in 1960. Although the secessionists had the advantage that Katanga was rich in mineral resources, enjoying close contacts with foreign businesses, they failed to build enough support to resist the power of the central state (though not before this crisis had precipitated a military *coup d'état* at the centre, and involved the intervention of the United Nations). Nigeria also went through a secessionist crisis in the 1960s, as will be explored in greater depth in the case study at the end of Chapter 4. It is worth noting at this point, however, that neither of these conflicts resulted in a permanent redrawing of Africa's international boundaries. The nation-state system endured.

The reason why Eritrean and South Sudan separatists succeeded where the Katangans and Biafrans failed relates to the level of power at the centre, and Eritrea's and South Sudan's historic claim to political and cultural autonomy. Eritrea, formerly a separate Italian colony, was federated with Ethiopia in 1952, a federation that many Eritreans rejected. After 20 years of guerrilla war, this territory finally gained its independence in 1993. This was because the Ethiopian state had imploded. A coalition of opposition movements from all over Ethiopia, including the EPLF, had joined forces and marched on Addis Ababa. The resulting fall of Haile Mariam Mengistu's regime created a power vacuum at the centre. No authority remained to enforce the unity of the nation. Consequently, in the talks between the opposition movements, Eritrean representatives were successfully able to negotiate independence for their region. Critically, given that this separate state was agreed by all parties, the wider international community recognised Eritrea's newly won sovereignty. Eritrea has thus survived, despite an inconclusive border war between Ethiopia and Eritrea in 1998–2000.

Similarly, South Sudan was governed by a separate administration to its northern neighbour during the colonial period. It was only in 1946 that the two territories were merged. North and South Sudan are also different culturally, with the south being dominated by Christian and animist beliefs, and the north very much part of the Muslim world. Broadly speaking, the older, greater Sudan was therefore split by a fracture line dividing Arab North Africa and Christian sub-Saharan Africa. Two prolonged civil wars (1955–1972 and 1983–2005) were prosecuted before a negotiated settlement held, and South Sudan became the continent's newest state in 2011. Again, given that the international community helped to broker this peace deal, and it was confirmed by a referendum, the creation of this new border enjoys international recognition.

Eritrea and South Sudan, however, it has to be stressed, were the exceptions to the rule. Elsewhere the colonial boundaries have remained intact, even when under considerable pressure. In the Great Lakes region of Central Africa, for example, the continent experienced its first regional war. Events, starting with Rwanda's genocide in 1994, first led to Uganda assisting rebels to topple the government in Kigali, and then saw Rwandan and Ugandan forces involved in DRC's (formerly Zaire's) civil war. Eventually this war would draw military support from a number of regional powers. Zimbabwe, Angola, Namibia, Sudan and Chad, as well as Rwanda and Uganda, all dispatched troops to fight in this conflict during the 1990s. The first decade of the twenty-first century saw continued overt and covert international intervention in this resource-rich, but security-poor, region of eastern DRC. It should be noted, however, that although sovereignty has been persistently violated in this part of the Congo, there have still been no efforts to alter this state's internationally recognised boundaries.

Despite the above examples of Eritrea's and South Sudan's independence, unsuccessful attempts at secession in Congo-Kinshasa and Nigeria, and occasions of states invading their neighbours, when the post-colonial period is taken as a whole, one has to acknowledge a remarkable recognition of the inherited colonial boundaries in Africa. This has produced a degree of peace many would not have predicted at independence. This is a significant achievement for nationalism in Africa.

The continent's international stability, however, comes at a price. In the first instance, one has to consider whether protecting weak states is beneficial in the long term. Although violence is avoided, these weak states are perpetually condemned to deal with cumbersome ethnic divisions and/or a lack of natural resources. European wars over the centuries have ensured that few weak states survive on this continent. The remaining

are largely ethnically cohesive and economically strong. In this light, the debate
ues among Africanists as to whether the OAU's decision to keep the inherited
.ry boundaries was ultimately the correct one.[21]

The commitment to nationalism has also proved costly in another area. It is one thing
to gain mutual respect for nations externally; it is another to suppress political competition internally in the name of national unity. Nation building was accompanied by
many states trying to dictate to, and exploit, civil society. Authoritarian edicts were
common, proclaiming exactly what the people had to do in the name of national unity.
Any dissent from this official nationalist line was deemed subversive by the political
leadership, and was dealt with accordingly.

Pluralist systems of conflict resolution had difficulty surviving in this environment.
There was little room for alternative views to be aired. If a challenge to a state's nationalist programme was channelled through ethnic mobilisation, it was dismissed as 'tribalism'. If this opposition stemmed from a particular part of the country, this region was
condemned as separatist. If just a minority within the population was involved, the
dissenters were told (or forced) to desist and were required to pull together with the rest
of the nation. Members of the political elite, in this respect, controlled the state as they
saw fit, becoming the self-proclaimed guardians of national unity.[22] In this sense, African
nationalism was very much a state-defined and state-led phenomenon. Civil society,
rather than actively shaping and participating in the nation-building project, became
instead merely its passive recipient.

The addition of a socialist dimension to this basic nationalist creed similarly failed to
improve things for civil society. The 'revolution', after all, was usually instigated from
above. Having selected an ideology that justified the centralisation of power, and the
suppression of private economic activity, the state elite was firmly in control. Indeed,
whether socialism, populism or state capitalism was promoted, all these ideologies had
the same result: the centralisation of power in the hands of a bureaucratic and political
elite. Although many African leaders were sincere about their commitment to their
chosen ideology, the inequality that grew between state and civil society left these leaders open to the charge that they were merely attempting to hide exploitative behaviour
through the creation of a 'false consciousness' among the masses.

This recurrent split between the interests of the state and those of civil society has, in
many parts of Africa, been the downfall of the nation-building project itself. Amílcar
Cabral, the leader of Guinea–Bissau's liberation movement, warned his guerrilla forces that
'the people are not fighting for ideas, nor what is in a man's mind. The people fight and
accept the sacrifices demanded by the struggle in order to gain material advantages, to live
better and in peace, to benefit from progress, and for a better future for their children'.[23] If
the state and its ideology do not serve civil society's interests, the masses will eventually
disengage from the state. As Chapter 10 will show, this is exactly what happened in a
number of African countries during the 1990s. The result was a slide towards state collapse.

However attractive an ideology may be, if it is not used to serve civil society's interests,
then in the long run it will be discredited. Ideology has to be accepted by, and not imposed
upon, the masses. Nationalism, in this respect, may have helped to maintain a degree of
international stability on the African continent since independence, but the way it was
applied to domestic public policy only resulted in a growing internal distrust between the
governors and the governed. This political disharmony had the effect of endangering the
very nation-building project itself. In this respect, the next chapter turns the book's attention to competing civil society 'ideologies', namely ethnicity and religion.

Case study: socialism and *ujamaa* in Tanzania

Tanzania is located on the east coast of Africa just below the Equator. It came into existence in 1964, when mainland Tanganyika and the Indian Ocean islands of Zanzibar came together to form the United Republic of Tanzania. The country has a varied topology: much of the mainland consists of a dry central plateau, but there is also a humid coastal strip, grassland (including the Serengeti), and even areas of semi-desert. The Great Rift Valley, and ancient volcanic activity on Tanganyika's borders, have produced some of the country's more spectacular features. There is the permanently ice-capped Mount Kilimanjaro, and the massive lakes of Victoria, Tanganyika and Malawi. By contrast, Zanzibar is a group of low-lying islands approximately 50 kilometres from the mainland, which boasts a hot and humid tropical climate (ideal for growing spices and fruit).

The nationalism pursued by the Tanzanian government after 1964 had at its heart similar goals to other brands of nationalism found elsewhere on the African continent. At the centre of these ideologies were the twin desires to build national unity and to foster economic development. Unity was very important for the stability of Tanzania, as over 120 ethnic groups can be found on the country's mainland. Similarly, there are 'racial' divisions among Tanzania's people. Alongside its African inhabitants, there are Asian Tanzanians, Arab Tanzanians and a smaller community of white Tanzanians. The population practises Islam, several denominations of Christianity and numerous traditional beliefs. Added to these differing social identities are potential clashes of interest between the residents of Zanzibar and those on the mainland.

Given these social divisions, the government's first task was to set about building a single nation within the inherited state boundaries. The aim was to enhance the unity generated by the independence campaign, and Julius Nyerere, Tanzania's first president, continued to urge his people to regard themselves primarily as Tanzanians, and only after this as Chagga, Arab, Asian or Shirazi. And this unity, indeed, has been Tanzania's post-colonial success story. There was relatively little ethnic conflict during Nyerere's leadership of Tanganyika and then Tanzania (1961–85).

Tanzanian nationalism, however, was less successful with respect to its second goal, that of economic development. With few natural resources to exploit, Tanzania has always relied heavily on agricultural production to generate wealth. At independence, the country was self-sufficient with regard to food, but this production was largely confined to smallholdings farmed by peasants. There were relatively few large commercial enterprises feeding the economy. The task of the state's economic planners in the post-colonial period was therefore to increase production. This, in turn, would generate greater surpluses, which could then be reinvested to develop the economy further. Like most African leaders, Nyerere considered capitalism to be an inappropriate method of generating this economic expansion. Instead, he advocated socialism as the correct ideology to follow. This would secure growth that could be shared by all Tanzanians.

Nyerere formulated his own genus of African socialism. Termed *ujamaa* (family-hood), this ideology was very much associated with the president personally. Like all other breeds of socialism, *ujamaa* was critical of individualism and capitalism. Instead, it advocated the public ownership of the means of production; it gave a special status to workers and peasants; and it had as its goal the creation of social equality. In this respect, it followed closely the classical socialist mantra, 'from each according to their ability; to each according to their need'. As Nyerere himself put it, 'Socialism, as a system, is in fact the organisation of men's inequalities to serve their equality....Its concern is to see that those who sow reap a fair share of what they sow'.[24]

Nyerere, however, did not believe Tanzania would benefit from a dogmatic application of Soviet-style socialism. He pointed out that:

> Africa's conditions are very different from those of the Europe in which Marx and Lenin wrote and worked. To talk as if these thinkers provide all the answers to our problems, or as if Marx invented socialism, is to reject the

Plate 3.3 Portrait of Julius K. Nyerere, president of Tanzania and leading African socialist thinker, 1979.

humanity of Africa and the universality of socialism. Marx did contribute a great deal to socialist thought. But socialism did not begin with him, nor can it end in constant reinterpretations of his writings.

Continuing with this theme, Nyerere stated that if Marx 'had lived in Sukumaland, Masailand or Revuma, he would have written a different book to *Das Kapital*, but he could have been just as scientific and just as socialist'.[25] In short, *ujamaa* was not an imported ideology, but rather it was a social blueprint that specifically aimed to address both African conditions and African needs.

Nyerere argued that Tanzanians 'have no more need of being "converted" to socialism than we have of being "taught" democracy. Both are rooted in our own past – in the traditional society that produced us'.[26] Instead of seeing socialism as being born out of class conflict, as it was in Europe, many African leaders considered that their predecessors had already practised socialism prior to the onset of colonial rule. African socialism was inherent in the notion of the extended family and the mutual co-operative nature of village communities. A member of these classless societies 'saw no struggle between his own interests and those of his community....We took care of the community, and the community took care of us'.[27]

Put simply, Nyerere saw *ujamaa*'s mission in the post-colonial era as the neutralisation of the vestiges of capitalism (and the embryonic class conflict) that colonialism had introduced to the continent. This involved recapturing the socialist ideals of traditional African society and adapting them to the modern era. In this respect, Tanzania was seeking a non-capitalist path of development. Why 'create capitalism, with all the individualism, the social aggressiveness and human indignities which it involves?' Nyerere asked.[28] By using the organisational capacity of the modern nation-state, and by harnessing new technology and production methods, Nyerere argued that *ujamaa* would produce a more harmonious path towards socialism.

Tanzania's commitment to *ujamaa* was confirmed with the Arusha Declaration of 1967. At a time when, elsewhere, a number of African socialist regimes were beginning to lose their way, and several others had fallen prey to military coups, Nyerere moved to reinforce Tanzania's ideological foundations and renew its socialist ideals. The Arusha Declaration aimed 'to create a society based on co-operation and mutual respect and responsibility, in which all members have equal rights and equal opportunities, where there is no exploitation of one person by another, and where all have gradually increasing levels of material welfare'.[29] To assist this transition to socialism, the Declaration highlighted four specific problems that had to be overcome: the potential inequalities between state employees and civil society; that capital development may come at the expense of human-centred development; that private capital was making profits that could be invested in development for all; and that there was an urban–rural imbalance evolving in favour of towns and cities.

Legislation was enacted to address all four of these issues. Tanzania's public servants and political elite have been more disciplined than most in the post-colonial era. The declaration prevented government leaders from undertaking additional employment, holding shares or renting out property. Salaries were also restrained. This prevented a 'bureaucratic bourgeoisie' emerging in Tanzania on the scale that occurred in other African states. Nyerere himself even went so far as to live and work in a village commune for a period of time, in order to stress that *all* Tanzanians had to work to secure economic development.

Similarly, the government kept to the Arusha Declaration's promise that human-centred development would be prioritised. Universal primary education was introduced, literacy campaigns were undertaken, and village health centres were built. As for the issue of nationalisation, most private capital in Tanzania (both indigenous and foreign) was taken into public ownership almost immediately. The aim was to make these enterprises serve the needs of the people collectively, rather than let them generate profits for private gain.

With respect to the fourth area highlighted by the Arusha Declaration, *ujamaa* is most associated with rural development. As this is the case, the remainder of this case study will concentrate on this specific programme.

Tanzania has one of the least urbanised populations in the world. *Ujamaa* therefore had to find a way of increasing national production by developing rural sectors of the economy. Yet Nyerere came up against the same realities that the German and British colonial administrators had faced before him. Tanzania's future prosperity relied upon disparate and scattered peasant smallholders, whose priorities lay chiefly in their own subsistence and not necessarily in the wider development of the national economy. Nor could these peasants be classed as a modern agricultural workforce, employing modern methods of production. Nyerere responded to this problem by attempting to house the majority of rural Tanzanians in model villages that would act as collectivist units of production.

The central idea behind the 'villagisation' programme was to combine tradition (village life of mutual assistance) with modern production methods (larger collective farms with access to technology). Economies of scale could be gained with the whole village combining to farm common land rather than their own separate plots. Rural Tanzanians would work together for the community, to provide both its subsistence and a surplus enabling the village to develop. The villages would also act as a point of contact for government officials to teach peasants modern agricultural techniques, and for them to supply technology (machinery and fertilisers). There was also the opportunity for the state to invest in the country's human resources. The majority of Tanzania's new schools and health centres, for example, were built in these *ujamaa vijijini*. Similarly, the villages served as centres of local democracy, with community members, aided by state administrators, making decisions for themselves. As Paul Kaiser observed, 'The process of villagisation was intended to integrate the logic of economic efficiency with the goal of social equality'.[30]

By 1977, over 13 million Tanzanians lived in *ujamaa* villages. This represented almost all the country's rural population. Some were attracted by the nationalist and socialist aims of the project. More were enticed by the government waiving its poll tax for these communities, the provision of schooling and basic welfare facilities, and the access to subsidised seeds and fertilisers. State coercion, however, was needed in later years to resettle more reluctant communities. Yet, despite this massive undertaking of social engineering, the *ujamaa* experiment failed to produce the levels of rural development required to keep Tanzania's economic expansion ahead of its population growth.

Goran Hyden argues that the *ujamaa vijijini* failed to meet their production targets because the state, and its ideology, failed to 'capture' the Tanzanian peasantry.[31] Members of these village communities certainly respected many of the social goals of *ujamaa* (living as a community, and having access to government-supplied technology and welfare), but they never really adopted the modern agricultural production methods advocated. This was because, even in their traditional societies, Africans were never collectivist farmers. They would certainly co-operate as a community to clear land, and offer mutual assistance at times of harvest or need, but the tradition was never to farm together, sharing the product of this labour.

A 'peasant mode of production' continued in the *ujamaa* villages. Common land was farmed collectively, but only after villagers had attended to their own individual plots first. In other words, subsistence gained from the individual plots was the main activity; collective work was only undertaken to raise additional income above this. Hyden concluded that 'To the peasants, work on the communal farm was never considered an end in itself. To them it remained a supplementary activity, to which attention was given when circumstance in the household permitted'.[32]

The villages, given their retention of the peasant mode of production, did not produce the efficiency of modern agricultural enterprises. 'It was not laziness as much as a different set of priorities and limited capacity that explain *ujamaa* shortfalls in rural areas. The peasants did not have a capitalist orientation and were thus unconcerned with the need for a surplus as an end in itself'.[33] With the peasantry largely content in producing only their subsistence, the wider national economy failed to 'take off'. This left the nationalist leadership without the economic development it promised, and, in many cases, not even with the funds to cover the initial costs of establishing these villages. Nyerere, in his review of Tanzania's progress to socialism written ten years after the Arusha Declaration, candidly admitted 'the truth is that the agricultural results have been very disappointing'.[34]

Ujamaa's lack of success in terms of rural production, however, cannot be blamed entirely on the peasantry remaining 'uncaptured'. The state itself must accept some of the blame. Administrative errors were made. People were occasionally settled in unproductive areas, inappropriate crops grown, and there was generally a lack of transport infrastructure, preventing the efficient movement of harvests. Mistakes of this kind are almost inevitable in a development project of this scale. It was in the interaction between the peasantry and local administrators, however, that the state let its *ujamaa* ideology down the most.

Faced with a peasantry reluctant to farm collectively, bureaucrats often returned to the same authoritarian and managerial styles of public administration experienced during the colonial years. What is more, in order to shore up their legitimacy under these circumstances, local administrators began to build patron–client relationships with their villages. Development funds were therefore now being absorbed in bureaucratic empire building, rather than being fully utilised in expanding production. With an uncaptured peasantry managed by patrimonial administrators, it is not surprising that most 'collectivist' *ujamaa* villages failed, by some degree, to reach the production levels attained by Tanzania's few remaining private (capitalist) farms.

The problem remained that Tanzania's economy was expanding at a rate slower than its population growth. The development envisaged at independence failed to emerge. Adaptations were made to the *ujamaa* ideology in an attempt to rectify these problems, and, indeed, Tanzania was one of the last countries in Africa to retain public policy based on the ideals of African socialism and self-reliance. The non-capitalist path of development was still being advocated even during the early 1980s, when neighbouring states were turning to international financial institutions (IFIs) to shore up their crumbling economies. Eventually, however, Tanzania succumbed too.

Forced by its crippling external debts, it agreed in 1986 to an IFI structural adjustment programme involving the liberalisation of the Tanzanian economy.

Yet before critics judge the *ujamaa* experiment as a total failure, they should acknowledge that Nyerere and his government administered a remarkably stable and equitable society. Tanzania was a country where levels of education and health care improved remarkably in the years after independence. Some of this work was undone with structural adjustment's application of 'market ideals' to the provision of public services. Universal primary education, for example, was lost, and health care became less accessible. Likewise, although a more liberal economy succeeded in bringing better economic growth in the twenty-first century, the distribution of this wealth is narrower. Politically, things are also more complicated. The mainland has had occasional occurrences of electoral violence since the introduction of multi-party competition, whilst political violence has become more common on the island of Zanzibar. In short, Tanzania has yet to find an ideology that can concurrently deliver unity and economic development. *Ujamaa* produced both welfare and a significant degree of social coherence, whilst the more liberal era has created increased wealth. To date, the Tanzanian nation-building project has yet to combine these two objectives.

Tanzania[35]			
Territory:	939,760 sq. km.	Population:	49.3 million
Colonial power:	(Germany) Britain	Independence:	1964
Major cities:	Dar es Salaam	Major ethnic groups:	Ewe
	Mwanza		Kabare
	Tabora		Masai
Urban population:	30 per cent		(among many others)
Languages:	Kiswahili	Life expectancy:	61 years
Infant mortality:	36 deaths/1,000 live births	Adult literacy:	68 per cent
Currency:	Tanzanian Shilling	Major exports:	Gold
Religions:	Traditional		Other precious metals
	Christian		Tobacco
	Hindu		Fruit and nuts
GDP per capita:	US$609		Coffee

Questions raised by this chapter

1. What role does ideology play in the practice of politics?
2. How does African nationalism differ from other nationalisms found elsewhere in the world?
3. Has the inherited nation-state structure benefited Africa in the post-colonial era?
4. To what extent did African socialist and Afro-Marxist regimes conform to the principles of 'classical' socialism developed in Europe?
5. Were populist and state capitalist administrations more successful at governing African states than their socialist-oriented counterparts?
6. To what extent has African civil society suffered in the post-colonial period as a result of state-sponsored ideologies?

Glossary of key terms

African socialism	A strain of socialism built more on African 'traditional values' (village communalism and co-operation) than the class struggle of classical Marxism–Leninism.
Ideology	A lifeguiding system of beliefs, values and goals affecting political style and action (R.D. Putnam).
Irredentism	A movement by members of one ethnic group to retrieve people and their territory across borders (Horowitz).
Nation	A collection of people bound together by common values and traditions, often sharing the same language, history and an affiliation to a geographical area.
Nationalism	The desire that the nation should be housed in its own sovereign state.
Nation building	The post-independence attempts to unite peoples, and develop economies, within Africa's inherited colonial boundaries.

OAU inviolable borders	The agreement among most OAU members in 1963 that the inherited colonial boundaries should remain, and be respected.
Populism	A political movement favouring the wishes and interests of 'ordinary people'.
Scientific socialism	A strain of socialism based on the class analysis of Karl Marx, later developed by V.I. Lenin.
Separatism	The desire for a region within a state to secede, forming its own (or joining another) sovereign state.
State capitalism	A policy that assists (local and foreign) free market activity, but still involves heavy state intervention in the economy.
Structural adjustment	Loan programmes that require borrowing countries to liberalise both their economies and their public policy.
Tribalism	The charge that groups continue to hold divisive 'outdated' ethnic allegiances which counter the state's goal of national unity.

Further reading

Ernest Gellner's general work on nationalism is an excellent place to start any further reading. This could be complemented by Basil Davidson's book, which concentrates specifically on the African continent, and Crawford Young's article, which explores how Africanists have used the concept of nationalism in their studies. In terms of the debate on the utility (or otherwise) of the inherited nation-state, Pierre Englebert and Rebecca Hummel provide a good analysis of why the colonial borders have survived, specifically looking at how national unity has defeated movements of secession in post-colonial Africa.

Sources that could be consulted to develop a deeper knowledge of African socialism include Chapter 4 of Harvey Sindima's book, Thomas Callaghy's article, and the introduction to Julius Nyerere's collection of speeches and writings. Those interested in scientific socialist African regimes should read Kenneth Jowitt's chapter in Carl Rosberg and Thomas Callaghy's book.

All of the above suggestions can be read in conjunction with case studies. Christopher Clapham provides a good account of the Marxist–Leninist revolution in Ethiopia; Adotey Bing looks at populist participation in Ghana; Goran Hyden has analysed the *ujamaa* experiment in Tanzania; while Crawford Young's book addresses several post-colonial African ideologies, illustrating his arguments with numerous examples taken from across the continent.

Bringing this literature more up to date, the journal article by Michael Kpessa and colleagues examines the relationship between nationalism and social and political cohesion, arguing that national unity has been undermined by the introduction of liberal economic policy since the 1980s.

Bing, Adotey. Popular participation versus people's power: notes on politics and power struggles in Ghana. *Review of African Political Economy*. 1984, 11(31), 91–104.

Callaghy, Thomas M. The difficulties of implementing socialist strategies of development in Africa: the 'first wave.' In: Carl G. Rosberg and Thomas M. Callaghy, eds. *Socialism in Sub-Saharan Africa: A New Assessment*. Berkeley, CA: Institute of International Studies, University of California, 1979. 112–29.

Clapham, Christopher. Revolutionary socialist development in Ethiopia. *African Affairs*. 1987, 86(343), 151–65.

Davidson, Basil. *The Black Man's Burden: Africans and the Curse of the Nation-State*. London: James Currey, 1992.

Englebert, Pierre and Rebecca Hummel. Let's stick together: understanding Africa's secessionist deficit. *African Affairs*. 2005, 104(416), 399–427.

Gellner, Ernest. *Nations and Nationalism*. Oxford: Blackwell, 2006.

Hyden, Goran. *Beyond Ujamaa in Tanzania: Underdevelopment and an Uncaptured Peasantry*. London: Heinemann, 1980.

Jowitt, Kenneth. Scientific socialist regimes in Africa: political differentiation, avoidance, and unawareness. In: Carl G. Rosberg and Thomas M. Callaghy, eds. *Socialism in Sub-Saharan Africa: A New Assessment*. Berkeley, CA: Institute of International Studies, University of California, 1979. 133–73.

Kpessa, Michael, Daniel Béland and André Lecours. Nationalism, development, and social policy: The politics of nation-building in sub-Saharan Africa. *Ethnic and Racial Studies*. 2011, 34(12), 215–33.

Nyerere, Julius K. *Freedom and Socialism: A Selection from Writings and Speeches, 1965–1967*. Oxford: Oxford University Press, 1970.

Sindima, Harvey J. Chapter 4. In: *Africa's Agenda: The Legacy of Liberalism and Colonialism in the Crisis of African Values*. Westport, CT: Greenwood, 1995. 89–123.

Young, Crawford. *Ideology and Development in Africa*. New Haven, CT: Yale University Press, 1982.

Young, Crawford. Evolving modes of consciousness and ideology: nationalism and ethnicity. In: David E. Apter and Carl G. Rosberg, eds. *Political Development and the New Realism in Sub-Saharan Africa*. Charlottesville, VA: University Press of Virginia, 1994. 61–86.

Notes and references

1 Putnam, Robert D. *The Beliefs of Politicians*. New Haven, CT: Yale University Press, 1973.

2 Anderson, Benedict. *Imagined Communities*. London: Verso, 1991. 6.

3 See Gellner, Ernest. *Nations and Nationalism*. Oxford: Blackwell, 1983. 1–2.

4 Vail, Leroy and Landeg White. Tribalism in the political history of Malawi. In: Leroy Vail, ed. *The Creation of Tribalism in Southern Africa*. London: James Currey, 1989. 151.

5 Cited in Mamdani, Mahmood. *Citizen and Subject: Contemporary Africa and the Legacy of Late Colonialism*. Princeton, NJ: Princeton University Press, 1996. 135.

6 Nyerere, Julius K. *Spearhead*. 1961. Reprinted in Paul E. Sigmund, ed. *The Ideologies of the Developing Nations*. New York: Praeger, 1963. 199. Original emphasis.

7 Jowitt, Kenneth. Scientific socialist regimes in Africa: political differentiation, avoidance, and unawareness. In: Carl G. Rosberg and Thomas M. Callaghy, eds. *Socialism in Sub-Saharan Africa: A New Assessment*. Berkeley, CA: Institute of International Studies, University of California, 1979. 148.

8 Zolberg, Aristide R. The Daka colloquium: the search for a doctrine. In: William H. Freidland and Carl G. Rosberg, eds. *African Socialism*. Stanford, CA: Stanford University Press, 1964. 118–19.

9 Touré, Ahmed Sékou. *The Doctrine and Methods of the Democratic Party of Guinea*. II. 24. Cited in Ottaway, Marina and David Ottaway. *Afro-Communism*. New York: Africana, 1986. 15.

10 Senghor, Léopold Sédar. *Afrique Nouvelle*. 11. Cited in Ottaway, Marina and David Ottaway. *Afro-Communism*. New York: Africana, 1986. 91.

11 Senghor, Léopold Sédar. *On African Socialism*. New York: American Society for African Culture, 1959. 32.

12 Barré, Mohamed Siad. Revolutionary resolve. *World Marxist Review*. 1976, 19(5), 26.

13 See Clapham, Christopher. Revolutionary socialist development in Ethiopia. *African Affairs*. 1987, 86(343), 151–65.

14 Cited in Ottaway and Ottaway. *Afro-Communism*. 9.

15 Jowitt. In: Rosberg and Callaghy. *Socialism in Sub-Saharan Africa*. 133.

16 Munslow, Barry, ed. *Africa: Problems in the Transition to Socialism*. London: Zed, 1986. 1.

17 See Yeebo, Zaya. Ghana: defence committees and the class struggle. *Review of African Political Economy*. 1985, 12(32), 66.

18 Robinson, Pearl T. Grassroots legitimisation of military governance in Burkina Faso and Niger: the core contradictions. In: Goran Hyden and Michael Bratton, eds. *Governance and Politics in Africa*. Boulder, CO: Lynne Rienner, 1992. 163.

19 Young, Crawford. *Ideology and Development in Africa*. New Haven, CT: Yale University Press, 1982. 184, 188.

20 Quoted in Neuberger, Benyamin. Irredentism and politics in Africa. In: Naomi Chazan, ed. *Irredentism and International Politics*. Boulder, CO: Lynne Rienner, 1991. 97.

21 See, for example, Herbst, Jeffrey. *States and Power in Africa: Comparative Lessons in Authority and Control*. Princeton, NJ: Princeton University Press, 2000. 112–13.

22 Clapham, Christopher. *Third World Politics: An Introduction*. London: Routledge, 1985. 62.

23 Cabral, Amílcar. *Palavras de Ordem Gerais*. Conakary: PAIGC, 1969. 23. Cited in Chabal, Patrick. Revolutionary democracy in Africa: the case of Guinea–Bissau. In: Patrick Chabal, ed. *Political Domination in Africa: Reflections on the Limits of Power*. Cambridge: Cambridge University Press, 1986. 84.

24 Nyerere, Julius K. *Nyerere on Socialism*. Dar es Salaam: Oxford University Press, 1969. 30. See also Nyerere, Julius K. *Freedom and Unity: A Selection from Writings and Speeches 1952–1965*. Dar es Salaam: Oxford University Press, 1966. 164.

25 Nyerere. *Nyerere on Socialism*. 41 and 42.

26 Nyerere. *Freedom and Unity*. 170.

27 Nyerere, Julius K. Africa's place in the world. In: *Symposium on Africa*. Wellesley, 1960. 157. See also Nyerere. *Freedom and Unity*. 164.

28 Nyerere. *Nyerere on Socialism*. 44.

29 Sindima, Harvey J. *Africa's Agenda: The Legacy of Liberalism and Colonialism in the Crisis of African Values*. Westport, CT: Greenwood, 1995. 103.

30 Kaiser, Paul. Structural adjustment and the fragile nation: the demise of social unity in Tanzania. *Journal of Modern African Studies*. 1996, 34(2), 229.

31 Hyden, Goran. *Beyond Ujamaa in Tanzania: Underdevelopment and an Uncaptured Peasantry*. London: Heinemann, 1980. *Passim*.

32 *Ibid*. 115.

33 *Ibid*. 114.

34 Nyerere, Julius K. The Arusha Declaration ten years after. *Africa Review*. 1977, 7(2), 13.

35 Statistics taken from United Nations Conference on Trade and Development. *UNCTAD Handbook of Statistics 2014*. New York: United Nations, 2014. Tables 8.1, 8.4 and 3.2.D; World Bank data http://data.worldbank.org/indicator/SP.DYN.LE00.IN (accessed 24 July 2015) and http://data.worldbank.org/indicator/SP.DYN.IMRT.IN (accessed 24 July 2015); and UNESCO data www.uis.unesco.org/DataCentre/Pages/regions.aspx (accessed 24 July 2015).

4 Ethnicity and religion

'Tribes', gods and political identity

Chapter outline

- Definitions of ethnicity
- The creation of 'tribes'
- Ethnicity as a method of modern political mobilisation
- Religion and African politics

    - African religions strengthening civil society
    - Islamist politics on the African continent
    - Instrumental religious political mobilisation

- State and civil society
- Case study: ethnicity, religion and the nation-state in Nigeria
- Questions raised by this chapter
- Glossary of key terms
- Further reading
- Notes and references

Social diversity, whether this be racial, ethnic, religious or economic in nature, is a prominent generator of political difference. Fault lines generated by these social cleavages can be found in most countries. Opposing interests are divided by social fractures, which in turn create political competition. Occasionally, violent conflict is the consequence. Exploring this chapter's twin focus on ethnicity and religion within twentieth-century Europe, for instance, notions of ethnicity played a key role in fuelling the Second World War, while more recently, in the 1990s, similar sentiments of ethnicity and religion brought devastation to the Balkans with the break-up of Yugoslavia. Even within the European Union, such tensions are common. The populations of Northern Ireland and Spain's Basque country, for example, know well enough the tragedy that such 'clannish' competition can bring.

This is not to say that expressions of ethnicity and religion always result in violence. Such desires and demands are usually channelled peacefully through political institutions, just like other clashes of interest within society. For example, Scotland secured its own parliament in 1997. Ethnic groups in the United States are also adept at constitutionally promoting their interests. Modern Germany has likewise successfully managed religious difference within its society, despite a history of conflict between Roman Catholics and Protestants in that country.

As in the West, political interaction on the African continent is also influenced by these twin considerations. Indeed, given that these states are relatively young, sentiments of ethnicity and religion are often as powerful as notions of the nationalism studied in the previous chapter. As such, when making decisions, political leaders in Africa not only have to think of the national interest, but also have to consider the reactions of the various ethnic and religious constituencies housed within their country.

This chapter explains the influence that ethnic and religious mobilisation has had on African politics during the post-colonial era. The first half of the chapter will concentrate on ethnicity. It will investigate how social scientists have defined ethnicity generally, and then explore ethnic identity specifically within the African context. It will be shown how modern ethnic identities play a key role in relations between governors and the governed on the continent. The second part of the chapter will then examine the impact of religion upon African politics. In both cases, the chapter argues that ethnicity and religion are not necessarily a hindrance to peaceful government. Although they can certainly cause political tension and violence, these two social forces can also act as a powerful counterbalance to state power, serving as a useful way for civil society to mobilise politically.

Definitions of ethnicity

A basic definition of an ethnic group would be *a community of people who have the conviction that they have a common identity and common fate based on issues of origin, kinship ties, traditions, cultural uniqueness, a shared history and possibly a shared language.* In this sense, an ethnic group is much like the 'imagined community' of the nation. Ethnicity, however, focuses more on sentiments of origin and descent, rather than the geographical imperative of a nation.

Notions of ethnicity become pronounced and political when they are used to distinguish one social group from another within a specific territory.[1] As such, this 'contested' ethnicity is of particular interest to political scientists. Scholars can learn a great deal from studying how ethnic groups relate to one other, and how these groups interact with broader social organisations such as the nation and the state. This is especially relevant in situations where more than one ethnic group resides within a single country.

The popular view is that an ethnic group is a smaller community found within a larger society. More recent immigrant communities within the United Kingdom, for example, have become known as 'ethnic minorities'. United States minority groups are also often defined in terms of ancestral origins (Irish-Americans, African-Americans, and so on). These interpretations of ethnicity are misleading, however. All individuals have ethnic allegiances, whether they regard themselves as belonging to a minority of a state's population or part of the majority. Being 'English' or 'Scottish' is just as much being part of an ethnic group as is being a member of the smaller British 'Afro-Caribbean' or 'Asian' communities. Ethnicity is therefore a sentiment expressed by both majority and minority populations, and political scientists have to monitor these expressions (just as they do with other sources of social cleavage). Social pluralism of this sort, after all, will result in differences of interest, which is the engine of politics itself.

The creation of 'tribes'

Ethnicity, or 'tribalism', is frequently used as an auto-explanation of political events in Africa. The media will often report that there has been violence on the continent because tribe 'A' has clashed with tribe 'B'. No further exploration of the cause of this violence is offered, or apparently needed. It is only natural, it is presumed, that ancient ethnic rivalries will result in conflict from time to time, as Africans are inherently 'tribalistic' and will therefore act in a 'tribalistic' manner.

This *primordialist* explanation sees African 'tribes' as something left over from the pre-colonial past. The argument states that historical loyalties, often demonstrated in a primitively savage fashion, have been brought into present-day politics. This will continue to be the case until the forces of modernisation make tribal associations redundant. They will disappear only when Africans develop a national consciousness, working together to enjoy the fruits of modern-day civilisation (as Westerners do in their nation-states). In the meantime, it is only normal that tribes will clash, sometimes violently.

Such 'tribalistic' interpretations of African politics, however, are worthless. A good political scientist has to go beyond such simplistic, not to mention racist, approaches to social pluralism on the continent. They should find out *why* tribe 'A' has entered into conflict with tribe 'B'. Conflict, after all, is not an unprompted phenomenon. Why was ethnic identity important in this confrontation? What was the specific cause of the dispute? Why has the clash happened at this time? Why was the altercation not contained by peaceful political bargaining, in the manner of most differences? These are the sort of questions that should be asked. The simple answer, 'tribalism', satisfies none of these inquiries. Ethnicity may often be the agent of political mobilisation in Africa, but it is rarely the primary cause of conflict.

Gérard Prunier made sure he asked such questions in his efforts to understand the 1994 genocide in Rwanda. Television viewers around the world simply could not grasp the fact that 800,000 people died over a three-month period in a series of massacres. It was difficult for them to remember who was killing whom, let alone *why* it was happening. It was easier to ignore the details and put it all down to African 'tribalism'. Yet Prunier is adamant: 'What we have witnessed in Rwanda is a historical product, not a biological fatality or "spontaneous" bestial outburst. Tutsi and Hutu have not been created by God as cats and dogs, predestined from all eternity to disembowel each other'.[2] There had to be a motive for these killings. The Rwandan genocide was no more 'tribalistic' or 'African' than the extermination of Jews by Nazi Germany or of North American natives by the United States army. All these events had specific historical introductions and immediate political imperatives.

Conflict in Africa needs to be explained in the same manner as conflict elsewhere in the world. In the Rwandan case, political scientists should look towards overpopulation, land competition, falling coffee prices, economic malaise, French neo-colonialism and Tutsi domination of the state, rather than resorting to racist primordial explanations. As Prunier pleaded, to allow the Rwanda killings to be 'misunderstood through simplified clichés would in fact bring the last touch to the killers' work, in completing their victims' dehumanisation…. To deny a man the social meaning of his death is to kill him twice, first in the flesh, then in the spirit'.[3]

The primordial 'tribal' argument is clearly wrong, as African ethnic groups are not simply ghosts from the past, or a residue left over from history. Ethnic groups remain an important form of social organisation today because they continue to serve contemporary social, political and economic needs. It is also a fact that African 'tribes' are *modern* social constructions. Indeed, largely having been formed no earlier than the late nineteenth century, African 'tribes' have actually gained in importance over the last 150 years. Ethnicity on the continent has not retreated in the face of modernisation, as the primordial argument suggests.

Few African communities could be defined as 'tribes' prior to colonialism. Of course, ethnic association was prominent before European authority arrived, but these earlier ethnic associations were much more fluid when compared with their modern regimented equivalents. In this sense, Aidan Southall talks of 'interlocking, over-lapping, multiple identities'.[4] There were certainly pre-colonial lineage groups, clans and kinship communities, but these were not, as yet, consolidated into larger 'tribes'. Neither was the membership of these groups necessarily set in stone. Loyalties changed over time, responding to migration, enslavement, military conquest or marriage, among other social forces. The ancestors of the Ghanaian citizens who today regard themselves as Akan, for instance, would have categorised themselves variously as Asante, Fante, Brong, Akim or Nzima in the past. Being described as part of a larger Akan 'tribe' would have meant very little to these people prior to the twentieth century.

This is why many Africanists refuse to use the term 'tribe', and others put this word in inverted commas. It is more accurate to talk about ethnic groups. In this manner, stereotypes of primordial, rather than socially constructed, communities can be avoided, as well as the many racist associations that are attached to the word 'tribe'. Why are Africans and not the Welsh or Texans referred to as tribes, for example? The images that are conjured up by this word obscure more than they illuminate. The more universal concept of 'ethnicity' is therefore more useful.

Why, then, did 'tribes' consolidate in the late nineteenth century and throughout the twentieth century? Why were more fluid ethnic associations abandoned at this point? Well, it is no coincidence that the process of 'tribalisation' emerged concurrently with the era of colonial rule in Africa. The continent's people gathered into tribes for two specific reasons. First, the administrative imperatives of imperial rule demanded this, and second, Africans themselves found these new ethnic identities to be advantageous within the new colonial political environment.

Once they had established their authority on the continent, Europeans had to make sense of the societies they now ruled. In the typically arrogant manner of the age, imperialism never really got to grips with the nature of existing kinship communities in Africa. Instead, colonial rulers attempted to mould reality to their own administrative requirements. As Crawford Young puts it, 'In the construction of its hegemony, the colonial state soon acquired a compulsion to classify. Particularly for the British and Belgians, administrative organization was rooted in a "tribal" image of Africa. The task of the ruler was to identify, rationalize, and streamline ethnic cartography'.[5]

Communities were therefore gathered together into regional blocs ('tribes') in order to make their political and economic management easier. Where conveniently distributed 'tribes' did not exist, the colonial authorities did their best to create them. Acting as amateur anthropologists, colonial officials assigned all their subjects to a 'tribe', often based on very dubious historical or ethnological research. Once categorised, a suitable chief would be appointed to act as an intermediary between this new ethnic group and the colonial state. Sometimes this would be an incumbent African leader; on other occasions the government would promote a more pliant candidate.

The Fulbe of northern Cameroon, for instance, were categorised as a single tribe by the imperial authorities. This enabled these people to be slotted neatly into the administrative mechanisms of the colonial state. In reality, a closer examination of this 'tribe' reveals extensive internal fault lines. Contained within this group are the Kirdi, a community the Fulbe had subjugated some 100 years earlier. Differing identities remained, as a consequence. The Fulbe, for example, had largely converted to Islam, whereas the

Kirdi continued to practise animist beliefs. Even within the Kirdi there were distinct groups, such as the Mundang, Tupuri, Guisiga, Massa, Mbum and Duru. Yet, for administrative purposes, all were now regarded by the colonial authorities as members of the single Fulbe 'tribe'.[6] Gone was the flexibility of pre-colonial identities, and, consequently, ethnic boundaries became less porous as the twentieth century progressed.

It was not just a case of 'tribes' being imposed on Africa, however. Many Africans themselves willingly took on these new identities to further their own political interests and those of their communities. This was particularly so for those who strove to be the intermediaries between the state and the 'tribe'. These individuals benefited from becoming leaders of larger communities, as well as gaining a degree of access to state institutions, and the spoils that this position unlocked. Chiefs often became richer and more influential as a result of colonial rule. Under these circumstances, it is not surprising that these intermediaries had an overriding interest in building the myth of the 'tribe'.

Similarly, many of the individuals who made up these 'tribes' also adopted the myth. To belong to a tribe enabled members to share the resources that their ethnic intermediaries extracted from the colonial authorities. This, after all, was the key conduit along which state-allocated goods were distributed. Conversely, not belonging to a tribe resulted in automatic exclusion from the competition for state spoils. Belonging to a tribe also offered individuals a degree of protection from the alien colonial authorities. There was greater security in numbers. It was therefore logical for ethnic associations to consolidate in this new political environment. States wanted to deal with 'tribes', so Africans responded by constructing the larger ethno-regional groups required. Leaders and followers alike involved themselves in inventing traditions and symbols to bind these 'imagined' communities together. History was manipulated to give the 'tribe' a long and honourable past. In this manner, while the colonial authorities were busy assigning Africans to 'tribes', Africans were busy building 'tribes' to belong to.

The above evidence suggests that African 'tribes' can be seen, in part, as *instrumental* social constructions, and certainly not as 'natural' or 'primordial' phenomena. Africans identify themselves as belonging to an ethnic group because it is in their interests to do so. Alongside the social benefits, cultural solidarity has become a method of securing tangible political power and economic advantage. In this sense, Robert Bates talks of ethnic groups being 'a form of minimum winning coalition, large enough to secure benefits in the competition for spoils but also small enough to maximise the per-capita value of these benefits'.[7]

Despite their cultural make-up, therefore, ethnic groups can be compared to other interest groups that can be found working within African political systems. Their representatives lobby the state, seeking resources and public policy measures that serve the group's interests. Individuals will identify themselves as belonging to this group, supporting it, because this is a method of securing new wells, medical centres, schools and roads, or a new factory for their community and region. This reality requires Africanists not to regard ethnic conflict as an exotic clash of cultures, but more simply as the perennial clash over scarce resources. It is not irrational primordial rivalry, in this respect, but simply familiar political competition: the politics of the 'pork barrel' with an African twist.

Ethnicity as a method of modern political mobilisation

Ethnicity is frequently portrayed as having been a hindrance to Africa's political and economic development in the post-colonial period. This has become the popular view, fuelled by nationalist arguments. Such a condemnation of ethnicity, however, is not necessarily warranted. Operating in the right political environment, ethnicity can be as progressive a force as any type of social organisation. Indeed, in the harsh arena of Africa's authoritarian one-party governments, ethnicity provided a rare degree of pluralism and representation.

No state is socially homogeneous. Social cleavage produces conflicting interests everywhere. In each country, different issues act as the primary point of mobilisation. Nationalism, class, religion and ideology are all favoured rallying cries that gather individuals together, enabling them to make their political demands to the state, and to society as a whole. So why should not ethnicity be a legitimate tool enabling groups to aggregate demands and mobilise politically? Ethnicity, after all, is the most obvious social divide on the continent.

Ethnicity has made a positive contribution to many post-colonial African countries in that it has managed to serve both state and civil society to some degree. Even in the most repressive of African countries, state elites were forced to acknowledge ethno-regional power. Although these leaders gave scant public recognition to this rival source of political strength, given that it grated against the official nationalist credo and their own elite interests, tacit concessions were nevertheless consistently made to sub-state groups. Cabinets, for example, were often a fine balancing act. Most ethnic groups had their own cultural brokers within this state institution. The failure to include leading members of each ethnic group within the executive would risk provoking a challenge to the regime from each absent region. Similarly, ethnic quotas were also exercised in bureaucratic appointments (the military, civil service, police and public agencies), as well as in the allocation of local budgets, and the allotment of state resources in general. Of course, there was not automatically an equal distribution of these resources, but the state elite knew that they would have to pay a political price if any group perceived itself to have been left out of these ethnic calculations.

In this sense, the state had to acknowledge ethnic demands, which resulted in it bargaining with each group, as well as acting as a mediator between them all. This in turn made the state, however grudgingly and limited, responsive to and representative of civil society. Donald Rothchild describes this state–ethnic relationship in terms of a 'hegemonial exchange'. This is where African states do not have enough power to impose themselves totally on civil society, as they cannot unilaterally impose their will on powerfully mobilised ethno-regional groups. As a result, the state has to win a degree of legitimacy from these ethnic groups to avoid full-scale regional challenges to its authority. This legitimacy is bought through the distribution of state-controlled resources. As Rothchild put it, 'as an ideal type, hegemonial exchange is a form of state-facilitated co-ordination in which a somewhat autonomous central state and a number of considerably less autonomous ethnoregional (and other) interests engage in a process of mutual accommodation on the basis of commonly accepted procedural norms, rules, or understandings'.[8] In other words, because the state cannot extend its hegemony totally over powerful ethnic groups, it negotiates with them instead (albeit from a position of strength). Ethnic groups, in return, relinquish any overt challenge to the state, as long as they feel sufficient resources are flowing into their region.

Of course, to Western eyes, this is an arrangement far removed from the ideals of liberal democracy. Yet it does provide a measure of stability and order within divided societies. The state and civil society are bound together by these political channels, with a degree of legitimacy and compliance being traded for a degree of representation. Many

African societies avoided violent confrontation for long periods of time through this 'hegemonial exchange'. Indeed, President Jomo Kenyatta of Kenya and Félix Houphouët-Boigny of Côte d'Ivoire took the art of ethnic balancing to a different plane, and consequently managed to govern over remarkably stable societies for decades. These 'Big Men' kept all their state's major ethnic brokers content by shuffling patronage opportunities and the allocation of state resources.

Three major potential problems, however, stand out in societies dominated by hegemonial exchange. The first could arise from a lack of skill, or will, to balance *all* the ethnic groups within the nation-state; the second problem relates to the massive inefficiencies that rule through hegemonial exchange generates; and the third is the reality that this basis of government only provides a limited degree of representation for those in civil society.

The first of these problems would arise if an ethnic group felt itself to be discriminated against by the state. Its members may perceive that they are being excluded from rights and resources enjoyed by other groups. The balancing act, using ethnic arithmetic, is difficult to maintain at the best of times, and miscalculations can often lead to conflict. There are also plenty of examples in post-colonial Africa where state elites *consciously* maintained an uneven ethnic balance. Where this occurred, the state became identified with one particular ethnic group (or groups). Instead of pursuing a policy of social inclusion, elites allocated a disproportionate amount of the country's resources to favoured regions. Under these circumstances, state coercion is needed to temper any opposition emanating from the excluded groups.

Hegemonial exchange also hinders the logical execution of public policy. It is simply inefficient for resources to be distributed according to demand, rather than need. If one ethnic group absorbs the bulk of a state's resources (simply because it is the most powerful), this results in weaker regions forfeiting their share. Site 'A', for example, may be the most practical place to build a state factory in terms of raw materials and transport links, but it may be that site 'B' is chosen instead because of the imperatives of ethnic balancing. Political stability, in this respect, is bought at the price of policy inefficiencies. Hegemonial exchange can also result in a lack of strategic planning. Short-term deals are the order of the day, instead of long-term considerations. President Milton Obote complained of Ugandan politicians in the 1960s that they did not act as if they were members of a national parliament. Instead, they resembled an 'assembly of peace conference delegates' involved in some curious game of 'Tribal Development Monopoly'.[9] Parochial ethnic interests, in post-colonial Africa, continually prevented public policy measures that could have brought greater national gains, rather than limited region benefits.

Above all, however, it is for its lack of opportunity for mass public participation that the hegemonial exchange model must be most criticised. Politics within these countries was the preserve of ethnic brokers and state officials. Rarely would the 'masses' become involved. Legitimacy, as a consequence, suffered. Indeed, with resources becoming increasingly scarce during the 1970s and 1980s, ethnic brokers often failed to deliver to their communities. Consequently, a split emerged between the mass of civil society on the one hand, and their ethnic intermediaries (parliamentarians, local councillors and traditional leaders) and state officials (politicians and bureaucrats) on the other. What is more, one-party state structures left no other avenues open for civil society to express its grievances. The result was a wholesale crisis of legitimacy for the African state. This is a theme taken up in more detail in Chapters 10 and 11, but it should be noted here that

Africans during the 1990s successfully demanded greater levels of representation and a move to multi-party politics.

This dramatic move towards multi-party competition certainly highlights the flaws in the hegemonial exchange model. In itself there is no problem with Africans mobilising along ethnic lines. Long-term stability and efficient development can only come, however, if this ethnic mobilisation occurs within a system that is more responsive to civil society's demands. Ethnic competition needs to be channelled through pluralist and democratic institutions. Likewise, ethnic considerations have to be balanced against the demands generated by other forms of social mobilisation (economic organisations, for example, or trade union or women's associations). Genuine pluralist representation across the whole of society fosters political legitimacy, not isolated and grudging concessions granted to ethnic groups by a dominant state.

Religion and African politics

As with ethnicity, religion has historically also been a social cleavage generating political competition within, and between, societies. Ever since humans have been in existence, individuals have been mobilising politically with reference to spiritual beliefs. European armies, for example, for 200 years, from the late eleventh century onwards, launched several crusades in an attempt to keep the holy sites of Jerusalem from Muslim control. More common in Europe were intra-faith conflicts between different denominations of Christianity. Entire countries were paralysed and devastated, occasionally for decades, while political and military disputes over religious ideas and the correct rituals of worship were resolved. Again, a political scientist should not attribute this conflict simply to intolerance and religion alone. Each of these political or violent acts had its own underpinning social and economic imperatives. Political interests were being acted out through religious mobilisation, and justifications offered by referring to holy scripture.

Religious competition in Europe, especially violent conflict, has declined over the last two centuries. This is because, relatively speaking, European countries have succeeded in separating church and state. The modern state minimally interferes in religious affairs, with faith becoming something practised in the private sphere. Governments may promote tolerance and protect the right of individuals to worship whichever god they choose (or no god at all), but the state no longer dictates doctrines and forms of religious observance for all. Certainly, issues of faith are still part of the political process (the violent hot-spots of Northern Ireland and the former Yugoslavia, for example, or the influence of the conservative Christian Right in US politics), but the West has come a long way from the Crusades and the Thirty Years War. Today, religion only plays a minor part in government deliberations and the formulation of public policy. By and large, the state commands the public realm, while religion is practised in the private domain.

African religions strengthening civil society

Indigenous African religions, like most traditional religions around the world, revolve around animist beliefs: the belief that the physical world is controlled by many kinds of spirits (of the earth, rivers, rain, sun, hunting and animals, for example). African religions also usually involve the worship of, and communicating with, ancestors and ghosts of the dead who have achieved partial divinity. Often this ancestor will be a hero, real or mythical, who founded the ethnic group concerned. These beliefs give a powerful *political* position to individuals, priests, lineage and clan elders, rainmakers, diviners, prophets, and other figures who act as inter-mediaries to the spirits. Witchcraft and sorcery are also still given widespread credence across Africa today, as many respect this traditional animist world of spirits and ancestors.

Often, this respect comes in the form of combining traditional beliefs with the more 'modern' faiths of Christianity and Islam. This is because, again like the rest of the world, Africa has been subject to the spread of alternative religious doctrines at different points in its history. Judaism, for example, established itself along the Mediterranean coast as far as Morocco, but it was almost completely superseded by Christianity early in the first century AD. This original and distinct form of Christianity is still practised in parts of Egypt and the Sudan, but it is Ethiopia that can boast some 1,600 years of continuous Christian worship, which is still observed today. From the seventh century onwards, the next wave of religious influence came from Islam, which replaced most of the early Christian churches. Islam spread through north Africa and across the Sahara via trading routes. This is, today, the dominant religion practised in the northern half of continental Africa. A second period of Islamic expansion was brought to the east coast by Arab traders and governors from the twelfth century onwards. Similarly, a second wave of Christianity, initiated by European missionaries in the nineteenth and twentieth centuries, came to dominate the southern half of the continent. This part of Africa is host to well-established and thriving churches of various Roman Catholic, Protestant and non-conformist denominations. With Islam dominating the north and practised in the east, Christianity commanding central and southern regions, and with animist beliefs found throughout the continent, post-colonial Africa was and remains a devoutly religious part of the world.

Plate 4.1 More than one million Zairian Christians gather for Pope John Paul II's mass at the Palace of the People, Kinshasa, Zaire, 5 April 1980.

Plate 4.2 Muslims praying, Al-Ubayyid, Sudan. Photographer: Alain Keler.

In terms of interaction with the post-colonial African state, these religious groups prove to be interesting. Just as with the ethnic groups discussed above, political leaders had to tread carefully with religious institutions. This was the area of civil society least subject to co-optation, bullying or coercion by the state (discussed later in Chapter 6). Politicians may have been promoting alternative ideologies and belief systems (nationalism, socialism, capitalism and populism, for example), but none of these ideas could supersede the notions of Christianity or Islam in African minds. As a result, whereas the state could readily ban or monopolise other civil society activity (opposition political parties or labour groups, for instance), churches and mosques always had to be given space to operate. In a one-party state this amounted to a rare luxury for any civil society organisation.

From time to time, state elites paid a price for their relative inability to co-opt or coerce religious institutions. These organisations occasionally became a rallying point and conduit for civil society to express grievances against the state. In apartheid South Africa, for example, when the white minority government had banned all other black opposition groups during the 1980s and early 1990s, leaving the liberation movement voiceless, it was church leaders who stepped into this political vacuum. Even the ruthless apartheid state had to think twice about closing churches and imprisoning congregations. Another example of religious leaders acting where nobody else could was Malawi in the 1990s (discussed in more detail in Chapter 11). Here church ministers used their uniquely uncensored pulpits to advocate an end to President Hastings Banda's authoritarian style of rule. These sermons had the effect of kick-starting Malawi's successful civil society campaign for multi-party democracy.

Islamist politics on the African continent

The above examples of the church or more liberal mosques engaging in overt political action tend to be rare. The primary concern of religious leaders, after all, is to look after their congregation's spiritual needs, not their political interests. These leaders will involve themselves with day-to-day political issues, but, generally, only when pushed by significant humanitarian considerations, and the lack of alternative avenues of opposition, do churches and mosques become the focus for larger-scale political mobilisation. This is because these organisations tend to follow the modern precedent of a separation of church and state. Religion is a private matter between an individual and their God. Worship may be conducted collectively and in public, but it is a part of life to be kept away from political competition.

Some Muslims, however, broadly termed *Islamists*, disagree that religion and the state should exist apart. Instead, Islamists argue that religion without authority is worthless (rejecting the converse liberal arguments that religion without individual freedom is worthless). Islamists point to the West, where religion has become detached from government, and they see decadent societies where greed, crime, materialism and a lack of community are rife. With church separated from state, the argument runs, public life in the West has become amoral in outlook.

Islam lends itself to a unification of religion and politics because it is a faith whose message regulates both the spiritual and temporal worlds. Interpretations of the Qur'an advise not only on matters regarding an individual's relationship with Allah, through the soul, but also on social conduct in the material world. Islam pervades all aspects of life. Consequently, there are Islamic teachings and interpretations on how individuals should not only pray, but conduct commerce, marry, rear children, socialise, and so on. It is the duty of all Muslims to adhere to and protect these holistic religious and social characteristics of Islam. This duty is the *jihad*, interpreted variously as the inner or external holy struggle, or war.

In terms of politics, Islamists underline this unification of the material and spiritual worlds. They advocate that the *shari'a* should not only be the guiding principle of personal behaviour, but also the responsibility of government. *Shari'a* law is a basic code of conduct for Muslims to follow. It addresses how one should worship (daily prayers, almsgiving, fasting and pilgrimage); it outlines the punishments for basic crimes (amputation of the hand for theft, and stoning for adultery, for example), and the legal system to try alleged offenders; it also states how Muslims should dress, what they should eat, and a whole host of other regulations. A state's implementation of *shari'a* correctly, Islamists argue, will bring justice, order and clarity to a society.

The Qur'an, however, in no sense provides a definitive legal code or constitution for government. No more than 80 verses of this text deal with these matters directly. This invites a good deal of debate and interpretation with regard to what *shari'a* should actually be in this political sense, let alone how it should be applied. Some Islamic scholars interpret the Qur'an very conservatively and literally. Ayatollah Khomeini, who came to rule Iran after the fall of the Shah in 1979, drew together some 3,000 rulings on the conduct of daily life in his *Explication of Problems*. These rulings decreed on a range of matters, from how Iranians should organise their laws of inheritance, to matters of personal hygiene, and how to slaughter animals correctly.[10] The Taliban regime in Afghanistan (1996–2001) had an even more conservative interpretation of the *shari'a*. They rejected modern science, seeking a return to a more traditional way of life. Other Islamic polities, such as Morocco and Indonesia, have far more liberal ideas of how these principles ought to impact on government. These two states see no problem in technology being part of a modern Muslim society.

Then there is the question of who should interpret the *shari'a*. Like all religions and belief systems, Islam has had its fair share of ideologues who insist that *their* interpretation of the Qur'an is the correct and only law. Other scholars advocate a democratic Islam where the interpretation of the *shari'a* is the equal right of all adults within society. Similarly, some Islamic movements advocate prosecuting the *jihad* by violent means, while others reject this out of hand. Despite these considerable differences over the precise nature of the Islamic state and how it governs, what is certain is that all Islamists reject the notion of the separation of religion and politics. Instead, they seek to install or maintain an Islamic republic in which public policy and social conduct are guided and determined by the *shari'a*.

Potentially, Islamist politics could have a massive impact on African states. This is because one-fifth of the world's Muslim population lives in Africa. In reality, however, this movement's impact on politics has, so far, been restricted as the vast majority of African states are currently *secular*, that is, they separate religion from the state. This is the nature of the societies left by the departing colonial powers at independence, and, by and large, most African Muslims are content to continue with this arrangement. Political mobilisation based on religion can be found, and many African religious leaders have gained political advantage, prominence and power though their spiritual position. Leading *marabouts* (Islamic teachers) in Senegal, for example, have acted as political intermediaries between their congregations (or brotherhoods) and the state for decades. They have also even occasionally acted as 'kingmakers', backing or breaking politicians' careers.[11] Despite this influence, Senegal remains a secular state. Only the governments of Libya and the Sudan have ruled in the name of Islam for periods of the post-colonial era, whilst Mauritania has been an Islamic republic since 1958.

Yet, despite the dominance of secularism, Islamist movements have become increasingly active and politically significant on the continent in the last three decades. Algeria set the trend when it came close to forming an Islamist government in 1992. That year saw the *Front Islamique de Salut (FIS)* win local, and then the first round of national, democratic elections. The Algerian army, however, fearful of Islamist rule, stepped in at this point and annulled the poll (sparking a decade of conflict in which some 100,000 people lost their lives). At the same time, stateless Somalia, and regions of the Sudan, began to host Islamist terrorist groups, with Islamist politics taking hold in these host societies. Interventions by peace keeping forces, and even the temporary invasion of Somalia by the Ethiopian army in 2006, have failed to lessen this activity. The fear in Western capitals is that links between local religious leaders and international terrorist groups will increase in these stateless environments. The fact that Egypt, Kenya, Tanzania and Morocco have all had Western-associated targets, notably embassies and tourist facilities, bombed on their territory has added to these fears. The West was also troubled by events in Egypt during 2011. Here, in the wake of the Arab Spring, the Muslim Brotherhood won power democratically. However, as with Algeria two decades earlier, the Egyptian army found this situation intolerable, and the military forcibly intervened in 2013 to restore a secular government.

Attracting most attention in recent years, however, has been the violence introduced by Islamist movements in parts of western Africa and the Sahel (a strip of territory stretching across the continent along the southern boundary of the Sahara Desert). Inspired by events in the Middle East, and mirroring the activities of Al-Qaeda, the Taliban and Islamic State, Islamist groups have resorted to armed force to try and impose their preferred forms of Islamic government on this part of the world. As will be seen in the case study below, for example, Islamists in Nigeria, most notably Boko Haram, began committing sophisticated terrorist attacks from 2010 onwards. This movement brought chaos to north-east, north-central and central Nigeria. Boko Haram also had a presence in Chad, Niger and Cameroon. Elsewhere, in 2013, a coalition of Islamist and other (secular) fighters sought to capture the state of Mali. A fractious insurgent alliance took on the Malian army, which itself was divided. This rebel force brought together Islamist groups exiled from Algeria during its civil war, those pledging allegiance to *Al-Qaïda au Maghreb Islamique*, Tuareg rebels and criminal gangs who had prospered through narcotic and human trafficking, taking advantage of the Malian government's inability to project its authority into the north of its territory. Only the intervention of French troops prevented the capital Bamako falling to this rebel coalition. France and the United Nations deployed troops to first turn back the insurgent forces, and then loosen the grip of these Islamist groups in north Mali. Similarly, across the continent, but still in the Sahel, the threat of *Al-Shabab* remains. This Islamist group, also with links to Al-Qaeda, failed to resist the Ethiopian army's intervention, and lost its hold of the Somali capital Mogadishu in 2006. Yet Al-Shabab fighters still control most of southern and central Somalia, and have exported terrorist atrocities to both Kenya and Uganda.

The above survey suggests that evolving Islamist activity and ambitions need to be recognised when studying African politics. There is certainly mounting support in many parts of the continent for Muslim beliefs to be reflected more overtly in public policy. It should be remembered, however, that the norm for the vast majority of African states is religious organisations (Christian and Muslim) exerting only measured political influence. Spiritual leaders interact with other interest groups within a secular political culture. There is no majority demand in any of these countries for religion to over-shadow secular politics.

Instrumental religious political mobilisation

This discussion on religion can be concluded by briefly building upon what was said at the end of the previous section addressing ethnicity. Religion enters politics not just for spiritual or moral reasons; often there are instrumental imperatives as well. Political, economic and social conditions affect the decision of anyone who decides to challenge the state using justifications of faith. One can certainly characterise, for example, an Islamist militant fighting in Algeria as a devout believer who is willing to lay down their life to wrestle the state from infidels. Yet, just as with the Rwandan genocide discussed above, to leave this as the sole explanation of the Algerian conflict tends to mislead. Again, the political scientist has to dig deeper. One should acknowledge the fact that the Algerian military has always stymied political representation in this country, as well as the fact that the timing of Islamist popularity coincided with chronic economic problems, and the stalling of the whole (secular) nation-building project. Thus an Islamist activist in Algeria is not just a devout follower of Mohammed's teachings; he or she is also someone who is aware of the acute social inequalities in their country. They also believe that the current political dispensation, particularly the power of the military, has contributed to these inequalities.[12] Essentially, this individual sees an Islamic republic providing a better future given a perceived failure of the 'Western' model of development in Algeria. It is not just blind faith that sees this person (violently or peacefully) express their opposition to the incumbent government; instrumental choices have been made as well. And what goes for Algeria follows for Mali, too. The attempt to establish an Islamic caliphate in the north of that country in 2013 was not solely about seeking to rule in Allah's name. It was just as much about attempting to break free from Bamako's political authority, rejecting the ineffective and

Table 4.1 Chapter summary: ethnicity and religion in African politics

Ethnicity	• A community solidarity based on shared ideas of origin, ancestry, tradition and culture
The creation of 'tribes'	• Ethnic groups dynamic and modern, not primordialist
	• 'Tribes' a product of colonialism and African responses to the imposition of the modern state
Ethnicity and political mobilisation	• Strong ethnic loyalties protect ethnic groups, to a degree, from state harassment
	• States often try to balance ethnic interests through the allocation of resources and the granting of political office
	• Relatively stable but inefficient and unrepresentative government created by 'hegemonial exchange'
Religion	• Traditional African beliefs based on animism and ancestor worship are still respected, and often combined with Christianity and Islam
	• An outpost of early Christianity is still strong in Ethiopia
	• Spread of Islam from seventh century onwards across north Africa, and later down the east coast of the continent
	• European missionaries bring Christianity to southern Africa from the nineteenth century onwards
Religious institutions as a conduit of civil society protest	• Religious organisations are potentially difficult for the state to suppress, due to popular support and moral implications
	• Churches and mosques occasionally become a conduit for civil society to protest against the state, especially when other avenues of opposition are blocked
Islamist politics in Africa	• Islamists are seeking to create Islamic republics where religion and the state are not separated
	• Government in Islamic republics focuses on implementing the *shari'a*
	• Most African Muslim countries are secular
	• Islamist movements are gaining influence in the Sahel

unrepresentative government to which those in the north of Mali had been subject for most of the post-colonial period.

State and civil society

Ethnic and religious sentiments are, of course, not the sole foundation for political relationships in Africa. They intermingle with other social considerations, such as class, 'race', ideology, gender and age, to mention but a few. Ethnicity and religion have, however, been particularly relevant to the political structure of post-colonial Africa. As such, they are concepts that reveal much about the general underlying theme of this book: the competition between the state and civil society on the African continent.

Nationalism was clearly the 'ideology' favoured by state elites. This was a tool that served them well in maintaining their authority over political institutions, and over society as a whole. The nation-state was promoted as the key to the future. Governors talked about opportunities arising from nation building, and discouraged alternative 'tribalist' loyalties. The nation-state, they argued, had to beat back any sub-national challenges to its authority. Only in this manner would the state be able to protect modern economic and political development. Similarly, religious leaders were encouraged only to operate in the private, and not the public, sphere. Nationalism was promoted as the only legitimate form of political mobilisation.

Despite the above protestations of African leaders, it was not necessarily true that ethnic and religious loyalties were counter-productive for a functional political environment. Indeed, in many cases, the pluralism that ethnic mobilisation brought, and the opportunity for expression that religious institutions gave to an otherwise closed political system, often proved beneficial. Ethnicity opened a channel of negotiation and bargaining between the nationalist state and civil society. Indeed, in a political environment of one-party states and authoritarian rule, many Africans received the bulk of their political representation through this channel, by way of membership of an ethnic group. Likewise, religious institutions acted as a safety valve. They allowed civil society to voice its grievances, should state oppression become unbearable. Unlike opposition political parties, only in a handful of cases did state elites manage to completely eradicate or neutralise these alternative sources of political power.

As the post-colonial period developed, Africans certainly came to see themselves as national citizens (for example, Zambians or Gambians), but they also held on strongly to identities at a sub-state level. This was because multiple identities served their interests well. Certain benefits could be gained from state institutions, but others derived from acting collectively with citizens who shared similar ethnic or religious identities. Africans were thus unwilling to do as their political leaders demanded and put all their faith in the nation-state. Indeed, it is as well that they did not do this. The fact remains that, during certain periods of the post-colonial period, ethnic and religious mobilisation brought Africans far more political rewards than affiliation to state institutions. In this respect, if nationalism was the ideological tool of the state, then ethnicity and religion remained valuable instruments of civil society.

Case study: ethnicity, religion and the nation-state in Nigeria

Nigeria is located on Africa's west coast, and is the continent's most populous state. Its topography consists of swamps and lagoons in the Niger River delta, giving way to areas of tropical forest and savannah up-country. In the far north, there are arid fringes where the Sahara Desert begins to impinge. Nigeria ranks as one of Africa's more developed states, having benefited from the export of its oil reserves. Ongoing conflicts of interest between various social groups, however, have hindered optimum political and economic development during the post-colonial period. Much of this conflict has encouraged political mobilisation along ethnic lines.

Contained within Nigeria's national boundaries are over 250 ethnic groups. The largest three of these have dominated Nigerian politics since independence in 1960. They each mobilise in a distinct geographical region. The northern Hausa-Fulani consist of 30 per cent of the country's total population; the western Yoruba furnish 20 per cent of the total; and the eastern Ibo account for 17 per cent. This observation, however, should not hide the fact that each of these regions is also home to numerous other, smaller ethnic groups. It should also be noted that the three dominant ethnic groups can be further divided into sub-groups. Twenty-nine distinct divisions can be identified within the Hausa-Fulani community, 12 within the Yoruba, and 32 within the Ibo.[13]

This last fact, that there are prominent sub-ethnic identities, reveals a great deal about the respective histories of the Hausa-Fulani, the Yoruba and the Ibo. Evidence from the past clearly shows that these communities are not primordial. They are ethnic groups that have been socially constructed in relatively modern times. Indeed, the creation of these 'tribes' is closely linked to the era of British imperial rule.

It is no coincidence, for example, that the three regions of independent Nigeria closely resemble the administrative boundaries of the colonial years. The northern region had previously been the Northern Protectorate, administered through indirect rule, relying on Fulani emirs as intermediaries. The eastern and western regions had been the Southern Protectorate, which had combined in 1906, after being run as two separate administrative areas prior to this. Despite the Northern and Southern protectorates being united to form a single Nigeria in 1914, each region retained considerable autonomy under colonial rule.

Given this distinct regional administrative pattern, it was only natural that 'tribes' would develop within, and identify with, these separate (northern, eastern and western) regions. This was a rational manner in which to lobby the colonial authorities for resources. In other words, mobilisation along ethno-regional lines proved to be the most effective method of building Robert Bates' 'winning coalitions'. Consequently, groups which had previously sought only loose affiliations now came together as 'tribes'. Such an instrumental consolidation of clans and lineage groups was also encouraged by the colonial authorities, who required larger groups for administrative purposes.

A brief examination of the creation of the western Yoruba 'tribe' illustrates this process well. The historical evidence shows how this group, far from being a primordial social formation, with its origins shrouded in the mists of time, is in fact a modern political and social construct.

Prior to colonial rule, there had been no such thing as a Yoruba political unit or identity. Indeed the word 'Yoruba' was not familiar to the people of south-west Nigeria until the nineteenth century. Instead, the individuals of this region regarded themselves as Oyo, Ketu, Egba, Ijebu, Ijesa, Ekiti, Ondo, or members of a number of other, smaller communities. Certainly, each group was aware of their neighbours, having established trading links and social contacts, and even through the waging of war, but none of these societies shared a larger 'Yoruba' identity. Similarly, although the groups may have had a common language in academic linguistic terms, different dialects meant that these languages were not always mutually intelligible.

Social relationships between the 'Yoruba' clans changed dramatically under colonial rule. The imperial authorities needed larger communities to reduce the costs and difficulty of administration. Missionaries also desired larger communities, and for these people to speak the same language. This would aid their conversion to Christianity. In this respect, a standard Yoruba vernacular was invented by missionaries (based on the Oyo dialect, that of the largest clan), and a Yoruba bible was printed. From this point onward, it was in the interests of the 'clans' to adopt this standard Yoruba language, as it became the medium of Western education and local Christianity. In addition, it was vital for individuals in this region to take on a broader Yoruba identity in order to be recognised by, and gain access to, the colonial state. A failure to bargain with the imperial authorities as a united force would have resulted in all the 'clans' losing out to other, more consolidated groups, found elsewhere in Nigeria. In short, ethnic coalitions were re-forged and enlarged to meet the demands and opportunities of the new modern state. And just as the Yoruba adapted, so did the Fulani-Hausa and the Ibo.[14]

It should be no surprise, then, that at independence, Nigeria's First Republic was dominated by these ethno-regional groupings. Indeed, the independence constitution rested firmly on this political reality. A federal system of three regions was established, which sought to recognise the needs, and balance the aspirations, of these dominant ethnic groups. Each region had a strong, relatively autonomous government, while the central administration concentrated on 'national' issues such as defence, foreign policy and international trade.

Nigerians, naturally enough, responded to this ethno-regional constitution by voting for their respective 'cultural brokers'. They charged their chosen candidates with the duty of capturing central federal resources, bringing these back to the regional community. Consequently, no powerful nation wide political party or constituency emerged. Local considerations dominated, and issues of ethnicity became increasingly politicised. Each region was governed by a political party that squarely identified with just one ethnic group. The Fulani-Hausa governed the north, the Yoruba the west, and the Ibo the east.

The First Republic's three-legged constitution, however, failed to institutionalise this ethnic balancing act within a stable political system. Too many suspicions existed between the regions. The Christian south feared the larger-populated Muslim north, while the 'underdeveloped' north feared the better-educated south. Similarly, the east and north resented the larger presence of westerners in the federal bureaucracy. Each region saw itself in a vulnerable position. What is more, the tripartite federal constitution ignored the aspirations of minority ethnic groups which could not break this political oligopoly of the Ibo, Yoruba and Hausa-Fulani.

Perhaps the greatest constitutional danger, however, lay with the fact that it was possible for two of the regions to join forces against the third. Indeed, soon after independence, the northern party formed a coalition with the eastern party and did just that. Later, they attempted to exploit an internal split within the isolated western Yoruba party. Using their majority in the national assembly, they created a fourth federal region in order to disperse the power of the Yoruba. The instability this created, along with economic mismanagement and labour agitation, left the way open for two military coups in 1966. The military intervened, they declared, to restore order and discipline.

This military intervention, however, precipitated even more political turmoil. Ibo politicians, unhappy with the northern (Hausa-Fulani) dominance of the military government, promptly led their western region to secession. An independent state of Biafra was declared in 1967. This was the low point in Nigerian aspirations of national unity, and probably the high point of political mobilisation based on ethnicity. The country would eventually be reunited, after three years of civil war, but not before up to two million 'Biafrans' had died as a result of the federal government's siege of the west.

Nigeria's first period of military rule lasted from 1966 to 1979. The generals attempted to tame ethnic mobilisation by installing nationalist political structures instead. Government was to become more centralised, and it aimed to produce national unity and economic development for the whole country. The number of regions (now states) in the federation, for example, increased from four to 12 in 1968, and then to 19 by 1976. This was an attempt to loosen the stranglehold of the three dominant ethnic groups, and open up opportunities for smaller communities (and other interests). Military rule, in many ways, also assisted the consolidation of power among national bureaucrats. Although ethnic balancing was still a feature of government appointments, political competition gradually became channelled more through federal structures, rather than the earlier regional dominance. The military also successfully protected Nigeria's national integrity. No real attempt at secession emerged after the 1967–70 civil war. This is not to say, however, that the country enjoyed political stability during this first period of military rule. Officers, disaffected with corruption within the bureaucracy and

Nigeria's poor economic management, overthrew their superiors in 1975, forming a successor military government.

The regime of Lieutenant General Olusegun Obasanjo returned Nigeria to civilian rule in 1979. The Second Republic had at its helm President Alhaji Shagari, leader of the National Party of Nigeria (NPN). It is true to say that the lion's share of NPN power lay in the northern region, but the support this organisation enjoyed among southern voters did give credibility to its pretensions to be a national party.

This Second Republic (1979–83) was very much an age of patronage, giving a good illustration of Donald Rothchild's 'hegemonial exchange' model. The federal government at the centre looked after its own interests, but also had to acknowledge ethno-regional power. Resources were distributed accordingly. As well as material goods and local budgets, political posts were also part of this ethnic arithmetic. The NPN itself, for example, made sure that the posts of President, National Chair, Vice President and Head of the Senate were rotated among party notables hailing from the north, east, west and central zones. The federal cabinet was also inclusive, representing all of Nigeria's major ethnic brokers. No one ethnic group could be perceived to be too dominant, nor could any of these groups be excluded.

The Shagari regime, however, was to fall to another military coup on New Year's Eve, 1983. Shagari had got his ethnic arithmetic right, but the army intervened because of this civilian administration's inability to manage the economy.

At a time when oil revenue was declining, the cost of corruption had become too destructive. As Shagari relied on ethnic patronage for its survival, corruption was hard to control. Politics had become centred on the short-term winning of state resources, and gaining access to the levers of power. Little long-term strategic political or economic planning could survive in this institutionalised system of political exchange. Resource capture and distribution had become more important to politicians and bureaucrats than the actual development of the economy that produced these resources. Nigeria had hit, head-on, the problems of inefficiency and legitimacy associated with the hegemonial exchange model.

The military administration of Major General Muhammadu Buhari failed to find any immediate remedies for Nigeria's economic problems, and his regime became increasingly authoritarian as it began to lose popular support. This prompted yet another military coup in 1985, in which Major General Ibrahim Babangida became head of state. Babangida imposed an economic structural adjustment programme, and promised a return to civilian rule by 1992. In this respect, the regime set about attempting to formulate a constitution that could manage Nigeria's social divisions more successfully than the democratic experiment of the Second Republic.

The Babangida constitution introduced a number of new ideas to Nigerian politics. First, the Armed Forces Ruling Council (AFRC) declared that former politicians, and its own members, would not be able to participate as elected officials in the Third Republic. Nor would the institutionalised ethnic balancing of the past be reproduced. Instead, Babangida opted for a two-party system, based on national, rather than regional, political competition. Both parties would have to gain support right across the country, if they were to win power.

True to its word, the Babangida regime invited political parties to form and compete to be one of the two legal political parties within the new constitution. Forty groups applied, and 13 were deemed to meet the national credentials set by the regime. The AFRC, however, later dissolved all 13 of these parties because, they claimed, they did not have a distinctive ideology (and were too closely linked to proscribed former politicians). Instead, the AFRC created two parties of their own, along with their accompanying manifestos. The transition to civilian rule stalled, however, when pressures from within the military led to the 1993 presidential election being annulled. The victor of this democratic poll, Moshood Abiola, was subsequently thrown into jail. Evidently, elements of the military enjoyed their taste of political power, and were not prepared to relinquish the reins of the state.

It was not until 1999 that multi-party democracy returned to Nigeria, when President Olusegun Obasanjo was duly elected to lead the Third Republic. That Obasanjo was a retired general, and had led the 1976–79 military government, clearly illustrates the 'veto' that the armed forces still held over Nigerian politics. Yet it should be noted that Nigeria is currently enjoying its longest period of civilian rule since independence. Elections have been held regularly, albeit with serious flaws in terms of violence and vote rigging. Obasanjo also made some inroads into the issue of corruption, removing several leading politicians from office. In 2007, Nigeria even experienced its first civilian-to-civilian transfer of power, when Obasanjo, having failed to amend the constitution to enable himself to enjoy a third term of office, made way for President Alhaji Umaru Musa Yar'Adua. After his death in office during 2010, Musa was in turn succeeded by Vice President Goodluck Jonathan, who won the subsequent multi-party elections of that year. Despite this more 'democratic' era, however, the difficulty of managing ethnic and religious differences has remained.

In terms of ethnicity, the Third Republic has been associated with political violence in the oil-producing Niger Delta region of the country. Activists, invoking sentiments of ethnicity, have mobilised against the federal government, complaining that local people gain little economic or social benefit from the oil extracted on their land. Profits, they argue, are siphoned off by federal authorities and transnational corporations. The struggle is portrayed as central government exploiting the local minority ethnic groups that inhabit the delta. Political conflict over inequality has taken on an ethnic dimension. Low-intensity insurgency has been the result.

It is religion, however, that has caused most conflict in the Third Republic. Since 1999, violence has accompanied the decision of 12 northern states in the federation to enforce full *shari'a* law. Although the *shari'a* had been practised in colonial Nigeria, the traditional unmitigated punishments (death by the sword, stoning, amputation and flogging) associated with *hudud* offences (such as theft, fornication, consumption of alcohol, and apostasy) had been outlawed under British indirect rule. Post-colonial Nigeria, until 1999, had maintained this position. One should not be surprised, therefore, that the reintroduction of the full *shari'a* penal code by these 12 states prompted inter-communal violence. Each instance of a judge passing an unmitigated sentence for a *hadd* crime precipitated riots, collectively costing hundreds of lives. Likewise, actions in Iraq and Afghanistan also periodically encouraged violence between Muslim and Christian neighbours.

At first glance, events in northern Nigeria appear to be a simple outpouring of faith, a clash of spiritual beliefs. The decision to impose full *hudud* penalties, after all, had local popular support. Yet the political scientist has to enquire why the governors of these 12 states chose this particular moment to restore *shari'a* law in the way that they did. A deeper analysis reveals the underlying politics behind this decision. The politicians may have been sincere about acting in the name of Allah, but instrumental interests were also being served.

First, it should be noted that northern interests had just been forced from power by the election of Obasanjo. The previous period of military rule had been closely associated with a powerful northern officer class. Invoking Islamic solidarity can therefore be seen as a defensive act. It was a vehicle for politicians to protect their northern homeland against any manoeuvring by the new democratically elected federal government.

Then there was the issue of corruption. Given the historic failure of the federal government to tackle this issue, would not the political system be cleansed by the full implementation of the *shari'a*? Citizens of the north supported the notion that it would. Reference to Islam could bring a much needed moral dimension to political conduct.

Also to be considered was the retreat of the state under structural adjustment programmes (discussed in depth in Chapter 9). Neo-liberal-inspired reforms had required the federal government to provide fewer social services nationwide. In the north, Muslim non-government organisations stepped into this social space. Islamic organisations could now be found operating in the health, education and even security sectors, providing what the state no longer could. Why not extend this faith-based public service to the 12 state governments themselves?

Thus, for these three reasons, the political environment was ripe for politicians to appeal to constituents using Islam as a rallying point. And this is exactly what they did. Religious mobilisation won popular support for the governors of the 12 states, together with their political factions. Faith was a vote winner and helped politicians secure office; the full reintroduction of *shari'a* law was the logical extension of this competition for political support and legitimacy.

Less legitimate has been the emergence of Boko Haram, and the introduction of organised religious violence into Nigerian society. This group's official name, *Jama'atu Ahlis Sunna Lidda'awati wal-Jihad*, translates as 'People Committed to the Propagation of the Prophet's Teachings and Jihad'. Local people, however, dubbed the group *Boko Haram*, loosely meaning 'Western education is forbidden'. Although its origins can be traced back to earlier Islamist activism, Boko Haram came to the fore in 2002, when its followers established a school and mosque complex in Maiduguri, northern Nigeria. The group's aim was to provide an authentic Islamic education, countering Western values that it perceived had damaged Nigerian society. As its reputation grew, this school recruited students and activists from across Nigeria and neighbouring states. Boko Haram's political ambition was to rid Nigeria of its corrupt government, and replace it with an Islamic caliphate.

In 2009 this movement turned to a violent jihad in the wake of clashes with state security forces that had resulted in hundreds of its supporters and police being killed. Despite Boko Haram's leader, Mohammed Yusuf, having been summarily executed after his arrest, fighters loyal to this movement have subsequently stepped up their insurgency. Initial attacks on local police stations soon escalated to assassinations, bombings (including Abuja itself), mass kidnappings (including schoolchildren) and military activity in the neighbouring states of Niger, Cameroon and Chad. Raids on villages and towns involving hundreds of Boko Haram fighters followed. By mid-2014, Boko Haram could claim control over 50,000 square kilometres of north-east Nigeria for its caliphate, with the Nigerian army struggling to contain this force. Five thousand lives had been lost in this insurgency, while over a million refugees were forced to flee from this part of the country.

Again, it would be too simplistic to put this violence down to religious extremism alone. One also has to consider the environment in which these terrorists operate. Social inequality, state corruption and a lack of political representation are also part of the problem. Even if the Nigerian government does find a way to defeat Boko Haram militarily, these underlying factors will invite future challenges to state authority. It will not be too long before another political grouping will appeal to religion or ethnicity in an attempt to win power.

Nigeria[15]

Territory:	580,768 sq. km.	Population:	173.6 million
Colonial power:	Britain	Independence:	1960
Major cities:	Abuja (capital)	Major ethnic groups:	Hausa
	Lagos		Yoruba
	Kano		Kano
	Abadan		Fulani
Infant mortality:	74 deaths/1,000 live births		250+ others
Currency:	Naira	Life expectancy:	52 years
Urban population:	46 per cent	Adult literacy	52 per cent
Religions:	Traditional	Exports:	Oil and gas
	Christian		Rubber
	Islam		Cocoa
GDP per capita:	US$1,555		Leather

Questions raised by this chapter

1. Why did Africans start consolidating on a 'tribal' basis in the nineteenth and twentieth centuries?
2. Do you consider African ethnic groups to be primordial or instrumental in nature?
3. Is the 'hegemonial exchange' model an appropriate form of government for African societies?
4. Have ethnic and religious identities assisted or hindered the political process in post-colonial Africa?
5. To what extent would the establishment of an Islamist government on the continent change the nature of African politics?

Glossary of key terms

Animist beliefs	Traditional beliefs that the physical world is controlled by many kinds of spirits (of the earth, rivers and rain, for example), which may also involve ancestor worship.
Distributive politics	A style of politics where state resources are distributed according to demand, rather than need. Political calculations override social or economic considerations.
Ethnic arithmetic	Calculations required to ensure that all ethnic groups within a society receive an appropriate share of state resources.
Ethnic brokers	Intermediaries or members of the state elite who represent the interests of, and seek resources for, their ethnic group.
Ethnic group	A community of people who have the conviction that they have a common identity and common fate based on issues of origin, kinship ties, traditions, cultural uniqueness, a shared history and possibly a shared language.
Hegemonial exchange	Where the state, unable to completely assert its hegemony over ethnic groups, exchanges resources and patronage in return for political compliance.
***Hudud* offences**	(Singular *hadd*). Crimes in *shari'a* law that warrant the most serious punishment. *Hudud* offences include theft, highway robbery, illegal sexual intercourse, drinking alcohol, and apostasy (the rejection of a former religious belief).
Islamism	The belief that Islam should dominate not only the spiritual world, but also the temporal world (including politics and government). Islamists seek to build an Islamic republic where there is no separation between church and state.
The *shari'a*	The religious code of Islam that regulates both public and private life. The *shari'a* informs correct behaviour with respect to banking, commerce, family relations, sexuality, hygiene and dress, among many other issues.

Further reading

Sources that could be consulted to develop a deeper knowledge of ethnicity in Africa include Crawford Young's chapter in David Apter and Carl Rosberg's book looking at how Africanists have studied the concept of ethnicity, as well as Louise de la Gorgendière, Kenneth King and Sarah Vaughan's edited collection which covers a remarkable amount of ground. For a detailed case study, Gérard Prunier's book on Rwanda is highly recommended, while those readers interested in how African ethnic groups consolidated as a reaction to colonial rule should consult the extremely informative book edited by Leroy Vail. The instrumentalist case of 'hegemonial exchange' is argued well in Donald Rothchild's essay. David Welsh has written an excellent article drawing together many of the above ideas on ethnicity, whilst Bruce Berman, Dickson Eyoh and Will Kymlicka's collection provides good illustrative case studies from across the continent.

In terms of how religion has influenced African politics, Jeff Haynes's book is recommended as a general introduction to the issues, while Gudrun Krämer's article is a good place to start exploring the concept of an Islamic republic. Those who wish to look at religion and politics in the case study country of Nigeria may want to read Ogbu Kalu's article on how *shari'a* law has been imposed in this country's northern states, and the problems and political tensions that this has created nationally and internationally. The book edited by Benjamin Soares and René Otayek provides a broader collection of country studies assessing the impact of Islam on African politics.

Berman, Bruce, Dickson Eyoh and Will Kymlicka, eds. *Ethnicity and Democracy in Africa*. Oxford: James Currey, 2004.

Gorgendière, Louise de la, Kenneth King and Sarah Vaughan, eds. *Ethnicity in Africa: Roots, Meanings and Implications*. Edinburgh: Centre of African Studies, University of Edinburgh, 1996.

Haynes, Jeff. *Politics and Religion in Africa*. London: Zed, 1996.

Kalu, Ogbu. Safiyya and Adamah: punishing adultery with shari'a stones in twenty-first century Nigeria. *African Affairs*. 2003, 102(408), 389–408.

Krämer, Gudrun. Visions of an Islamic republic: good governance according to the Islamists. In: Kai Hafez, ed. *The Islamic World and the West: An Introduction to Political Cultures and International Relations*. Leiden: Brill, 1997. 33–45.

Prunier, Gérard. *The Rwanda Crisis 1959–1994: History of Genocide*. London: Hurst, 1995.

Rothchild, Donald. State–ethnic relations in middle Africa. In: Gwendolen M. Carter and Patrick O'Meara, eds. *African Independence: The First Twenty-Five Years*. Bloomington, IN: Indiana University Press, 1985. 71–96.

Soares, Benjamin F. and René Otayek, eds. *Islam and Muslim Politics in Africa*. New York: Palgrave Macmillan, 2007.

Vail, Leroy, ed. *The Creation of Tribalism in Southern Africa*. London: James Currey, 1989.

Welsh, David. Ethnicity in Sub-Saharan Africa. *International Affairs*. 1996, 72(3), 477–91.

Young, Crawford. Evolving modes of consciousness and ideology: nationalism and ethnicity. In: David E. Apter and Carl G. Rosberg, eds. *Political Development and the New Realism in Sub-Saharan Africa*. Charlottesville, VA: University Press of Virginia, 1994. 61–86.

Notes and references

1 Calhoun, Craig. *Nationalism*. Buckingham: Open University Press. 1997. 40.

2 Prunier, Gérard. *The Rwanda Crisis 1959–1994: History of a Genocide*. London: Hurst, 1995. 265 and xi–xii.

3 *Ibid*. xii.

4 Southall, Aidan W. The illusion of tribe. *Journal of Asian and African Studies*. 1970, 5(1), 36.

5 Young, Crawford. *The African Colonial State in Comparative Perspective*. New Haven, CT: Yale University Press, 1994. 232.

6 See Kofele-Kale, Ndiva. Class, status, and power in post-reunification Cameroon: the rise of an anglophone bourgeoisie, 1961–1980. In: Irving Leonard Markovitz, ed. *Studies in Power and Class in Africa*. New York: Oxford University Press, 1987. 138.

7 Bates, Robert H. Modernization, ethnic competition, and the rationality of politics in contemporary Africa. In: Donald Rothchild and Victor A. Olorunsola, eds. *State Versus Ethnic Claims: African Policy Dilemmas*. Boulder, CO: Westview Press, 1983. 164.

8 Rothchild, Donald. State–ethnic relations in middle Africa. In: Gwendolen M. Carter and Patrick O'Meara, eds. *African Independence: The First Twenty-Five Years*. Bloomington, IN: Indiana University Press, 1985. 72–3.

9 Obote, A. Milton. *Proposals for New Methods of Election of Representatives of People to Parliament*. Kampala: Milton Obote Foundation. 6–7. Cited in Rothchild. In: Carter and O'Meara. *Africa Independence*, 1970. 94.

10 See Haynes, Jeff. *Religion in Third World Politics*. Buckingham: Open University Press, 1993. 35.

11 See, for example, Villalón, Leonardo A. *Islamic Society and State Power in Senegal: Disciples and Citizens in Fatick*. Cambridge: Cambridge University Press, 2007.

12 Zoubir, Yahia. Algeria: Islamic secularism and political Islam. In: Rolin G. Mainuddin, ed. *Religion and Politics in the Developing World: Explosive Interactions*. Aldershot: Ashgate, 2002. 84.

13 Jinadu, L. Adele. Federalism, the consociational state, and ethnic conflict in Nigeria. *Publius*. 1985, 15, 77.

14 Law, Robin. Local amateur scholarship in the construction of Yoruba ethnicity, 1880–1914. In: Louise de la Gorgendière, Kenneth King and Sarah Vaughan, eds. *Ethnicity in Africa: Roots, Meanings and Implications*. Edinburgh: Centre of African Studies, University of Edinburgh, 1996. 65–87.

15 Statistics taken from United Nations Conference on Trade and Development. *UNCTAD Handbook of Statistics 2014*. New York: United Nations, 2014. Tables 8.1, 8.4 and 3.2.D; World Bank data http://data.worldbank.org/indicator/SP.DYN.LE00.IN (accessed 24 July 2015) and http://data.worldbank.org/indicator/SP.DYN.IMRT.IN (accessed 24 July 2015); and UNESCO data www.uis.unesco.org/DataCentre/Pages/regions.aspx (accessed 24 July 2015).

5 Social class

The search for class politics in Africa

Chapter outline

- Marx on social class
- The problems of exporting Marx to Africa
- The African mode of production
- A more flexible look at social class in Africa
- Identifiable social groups within African society

    - The peasantry
    - The proletariat
    - The commercial bourgeoisie
    - The bureaucratic bourgeoisie
    - Traditional leaders
    - Informal-sector entrepreneurs
    - An international bourgeoisie

- The value of class analysis in explaining African politics
- State and civil society
- Case study: social class in Botswana
- Questions raised by this chapter
- Glossary of key terms
- Further reading
- Notes and references

The next political concept used to investigate post-colonial Africa is a trusty tool of all social scientists, the notion of class. This concept is invaluable to those studying politics because it is an excellent way of identifying the age-old battle between the 'haves' and 'have nots' within society. Class, in this sense, is the study of inequality, and where inequality exists, relationships between competing groups will follow. Politics will determine how such conflict is resolved. Indeed, Marxists believe class to be the defining feature of any society. As Marx and Engels wrote in their *Communist Manifesto*, 'The history of all hitherto existing society is the history of class struggles'.[1]

Initially, this chapter will use the ideas of Karl Marx to subject African states to class analysis. Such analysis will certainly highlight class relations operating on the continent. Marxism, however, has its limits when it comes to Africa. This is why other theories are presented in the second half of the chapter, giving perhaps a more accurate picture of how 'classes' have competed for power in the post-colonial era.

Marx on social class

Karl Marx provided a model of society that was governed by class conflict. His ideas help to identify competing groups within society, and the basis of the relationship between these groups. Marx, however, went beyond mere description, adding dynamism to class analysis. He argued that class formation is inherently related to the progression of history. Indeed, he considered class conflict to be the motor of all history.

The key to understanding Marxist class analysis, especially within the African environment, is to recognise what is meant by the *means of production*. The owners of the means of production constitute the ruling class, and are therefore in a position to exploit the rest of society. As Friedrich Engels explained, 'the determining factor in history is, in the final instance, the production and reproduction of immediate life'.[2] In other words, all people have to produce at least their subsistence needs (food, shelter and clothing) to survive. This is a basic fact of life. Achieving this goal, however, is much easier for the owners of the means of production than it is for the masses. The means of production are, therefore, the material factors such as land, tools and machinery that help human beings produce these subsistence needs, and any economic surplus beyond this.

Classes form in relation to the means of production. Under the capitalist mode of production, for example, society divides into two classes: the bourgeoisie and the proletariat. Landlords and capitalists form the ruling bourgeois class as they secure a good standard of living, and political power, by using their ownership of these means of production (land and machinery). From this position they exploit the mass proletariat.

The proletariat, by contrast, struggles. Its members do not own any means of production, yet they still have to produce in order to meet their subsistence needs. They therefore have to gain access to (the bourgeoisie's) productive forces, and this comes at the price of exploitation. The proletariat is vulnerable because it only has its labour to sell. It has no option but to work for the bourgeoisie.

The ruling class is exploitative because it does not pay the full value for this labour. Capitalists pay enough to ensure that the workforce can reproduce itself, ensuring the survival of a labour force, but they share little of the profit from this productive process with the proletariat. Most of the surplus, even though it is generated by the toil of the workers, is retained by the bourgeoisie to maintain their higher standard of living, and to reinvest in further exploitative ventures. In this manner, members of the proletariat are reduced to mere units of production, working for the ruling class in their factories and on their land.

Naturally enough, this class exploitation is reflected within the structure of the state. The bourgeoisie is hegemonic, and thus itself commands the government. Consequently, the government always supports the interests of the bourgeoisie over those of the proletariat. As Marx himself put it, 'The executive of the modern state is but a committee for managing the common affairs of the whole bourgeoisie'.[3] The entire political system is therefore geared towards serving this ruling class.

This is how Marx, writing in the nineteenth century, saw the development of modern society. He observed: 'Our epoch, the epoch of the bourgeoisie, possesses... this distinctive feature: it has simplified the class antagonisms. Society as a whole is more and more splitting up into two hostile camps, into two great classes directly facing each other: Bourgeoisie and Proletariat'.[4]

Marx's work assists political scientists in that it not only helps to identify classes, but also puts the relationship between these classes within a historical framework. Underlying all Marx's work is the idea of 'revolution'. Classes have formed, consolidated, and then fallen to new class formations throughout history. In this respect, it was Marx's belief that the process of class evolution would not end with capitalism. Europe had passed from a feudal mode of production to one where capitalism dominated. Now there was one more stage to go. Revolution would defeat capitalism, ushering in socialism.

The key to capitalism's downfall would be that this mode of production did indeed create a mass proletariat. Given their exploitation by the ruling class, and the reality that this working class far outnumbered their oppressors, the proletariat would eventually become uncontrollable. At first, workers would protect their interests via collective action such as trade union activity, and then a revolutionary movement would develop, completing the transition from capitalism to socialism. The proletariat would take the state from the bourgeoisie by force. After the revolution, socialism would create a classless society, where inequality and exploitation would be at an end. In the words of Karl Marx, 'What the bourgeoisie, therefore, produces, above all, is its own grave-diggers. Its fall and the victory of the proletariat are equally inevitable'.[5]

The problems of exporting Marx to Africa

However brilliant Karl Marx was, he could not escape his own mortality. Naturally enough, Marx's work is largely a critique of nineteenth-century European capitalism. This is the world he knew. Through Marx's writings much can be learnt about this period, and in terms of the foundations that he laid for contemporary study, no other individual has offered more to the social sciences. The modern world, however, is a different place to the one evaluated by Marx. Even within today's European capitalist systems, Marxist analysis has hit several fundamental problems (mostly to do with a growing middle class and the absence of a revolutionary working class). Outside Europe, there is even less empirical evidence to support Marx's thesis. Africa tests the idea that the Marxist paradigm of class analysis has a universal application.

Africa, at first glance, is not open to classical Marxist interpretation because the continent has not been fully penetrated by the capitalist mode of production. Chapter 2 certainly showed how imperialism drew various sectors of the colonial economy (mining and plantation farming, for instance) into the capitalist world system, but capitalism did not come to dominate all economic activity within African states, and still does not do so today.

The lack of widespread industrialisation on the continent is clear evidence of a lack of capitalist penetration. South Africa apart, there have been no real industrial revolutions within African states. It is therefore not surprising that the accompanying social relations created by the capitalist mode of production are also absent. Few African states have a proletariat to speak of, while there is also a distinct lack of any classical bourgeoisie. And with no bourgeoisie and no proletariat, there is no Marxist revolutionary dynamic pushing forward the transition of history from capitalism to socialism.

Considering these facts, many have described Africa as being classless. This was certainly the view of several African nationalists who led their countries to independence. Instead of class, the communalism of traditional Africa was emphasised. Village life, based on inalienable land rights for all, community co-operation, and leaders being both responsible and accountable to their people, was portrayed as the typical form of social relationship on the continent. In this respect Tom Mboya, a Kenyan nationalist, argued: 'The sharp class divisions that once existed in Europe have no place in African socialism and no parallel in African society. No class problems arose in traditional African society and none exist today among Africans'.[6] Other nationalist politicians agreed with Mboya. Nyerere, Senghor and Sékou Touré all stressed that there was a common ownership of the means of production (as all had access to land), while African leaders served rather than exploited their people.

Clearly, then, the bulk of Marx's work is not applicable to explaining post-colonial African politics. This, however, should come as no surprise. Marx died before the twentieth century began, and never sought to analyse social classes on the African continent. Yet, just because African conditions cannot be shoehorned into dominant European explanations of class, this is not to say that class and class conflict were, and are, absent in African states. Indeed, the next section of this chapter shows nationalist arguments of classlessness to be unfounded. It will show that social relationships determined by class (or, at least, by inequality) have been at the forefront of African politics since early times, and continue to play a major part in African politics today.

The African mode of production

Many students struggle to understand social relationships within African states because they find it difficult to distance themselves from the capitalist mode of production. This, after all, is where Marx produced his best work, and it is also the area where most apprentice political scientists cut their teeth when learning about the class dimension to politics. It is a fact, however, that Africa has not been fully penetrated by capitalism. Africanists therefore have to look beyond just this one, capitalist mode of production.

This is not to say that capitalism is totally absent on the African continent. It has increasingly penetrated and captured strategic sectors of all African economies. Yet, today, many Africans still undertake the same economic activities that their forebears practised for generations. Many peasant farmers, for example, only have limited contact with the capitalist market, as they own their means of production (land and basic farming tools). Consequently, peasants produce largely for themselves, avoiding the exploitation of a bourgeois class. In this sense, class relations on the continent are not only a product of the capitalist mode of production, but are also still influenced by *pre*-capitalist modes of production.

African historians, especially in the 1960s and 1970s, spent a great deal of time trying to identify the nature of these pre-capitalist modes of production. This was undertaken to reveal more about the current social forces that were still operating in tandem alongside the initial penetrations of capitalism. The starting point for these historians consisted of the supplementary writings that Karl Marx himself had penned considering modes of production other than capitalism.

In Europe, for example, Marx argued, feudalism had preceded capitalism. Africanists, however, found little evidence of this type of class relationship ever existing in Africa. Feudalism was based on relationships between landlords who extracted a surplus from the serfs farming their land. In Ethiopia, something akin to feudalism existed, as an 'aristocracy' did own land, but this was not the case in most of Africa. It is the norm for each family within a community to have an inalienable right to land, and without landlords feudalism cannot exist.

Undaunted, historians of the continent sought to identify an alternative, unique 'African mode of production'. Some Africanists, for example, pointed to 'tribute' or 'lineage' modes of production fostering class formation. In these societies, certain families received gifts and tribute as a result of their status as hereditary or religious leaders. Consequently, these families came to form the ruling elites, holding positions of political power over their followers. Other historians highlighted external commerce as a source of surplus accumulation. Complex social formations were created in West Africa, for example, by trans-Saharan commerce and the slave trade. The surplus that this exchange generated created merchant classes, who then went on to translate this economic power into political power. Similarly, conquest could produce a surplus, and thus a ruling class. Instead of exploiting domestic societies, military raids against neighbouring societies generated wealth that was then transformed into political power back at home.

Presumably there are an infinite number of modes of production that have existed in African (and world) history. Different modes have been created by different local conditions. This, of course, makes class analysis much more complex. Gone is Marx's relatively simple model of two capitalist classes: bourgeoisie versus proletariat. Yet this search for the African mode of production has been extremely useful for those interested in modern African politics. These scholars have shown that pre-colonial Africa did not host utopian classless societies. Historical African ruling elites were just as adept at exploiting the masses as their European contemporaries. Additionally, this scholarship has highlighted the pre-capitalist modes of production themselves. This knowledge is extremely important, because it is these modes that are still interacting with the more modern capitalist mode on the continent today.

Africa, in this respect, currently straddles both pre-capitalist and capitalist modes of production. Uneven development means that capitalism has a great deal of influence, but it has yet to completely replace its predecessor. Much about African politics can therefore be explained by the interaction, or the *articulation*, between these two modes of production. African class formation is thus a complex mixture of the traditional and modern. Notions of 'tribute', for example, are as much a reality as capitalist-induced 'wage labour'. Similarly, Africa is still home to the spectacle of economically powerful urban business people (theoretically the owners of the means of production) returning home in their Mercedes Benz to respect the authority of their village chief. As Marx put it, 'No social order is ever destroyed before all the productive forces for which it is sufficient have been developed, and new superior relations of production never replace older ones before the material conditions for their existence have matured within the framework of the old society'.[7] African states today have highly complex class structures as they represent this articulation between pre-capitalist and capitalist modes of production, and (unfortunately for analysts) complex class structures result in complex systems of class politics.

A more flexible look at social class in Africa

Africanists have been left with the task of trying to analyse these intersections of modes of production. Much illuminating work has been produced on this issue. Yet, despite all this academic activity, basic questions still remain. What, for example, does all this Marxist theory actually reveal about the day-to-day realities of political interaction in post-colonial Africa? It is, no doubt, essential to know that African societies do not have simple class conflicts between a bourgeoisie class and a proletariat, but what exactly is the nature of class conflict on the African continent? In the remainder of this chapter, the answers to these questions are sought by first identifying common social groups found in African states, and then addressing the consequences of the competition between these groups.

In this respect, it is now time to move beyond rigid Marxist doctrine. Marx's ideas have to be adapted and built upon. It is certainly wise to use the foundations explored in the paragraphs above, but even Marxists concede that, given that classes are still forming in Africa, class alliances and class consciousness are bound to be complex. Even more sceptical are the non-Marxists. Many consider grand European-constructed models of class analysis to be more of a hindrance than a help in the African case. They seek other explanations of social interaction, and talk of 'elites' and 'groups' rather than 'classes'.

Whoever is correct, there is no doubt that Marx's unyielding economic determinism loses some of its precision in such a complicated social environment. A more flexible conceptual framework is needed to identify African social groups. In a sense, something more descriptive and less dynamic than Marx's ideas works best under African conditions.

Identifiable social groups within African society

Under such conditions, Max Weber's notion of *status* as a determinant of social class is useful. This approach distances the scholar from myopic economics and associated modes of production. Instead, issues of power and social position come to the fore. Structural functionalist ideas of tying class definitions to occupation and income can also help. Indeed, anything concrete and empirically based is most welcome when trying to identify social groups within Africa's complex societies. Discussed below (and summarised in Table 5.1) are the continent's more recognisable social classes.

At independence, broadly similar social groups could be found in most African states. At the top of the hierarchy was an elite of educated bureaucrats and professionals. These were the Africans who had benefited most from the days of colonial rule, and who were set to profit yet again as those most closely associated with the institutions of the post-colonial state. Independent African states also often had a small merchant class of entrepreneurs who had found a niche within the capitalist market that, up to this point, had been dominated by the imperial authorities. Then there were the traditional leaders who had either weathered the storm of having their authority tempered by the colonial state, or had actually benefited from imperial rule. Further down the social hierarchy was usually a small proletariat working in the continent's mines, its limited manufacturing industry or its transport sector. The vast majority of Africans at independence, however, were peasants, whose central economic activity involved farming smallholdings. Events that determined the nature of post-colonial African politics, in part, would be defined by how these social groups interacted. This being the case, each class needs to be investigated in greater depth.

The peasantry 'the masses'

It is the peasantry, rather than a proletariat, which can be described as 'the masses' in African societies. Teodor Shanin describes peasants as 'small agricultural producers, who, with the help of simple equipment and the labour of their families, produce mostly for their own consumption (direct or indirect) and for the fulfilment of obligations to holders of political and economic power'.[8] The peasantry is thus a class of individuals whose main economic activity is providing their own subsistence from small-scale farming, and whose social focus is that of the village community. African tradition and custom usually dictate that these people have free access to land. In this sense, they control their own means of production, and can therefore limit their need to interact with the capitalist market. Peasants, however, will become involved with this market to secure products that cannot be produced on their own smallholdings (cooking oil, kerosene, consumer goods and school fees, for example), or to meet the demands of political authority (taxation or tribute).

Self-sufficiency certainly reduces this class's potential for being exploited by other classes, but since peasants make up the vast bulk of Africa's population, they are the main target for exploitation by those above them in the social hierarchy. Peasants are particularly vulnerable because they are the individuals furthest away from the state. They have little access to government institutions and the power that these institutions bring.

Yet, despite being the most exploited social group, their isolation and traditional beliefs make the African peasantry a rather conservative class. There is little evidence in the post-colonial period of peasants mobilising, as a class, to challenge their oppressors. The liberation struggles against white-minority rule in Mozambique and Zimbabwe may be the exception, but there certainly has not been a revolutionary peasant movement similar to those found in China or Vietnam during this same period. As Colin Leys observes, 'it really requires a rare combination of tyranny and misery to produce a peasant revolt, let alone a peasant revolution'.[9]

The most common way for the African peasantry to retaliate against its exploiters is simply to try to keep out of harm's way. As the peasantry controls its own basic means of production, through having access to land, it can withdraw from the capitalist market. If state-imposed taxes become too high, or a derisory price is being offered for cash crops grown for the market, then peasants simply disengage. They avoid this 'external' economy, and revert to basic subsistence farming, relying on their self-sufficiency to survive, or seek profits from 'informal' economies instead. Indeed, as will be discussed in Chapter 10, the 1980s and 1990s saw mass peasant disengagement in many African countries, resulting in state structures coming close to collapse.

There are, however, opportunities created by the capitalist mode of production. Peasants do often supplement their smallholding subsistence with external sources of revenue. Indeed, both colonial and post-colonial governments encouraged this, often *forcing* peasants out of their subsistence way of life. Taxes, for example, were imposed by state authorities to coerce peasant farmers into the capitalist market. To pay these taxes, peasants had to sell their labour as migrant workers, or use some of their land to grow cash crops. Where there was still resistance to entering the capitalist economy, further pressure was exerted. During colonial times in the Belgian Congo and Mozambique, for example, forced labour was introduced. Peasants were compelled to leave their smallholdings for a period of time each year to undertake employment determined by the state. Post-colonial methods of creating a labour force were less harsh. Several states did, however, oblige smallholders to use a proportion of their land to produce cash crops for the market. In Marxist terms, peasants were being partially drawn out of their pre-capitalist mode of production, and being exposed to the modern economy of the capitalist mode of production.

Indeed, it is in the interest of the ruling class to keep the peasantry trapped between the old and the new modes of production. This allows capitalists to pay migrant labourers wages below the level of reproduction. In other words, mine owners and farm managers rely on the fact that peasants are also producing for themselves back on their smallholdings (farmed in their absence by their families). As workers have this additional source of subsistence, wages can be kept low. If they were a classical working class, with only their labour to sell, and no other means of production, higher wages would have been essential. This, however, was not the case. In the 1950s, African migrant workers were earning half the income of more permanent labourers in private industry, and a quarter of that of public service employees.[10] A disparity between the wages of this temporary labour force and their fully proletarianised colleagues still exists today.

In summary, peasants can be defined by their reliance on smallholding farming. Yet members of the family will often seek additional income and goods from the market by selling their labour and growing cash crops. Many peasants therefore have one foot in the traditional subsistence economy and one foot in the modern capitalist economy, forming what could be termed a 'peasantariat'.[11]

The proletariat

As was seen above, the absence of a mass proletariat is the key difference between European and African class formations. Levels of industrialisation in Africa simply cannot sustain a working class forming a majority of a state's population.

Africa can, however, provide examples of isolated pockets of working-class consciousness. Organised labour can be found among the miners of Zambia's Copperbelt, for instance, amid the dockers of Dar es Salaam, and among railway workers in Ghana, but this is not a common form of class expression. Indeed, these workers' privileged position makes them almost an 'aristocracy of labour', rather than a proletariat. They enjoy the security of relatively stable employment, and income levels above those of their peasant compatriots. These benefits make African proletarians less likely to challenge the status quo, as they are not to be found at the bottom of the social hierarchy.

Only in South Africa, where the trade union movement played a major role in the fight against apartheid, has a proletariat emerged that is in any way akin to the Marxist model. This was a result of an industrial revolution in South Africa, absent elsewhere on the continent. Yet even here many of the workers are still migrants, relying on their families back in the 'homelands' to produce part of their subsistence.

The commercial bourgeoisie

The African commercial bourgeoisie is the closest social group this continent has to offer by way of Marx's notion of a (classical) bourgeoisie. They are predominantly merchant groups that developed despite the trading constraints imposed by colonial and post-colonial governments. Capitalists involved in small-scale commercial farming and manufacturing industry can also be found on the continent, but so far these entrepreneurs are generally not so numerous as their merchant colleagues.

These traders, small manufacturers and farmers do indeed own their means of production, but have not yet developed into a dominant bourgeoisie. In this sense, many within this class could be described as petit bourgeois. They are only minor owners of productive property, whose exploitation of other classes is limited. Usually this exploitation amounts just to the mark-up they can place on commodities sold in their shops. Economic power is limited because most goods first have to be obtained from foreign suppliers.

In many African states, this commercial bourgeoisie often has a large non-African ethnic contingent. Lebanese traders are prominent in West Africa, for example, while Asian merchants dominate East Africa. Elsewhere, a 1980 survey of Kisangani revealed that nearly half of the locally owned businesses in this Congo-Kinshasa town were run by Greeks and Asians.[12] In former settler societies, such as South Africa and Zimbabwe, the pattern is similar. The big commercial farms will be owned by 'Europeans', as will the larger industrial concerns. This is why Robert Mugabe's regime targeted white farmers as part of Zimbabwe's land redistribution programme of 2000 (discussed in more detail in Chapter 11).

Whether indigenous or not, having remained relatively small for the majority of the post-colonial period, this commercial group cannot be described as the dominant or ruling class. Up to now, Africa has not had a significant classical bourgeoisie. As the following paragraphs testify, scholars have had to look elsewhere to find the truly powerful groups within African societies. Yet Africa's economic upturn in the twenty-first century has led to this commercial bourgeoisie becoming more numerous and more powerful. This development, and its impact on the make-up of the ruling class, is discussed in the final chapter as part of a broader analysis of this 'Africa Rising' phenomenon. In the meantime, this chapter will move on to consider the prevailing class in the post-colonial period: the bureaucratic bourgeoisie. It is these controllers of the state, who have so dominated African politics since independence, that this newly empowered commercial bourgeoisie is beginning to challenge.

The bureaucratic bourgeoisie

Given that Africanists have to approach the concept of class with flexibility, they would do well to take the advice of Max Weber. He stated, '"Economically conditioned" power is not, of course, identical with "power" as such. On the contrary, the emergence of economic power may be the consequence of power existing on other grounds'.[13] This has been a theme taken up by neo-Marxists and liberals ever since Marx laid the foundations for the modern era of class analysis.

Such scholars argue that Marx's work is too reductionist. As Nicos Poulantzas put it, classical Marxist analysis suffers from 'economism'. The complete subordination of class formation to economic determinants obscures too many political factors that are also important. Indeed, Poulantzas went on to argue that these political factors could produce periods in history when the dominant economic class actually fails to control the state. The owners of the means of production are, therefore, not necessarily the ruling class. Instead, a *political* elite may be dominant.[14] Presumably the chances of this occurring are increased in more confused periods of articulation, when class formations are immature or decadent, respectively, and are consequently less influential.

In the search for African ruling classes, then, it is wise still to lean heavily on Marx's work. After all, the dominant group will still use its position to exploit the masses, accumulating capital at their expense. The point is, however, that it may be that this ruling elite uses *political* strength, more than *economic* power, to achieve and maintain its position of dominance.

In this respect, Stanislaw Ossowski considered not only the means of production as a defining feature of class, but also the means of consumption and the means of compulsion.[15] Richard Sklar built on Ossowski's work, applying it directly to African states. The ruling class on this continent, Sklar argues, is more usefully identified in relation to the political realm, rather than to the economic realm.[16] The dominant elite is not necessarily the group that *owns* the means of production, but is more likely to be the group that *controls* the means of production. In other words, a politically advantaged class has the power to take economic surplus from wherever it finds it within the country. This class has little part in producing a surplus itself, but still has the ability to appropriate the capital generated for its own members' use.

Not surprisingly, if political power is so important in identifying ruling classes in Africa, this class is going to use the state itself as its main conduit of privilege. Indeed, as early as 1962, René Dumont was talking of 'a "bourgeoisie" of a new type, that Karl Marx could hardly have foreseen: a bourgeoisie of the public service'.[17] The African state became a tool for accumulation, offering possibilities of social mobility. Instead of the state merely being the executive committee of the bourgeoisie, assisting this class in its exploitation via private commercial activities, it is the state itself that becomes the central tool of accumulation for the bourgeoisie. Individuals in Africa, therefore, gain increasing power the more closely they are associated with state institutions, and political power brings economic rewards. Hence the ruling class found in Africa is a political *bureaucratic bourgeoisie* (also termed a state, organisational or managerial bourgeoisie), not an economic, commercial or industrial bourgeoisie.

This bureaucratic bourgeoisie is predominantly an urban coalition consisting of ministers, party officials, members of parliament, bureaucrats, military officers, the managers of public industries and, indeed, anyone else who exploits their command over state institutions. As a class, this group has its historical roots within the colonial administration. As was seen in Chapter 2, an educated African elite was employed by the colonial service to act as junior administrators and professionals. As the group consolidated, this petit-bourgeoisie of bureaucrats, doctors and teachers formed the backbone of the nationalist movements that won Africa's independence. Their reward at liberation was accession into their former colonial masters' jobs.

This bureaucratic bourgeoisie has proved very proficient in converting political power into economic gain. Its members profit not only from their state salary, but also from the trappings of office (such as cars, expense accounts, education for children, health care, and access to cheap, even non-repayable, loans). Then there are the prebends (stipends of office) that state employment provides. These benefits include simple corruption: the pocketing of a proportion of the money handed over in payment for government services (such as export licences, legal fines, passports, or even the registration of births and deaths – indeed, anything that needs an official stamp or signature). Alternatively, there are opportunities for collecting commission for services rendered (a 'gift', maybe, for awarding a state contract to the right person). In many cases, bureaucrats make much more money from 'backhanders' than they do from their official salaries. Indeed, state salaries are artificially low, as employees know that they can use their position of power as a springboard for accumulation. Association with state institutions has therefore become the key to a higher standard of living in post-colonial Africa. Ndiva Kofele-Kale, for example, has calculated that the bureaucratic bourgeoisie makes up about 2 per cent of Cameroon's population, yet it grosses a massive one-third of this state's national income.[18]

With the state being at the heart of the bureaucratic bourgeoisie's power, the most common expression of class consciousness from this group relates to the defence of its command over state structures. This leads to conflicts between the bureaucratic bourgeoisie and other classes. The bureaucratic bourgeoisie may clash with the commercial bourgeoisie, for instance. In the Democratic Republic of the Congo (Congo-Kinshasa/Zaire), the state neutralised the threat of an independent commercial bourgeoisie in one dramatic act. On 30 November 1973, President Mobuto Sese Seko nationalised nearly all of the private sector within this country, and confiscated all foreign-owned businesses. The control of these concerns then passed directly to the state and its clients. Indeed, all over Africa, the bureaucratic bourgeoisie attempted to keep as much economic activity as possible within the public sector where it could be controlled and utilised by the state elite (rather than give away power to a commercial bourgeoisie within the private sector). Just how this bureaucratic bourgeoisie has hampered Africa's development by siphoning off economic surplus for its own interests is discussed in Chapter 10. For now it is sufficient to note that the bureaucratic bourgeoisie is the group that has wielded most power in post-colonial African politics.

Traditional leaders

The emergence of a bureaucratic bourgeoisie as the dominant group within African societies has not totally eclipsed sources of traditional authority. Old elites still have a role to play in the modern African state. Swaziland, for example, has retained a monarchy whose ancestors ruled this territory in pre-colonial times. Many other states have also seen traditional leaders use their historic authority as a springboard to occupy positions of power within modern political systems.

These traditional leaders do not necessarily always refer to history. They may use custom to gain part of their authority, but to rely solely on the past would find these individuals rapidly sidelined. Just as chiefs and monarchs adapted to colonial rule, gaining what they could from imposed imperial administrative structures, the following generation modernised themselves to retain power within post-colonial societies. Many of the old 'aristocracy', for example, played prominent roles in the nationalist movements that ended European rule. Nelson Mandela, in this respect, was not only the leader of the African National Congress of South Africa, but he also hailed from a leading family in the Transkei. In the post-independence era, chiefs often became local party dignitaries, local members of parliament, or heads of regional government. Many state presidents also have powerful family connections. In this manner there is a strong continuity of authority running from pre-colonial times, through the years of imperial rule, right into the modern era.

Informal-sector entrepreneurs

Another group found within African societies that defies classical Marxist analysis is what can be termed 'informal-sector entrepreneurs'. These individuals make a living from petty trading, often straddling the line between legal and illegal activities. The closest category to this group that Marx wrote of was a 'lumpenproletariat'.[19] He used this word to identify an 'underclass' of society: thieves, prostitutes, vagabonds, beggars and the like (who were far from gaining class consciousness).

A lumpenproletariat is too inaccurate and insulting a term to use, but there is a large social group in most African societies that occupies this underclass position, especially if the continent's large mass of unemployed is added to this category. These people attempt to produce their subsistence from casual work and small-scale entrepreneurial activities. Urban women, for example, many of whom have rejected their 'rural yoke', can be found in African cities in occupations such as small wholesalers running markets, beer brewers, or vendors of food or handicrafts on the streets.[20]

Such entrepreneurial activities frequently involve breaking the law. Street traders, for instance, rarely pay taxes or obtain the appropriate commercial licences from the state. Indeed, with the growth of the informal sector generally in African countries, numerous smugglers, 'black market' money changers and 'hawkers' of all descriptions can also be added to this social category. Although lacking class consciousness and organisation, due to their fragile and nefarious position, these individuals have played an important role in post-colonial political activity. These vulnerable people, especially in urban areas, often made up the foot-soldiers of any 'bread riots' directed against state authority. Allied to students and workers, these groups, in the bluntest of manners, can deliver considerable political clout.

An international bourgeoisie

So far, this social survey has focused on the domestic arena. Peasants and a small prole-tariat are exploited by a bourgeoisie that largely derives its power through the mecha-nism of state institutions. Operating at the fringes of society are 'informal-sector entrepreneurs', and also present is a commercial bourgeoisie, although this latter group is overshadowed by the bureaucrats, as they have failed to muster enough political power to compete with the ruling class.

Together, the bureaucratic and commercial bourgeoisie can be termed a *national bour-geoisie*. Yet the problem remains that neither of these groups owns the means of production to any great extent. As such ownership is paramount to Marxist class analysis, academics of this school have continued the search for Africa's true ruling class. Many consider that they have found this dominant group by linking their analysis to theories of underdevelop-ment and dependency. This paradigm locates the real bourgeoisie outside Africa.

Dependency theorists argue that it is the owners of international capital that form the true ruling class, not only in Africa, but across the globe. Transnational corporations and international financial institutions are hegemonic. In this respect, members of indige-nous national bourgeoisies in the Third World are just agents or lackeys of this *interna-tional bourgeoisie*. They are merely collaborators, or *compradors*, to use the terminology of the dependency theorists.[21]

Officials within African states, therefore, act as debt collectors for external agencies, receiving international backing and taking a minor share of the profits for their services. These *compradors* are in the business of facilitating foreign capital, often at the expense of the national interest. In other words, state officials will look after the needs both of international capital and of themselves before they consider what course of action is suit-able for their country. This line of reasoning explains why the national bourgeoisie holds power despite not actually owning the means of production. The true bourgeoisie oper-ates from the Western capitalist countries, exploiting the masses of the Third World, while the local, national bourgeoisie only occupies an intermediary position in this world economy. *Compradors* therefore gain their power from being agents of, rather than owners of, the means of production.

This dependency school of thought dominated studies of class in Africa throughout the 1970s and 1980s, and still holds great sway today. In recent years, however, many Africanists have been seeking to revise this paradigm. They argue that dismissing the national bourgeoisie as a mere *comprador* class is too reductionist.

A more subtle analysis of the continent's local dominant groups is required. Relating African states to worldwide theories of underdevelopment explains a great deal, but relegating Africa to just a footnote of the wider international political system diverts scholars from explaining African realities. What about political events generated by internal class conflict? What about the divisions within the national bourgeoisie (the battle between the commercial and the bureaucratic wings, for example)? There is also a question about the actual level of autonomy these '*compradors*' enjoy.

The reality is that, in the post-colonial period, peripheral states have selected different economic development strategies; groups within them have accumulated capital creating internal politics of inequality; governments have changed trading partners; and local leaders have selected different public policy options. There is a considerable degree of autonomy for locally dominant state elites to exercise. Indeed, the national bourgeoisie may even act against the interests of international capital. Several states in the post-colonial period, for example, have nationalised the assets of foreign companies operating within their territory. In this respect, African bourgeoisies are as keen as any other bourgeoisie to make a profit and protect their position of power. They are quite willing to tap into sources of international capital if this is beneficial, especially as sources of indigenous capital are limited, but they will also use their autonomy to protect their interests against international capital should this be possible and necessary. They may have to work within the constraints of the international economy, but this does not make the national bourgeoisie a passive, subservient and powerless class. To think this is to profoundly misunderstand the national bourgeoisie's role within African politics.

The value of class analysis in explaining African politics

These, then, are the more obvious social groups that can be identified within African states. But how useful is class analysis under African conditions? To what degree do the preceding paragraphs really contribute to an explanation of African politics? For the political scientist whose knowledge is based mainly on studying Western societies, the above exercise is invaluable. Western-formulated models of class, particularly Marxism, are almost as useful in how they fail to conceptualise African class formations as they are in providing an understanding of African politics. These models highlight the significant differences between Western classes and those found on the African continent. It is not all negative, however. An adaptation of classical class theories does help to identify the main groups within African societies, and they also put these classes in a historic framework, pointing to the articulation between pre-capitalist and capitalist modes of production.

Yet the fact remains that Africa is not willing to be shoehorned into the models most used by social scientists in the West. Class analysis is meant to simplify things. Academic work is easier if a society only has two classes, a competing bourgeoisie and proletariat. Of course, reality itself is never this simple, even in mature capitalist countries, but in Africa things remain complex even after conceptual short cuts have been taken. The articulation between modes of production ensures this. Instead of two classes, the African 'masses' are divided into peasants and a small group of proletarians, while the bourgeoisie comprises at least three factions (commercial, bureaucratic and international), of which the dominant African branch is an administrative class that has its social base in the state itself, rather than civil society as Marx himself argued. And somewhere among

Table 5.1 Chapter summary: African social groups

Social group	Characteristics
Peasants *(small-scale farmers, producing largely for their own consumption)*	• Majority of the population • Based in small rural communities • Involved primarily in subsistence agriculture • Family is the main unit of production • Limited contact with the capitalist economy • Occupy an 'underdog' position in society
Proletariat *(wage earners within capitalist societies who rely on selling their labour)*	• Small proportion of the population • Landless rural labourers • Urban labourers (industry, mining, transport, etc.)
Informal-sector entrepreneurs *(individuals making a living from petty trading, often involving illegal activities)*	• Not permanently employed in formal economy • Often irregular/insecure work • Often unlicensed/illegal • Street vendors • Money changers/lenders • Smugglers • Petty thieves • Prostitutes
Petty bourgeoisie *(minor owners of productive property whose exploitation of labour is limited, or the lower ranks of the salaried state bureaucracy)*	• Predominantly male • Self-employed artisans • Small farmers employing labour • Small traders • Teachers • Soldiers • Lower ranks of public service
Bourgeoisie	• The ruling class
National bourgeoisie *(the indigenous ruling class)* a. Commercial bourgeoisie *(the classical bourgeoisie as defined by Marx in his studies of Western capitalist societies)*	• Predominantly male • A small proportion of the population • Largely in the trading and agricultural sector (rather than manufacturing) • Entrepreneurs • Business interests • Commercial farmers • Land owners
b. Bureaucratic bourgeoisie *(those who 'control' rather than 'own' the means of production, exploiting their command over the institutions of the state to accumulate capital)*	• Largely urban • Educated • State decision makers • Political class (MPs, ministers, party officials, etc.) • Civil servants • Military officers • Public managers (e.g. in nationalised industries) • Professionals (public sector)
c. Comprador bourgeoisie	Any section of the national bourgeoisie which acts as an agent for the international bourgeoisie

(Continued)

Table 5.1 Chapter summary: African social groups (Continued)

Social group	Characteristics
International bourgeoisie *(international capitalists based in the 'North' who exploit the 'peripheral' economies of Africa, and other areas of the 'South')*	The ultimate ruling class according to underdevelopment/dependency theorists • Transnational corporations • International financial institutions
Traditional rulers *(those whose authority is based mainly on tradition and custom)*	• Clan heads • Chiefs • Paramount chiefs • Emirs • Monarchs, etc.

this mix, a place has to be found for traditional leaders and informal-sector entrepreneurs. Add notions of what Marxists call 'false consciousness' (ethnic or religious loyalties, for example), and the picture gets even more confused. A point has to be reached where Africanists have made so many adaptations to classical models of class that the whole exercise should be abandoned and new ideas of social groups put forward.

One such alternative approach is based on the fact that ruling groups are rarely homogeneous in Africa. The elite holding power is perhaps more usefully seen as a coalition of competing factions, rather than a single consolidated class. At the most basic level, for example, the national bourgeoisie is partly commercial and partly bureaucratic. Within the bureaucracy itself there are splits between the military and civilian wings. Factions mobilising around ethnic identities and charismatic individuals are also prominent within African political systems. As a result, there is internal competition within the ruling group. Many state elites simply represent too many interests for the coalition to survive long. The various factions want different things, and hold little class solidarity with their allies. Consequently, many African governments are particularly vulnerable to shifting alliances within the ruling group. Witness the number of military *coups d'état* experienced by certain African states in the post-colonial period.

This reality of power is why some scholars talk of African politics being underwritten by a 'hegemonic drive'.[22] No longer is class conflict solely between the bourgeoisie and the proletariat, or corresponding pre-capitalist and capitalist groups; it is more about groups and individuals co-operating and competing in order to capture the power of the state. Social alliances are not therefore based on class solidarity, but on the willingness to co-operate with strategic allies in order to receive more of the spoils associated with the state. Under these circumstances, social leaders will search each other out, to see if their corresponding factions can do business together.

Jean-François Bayart, in this respect, talks of the 'assimilation of elites'.[23] Powerful groups within society will respect each other's position, forming an uneasy ruling coalition, a 'hegemonic bloc'. The members of this coalition, and their position within it, will constantly change, but all realise that to compete too hard would be to risk political turmoil and the possibility of losing access to the state altogether. Nobody wishes to give up this opportunity to accumulate, so the elites have to co-operate to some degree. Bayart therefore argues that classical class categorisations are misleading, as they artificially obscure the component parts of this hegemonic bloc.

Links are forged between the different factions. Note, for example, how once the bureaucratic bourgeoisie has accumulated wealth via its control over state structures, not all this wealth is spent on ostentatious consumption. Members of the bureaucratic bourgeoisie will also invest in commercial projects. They set up businesses and buy property, often using their position within the state to facilitate this. A bureaucrat, for example, may allocate him- or herself a plot of government land, usher through planning permission, and negotiate a loan from the state bank to build property for renting. Many state managers, in this respect, accumulate significant private commercial empires during their term of office. State assistance is also extended to the family, friends and clients of the bureaucrats. Such entrepreneurial activity by state officials closes the gap between themselves and the members of the commercial bourgeoisie also found within the ruling hegemonic bloc.

Links between other elites also form. Political alliances between traditional leaders and the state executive are common, for example, as are those between trade union leaders and the Department of Labour. Indeed, the ruling coalition tends to co-opt the leaders of all the important factions within society, hence the term 'assimilation of elites'. As Bayart puts it, these are the people, after all, who 'drive the same Mercedes, drink the same champagne, smoke the same cigars and meet in the same VIP lounges at airports'.[24] Having a similar level of power and the same desire to consolidate their hold on state institutions, it is not surprising that these leaders, even if they do not share cognate class backgrounds, join to form a hegemonic bloc. This is how a collection of leaders as diverse as business people, bureaucrats, soldiers, chiefs, trade union activists, ethnic brokers and women's representatives can assimilate themselves into a state's ruling elite.

State and civil society

The above evidence confirms that social class is an important factor influencing the central theme of this book, namely the relationship between state and civil society. Scholars may differ on how to identify these groups, and also disagree about the nature of these social formations, but what is certain is that African societies cannot be described as classless. Inequality does exist.

Unfortunately, class politics in Africa cannot be reduced to a simple competition between bourgeoisie and proletariat. This, of course, reduces the attractiveness of using class as an analytical tool. Yet the fact that the continent is host to numerous complex societies, harbouring varied group dynamics, should come as no surprise. Even Europe has moved on, with the social divisions that inspired Marx's model of capitalist relations now being less obvious. Perseverance, however, does allow Africanists to identify various common social groups within African societies, and, as will be seen later in the book, the interaction between these groups has determined much of the continent's post-colonial political history.

Indeed, it is still possible to apply a simplistic model to African social relations, avoiding the complications of Marxist analysis. Since independence, the continent has staged a battle between two separate parties. It is the age-old conflict between the haves and the have-nots which were referred to at the beginning of this chapter, and in this case, between state and civil society. As the Ghanaians put it, Africa's post-colonial political environment has been dominated by a divide between the 'big men' and the 'small men'.[25]

The big men, inevitably, are those individuals who have access to state institutions. Association with the state, after all, has been the key to social advancement on the continent in modern times. Once this access had been achieved, individuals commanded a share of the means of compulsion, bringing opportunities for both accumulation and political power. Class in Africa is therefore more to do with access to political power than with owning the economic means of production. The result has been the building of hegemonic coalitions across the continent, where leading members of society have been assimilated into state elites. It is these sometimes fragile hegemonic blocs that have been at the heart of African politics in the post-colonial period. Just how these big men have used their power, and engaged the small men within civil society, is the subject of the next chapter, which addresses the issue of legitimacy.

Case study: social class in Botswana

Botswana is a landlocked country of just 2 million people located in Southern Africa. Most of this territory is dominated by the Kalahari Desert, which partially explains why, at independence, Botswana was one of the poorest countries in the world. Yet, today, Botswana is often cited as Africa's 'miracle'.[26]

What this country has achieved in the post-colonial period is remarkable. From independence in 1966, Botswana has enjoyed sustained economic growth. Indeed, it has been one of the world's fastest growing economies during these years. Per capita gross national product (GNP) expanded from less than US$100 in 1966 to over US$7,500 by 2009. Moreover, Botswana is the only mainland African state to have retained an unbroken record of liberal democracy since decolonisation. The country's first multi-party election was held in 1965, and similar polls have been repeated every five years since that date. This political stability is all the more striking when one considers Botswana's location, for most of its existence, on the doorstep of the potentially disruptive influence of apartheid South Africa.

Initial post-colonial development strategies were based on cattle and the export of meat. This, after all, was Botswana's only significant commercial activity prior to independence. From the 1970s onwards, however, the country's fortunes were dramatically transformed by the discovery of diamonds. Local mining contributed little to the economy of the British protectorate of Bechuanaland, but, by 2007, this sector of the economy had expanded to account for more than one-third of Botswana's gross national income.

A state's politics, however, are influenced by factors beyond just macroeconomic indicators and regular elections. This case study seeks to introduce Botswana by analysing another important political determinant: the issue of class.

Like all societies, Botswana has been host to social groups competing for power. Ruling classes historically relied on their ownership of the main economic commodity, cattle, as their basis for power (as land, the more common European means of production, was held in common). Traditional elites in this part of Africa had been a cattle-owning class for centuries. This commodity provided the surplus wealth that underpinned their political authority. Even with the arrival of colonialism, traditional leaders managed to maintain their position as a ruling class.

Following the path of indirect rule, British administrators relied on these leaders as intermediaries of government. Then, as Africa entered the era of decolonisation, many members of this traditional cattle-owning elite went on to play a significant role in the nationalist movement. They consequently gained influence within the structures of the post-colonial state.

As was the case with other African states, however, elites whose authority was rooted in tradition or commerce did not rule alone. It was a bureaucratic bourgeoisie that expanded most, both in size and power, during the post-colonial era. As the economy grew, so did the state apparatus that managed it. New social provision (for example, education and health) also required a bigger bureaucracy. More individuals were being employed to run state institutions, which provided these officials themselves with opportunities to enhance their political power and economic wealth.

Indeed, a trend developed where bureaucrats ran directly for political office, resulting, in time, with them taking over from the older generation of nationalist leaders. Civil servants thus crossed the divide and became politicians. In short, a 'bureaucratic' bourgeoisie formed and came to dominate Botswanan politics, a fact determining that, despite the holding of free and competitive elections, only one party, the Botswana Democratic Party (BDP), has held office since independence.

A thumbnail biography of Botswana's first president illustrates the nature of this ruling elite. Seretse Khama led Botswana from independence in 1966 until his death in 1980. He was a hereditary chief of the Bamangwato, and a direct descendant of Khama III (a 'national hero' who had united the Tswana people and negotiated wisely with the European authorities in the nineteenth century). Seretse Khama was well educated. He studied in South Africa, and completed his schooling at Oxford University in the United Kingdom. Khama, in this sense, was fully in touch with European society, and would eventually marry a British woman. His hereditary and educational credentials brought him to the head of Botswana's nationalist movement, and he helped to form the BDP in 1962. Khama was also a relatively wealthy individual, having purchased land in the new freehold areas of the country and farmed cattle. In this respect, Seretse Khama was almost an 'assimilation of elites' or a 'hegemonic bloc' by himself. He had strong links with traditional society, the modern political elite, the bureaucracy and the commercial sector. Khama was a natural candidate for state president, as he could represent all the elites that came together to form the post-colonial ruling coalition.

The Botswanan ruling elite, like many of its counterparts elsewhere on the continent, also sought to prosper through contacts with international capital. Dependency theorists would define this group as a *comprador* class, acting as agents for foreign capitalists rather than serving their own people. Indeed, the Botswanan government went out of its way to encourage transnational corporations (TNCs) to mine the country's resources. De Beers, for example, developed the diamond mines that are at the heart of the country's economy, and by giving that company a monopoly over the extraction of Botswana's diamonds, the government certainly opened itself up to charges that it was assisting acts of neo-colonialism, merely overseeing the stripping of Botswana's assets by these TNCs. It cannot be denied, however, that foreign management of the mines, using foreign capital and technology, produced vast sums of money available for public spending. Botswana, as a result, has comparatively good health, education and welfare provision when compared with the rest of Africa. The government also cultivated a good relationship with international aid donors. Attracted by its stability and good human rights record, donors gave generously to Botswana in the post-colonial period.

Class analysis, however, is not just about the 'haves' within society. Outside the hegemonic bloc, the masses in Botswana, like those all over Africa, bore the brunt of elite exploitation. Although class conflict is perhaps more muted in Botswana than elsewhere on the continent because of the democratic links between state and civil society, there is certainly still evidence of class relationships influencing political actions.

With regard to the structure of labour, for example, it is in an elite's interests to keep wage earners as migrant labourers, rather than encouraging them to develop into a more stable proletariat. A more permanent proletariat, after all, would find it easier to organise and challenge these elite interests.

Bechuanaland was established as a protectorate in 1885, essentially to act as a vast labour reserve for South Africa. As occurred all over southern Africa, peasants were taxed and had their land rights curtailed in order to force them into the wage economy. For the majority, this meant seeking work in South African mines. By 1943, half of all Botswanan males aged 15 to 44 were supplementing production on their smallholdings by working as miners for part of the year.[27] They were a 'peasantariat'. Independence, and the development of mining in Botswana itself, has seen the 'nationalisation' of this workforce. Yet peasants are still employed as migrant labour, not as a more skilled permanent workforce. In this way the demands of modern capital are met, but the costs of labour are minimised.

Reflecting its alliance with the domestic commercial bourgeoisie and the TNCs, the Botswanan government (the bureaucratic bourgeoisie) also tended to favour the interests of capital, rather than labour, in the post-colonial period. Labour organisations were tightly controlled to create a more advantageous environment for TNCs. In 1991, for example, 50,000 workers went on strike in Botswana. The government responded by dismissing 18,000 public employees, only agreeing to re-instate them on less favourable contracts. Botswana has also yet to adopt several key standards drawn up by the International Labour Organization.[28]

As well as its coalition partners, the Botswanan bureaucratic bourgeoisie is also adept at serving its own interests. In 1992–93, for example, 10 per cent of Botswana's budget was spent on defence. In particular, vast sums of money were allocated to the building of a military airbase outside Molepolole during the 1990s. Such non-productive defence investments, in terms of sustainable development, are questionable in such a fragile economy, especially since the demise of apartheid has removed any major military threat to Botswana. Instead of investing this capital in rural development, the bureaucratic bourgeoisie is spending money on itself.[29] The state contracts and state employment involved in the Molepolole airbase, after all, create far more opportunities for patronage than would numerous small-scale community projects. Bureaucrats are thinking more of what public programmes will bring for themselves in the short term, rather than of economic development that would benefit the whole population in the long term.

Given these examples, there is little doubt that there is inequality in Botswana, laying the foundations for class politics. Although the political elite have provided for their people more so than most African states, it is still a reality that not everybody has benefited equally from the country's impressive economic growth. For example, less than a quarter of the population is involved in the wage economy, while most do not own enough cattle to benefit from the decision to develop this industry. Indeed, arguments that Botswana has experienced economic growth, but without an accompanying income redistribution of the same magnitude, are backed by the fact that most Batswana cannot even produce their own subsistence. They rely on relatives in the urban areas to supplement their income. Statistics show that 40 per cent of the population share just 10 per cent of the national wealth, while the top 20 per cent own 61.5 per cent of this sum.[30]

There is no doubt, however, that the citizens of Botswana are better off than most Africans. Despite there being evidence of a ruling class that has used its political power to facilitate its own economic accumulation, the bureaucratic bourgeoisie has not consumed all Botswana's wealth. Corruption, rent seeking, and the general misappropriation of state resources for personal gain are simply not at the levels practised elsewhere on the continent. Wealth has been distributed, to a degree, to the whole population. From scant social provision at independence, Botswana now has an extensive primary health care network, and most Batswana enjoy free schooling for a 10-year period. What is more, the ruling elite did not resort to authoritarianism to protect their interests. They have successfully accommodated the 'peasantariat' by maintaining a multi-party political system. It may be that just one party has been continually elected to office since independence, but this democratic longevity is unique in post-colonial Africa. Given its respect for human rights and democracy, and its efforts to provide public services, Batswana are content to continue to vote for the ruling BDP. Thus the bureaucratic bourgeoisie's position of power has been maintained. As Jack Parson put it, participatory politics and the ruling elite's not inconsiderable attention to the welfare of the masses, on a continent where these are usually conspicuously absent, have blunted the otherwise 'sharp edge of class politics' in Botswana.[31]

Botswana[32]

Territory:	582,000 sq. km.	Population:	2 million
Colonial power:	Britain	Independence:	1966
Major cities:	Gaborone (capital)	Ethnic groups:	Batswana
	Francis Town		San
	Molopolole	Languages:	Setswana
Urban population:	57 per cent		English
Life expectancy:	47 years	Adult literacy:	87 per cent
Infant mortality:	36 deaths/1,000 live births	Exports:	Diamonds
Religion:	Traditional		Copper-nickel
	Christian		Gold
Currency:	Pula		Meat
GDP per capita:	US$7,191		Vehicles and parts

Questions raised by this chapter

1. To what extent can Karl Marx's model of class be applied to African societies?
2. Is there a pre-capitalist 'African mode of production'?
3. How does the articulation between modes of production affect African class formations?
4. Can African classes be defined solely by the means of production, or do political and social considerations also play a prominent role?
5. Should the ruling elite in African states be termed a 'class', or is it more a coalition of elites forming a 'hegemonic bloc'?

Glossary of key terms

African mode of production	A pre-capitalist mode of production sought by Marxists, akin to feudalism preceding capitalism in European societies.
Aristocracy of labour	Where the proletariat is socially and economically relatively advantaged within society.
Articulation between modes	A period when remnants of the passing mode of production still operate alongside new social relations generated by a more modern ascendant mode of production.
Assimilation of elites	The formation of a ruling coalition consisting of leading representatives from the most powerful groups within society.
Bourgeoisie	The ruling class in the capitalist era of history, whose power is based on their ownership of the means of production.
Bureaucratic bourgeoisie	Those who 'control' rather than 'own' the means of production, exploiting their command over the institutions of the state to generate power and privilege.

Commercial bourgeoisie	The classical bourgeoisie, based on trade and manufacture, as defined by Marx in his studies of Western capitalist societies.
Comprador	Any section of the national bourgeoisie which acts as an agent for the international bourgeoisie.
Hegemonic bloc	A political coalition seeking the capture of state power.
Informal-sector entrepreneurs	Individuals gaining their subsistence from (often illegal) petty trading and services.
International bourgeoisie	International capitalists based in the 'North' who exploit the 'peripheral' economies of Africa, and other regions of the 'South'.
Means of production	The materials needed to produce human subsistence and economic surplus (land, machinery, etc.).
National bourgeoisie	The indigenous ruling class.
Peasants	Small agricultural producers, producing largely for their own subsistence.
Petit-bourgeoisie	Minor owners of productive property whose exploitation of labour is limited.
Proletariat	Wage earners within capitalist societies who rely on selling their labour.
Traditional leader	Those whose authority is based mainly on tradition and custom.

Further reading

For anyone interested in a classical Marxist explanation of class formation and conflict, there is no better starting point than Marx and Engels's *Communist Manifesto*. With respect to social class specifically in Africa, Crawford Young's examination of how Africanists have tackled this issue would be a valuable read. Catherine Coquery-Vidrovitch's work on the African mode of production was at the centre of this particular debate in the 1970s, and her chapter in the book edited by Peter Gutkind and Immanuel Wallerstein is particularly useful. On the idea that not only economic production but also political power has an important role to play in African class analysis, see Richard Sklar's article. Similarly, Immanuel Wallerstein's paper puts African class formations in the context of the broader international economy. For a more recent look at how Africanists view class analysis, Chapters 6 and 7 of Jean-François Bayart's seminal book *The State in Africa* introduce the idea of the ruling class in Africa being an assimilation of elites, forming a hegemonic bloc. Catherine Boone's chapter in Joel Migdal, Atul Kohli and Vivienne Shue's collection provides an excellent general discussion of the ideas raised in this chapter, while those readers wanting to know more about class politics in Botswana should turn to Jack Parson's article and Abdi Ismail Samatar's book.

Bayart, Jean-François. *The State in Africa: The Politics of the Belly*. London: Longman, 1993.
Boone, Catherine. States and ruling classes in post-colonial Africa. In: Joel S. Migdal, Atul Kohli and Vivienne Shue, eds. *State Power and Social Forces: Domination and Transformation in the Third World*. Cambridge: Cambridge University Press, 1994. 108–40.

Coquery-Vidrovitch, Catherine. The political economy of the African peasantry and modes of production. In: Peter C.W. Gutkind and Immanuel Wallerstein, eds. *The Political Economy of Contemporary Africa*. Beverly Hills, CA: Sage, 1976. 90–111.

Marx, Karl and Friedrich Engels. *Communist Manifesto*. London: Penguin, 1967.

Parson, Jack. The trajectory of class and state in dependent development: the consequences of new wealth for Botswana. In: Nelson Kasfir, ed. *State and Class in Africa*. London: Frank Cass, 1984. 39–60.

Samatar, Abdi Ismail. *An African Miracle: State and Social Class Leadership and Colonial Legacy in Botswana Development*. Portsmouth, NH: Heinemann, 1999.

Sklar, Richard. The nature of class domination in Africa. *Journal of Modern African Studies*. 1979, 17(4), 531–52.

Wallerstein, Immanuel. Class and class-conflict in contemporary Africa. *Canadian Journal of African Studies*. 1973, 7(3), 375–80.

Young, M. Crawford. Nationalism, ethnicity and class in Africa: a retrospective. *Cahiers d'Études Africaines*. 1986, 26(3), 421–95.

Notes and references

1　Marx, Karl and Friedrich Engels. *The Communist Manifesto*. Harmondsworth: Penguin, 1967. 79.

2　Engels, Friedrich. *The Origin of Family, Private Property and the State*. London: Lawrence and Wishart. 1972. 71.

3　Marx and Engels. *The Communist Manifesto*. 82.

4　*Ibid*. 80.

5　*Ibid*. 94.

6　Mboya, Tom. African socialism and its application to planning in Kenya. *Sessional Paper No.10*, 1965. Cited in Katz, Stephen. *Marxism, Africa and Social Class: A Critique of Relevant Theories*. Montreal: Centre for Developing Area Studies, McGill University, 1980. 9.

7　Marx, Karl. *A Contribution to the Critique of Political Economy*. Moscow: Progress Publishers, 1970. 21.

8　Shanin, Teodor, ed. *Peasants and Peasant Societies: Selected Readings*. London: Penguin, 1988. 4.

9　Leys, Colin. Political implications of the development of peasant society in Kenya. In: Peter C.W. Gutkind and Peter Waterman, eds. *African Social Studies*. London: Heinemann, 1976. 356.

10　Magubane, Bernard. The evolution of class structure in Africa. In: Peter C.W. Gutkind and Immanuel Wallerstein, eds. *The Political Economy of Contemporary Africa*. Beverly Hills, CA: Sage, 1976. 183.

11　Parsons, Jack. The peasantariat and politics: migration, wage labour and agriculture in Botswana. *Africa Today*. 1984, 31(4), 5–25.

12　Cited in Young, Crawford and Thomas Turner. *The Rise and Decline of the Zairian State*. Madison, WI: University of Wisconsin Press, 1985. 108.

13　Weber, Max. The distribution of power within the political community: class, status, party [1914]. In: H.H. Gerth and C. Wright Mills, eds. *From Max Weber: Essays in Society*. London: Routledge and Kegan Paul, 1948. 180.

14　Poulantzas, Nicos. The problem of the capitalist state. *New Left Review*. 1969, November–December, 67–78.

15　Ossowski, Stanislaw. *Class Structure in the Social Consciousness*. London: Routledge and Kegan Paul, 1963. 185.

16　Sklar, Richard. The nature of class domination in Africa. *Journal of Modern African Studies*. 1979, 17(4), 531–52.

17　Cited in Young and Turner. *Rise and Decline of the Zairian State*. 110.

18 Kofele-Kale, Ndiva. Class, status, and power in post-reunification Cameroon: the rise of an Anglophone bourgeoisie, 1961–1980. In: Irving Leonard Markovitz, ed. *Studies in Power and Class in Africa*. New York: Oxford University Press, 1987. 156.

19 Marx, Karl. *Capital*, 1. London: Penguin, 1976. 797.

20 Coquery-Vidrovitch, Catherine. *African Women: A Modern History*. Boulder, CO: Westview, 1997. 75–82.

21 *Comprador* is the Portuguese word for 'purchaser'.

22 See, for example, Chapter 13 of Chabal, Patrick. *Power in Africa: An Essay in Political Interpretation*. Basingstoke: Macmillan, 1992.

23 Bayart, Jean-François. *The State in Africa: The Politics of the Belly*. London: Longman, 1993. 218–27.

24 *Ibid*. 94.

25 Price, Robert. Politics and culture in contemporary Ghana: the big-man small-boy syndrome. *Journal of African Studies*. 1974, 1(2), 173–204.

26 For example, see Samatar, Abdi Ismail. *An African Miracle: State and Social Class Leadership and Colonial Legacy in Botswana Development*. Portsmouth, NH: Heinemann, 1999.

27 Parson, Jack. The trajectory of class and state in dependent development: the consequences of new wealth for Botswana. In: Nelson Kasfir, ed. *State and Class in Africa*. London: Frank Cass, 1984. 44.

28 Molutsi, Patrick P. International influences on Botswana's democracy. In: Stephen John Stedman, ed. *Botswana: The Political Economy of Democratic Development*. Boulder, CO: Lynne Rienner, 1993. 59.

29 See Good, Kenneth. Corruption and mismanagement in Botswana: a best-case example? *Journal of Modern African Studies*. 1994, 32(3), 506–9.

30 Parson, Jack. Liberal democracy, the liberal state, and the 1989 general elections in Botswana. In: Stephen John Stedman, ed. *Botswana: The Political Economy of Democratic Development*. Boulder, CO: Lynne Rienner, 1993. 84.

31 *Ibid*. 86.

32 United Nations Conference on Trade and Development. *UNCTAD Handbook of Statistics 2014*. New York: United Nations, 2014. Tables 8.1, 8.4 and 3.2.D; World Bank data http://data.worldbank.org/indicator/SP.DYN.LE00.IN (accessed 24 July 2015) and http://data.worldbank.org/indicator/SP.DYN.IMRT.IN (accessed 24 July 2015); and UNESCO data www.uis.unesco.org/DataCentre/Pages/regions.aspx (accessed 24 July 2015).

6   Legitimacy

Neo-patrimonialism, personal rule and the centralisation of the African state

Chapter outline

- Centralisation of the African state

  - The one-party state
  - The subordination of 'peripheral' state institutions to the core executive

- Personal rule

  - The characteristics of personal rule

- The search for legitimacy

  - Clientelism

- State and civil society
- Case study: personal rule in Côte d'Ivoire
- Questions raised by this chapter
- Glossary of key terms
- Further reading
- Notes and references

Legitimacy should be at the heart of any government. Without it, coercive measures must be deployed to maintain authority, and it is far more productive to keep a society content by providing for its needs than it is for a self-interested ruling elite to seek compliance through violence. The social contract between the rulers and the ruled should therefore be one based on trust and respect, not on fear and coercion. As such, legitimacy can be defined as *a psychological relationship between the governed and their governors, which engenders a belief that the state's leaders and institutions have a right to exercise political authority over a society*. Legitimacy will convince, rather than force, citizens to obey the state.

Max Weber identified three pure sources of legitimacy: traditional, charismatic and legal-rational authority.[1] Traditional legitimacy rests on a society's culture and history. Few subjects in medieval Europe, for example, questioned the right of monarchs to rule over them, given that hereditary succession, and the divine right of kings, was well established by this time. Most believed that this was how God chose to order the temporal world, and consequently subjects obeyed the head of state as tradition demanded.

With charisma, Weber's second source of legitimacy, individuals choose to follow and obey simply because of their leader's personality or the ideals the leader imparts.

Warlords, and religious teachers, for example, rely on charisma to generate legitimacy among their constituencies.

It was legitimacy based on legal-rational government, however, that was meant to underlie state authority in post-colonial Africa. This was to be provided by liberal democratic institutions left by the imperial powers. Legal-rational government, in this respect, is government based on a social contract. Citizens obey the state because state institutions have been specifically constituted to serve their interests. Governments rule on the citizen's behalf, formulating, executing and enforcing laws designed to advance the collective good. In doing this, those within the state officiate impersonally, putting society's interests above their own. A bureaucratic culture of public service overrules any ideas officials may harbour about using state institutions for their own private gain. In return for this beneficial and rational system of government, citizens are obliged to obey state laws. It is legal-rational legitimacy that underpins the relationship between state and society in the current democracies of Europe and North America.

Yet legal-rational institutions did not prosper in Africa after independence. Liberal democracy was soon abandoned. At first glance, the continent's political institutions, such as parliaments and executives, may seem familiar, but a closer examination reveals these institutions to be very different from those found in the West. The façade of a legal-rational bureaucracy may remain, but behind this façade lies a completely different political environment. As will be seen, 'personal rule' superseded any notions of 'legal-rationalism', and this was achieved by centralising political activity. Power was removed from civil society and peripheral institutions of the state, and hoarded instead within the core executive, often with just one individual being dominant. And with legal-rational legitimacy lost through this 'centralisation of the state', alternative representative links had to be forged between state and society. Patronage, based on the distribution of state resources, became the main bond between the governors and the governed in post-colonial Africa. In short, the continent's leaders took the inherited modern states, adapted liberal democratic institutions to their own interests, and then 'patrimonialised' the whole system. The current chapter is designed to explain further these two processes: the *centralisation of the African state* and the accompanying *neo-patrimonialisation of government*.

Centralisation of the African state

Representative, accountable and efficient government usually requires political power to be distributed across society. No one area should become hegemonic. Within the state itself, for example, there should be a number of branches of government acting as checks and balances upon one another. Such a 'separation of powers' deters a dangerous accumulation of authority within a single area of government.

Similarly, power should also be dispersed between the state and civil society. State institutions should not come to monopolise the political process. Political parties must be able to compete fairly for control over the state, and interest groups should be able to influence the making of public policy. The absence of such pluralism risks the state becoming 'inverted', turning in on itself, and concentrating more on serving its own interests rather than those of the society it serves.

Along with a separation of powers, and links between state and civil society, a representative state should also in the final analysis be accountable to 'ordinary' people. Multi-party elections, involving a universal franchise, are perhaps the best way of ensuring this accountability. These polls reduce the opportunities for state power to be abused by state officials either alone, or in an exploitative alliance accommodating elites within civil society. Only if power is diffused evenly among these three elements of society (the state, civil society groups and the electorate as a whole) can representation and accountability be guaranteed.

In a centralised state, by contrast, there is a dangerous concentration of power. Dispersal is limited. A centralised state can be found where centrifugal forces have resulted in political power shifting away from those within civil society and 'peripheral' state institutions. Instead, power accumulates in specific core areas, usually within the executive branch, and most often within the office of the president or prime minister. Individuals within the core executive seek to monopolise all formal political activity within society.

The key to a centralised state maintaining this concentration of power is the limitation of opportunities for organised opposition. No rival source of power can be endorsed or tolerated by the political elite. Opposition political parties, for example, are often outlawed. Only the official party of the state is permitted to campaign, and even here the ruling elite usually tightly controls the one party.

Indeed, the elite does not confine its political monopoly to neutralising challenges through formal political channels. It also restricts opposition emanating from within civil society. Labour unions, professional groups and other voluntary associations are commonly heavily influenced or co-opted by the government of a centralised state. Co-option usually involves civil society leaders being offered positions within the state structure, giving them a stake in the status quo. Potential sources of opposition thus become 'decapitated', as these social movements lose their leaders to the state elite. As they say in Cameroon, 'the mouth that eats does not speak'.[2] Voluntary associations that resist this pressure and continue to maintain their independence from the state will be harassed or banned out of existence. Nigeria's execution in 1995 of Ken Saro-Wiwa, and eight other campaigners for Ogoni community rights, is a single brutal example among tens of thousands that demonstrate the lengths to which leaders will go to protect their monopoly of political power.

Similarly, economic functions, which are largely located within civil society in the West (private sector activities, such as the production, distribution and sale of goods), are also dominated by government institutions in a centralised state. To leave these economic activities to the free market would risk empowering individuals operating outside state institutions. It is almost as if for the state, or at least those at its core, there is no limit to their ambition over what they should control. When the centralisation process is complete, no potential source of opposition remains, either inside or outside state structures.

Ghana in the 1960s illustrates this phenomenon of state centralisation well. In 1957, Kwame Nkrumah's Convention People's Party (CPP) won Ghana's multi-party independence elections, and formed a government under the inherited Westminster-style constitution. Although the CPP had won considerable electoral support, it faced organised opposition in several regions of the country. In particular, the Ashanti were seeking a degree of autonomy. Nkrumah refused to tolerate any such 'separatism'. The CPP's first step, therefore, was to use its parliamentary majority to outlaw 'tribal'-based organisations with the 1957 Avoidance of Discrimination Act. With this single piece of legislation an important conduit of civil society mobilisation, namely ethnicity, was stifled. Regional assemblies were also proscribed. A year later, Parliament passed the Preventative

Detention Act. This measure, suspending habeas corpus, was used to detain political dissidents who continued to oppose the CPP. Leading opposition members were intimidated, imprisoned or forced into exile. Similarly, traditional leaders were stripped of their constitutional powers and sidelined into an advisory House of Chiefs. Next it was the turn of Ghana's independent system of justice. The judicial branch was circumvented by establishing special courts to hear political cases of treason and sedition. These trials were overseen by judges appointed directly by Nkrumah himself. Given all these measures, it was not surprising that when it came to the 1964 referendum asking the Ghanaian people whether they wanted a one-party state, there was no organised opposition left to campaign against this final act of centralisation. The one-party state was approved by 2,773,920 votes to 2,452.

Since the centralisation of the state is such an important factor in understanding post-colonial African politics, the next two sections of this chapter concentrate on two common components of the process: the neutralisation of party political opposition, with the establishment of a one-party state; and the manipulation of power within the state itself, where the core executive bypasses 'peripheral' institutions such as parliaments, local government and the judiciary.

The one-party state

Moves towards a one-party state were not portrayed by the political elite as an exercise of naked power accumulation. African leaders put forward strong arguments justifying this centralisation of the state. Kwame Nkrumah dismantled the multi-party system in Ghana because he declared this system to be socially divisive; Félix Houphouët-Boigny did likewise in the Côte d'Ivoire on the grounds that no opposition actually existed; Sekou Touré opted for single-party structures because Guinea's socialist ideology demanded this; while Julius Nyerere favoured the one-party state because he considered it the most appropriate way to build democracy in Tanzania. The vast majority of African countries underwent a process of centralisation, and each leader had their own set of justifications for the constitutional amendments deployed.

At the time, these justifications rang true. Many Africans, and indeed many Africanists in the West, welcomed these changes. After all, they agreed, there was no reason why democracy in Africa had to mimic Western multi-party competition, especially in view of the fact that this pluralist form of democracy had no historical roots on the African continent.

In terms of justification, most leaders cited 'unity' as the main reason for curtailing multi-party activity. Given the alien nature of the colonial state in Africa, independent governments inherited ethnically divided societies, many with separatist tendencies. If these sub-national forces had remained unchecked, it was argued, the authority of the national government, and the very integrity of the state itself, might have been threatened. In this sense, nationalist leaders insisted that African countries could not yet afford multi-party structures. Africans would mobilise along ethnic lines, and political competition of this nature would simply pull the nation apart. Instead, institutions fostering unity were required, and the institution that would contribute most to the nation-building project would be the single party. Just as George Washington had warned of the 'baneful effects of the spirit of party' 200 years earlier in the United States, African nationalist leaders such as Nyerere similarly argued that multi-party systems could only bring misfortune during these 'vital early years' of independence.[3]

It also has to be remembered that the nationalist movements which imposed these one-party states enjoyed considerable support from the electorate. Most gained their initial legitimacy from liberating their countries from colonial rule, subsequently gaining landslide victories in the independence elections. Many of these countries were practically de facto one-party states anyway. Tanzania, for example, had just one (independent) opposition MP sitting in its parliament before the one-party state was created in 1965. Why should Tanzania, it was argued, suffer a Westminster-style multi-party constitution when its people had selected representatives from only one party? Would it not be better to have a political system that best reflected African realities?

Nationalist leaders were also quick to point out that there was no tradition of multi-party democracy in Africa. An adversarial political culture, it was argued, was alien to the continent. Nationalists considered it foolish to adopt political institutions that had largely evolved out of Europe's need to manage social inequality and class conflict. Africa was largely devoid of these social cleavages. Once again, it was proposed that African political institutions should reflect African customs. Leaders, such as Senghor and Nyerere, invoked a romanticised interpretation of the past by describing how their forebears had traditionally met as communities, rather than as individual contestants, in order to make political decisions. Under a village tree, elders would talk over an idea until consensus was reached. Thus consensus, not competition, was the key to African politics. It therefore followed that a one-party model was the best method of recreating this style of consensus politics within the inherited modern state.

Economic arguments were also used to justify the one-party state. African presidents advocated, as a response to historical underdevelopment, strong leadership within the new independent states. This was the best way to precipitate economic 'take-off'. Africa, in this respect, could not afford the inefficient 'short-termist' policies and resource bargaining that multi-party competition encourages. Instead, prioritised strategic economic management was needed, provided by a one-party state. After all, at this time the Soviet Union provided a successful model to follow. The one-party state there had overseen remarkable economic growth in the post-war period.

Unity, lack of opposition, tradition and the imperatives of economic development, then, were all put forward as justifications for the creation of the one-party state. Even today, many of these arguments deserve respect. Yet it has to be said that the one-party state's performance in Africa was poor. With the benefit of hindsight, it can be seen that none of these original justifications stood the test of time. Despite the different varieties of the one-party model executed across the continent, several common flaws can be found regarding this political experiment. This explains why, in the 1990s, popular pressure forced the vast majority of African states to abandon their one-party structures (as will be seen in Chapter 11).

The problem with the one-party state was that, in practice, this system reduced links between the state and civil society, and between governors and governed generally. The main function of a party in a political system is to act as an intermediary. Leaders use party institutions to remain in touch with the people, while civil society utilises party structures in order to channel their demands through to the political decision makers. Where leaders consistently fail to respond to the demands of society, legitimacy is lost.

In the first few decades of independence, as a consequence of the lack of open political competition, many politicians and bureaucrats took their privileged position for granted. Indeed, with no rival parties threatening to replace them, these elites abused their position within the state. For example, as was shown in the previous chapter, single-party structures encouraged corruption and the formation of an exploitative bureaucratic bourgeoisie. Multi-party competition could have potentially broken the monopoly of this ruling elite. New ideas and new personnel from civil society could have been introduced through regular competitive elections. Such non-violent regime change, however, simply did not occur in post-colonial Africa. There were no peaceful channels of conflict resolution available to remove self-interested elites. Consequently, political succession, if there was any, was confined to military *coups d'état* in the first three decades of African independence.

The arguments for one-party rule in Africa become even less convincing when one considers how these parties actually fared in the post-colonial political environment. Instead of being key institutions at the heart of the nation-building project, binding state and civil society together, most of these organisations atrophied after independence. Following the general trend of the centralisation of the state, the power that parties had enjoyed during the anti-colonial campaign diminished. This power was transferred from the party to the core executive, following the party leaders themselves as they took up their positions within the new independent state. In this respect, single parties rarely became key institutions of policy making and debate in post-colonial Africa. Members instead deferred to the leadership, allowing the party to degenerate.

It was not just the power of parties, however, that was usurped by this political elite operating at the apex of the executive. African parliaments, local government and judicial branches also became subordinate to the executive.

The subordination of 'peripheral' state institutions to the core executive

Generally speaking, parliaments all around the world lost a degree of power to their executives in the twentieth century. In post-colonial Africa, however, this power loss was extreme. Most of the continent's national assemblies became mere appendages to their executives during this period.

The restriction of Kenyan parliamentary influence proves an interesting illustration of this process. Between independence in 1963 and constitutional amendments that made Kenya a one-party state in 1982, there were relatively competitive elections for members of parliament. This was despite the fact that the Kenya African National Union (KANU) was the sole active political party for much of this period, making Kenya a de facto one-party state.

KANU members would compete among themselves to have their name put forward as an official KANU candidate, and thus the uncontested MP for a particular constituency. Although KANU's Executive Committee had a final veto, and all candidates had to swear allegiance to the party, its policies and the president, any adult Kenyan was eligible to stand for election to Parliament. These primary elections proved to be genuinely competitive. In the 1969 contest, for example, 77 incumbent MPs were defeated, including five ministers and 14 assistant ministers.[4] By comparison, fewer incumbents are removed in most United States elections.

African one-party structures, however, simply did not offer the level of political choice that Western electorates enjoy. Even in the relatively few cases where elections were more open (for example, Kenya and Tanzania in the 1960s), African parliamentary candidates rarely stood on issues or policies. They failed to offer choice between political alternatives. This was not possible as political decision making only took place in the higher echelons of the executive, and not in Parliament. As Goran Hyden and Colin Leys remarked in their study of the 1969 Kenyan general election, 'It is very difficult to identify any policy decision or legislative act which is traceable to the electoral outcome'.[5] Certainly there was a greater degree of linkage where more open one-party elections were held, but even here civil society's influence on public policy was limited. Instead, voters were looking for lobbyists who could secure state resources for their constituency (for example, cheaper fertilisers, new water supplies, or employment opportunities). The MP had to keep the resource 'tap' turned on, and 'the life chances flowing'.[6] Failure to win these state resources would result in constituents voting for an alternative candidate in the next primary election (hence the large turnover of personnel in Kenya's 1969 poll). Linkage, however, was limited to the local accountability of MPs to their constituents, judged on this ability to secure resources.

In this respect, African executives retained a monopoly over political decision making within their societies. On the rare occasions when MPs did challenge the executive, they often found their access to state patronage limited, or worse. For these reasons, it was advisable for MPs to concentrate on local resource issues, rather than wider national or international affairs. One MP who did challenge the presidential elite was Kenya's J.M. Kariuki. After he died in suspicious circumstances in 1975, the angered Kenyan parliament went against the wishes of President Jomo Kenyatta by mounting its own investigation into the role of the security forces in Kariuki's death. Kenyatta responded by dismissing those junior ministers who supported the investigation, while the ringleaders of this parliamentary 'revolt' were promptly detained. Subsequently, the executive made sure that the Kenyan Parliament would never exercise this level of independence again, and Kenyatta's successor, Daniel arap Moi, confirmed this position when he altered the constitution and made Kenya a *de jure* one-party state in 1982.

Of the liberal democratic institutions that African states inherited after independence, local government structures were the most established. This was because a majority of the imperial powers favoured indirect rule, and as part of the decolonisation process most encouraged local democracy as a stepping stone to full self-determination. Often, colonial administrators would grant local autonomy to nationalists in order to delay giving full independence to the territory. After independence, however, the strength of local democracy on the continent declined precipitously.

The problem with this form of governing was that it involved distributing political authority horizontally, rather than hierarchically. Given that, in a centralised state, leaders will not tolerate uncontrolled concentrations of political power outside core institutions, local government was doomed. Consequently, locally elected and accountable institutions were removed, replaced by officers and agencies directly controlled from the centre. In this respect, local *government* was replaced by local *administration*. Issues such as education, health, road maintenance and the collection of taxes were all now overseen by regional administrators who reported to, and took orders from, their superiors in the state capital. As a result, national rather than local initiatives came to dominate, while local communities had little influence over the policy-making decisions that most affected them. The executive, again, was in the driving seat.

Just as parties, legislatures and local government lost power to the executive in postcolonial Africa, so did the judicial branch of government. In legal-rational states, although most courts do not have official policy-making roles, they are still powerful institutions. They gain their authority from their function of maintaining the rule of law. All within society, including the law makers themselves, have to respect the courts' judgements. Even the judiciary, however, was sidelined by the centralised African state. In a political environment where executives were so powerful, laws became arbitrary. Politicians and bureaucrats felt disinclined to obey the constitution if their private interests were threatened. Laws became less binding on those who ran the state, while those in civil society were still expected to conform. Indeed, some leaders blatantly took the law into their own hands, paying little heed to the statute book. Idi Amin's Uganda, Jean-Bédel Bokassa's Central African Republic and Macías Nguema's Equatorial Guinea were extreme examples of this, with presidential operatives literally getting away with murder, but even in states where leaders were more constitutionally minded, the executive still tended to find ways to ensure that the judicial branch did not interfere with 'political' matters.

With this centralisation of power in the hands of the core executive, in many senses independent African states had reverted to the hierarchical, centralised and autocratic model of government found earlier under colonial rule. Government was controlled from the centre, and civil society played little part in the formal political process. Yet post-colonial Africa was different from imperial rule in one vital respect: the continent was now governed by *personal* (rather than institutional) rule, combined with *clientelism* to retain legitimacy. It is to personal rule and clientelism that the chapter now turns.

Personal rule

Colonialism brought 'legal-rational' institutional states to Africa. Within this form of political order, offices and institutions are established, based on legal authority, to carry out the functions of government. Civil society supports these institutions as they follow patterns of accepted rules. Both those in government and those in wider society know where they stand. Each side abides by clearly defined laws and practices, and the entire governing process gains predictability. In short, institutional norms take precedence over personal whims, and this is where legitimacy is generated.

There is also a clear distinction between private and public roles within a legal-rational system of government. It is illegal, or at least immoral, for the private interests of officials to interfere with their public duties. The public interest is paramount. In this respect, Max Weber declared this institutional legal-rational model to be the most efficient form of government.[7]

Yet, as has been seen, post-colonial African states do not always follow this legal-rational pattern. The rule of law is not always guaranteed, and many public officials use their position within the state to serve their own, and not just the public, interest. In this sense, African politics more often resemble the environment described in Machiavelli's *The Prince* rather than that depicted in Montesquieu's *Spirit of the Laws*. This does not necessarily mean, however, that African societies are anarchic. Political order and legitimacy do still exist in Africa, they are just of a different type. Given this failure of legal-rational institutions in post-colonial Africa, Africanists have attempted to explain the continent's politics in terms of *personal rule*.

The purest form of personal rule is patrimonialism. This is a form of political order where power is concentrated in the personal authority of one individual ruler. The leader gains this position from their status in society. They may be bound by traditions or customs, but there are no legal-rational constraints on government. The leader is above the law, and indeed often *makes* the law by personal decree. In this respect, patrimonial leaders treat all political and administrative concerns of state as their own personal affairs. The state is their private property, and the act of ruling is consequently quite arbitrary.

No modern system of government can be managed by just one person, however, but instead of building legal-rational institutions to carry out the duties of the state, patrimonial leaders distribute offices as patronage among close relatives, friends and clients. As a result, all these lesser officials have to demonstrate personal loyalty to the leader in order to maintain office. In this respect, clients are retainers tied to their benefactor, rather than salaried officials serving the government institutions in which they are employed. Loyalty to the leader brings rewards. Clients are free to exploit their position of authority, creating their own fiefdoms. Historical examples of patrimonialism include the monarchical and religious states of medieval and early modern Europe.[8]

It is true that many characteristics of patrimony can be readily identified in post-colonial Africa. Yet it cannot be said that these African regimes are purely patrimonial. Patrimony derives from tradition, and legal-rational institutions will play no part in this form of political order. By contrast, legal-rational institutions may have been weak in post-colonial Africa, but they did still exist and function (as any modern state requires). As this is the case, there is a fusion between patrimonialism and legal-rational institutions on the continent. Private interests are pursued within political structures that have a legal-rational façade. In this sense, the modern African state is the domain of the presidential monarch rather than of a purely patrimonial figure. Christopher Clapham is therefore correct when he suggests that the term *neo-patrimonialism* is more accurate.[9] Robert Jackson and Carl Rosberg prefer to use a completely separate phrase, and talk of post-colonial Africa being dominated by 'personal rule'.[10]

The characteristics of personal rule

African personal rule can be characterised as authoritarian, arbitrary, ostentatious and inefficient. It has produced fragile governments, even in states where presidential monarchs have reigned for decades. This personalised political system has also created administration that is based on factions, rather than institutions and officials working together. It is worth taking time to examine the characteristics of personal rule a little more closely.

The vast majority of African leaders in the period between independence and the democratic reforms of the 1990s achieved high office either by being in the vanguard of their country's nationalist movement, or by leading military coups. As such, many regarded themselves as the 'father' of their nation, and such self-perception encouraged these leaders to act as if they were above the law. Authoritarianism is very much a characteristic of personal rule. To protect their own position, presidential monarchs frequently resorted to the coercive resources of the state. Individual challengers were intimidated by the security forces, or even assassinated, while group challenges were countered by bannings, harassment, election manipulation and the withholding of state resources from regions where dissidents drew their support.

Personal rule also brought continuity to Africa's leadership. By contrast to legal-rational systems, where leaders tend to change at regular intervals, more permanent 'Big Men' have been a feature of the post-colonial period. Skilful politicians such as Tunisia's Bourguiba, Cameroon's Biya, Congo-Kinshasa's Mobutu, Malawi's Banda, Côte d'Ivoire's Houphouët-Boigny, Zambia's Kaunda, Tanzania's Nyerere, Kenya's Kenyatta and Moi,

Gabon's Bongo and Zimbabwe's Mugabe (the list goes on) were the key political influences within their respective countries during the first few decades of independence. Only in the late 1980s and the 1990s, when old age and the arrival of multi-party elections began to take their toll on the Big Men, was this longevity of personal rule broken.

Personal rule is also often ostentatious. In the West, attempts are made to distinguish between the individual and the office that they hold. In Africa, no such effort was made. Presidential monarchs linked their private and public interests, and many sought to display the wealth they had accumulated as a result of high office. Consequently, African leaders operated in a world of private jets, motorcades, limousines, palatial residences and ceremony. In two more extreme cases, Félix Houphouët-Boigny made his home village of Yamoussoukro the capital of Côte d'Ivoire, building a US$360 million cathedral in the process, while Jean-Bédel Bokassa spent US$20 million on his own coronation as Emperor of the Central African Republic (bankrupting the state in the process).

Symbols of the president are also important. As well as the leader's photograph and a report of his (rarely her) movements, however inconsequential, appearing in the press on a regular basis, portraits will be displayed in prominent public places as well as in private homes. T-shirts and posters will be produced featuring the image of the president; stadiums, schools and hospitals will be named after him. All in all, nobody will be left in any doubt as to who actually runs the country.

Personal rule is also arbitrary. As Weber observed of patrimonial leaders, neo-patrimonial autocrats may 'refuse to be bound by formal rules, even those that they have made themselves'.[11] The rule of law cannot be taken for granted in such political systems. Post-colonial African leaders ignored rules, bent rules, and made new rules to serve their own interests. The rules of the game were often changed overnight. In this manner, opposition forces, as well as the presidential monarch's own followers, were kept out of kilter, while the leader himself was free to satisfy his own personal whims. As a result, African politics were somewhat unpredictable. The whole of society was denied the security that legal-rational systems produce.

Another characteristic of personal rule is that it encourages competition among intra-governmental factions. In their seminal study of personal power in Africa, Jackson and Rosberg describe how this system

> is a dynamic world of political will and action that is ordered less by institutions than by personal authorities and power; a world of stratagem and countermeasure, of action and reaction, but without the assured mediation and regulation of effective political institutions. Political power is capable of being checked and stalemated in Africa, as elsewhere, but less by institutions than by countervailing power.[12]

This breeds a political environment of factionalism, schisms, purges and coups. Groups will jockey for position under the leader, offering support in return for resources and patronage, but if the leader is perceived to be weak, these previously loyal lieutenants will not hesitate to challenge the president's authority. Many African states suffered when this personalised rivalry failed to be contained within the political system. Competition spilt over into instability and violence, and the military was often the beneficiary by staging a *coup d'état*. Even the longest-serving presidential monarch is vulnerable to this factional competition, should it get out of hand.

Yet it is often in the leader's interests to foster controlled factional rivalry. If they are distracted by competition, the lower political ranks cannot mount a challenge for the ultimate prize, the presidency itself. President Mobutu Sese Seko of Zaire (today's Democratic Republic of the Congo, DRC) was one of the foremost proponents of seeing off potential competitors and managing his 'courtiers'. Richard Sandbrook wrote of Mobutu's reign:

> No potential challenger is permitted to gain a power base. Mobutu's officials know that their jobs depend solely on the President's discretion. Frequently, he fires cabinet ministers, often without explanation. He appoints loyal army officers and other faithfuls as provincial governors, but only to provinces outside their home areas. And he constantly reshuffles and purges his governors and high army command. Everyone is kept off balance. Everyone must vie for his patronage. Mobutu holds all the cards and the game is his.[13]

It took 32 years before Mobutu was finally deposed.

Above all, personal rule breeds inefficiency. As was seen in Chapter 4 addressing ethnicity, African administrations tend to allocate resources on the basis of demand, not need. Personal rule contributes to this problem. Powerful factions will receive control over the lion's share of the state's resources, leaving less well-represented groups at a disadvantage. Similarly, public policy receives little feedback or scrutiny under a system of personal rule. There is little incentive to evaluate policy systematically in a country where success or failure is neither rewarded nor punished by an electorate. Indeed, nobody is in a position to challenge the presidential monarch's chosen policy anyway. To leave the final words of this assessment of personal rule to Jackson and Rosberg:

> the concept of governance as an activity of guiding the ship of state toward a specific destination – the assumption of modern rationalism and the policy sciences – fits poorly with much political experience in contemporary Black African countries. In African countries governance is more a matter of seamanship and less one of navigation – that is, staying afloat rather than going somewhere.[14]

The search for legitimacy

Even in a neo-patrimonial state led by personal rule, a degree of legitimacy has to be generated. Political authority cannot rest on coercion alone. Bokassa, Amin and Macías Nguema came closest to achieving this, in the Central African Republic, Uganda and Equatorial Guinea, respectively. They ruled by confiscation rather than conciliation, but even here the utility of violence had its limitations.[15] It was a case of diminishing returns. Violence is very effective in the short term, but over longer periods of time, coercion only stimulates opposition and counter-violence. Therefore the skilful personal ruler uses a combination of coercion *and* legitimacy in order to maintain government and social order.

Yet how is this legitimacy generated? Weber's pure sources of legitimacy only tell part of the story. Legal rationalism is limited because of the neo-patrimonial nature of the state. Charisma is more of a factor, with Africans deferring to the 'Big Men' and the ideologies of nationalism they preached, but again this alone did not produce enough support. In the final analysis, it was material provision that contributed most to legitimising Africa's one-party states. Personal rulers relied on the distribution of state resources in order to 'buy' legitimacy for their regimes. As long as patrons could nourish their own followers, through the manipulation of public goods and institutions, they were safe. Therefore it was rewards for clients, distributed through the mechanism of *clientelism*, that became the key substitute for the legitimacy lost after Africa's independent liberal democratic institutions were dismantled, and personal rule was installed.

Clientelism

Christopher Clapham describes clientelism as 'a relation of exchange between unequals'.[16] It is a mutually beneficial association between the powerful and the weak. A patron extends public office (a salary and access to the state), security (freedom from violence) and resources (such as wells, roads and medical centres) to his or her clients. In return, the client offers support and deference that help to legitimise the patron's elevated position. In this respect, clientelism is a form of political contract.

Clientelism has permeated African societies from top to bottom. It is not just a case of presidential monarchs exchanging patronage for support among their immediate lieutenants within the heart of the state. There is a whole chain of patron–client networks that spread out from this point. This web connects the president, through numerous links down the chain, to the lowly peasant. Each client uses the resources received from the patron above them to build their own patronage empire. Individuals therefore simultaneously act as a client of a superior, and as a patron to those below them. For example, the presidential monarch is the patron to his lieutenants, but the lieutenants use a proportion of this patronage to recruit clients of their own, from among middle-ranking bureaucrats. These middle-ranking state officials, in turn, have clients lower down the administrative hierarchy. The chain of clients and patrons extends all the way down to local patrons, who may have a particular village as their client base. In this respect, clientelist networks are 'vertical threads' binding whole societies together which, in turn, create political stability and order.[17]

Clientelism is particularly important in Africa, as it provides political channels that are absent elsewhere in society. In an environment where personal rulers have a monopoly on formal political activity, and all independent political associations are banned, client–patron networks do represent a limited form of political exchange. They help to bring civil society back into the political arena, albeit to a small degree. Lesser patrons are tolerated by the elite, as the whole mechanism is reliant on the presidential monarch providing the largest input of state resources. It is the ultimate 'trickle-down' system. The leader relies on the network to ensure that his patronage permeates through the whole of society. The greater the number of people who feel that they benefit from this political system, the more legitimacy and support the regime receives.

Legitimacy that is founded on patronage, however, is fragile. Although clientelism avoids violence, and is mutually beneficial to the two parties concerned, it is nevertheless an asymmetric contract. The whole relationship is forged on the recognition and acceptance that there is inequality between the two parties. Patrons will retain as much wealth as possible for themselves, only passing on the resources they consider necessary to keep clients loyal. In post-colonial Africa, resource distribution was usually kept to a minimum. This was because there was no alternative political market where clients could maximise their rewards by selling their loyalty to the highest bidder. As a result, most Africans in the first few decades of independence settled for trying to get what they could from the existing patrons. The alternative path, that of contesting the status quo, was too costly. Clients risked losing out entirely if they challenged their existing patrons. Clientelism thus provided stability and legitimacy in post-colonial Africa. Yet this system of legitimacy relied too heavily on material provision. As will be seen in Chapter 10, once the patronage began to dry up due to economic difficulties in the 1980s and 1990s, so did the legitimacy supporting personal rule. Without the distribution of resources, presidential monarchs could no longer offer their chain of clients any reason to support them, apart from the threat of violence.

State and civil society

In terms of this book's underlying theme, the process of centralisation clearly advantaged the state at the expense of civil society. Gone were the pluralist institutions left by the imperial powers at decolonisation. Power was drained from civil society and

Table 6.1 Chapter summary: characteristics of a centralised state, personal rule and clientelism

Characteristics of a centralised state	• Accumulation of power in the executive branch, often in the office of the president or prime minister • Political mobilisation initially through just one official party that is ultimately sidelined • Civil society excluded from influencing state decision making • Sources of political opposition co-opted, harassed or eliminated • Limited respect for human rights • Absence of competitive elections • Local government, parliament and the judiciary bypassed by ruling elite • Strong security laws at the disposal of state leaders • State plays a dominant role in the economy, elements of a command economy • State often led by one dominant charismatic individual exercising personal rule • Legitimacy generated by neo-patrimonialism and clientelism
Characteristics of personal rule	• State led by one dominant charismatic individual • State institutions and authority treated as private, rather than public, property • Relies on clientelism to generate legitimacy throughout society • Ostentatious display of wealth by leaders • Arbitrary rule replaces the rule of law • Factional competition rife within ruling elite • Inefficient government, more about nurturing the client–patron network than managing public policy
Characteristics of clientelism	• A relation of exchange between unequals • Positions of power within the state used to generate patronage • Chain of patrons and clients extends deep into society • Generates minimal levels of legitimacy

'peripheral' institutions of the state, and amassed instead within the core executive. This would be the foundation on which presidential monarchs would exercise personal rule.

Africa's neo-patrimonial political structures did, however, maintain a modern state system after independence. Several countries did occasionally descend into periods of chaos and anarchy, but, on the whole, Africans lived under governments that offered a degree of stability and order. Indeed, in societies where national identities were fragile and resources scarce, it was argued that a highly centralised state was appropriate. Leaders reasoned that 'alien' liberal democratic institutions would most likely only serve to tear apart the freedom and self-determination that Africans had won at independence. Under a centralised system, fragmented societies could be bound together, enabling all to enjoy the benefits of the modern state.

These benefits, however, failed to materialise. Civil society was particularly disadvantaged. Indeed, all alternative political mobilisation was promptly co-opted or brutally crushed. The patronage offered in lieu of this civil society representation was flawed. Clientelism cannot work without the exploitation of clients by patrons. The political elite, in this respect, preyed on the vulnerability of their people. Patrons distributed some of their wealth into the network, but the priority was to serve their own personal needs first. The state bureaucracy prospered while civil society remained constrained. It was not a relationship of equal exchange.

The centralised state also failed to produce consistently strong government. Healthy states reflect the needs of their people, and seek advice and expertise from civil society. Conversely, centralised states destroy many of their links with society. Institutions that could have provided advice and feedback on policy, suggesting alternative approaches, as well as acting as a safety valve for dissent, were dismantled soon after independence. Instead, core executive institutions, and their leaders, relied on their own counsel and expertise. This is how the most powerful personnel at the heart of the African state often lost touch with their people. The gulf between state and civil society grew.

In states blessed with a sufficient resource base, such a gulf between the rulers and the ruled may not have been a problem. Resources could have been provided through client–patron networks to offset any misgivings Africans may have had about their governments. On a continent, however, where wealth is limited, this lack of linkage between state and civil society often proved fatal. Inefficient and corrupt regimes that did not have the resources to 'buy off' civil society experienced regular crises of legitimacy. Coercion could be used to plug this 'legitimacy gap', but violence has a limited political utility. Governments that could no longer feed the client–patron network were left vulnerable. In this respect, witness the number of military coups on the continent during the 1960s, 1970s and 1980s.

By the end of the 1980s, the game was up. As a consequence of economic failure, there were no longer enough resources to maintain requisite levels of legitimacy. Patron–client networks shrank, and as a consequence some territories spiralled into state collapse. In others, presidential monarchs attempted to liberalise their regimes. Multi-party competition was reintroduced in a last-ditch effort to retain power (see Chapter 11). The era of the centralised state and personal rule, at least in its extreme form, was now at an end.

Case study: personal rule in Côte d'Ivoire

Côte d'Ivoire is home to some 20 million people in West Africa. Located on the Gulf of Guinea, its environment ranges from lagoons on the Atlantic coast and rainforest in the south, to plains in the north. After being formally colonised by the French in 1893, this territory gained its independence in 1960. The most striking feature of Côte d'Ivoire in the post-colonial period was its initial economic growth. The country outstripped the performance of most of its neighbours, and was second on the continent only to South Africa in the per-capita income it raised. This Ivorian 'economic miracle', however, became somewhat tarnished in the 1980s and 1990s as a result of unstable cocoa and coffee prices. Worse was to come with the turn of the twenty-first century, when the country dramatically succumbed to devastating political unrest.

Politically, the first three decades of independence in Côte d'Ivoire were dominated by one individual, Félix Houphouët-Boigny. He was the focus of all state activity, masterminding the centralisation of the state. Houphouët-Boigny exercised personal rule from the office of the president, gaining legitimacy for his

Plate 6.1 Portrait of Felix Houphouët-Boigny, President of Côte d'Ivoire and skilled manager of patronage, 1976. Photographer: Richard Melloul.

regime through a complex patron–client network that cast his influence into all areas of Ivorian society.

Preparations for the one-party state started early. The Parti Démocratique de la Côte d'Ivoire (PDCI) purposefully went about absorbing significant opposition groups into its ranks between 1952 and 1957. Consequently, the PDCI became Côte d'Ivoire's ruling party when it won a large majority in the independence elections. It was helped by the fact that the electoral system involved only national party lists. There were no regional constituencies which would have allowed smaller, ethnically mobilised parties to establish a regional power base. Instead, each party had to compete for electoral support nationally. The PDCI leadership also kept secret who had been selected as official candidates from among its ranks until just before polling day. This ensured that rejected nominees would not stand as independent candidates, or collectively organise as a separate opposition party.

Once in power, the PDCI followed classic tactics of establishing a one-party state. It absorbed elements that could challenge its political monopoly, while at the same time eliminating lesser sources of opposition through electoral manipulation and intimidation. However, once the PDCI had successfully mobilised mass nationalist opposition against colonial rule, and had then seen off any residual opposition after independence (creating a de facto one-party state), Houphouët-Boigny let the PDCI atrophy. Elections for party posts became increasingly infrequent, while little effort was directed at maintaining the PDCI's links with the Ivorian people at a grass-roots level. Indeed, party structures degenerated until they became merely sources of patronage. As the *Africa Contemporary Record* reported in the early 1970s, the PDCI acted as a kind of British House of Lords, where the old party faithful could be retired with dignity and a source of income, but without extending them too much political power.[18] Of the PDCI's membership, only the elite leadership within the Political Bureau retained any real power, and this bureau consisted of Houphouët-Boigny's trusted lieutenants who already occupied high office within the core executive. The party was becoming, in Frantz Fanon's phrase, a 'skeleton of its former self'.[19]

Côte d'Ivoire displayed all the characteristics of a centralised state between 1960 and 1990. Any source of opposition was rapidly absorbed if possible, or suppressed. Houphouët-Boigny declared that 'competition is healthy for sport, but in politics, what must triumph is team spirit'.[20] In this respect, no independent source of political power was allowed to develop. Associations within civil society, for example, were either co-opted or dismantled by the state. Trade union leaders, for instance, were given positions in the government, but labour campaigners who continued to operate outside the state were imprisoned. Similarly, the PDCI's youth wing co-opted organisations of younger Ivorians, while traditional leaders were urged to join the Syndicat des Chefs Coutumiers (a state-sponsored talking shop with Houphouët-Boigny as its honorary president).[21] The banner used as a backdrop at the PDCI's first conference after independence summed up the Ivorian political environment well. It read, 'A single party, for a single people, with a single leader'.[22]

The legislative and judicial branches of government, as well as local government, also lost out to the core executive as a result of Houphouët-Boigny's centralisation of the state. Local councils fell into disuse, and were replaced by regional administrations directed from the centre. Similarly, the National Assembly became more of a forum to legitimise Houphouët-Boigny's policy choices, rather than an institution willing to debate and resolve differences over proposed public programmes. Following this pattern, the judiciary was also usurped, in this case by the establishment of special courts to hear political cases. The level of judicial independence that these courts observed is indicated by the fact that these trials took place in the president's own residence.

At the epicentre of this centralised political system was Félix Houphouët-Boigny himself. The president effectively held a private monopoly over Côte d'Ivoire politics until his death in 1993. Jackson and Rosberg described Houphouët-Boigny as an 'anti-politician'. This is because he was a ruler who attempted to remove politics from the public realm.[23] Individuals occupying a position in the state below the president were merely Houphouët-Boigny's personal administrators and clients. As such, politicians or bureaucrats who sought high office in Côte d'Ivoire could only achieve this with Houphouët-Boigny's explicit approval. The president's lieutenants would be issued conditional licences to do his bidding. They used Houphouët-Boigny's patronage to build their own fiefdoms and client bases, but if they failed to serve the leader loyally, they would soon lose their position in the state and the wealth that this generated.

Indeed, Houphouët-Boigny's court was a very tight-knit community. Many individuals held interlocking posts within the three key institutions of state: the PDCI's Political Bureau, the National Assembly, and the Economic and Social Council. Tessilimi Bakary has calculated that just 320 individuals held 1,040 positions within these institutions between 1957 and 1980.[24] As every young Ivorian knew, it was only possible to be adopted by the system, and perhaps even reach the higher echelons of the executive, if they conformed to the rules of the political game. Above all, loyalty had to be expressed at all times to the paramount patron, Houphouët-Boigny himself.

This is where Houphouët-Boigny gained his legitimacy. After all, the Ivorian state offered very little to civil society by way of legal-rational institutions. Democratic structures had been dismantled and public participation in the policy process curtailed. Instead, Houphouët-Boigny's system of personal rule relied on distributing rewards for continued political support. In this respect, the president believed that patronage, funded from economic growth, could be a substitute for political participation. Legitimacy would come from material provision. Hence, Houphouët-Boigny placed himself at the apex of a client–patron network that permeated deep into Ivorian society. The longevity of Houphouët-Boigny's regime

(1960–93) is testament to the presidential monarch's ability to maintain these networks.

Perhaps the most obvious evidence of Houphouët-Boigny's patronage system can be seen at a local level. State resources were offered to local communities who supported the president. After a period of transient political dissent elsewhere, the town of Adjamé, for example, received a publicly funded marketplace in the mid-1960s. At the market's opening ceremony, Minister of State Auguste Denise thanked the local population, on behalf of 'our president, the government, and the political directors of the Party' for the loyalty they had shown during this wave of anti-government protests.[25] Similarly, the annual independence celebration, the Fête Nationale de l'Indépendance, was moved each year in order to reward, or seek favour from, a particular region.[26] Of course, for a local community to really benefit, they had to promote one of their number into the cabinet itself. Ministers of Construction and Town Planning, for example, frequently awarded their home towns lucrative development schemes.[27] It was Houphouët-Boigny's own village of Yamoussoukro, however, that benefited the most. It became Côte d'Ivoire's new capital, and the location for the president's own gift to his country, a multi-million-franc basilica, which, when constructed, was the largest church in the world.

Towards the end of Houphouët-Boigny's life, however, increasing numbers of Ivorians began to demand representation from their state. Patronage could no longer buy off this more coherent challenge to personal rule. The people of Côte d'Ivoire joined civil societies elsewhere on the continent in demanding a return to multi-party democracy in the late 1980s and the 1990s. This was a direct consequence of poor economic performance, on the back of falling coffee and cocoa prices, which resulted in shrinking client–patron networks. Houphouët-Boigny no longer controlled a large enough state income to keep his patron–client networks in good order.

At first, as he had since 1960, Houphouët-Boigny argued that multi-party competition could not come to Côte d'Ivoire until the nation was fully united. In 1985, however, political liberalisation began. Open competition was allowed for PDCI National Assembly nominations. Despite this concession, the campaign for multi-party democracy expanded, and by 1990, Houphouët-Boigny had been forced to compete in his first multi-party contest for the post of president (after holding this office for 30 years). Although he won this poll by a landslide margin, confirming his position as the paramount patron and presidential monarch, the centralised state had been weakened and notions of legal-rational legitimacy advanced. Houphouët-Boigny's death in 1993 coincided with this transition to a more complicated political age.

The immense political skill displayed by Houphouët-Boigny became even more apparent in the years after his death. No individual or party has been able to generate sufficient legitimacy (or coercion) to calm the chaos that underpins the politics of Côte d'Ivoire. Although Houphouët-Boigny's successor, Henri Konan Bédiè, managed to win (disputed) multi-party elections in 1995, he could only maintain his authority by intimidating opposition parties, and by altering the constitution to give the president draconian powers. Bédiè ruled a country that was subjected to regular political protests, ethnic tensions, labour strikes and student demonstrations.

Eventually, in 1999, a military coup removed Bédiè, and unleashed a period of even greater political uncertainty. While the politicians squabbled over the terms of a reconciliation, political violence escalated. This developed into a full-scale rebellion in 2002, which was only quelled by the intervention of French and Economic Community of West African States (ECOWAS) peacekeepers. Although a Government of National Reconciliation was formed in 2003, it is evident that the politics of Côte d'Ivoire have deteriorated considerably. Factions continued to jostle for power within the 'government of national unity', with the promised General Election being postponed four times. When the poll was eventually held in 2010, the result was disputed. The incumbent, Laurent Gbagbo, refused to accept defeat, and widespread violence ensued. Again, it took international intervention to restore order, in the form of the UN and French troops. Amongst this political chaos, some Ivorians are looking back to the Houphouët-Boigny period with rose-coloured spectacles. They remember the stability that the 'Big Man' created, rather than the details of the personal rule mixing centralisation, patronage, legitimacy and coercion.

Côte d'Ivoire[28]

Territory:	322,462 sq. km.	Population:	20.3 million
Colonial power:	France	Independence:	1960
Major cities:	Abidjan	Ethnic groups:	Akan
	Bouaké		Volaïque
	Yamoussoukro (capital)		Mane Nord
Languages:	French		Krou
	Baoule	Urban population:	53 per cent
	Dioula	Life expectancy:	51 years
	Bete	Adult literacy:	41 per cent
Infant mortality:	71 deaths/1,000 live births	Exports:	Cocoa
Religion:	Traditional		Oil
	Christian		Rubber
Currency:	CFA franc		Fruit
GDP per capita:	US$1,230		Gold

Questions raised by this chapter

1. Were African leaders justified in centralising their states and imposing one-party rule?
2. How democratic were the more open parliamentary elections found in states such as Kenya and Tanzania?
3. Why did local government and independent judiciaries not prosper in Africa's centralised states?
4. Was African personal rule an efficient form of government?
5. To what extent did clientelism legitimise personal rule in post-colonial Africa?

Glossary of key terms

Centralisation of the state	A process whereby power is drained from civil society and 'peripheral' institutions of the state, and concentrated instead within the core executive.
Clientelism	A largely instrumental political relationship that exists when an individual of higher socio-economic status (the patron) uses their influence and resources to provide protection or benefits, or both, for a person of lower status (the client), who, for their part, reciprocates by offering general support and assistance to the patron.[29]
Client–patron network	The series of vertical links that bind patron and client, where the client of one patron often commands their own patronage network lower down the chain.
Legal-rational political order	Political authority built on impersonal state institutions which govern respecting acknowledged patterns of rules.
Legitimacy	A psychological relationship between the governed and their governors which engenders a belief that the state's leaders and institutions have a right to exercise political authority over the rest of society.
Neo-patrimonial rule	A system of government where patrimonial rule (see below) is exercised through the remnants of legal-rational institutions.
One-party state	A system of government where formal political mobilisation is channelled through a single state-sponsored party. Opposition parties are outlawed.
Patrimonial rule	Political authority based on an individual, where the state itself, and the affairs of state, are the personal interests of the ruler. All within this political system owe their position and loyalty to the one leader.
Personal rule	A system of government where one individual, commanding the heights of state institutions and patron–client networks, dominates political activity within a territory.

Further reading

Two books well worth reading on the centralisation of the African state and the move to one-party rule are Aristide Zolberg's *Creating Political Order* and the volume edited by James Coleman and Carl Rosberg. These two books, although dated now, give a flavour of events and the debate held at this time. For a more institutional and specialised look at government within the one-party state, Philip Mawhood's *Local Government in the Third World* is an interesting read.

The seminal volume on personal rule in Africa is Robert Jackson and Carl Rosberg's aptly named *Personal Rule in Black Africa*. Selections from works by Robert Fatton (Chapter 3) and Richard Sandbrook (Chapter 5) also make some useful points on this phenomenon in their more general books on African politics. In terms of a country study, the African one-party state and personal rule are analysed eloquently by Crawford Young and Thomas Turner's work on Zaire.

For those interested in the concepts of legitimacy and client–patron networks, Max Weber's work on legitimacy is still fascinating, while a good starting point for further reading on clientelism is the book edited by Christopher Clapham.

Clapham, Christopher, ed. *Private Patronage and Public Power*. London: Pinter, 1982.

Coleman, James S. and Carl G. Rosberg, eds. *Political Parties and National Integration in Tropical Africa*. Berkeley, CA: University of California Press, 1970.

Fatton, Robert. *Predatory Rule: State and Civil Society in Africa*. Boulder, CO: Lynne Rienner, 1992.

Jackson, Robert H. and Carl G. Rosberg. *Personal Rule in Black Africa: Prince, Autocrat, Prophet, Tyrant*. Berkeley, CA: University of California Press, 1982.

Mawhood, Philip, ed. *Local Government in the Third World: The Experience of Tropical Africa*. Chichester: John Wiley & Sons, 1983.

Sandbrook, Richard. *The Politics of Africa's Economic Stagnation*. Cambridge: Cambridge University Press, 1985.

Weber, Max. The types of authority and imperative co-ordination. In: Talcott Parsons, ed. *The Theory of Social and Economic Organization*. New York: Free Press, 1964. 324–92.

Young, Crawford and Thomas Turner. *The Rise and Decline of the Zairian State*. Madison, WI: University of Wisconsin Press, 1985.

Zolberg, Aristide R. *Creating Political Order: The Party-States of West Africa*. Chicago, IL: Rand McNally & Company, 1966.

Notes and references

1 Weber, Max. The types of authority and imperative co-ordination. In: Talcott Parsons, ed. *The Theory of Social and Economic Organization*. New York: Free Press, 1964. 324–92.

2 Cited in Bayart, Jean-François. *The State in Africa: The Politics of the Belly*. London: Longman, 1993. 188.

3 George Washington's Farewell Address, 1796; and Nyerere, Julius K. *Spearhead*. 1961. Reprinted in Sigmund, Paul E., ed. *The Ideologies of the Developing Nations*. New York: Praeger, 1963. 201.

4 Hyden, Goran and Colin Leys. Elections and politics in single-party systems: the case of Kenya and Tanzania. *British Journal of Political Science*. 1972, 2(4), 396.

5 *Ibid*. 400.

6 Sylvester, Christine. Whither opposition in Zimbabwe? *Journal of Modern African Studies*. 1995, 33(3), 421.

7 Weber. The types of authority and imperative co-ordination. In: Parsons, ed. *The Theory of Social and Economic Organization*.

8 *Ibid*. 346–54. See also Medard, Jean-François. The underdeveloped state in Tropical Africa: political clientelism or neo-patrimonialism? In: Christopher Clapham, ed. *Private Patronage and Public Power*. London: Pinter, 1982. 178; And also Young, Crawford and Thomas Turner. *The Rise and Decline of the Zairian State*. Madison, WI: University of Wisconsin Press, 1985. 165.

9 Clapham, Christopher. *Third World Politics: An Introduction*. London: Routledge, 1985. 48.

10 Jackson, Robert H. and Carl G. Rosberg. *Personal Rule in Black Africa: Prince, Autocrat, Prophet, Tyrant*. Berkeley, CA: University of California Press, 1982.

11 Weber, Max. Feudalism, ständestaat and patrimonialism. In: Guenther Roth and Claus Wittich, eds. *Max Weber: Economy and Society*. Berkeley, CA: University of California Press, 1978. 1084.

12 Jackson and Rosberg. *Personal Rule in Black Africa*. 12.

13 Sandbrook, Richard, with Judith Barker. *The Politics of Africa's Economic Stagnation.* Cambridge: Cambridge University Press, 1985. 92.

14 Jackson and Rosberg. *Personal Rule in Black Africa.* 18.

15 Bayart. *State in Africa.* 174.

16 Clapham, Christopher. Clientelism and the state. In: *Private Patronage and Public Power.* 4.

17 *Ibid.* 31.

18 Legum, Colin, ed. *Africa Contemporary Record: Annual Survey and Documents 1972–73.* London: Rex Collings, 1973. B628.

19 Fanon, Frantz. *The Wretched of the Earth.* Harmondsworth: Penguin, 1967. 137.

20 Cited in Rondos, Alex. The team spirit in Ivory Coast. *West Africa.* 1980, 3274, 694.

21 See Zolberg, Aristide R. Ivory Coast. In: James S. Coleman and Carl G. Rosberg, eds. *Political Parties and National Integration in Tropical Africa.* Berkeley, CA: University of California Press, 1970. 83.

22 Zolberg, Aristide R. *Creating Political Order: The Party-States of West Africa.* Chicago, IL: Rand McNally & Company, 1976. 100.

23 Jackson and Rosberg. *Personal Rule in Black Africa.* 145.

24 Bakary, Tessilimi. Elite transformation and political succession. In: I. William Zartman and Christopher L. Delgardo, eds. *Political Economy of the Ivory Coast.* New York: Praeger, 1984. 24.

25 Cohen, Michael A. *Urban Policy and Political Conflict in Africa: A Study of the Ivory Coast.* Chicago, IL: University of Chicago Press, 1974. 89–90.

26 Cohen, Michael A. The myth of the expanding centre: politics in the Ivory Coast. *Journal of Modern African Studies.* 1973, 11(2), 231–45.

27 Cohen. *Urban Policy and Political Conflict in Africa.* 90–1.

28 Statistics taken from United Nations Conference on Trade and Development. *UNCTAD Handbook of Statistics 2014.* New York: United Nations, 2014. Tables 8.1, 8.4 and 3.2.D; World Bank data http://data.worldbank.org/indicator/SP.DYN.LE00.IN (accessed 24 July 2015) and http://data.worldbank.org/indicator/SP.DYN.IMRT.IN (accessed 24 July 2015); and UNESCO data www.uis.unesco.org/DataCentre/Pages/regions.aspx (accessed 24 July 2015).

29 Here I am paraphrasing Scott, James C. Patron–client politics and political change in Southeast Asia. *The American Political Science Review.* 1972, 66(1), 92.

7 Coercion

Military intervention in African politics

Chapter outline

- African military *coups d'état*
- Why has Africa experienced so many military coups?
- Problems facing military rulers
- The outcomes of military rule in Africa
- State and civil society
- Case study: Uganda's 1971 military coup
- Questions raised by this chapter
- Glossary of key terms
- Further reading
- Notes and references

A state's very existence rests on its authority. Where sufficient authority is present, citizens believe it is in their interests to respect state institutions and conform to their laws. The result is a stable political order where individuals defer to their government. Conversely, if a state loses its authority, confusion reigns, and established channels of conflict resolution decay. Groups take advantage of this situation, and compete with the failing elite, and with each other, in their attempts to mould a new political order. Such an environment often results in the political process being abandoned altogether, and violence ensuing.

Political authority stems from two basic sources: legitimate authority, and the power of coercion. The previous chapter discussed the concept of legitimacy, where citizens *voluntarily* defer to the state. As Max Weber pointed out, they may do this as a result of tradition, charismatic leadership, or as a mark of respect for legal-rational institutions.[1] In addition, legitimacy can be enhanced by a state's provision of material goods and services (the welfare state in Western Europe, for instance, or in Africa's case, provision through client–patron networks). In short, individuals are persuaded to support the state because of the positive benefits that they gain from this form of social organisation.

The other side of the authority coin, however, is coercion. Violence is a tool that that states can use to retain control over civil society even when there is an absence of legitimacy. The state's agencies of coercion can be unleashed against citizens in order to *force* them, rather than persuade them, to accept a certain political order. As civil society can rarely match these coercive resources, state violence, or the threat of such violence, will result in citizens obeying their political rulers for fear of what would happen if they did not. Coercion in this instance can therefore be defined as *the use or threat of violence to achieve a political or social purpose.*

The reality is that all states use a combination of these two basic sources of authority. In the West, legitimate authority is relied upon far more than coercion, but even here coercion is still utilised as a tool of government. Armies, police forces, courts and prisons, for example, will all be used to deter and punish lawbreakers. The rule of law has to be maintained, and, at times, violence may be required to ensure this. Elsewhere in the world, state coercion is more widespread, with violence readily being used as a substitute for legitimacy. This is often because state authority is being used to secure narrower group interests rather than the national interest. The ruling elite withholds goods and services that could have been used to generate legitimacy among citizens, and violence is deployed to maintain order instead. The fact remains, however, that whether they serve the many or the few, all states need institutions of coercion in order to preserve their authority.

This reality has proved to be of particular significance in the evolution of post-colonial African politics. Coercive agencies may be a necessity of government, but it is essential in democratic regimes that the military and the police, as the custodians of state violence, remain subservient to political leaders. This has not been the case in Africa. On numerous occasions, soldiers have used their access to violence to instigate military *coups d'état*. In effect, those who were employed to manage violence on behalf of the state chose to turn this violence on the state itself, in order to capture political power for themselves.

Given the frequency of these military coups, any book introducing the politics of post-colonial Africa has a duty to analyse this intervention in detail, and this is the task of the current chapter. Structurally, three vital questions are asked. First, why have so many coups occurred? Second, what problems arise when military, rather than civilian, personnel take up the reins of government? And third, what have been the outcomes of military rule? The answers to these three questions show how the military had few political rivals on the continent that could match their power. Yet toppling the old regime proved much easier than establishing an effective replacement government. The military soon found out that, despite their resources of coercion, government cannot be based solely on the capacity to inflict violence. Coercion may result in a population's acquiescence in the short term, but a more stable political order requires the state to generate legitimate authority as well. Most of Africa's military governments struggled to do this. Consequently, yet more political instability followed.

African military *coups d'état*

The military is an integral part of any government. Yet, as noted above, it is imperative, in a democratic society, that the military acts solely in the public interest. As soon as this immense power is used to further private interests, benefiting the military itself or an allied political elite, democracy is lost. Democratic (legal-rational) rules demand that the military is politically neutral, and its institutions are subordinate to civilian government.

Despite this professional ethic of impartiality and obeying civilian superiors, all security forces participate in the political process to some degree. Even in democracies, high-ranking officers are involved in making defence policy, as well as engaging with budgetary matters concerning the funding of their forces. Similarly, liberal democracies have also seen members of the military attain high office (examples include US president Dwight Eisenhower and French president Charles de Gaulle). The difference between professional soldiers with political ambitions in the West and their African counterparts, however, is the fact that officers such as de Gaulle and Eisenhower, before they took office, first resigned their military command. They then went on to participate in the electoral process, as civilians, conforming to democratic norms. In short, de Gaulle and Eisenhower relinquished their access to the coercive powers of the state before they competed for political power. African coup leaders, by contrast, became heads of state illegally. Usually, their sole credential for gaining political power was the threat of violence they could still exert as active military officers.

A military *coup d'état* can be defined as *a sudden illegal displacement of government in which members of the security forces play a prominent role*. Coups can be reactionary or revolutionary, bloody or bloodless. They must, however, be sudden, lasting a matter of hours or days, rather than weeks.[2] Military coups, in this respect, differ from other types of political succession. They should not be confused with regime change instigated by democratic election, foreign invasion, more widespread internal rebellion, or any combination of these.

There were 71 military *coups d'état* in Africa between 1952 and 1990. These resulted in the toppling of governments in 60 per cent of the continent's states (see Table 7.1). Some of these countries (such as Cape Verde and Equatorial Guinea) experienced just one coup, most were subjected to two or three, while other states (such as Benin, Burkina

Table 7.1 African military coups since independence

State	Date of independence	1950s/ 1960s	1970s	1980s	1990s	2000s	2010s	Total
Algeria	1962	1965			1992			2
Angola	1975							0
Benin	1960	1963 1965 1965 1967 1969	1972					6
Botswana	1966							0
Burkina Faso	1960	1966	1974	1980 1982 1983 1987			2014	7
Burundi	1962	1966	1976	1987	1996			4
Cameroon	1960							0
Cape Verde	1975							0
Central African Republic	1960	1965	1979	1981		2003		4
Chad	1960		1975					1
The Comoros	1975		1975 1978	1989	1999	2001		5
Congo, DRC	1960	1965						1
Congo, Rep.	1960	1963 1968	1977 1979					4
Côte d'Ivoire	1960							0
Djibouti	1977							0
Egypt	1922	1952 1954					2011 2013	4
Equatorial Guinea	1968		1979					1
Eritrea	1993							0
Ethiopia	—		1974					1

Table 7.1 African military coups since independence (Continued)

State	Date of independence	1950s/ 1960s	1970s	1980s	1990s	2000s	2010s	Total
Gabon	1960	1964						1
The Gambia	1965				1994			1
Ghana	1957	1966	1972 1978 1979	1981				5
Guinea	1958			1984		2008		2
Guinea–Bissau	1974			1980		2003	2012	3
Kenya	1963							0
Lesotho	1966			1986	1991 1993			3
Liberia	1847			1980				1
Libya	1951	1969						1
Madagascar	1960		1972					1
Malawi	1964							0
Mali	1960	1968			1991		2012	3
Mauritania	1960		1978	1980 1984		2005 2008		5
Mauritius	1968							0
Morocco	1956							0
Mozambique	1975							0
Namibia	1990							0
Niger	1960		1974		1996 1999		2010	4
Nigeria	1960	1966 1966	1975	1983 1985	1993			6
Rwanda	1962		1973					1
São Tomé and Principe	1975				1995			1
Senegal	1960							0
Seychelles	1976		1977					1
Sierra Leone	1961	1967 1968			1992 1996 1997			5
Somalia	1960	1969						1
South Africa	1910							0
Sudan	1956	1958 1964 1969		1985 1989				5
Swaziland	1968							0
Tanzania	1964							0
Togo	1960	1963 1967 1967						3
Tunisia	1956							0
Uganda	1962		1971 1979	1980 1985				4
Zambia	1964							0
Zimbabwe	1980							0
Total		29	22	20	14	6	6	88

Faso, Ghana and Nigeria) were locked into a regular rhythm of coup and counter-coup. Exaggerating, to reflect the mood of this era when military rule became the norm instead of the exception, US diplomat George Ball wrote in his memoirs: 'During the years I was in the State Department, I was awakened once or twice a month by a telephone call in the middle of the night announcing a coup d'état in some distant capital with a name like a typographical error'.[3] Relief from these military takeovers only came in the 1990s. During this decade, the number of coups reduced significantly, with regime change now more likely to be prompted by mass rebellion or democratic elections.

The pattern was familiar in the 1960s, 1970s and 1980s. A faction of the military, usually led by middle-ranking or junior officers, or very occasionally by non-commissioned officers, would seize government buildings and communication centres, and then detain the president and the cabinet or force them to flee. Once these symbols of the state had been captured, the coup plotters would then use the radio station to broadcast to the nation. They explained how the civilian government's corruption and ineptitude had made it the military's duty to intervene, and they promised to withdraw to barracks as soon as a just and disciplined society had been restored. In this respect, African military coups were relatively peaceful affairs. Casualties were usually confined to the small participating factions, while many were entirely bloodless. This was because few in society were prepared to defend the outgoing, usually illegitimate, administrations. Other forms of regime change in Africa, such as insurgency campaigns or civil war, or even

Plate 7.1 Sudanese troops relax in Khartoum following the 1969 coup that installed General Gaafar al Numeiry as president.

democratic elections, have often prompted far more violence. The military *coup d'état* was quick and simple: 'Get the keys to the armoury; turn out the barracks; take the radio station, the post office and the airport; [and] arrest the person of the president…'.[4]

Given the impact that the military has had on post-colonial African politics, it is right that this book should investigate these *coups d'état* in detail. It should also be noted, however, that such an analysis does tend to mislead, bolstering a 'continent of coups' stereotype. The military may be influential in Africa, but at no time have they enjoyed a total, continent-wide monopoly over the political process. Sixty per cent of African states experienced military rule at some point between independence and 1990, but this obviously means that 40 per cent did not. Morocco and Mauritius, for example, have remained under civilian control for the entire post-colonial period, as have Kenya and Tanzania and Southern African states. Even those countries that did succumb to military rule often enjoyed long periods of civilian government, either prior to the takeover or after the army had returned to barracks. The Gambia, for example, maintained a multi-party democracy for 30 years before a coup in 1994. In short, it should be borne in mind when reading this chapter that not all African countries are, or have always been, the domain of a uniformed dictator.

Why has Africa experienced so many military coups?

All coups involve a short circuit of the 'normal' political process, creating an opportunity for violence to become the deciding factor. The military takes advantage of this opportunity, and captures the state for itself. It has proved difficult, however, to draw accurate comparisons beyond this simple reality. This is because every military *coup d'état* is different. They affect all forms of government (democracies, personal regimes, and even existing military administrations), they are a consequence of different motives (altruistic nationalism, selfish desire or ideological zeal), and they result in numerous types of rule (autocratic/democratic, liberal/socialist, conservative/revolutionary, and many that defy simple categorisation). Yet, since military coups have influenced so many political systems across the globe, political scientists have tried hard to isolate common factors that lead to these regime displacements.

One such typology of *coups d'état* involves three categories: the 'guardian coup', the 'veto coup' and the 'breakthrough coup'.[5] In a guardian coup, the military intervenes in order to rescue the state from civilian mismanagement. The men in uniform consider it their patriotic duty to replace their incompetent civilian predecessors. Under the military 'guardians', corruption and inefficiency are targeted, and politicians of the old regime are purged. In many cases, the military then (eventually) live up to their promise of returning to barracks, once they consider that discipline has returned to the political process. Despite this political upheaval, the 'guardians' usually leave society and the economy largely unchanged. Nigeria, for example, could be considered to have experienced several guardian coups in the post-colonial period.

Veto coups, on the other hand, are prompted by social changes that directly threaten the interests of the military and their allies. The security forces calculate that they cannot stand idly by while a new group in society takes over the state. This type of coup has been more common in Central and South America, where the military has prevented Leftist movements from capturing state power, but Africa has examples, too. The 1992 and 2013 takeovers in Algeria and Egypt, respectively, can be classed as veto coups. Here the secular military intervened because it feared the outcome of multi-party elections. In both cases, Islamist movements were poised to exercise political power that they had won, or were about to win. The military, concerned about its position within such a regime, opted to eliminate this risk, aborted the democratic process, and took power itself.

The last of these three broad categories is the breakthrough coup. This is where the military ousts an outdated (authoritarian or traditional) regime, seeking to change society entirely. The *coup d'état* becomes a revolutionary break from the past. In effect, the army becomes the 'vanguard' of this revolution. Ethiopia experienced a breakthrough coup in 1974, when the military, allied to other movements, established a socialist state in the wake of Emperor Haile Selassie's 44 years of 'traditional' rule.

This simple typology of coups, however, has to be expanded. Political scientists have dug deeper in an attempt to explain why military takeovers occur, and two major schools of thought have come to dominate. The first group of scholars emphasise the state's socio-political environment. These 'environmentalists', such as Samuel Huntington and Samuel E. Finer, argue that *coups d'état* are most likely to occur in states that lack institutionalised political cultures, which also suffer economic hardship and social division.[6] The second school of thought focuses more on the organisational ability and character of the military itself. Academics such as Morris Janowitz point to the patriotism, discipline, professionalism and cohesion found at the heart of military service. He argues that these factors eventually compel soldiers to intervene to rid their state of inept and corrupt civilian governments.[7]

It seems artificial to separate these two contributing factors. Military coups occur in Africa, first, because the socio-political environment encourages this, and second, because there exist on the continent military establishments which are organised and motivated enough to take advantage of this situation. Moreover, patriotism and professionalism are not the sole determining factors. Soldiers also rebel to further their *own* corporate and personal interests.

Ultimately, the military intervenes in the political process because it can. In terms of coercive power, soldiers control the most puissant institutions of the state. They are, after all, the individuals who have direct access to instruments of state violence. Many coups may be bloodless, but this should not disguise the fact that the military has the organisational ability and technology to take on any other group within the state, or, indeed, within civil society. Consequently, if the military is willing to use violence to secure political goals, few can stand in its way. Yet this fact alone does not explain why military coups have occurred so often in Africa. Globally, the vast majority of modern states maintain armies, but only a few of these have broken their professional ethic of non-intervention.

This is why Huntington and Finer argue that the military needs not only the ability but also the right socio-political environment before it is persuaded to intervene. Particularly relevant, in this respect, is the fact that most African economies throughout the post-colonial period failed to meet expectations of development. This often left Africans discontented, and it damaged levels of legitimacy. Ruth First, for example, argues that Kwame Nkrumah's regime was brought down by the plummeting price of cocoa in the mid-1960s, just as much as it was by Ghana's army and police force.[8] Similarly, social division, especially the ethnic and class conflicts discussed earlier, in Chapters 3 and 4, will also act to destabilise many African governments.

Then there is the question of political culture. Due to their social and economic problems, African states need strong institutions to manage the political conflict found on the continent. As was seen in Chapter 6, however, African regimes tend more towards personal rule rather than towards legal-rational structures. Consequently, most Africans are excluded from the political process. This puts the continent into Finer's category of 'minimal political culture', as opposed to the 'mature political cultures' of the West.[9] As such, African regimes are left particularly vulnerable to crises of legitimacy, when these emerge.

In the West, legal-rational channels of political renewal can be utilised to address political crises, whether these are constitutional, social or economic in origin. For example, a general election can be called, a coalition government formed, or a constitutional dispute referred to the courts. The political system can absorb these shocks, and the conflict can be resolved peacefully and rationally. In pre-1990s Africa, however, with no electoral mechanisms available to ensure a stable change of government, non-violent regime renewal was not available. And as soon as violence becomes the defining mechanism of regime change, the military, with its superior access to the resources of coercion, becomes a key political player. As Huntington argued, in a state that lacks authority, competing social groups employ

> means which reflect [their] peculiar nature and capabilities. The wealthy bribe; students riot; workers strike; mobs demonstrate; and the military coup. In the absence of accepted procedures, all these forms of direct action are found on the political scene. The techniques of military intervention are simply more dramatic and effective than the others because, as Hobbes put it, 'When nothing else is turned up, clubs are trumps'.[10]

This is where Huntington's and Finer's environmental causes of coups run into Janowitz's emphasis on the character and professional ethics of the military. With a crisis of legitimacy threatening the very existence of the nation-state, soldiers feel that they have to act. The military is not only a strong institution within the state because of its capacity to invoke violence; armed forces are usually also highly organised, cohesive, loyal and hierarchical organisations. Their command structure ensures that a disciplined army can get things done. This is why the military holds failing civilian governments in contempt. In this respect, Janowitz talks of the army's 'ethos of public service' and 'national identity', which combines 'managerial ability with a heroic posture'.[11] The military is forced to intervene in the political process as no other group can govern effectively. The patriotism and nationalism that keep the military away from the machinery of political administration in Western states are the same characteristics that require officers to rebel in African countries. A body entrusted with the defence of the realm cannot sit idly by while civilians destroy the state as effectively as any invading army could. Under such circumstances, a 'guardian coup' ensues.

There is no doubt that the characteristics of the military can certainly encourage rebellion when a government's legitimacy is lost, but, again, this does not entirely explain why the military intervenes. Almost all African countries have experienced economic and social problems in the post-colonial period, yet not all of them have encountered military takeovers. Similarly, the 'guardian coup' is often too romantic a concept to explain actual events. The army does not always operate solely in the *national* interest. In the final analysis, a coup will only occur if members of the military feel it is in *their* interests to overthrow political leaders. Certainly they command the organisational ability and technology to do this, and need to be prompted by the right social environment, but, ultimately, military takeovers stem from the military's own interests.

In this respect, despite its professional ethics, the military in Africa has to be regarded as just another faction of the ruling elite. Indeed, Christopher Clapham describes it as the 'armed wing of the bureaucratic bourgeoisie'.[12] Due to the continent's lack of legal-rational institutions, the military has to compete to protect its own corporate interests among the day-to-day political manoeuvrings of other factions within the state. The military simply cannot afford to divorce itself from this political exchange, as nobody else will protect its interests within the political cauldron where all groups are seeking to maximise their share of state power. As a result, from time to time the military may have to put pressure on civilian groups to recognise its demands. This pressure may turn into a full-scale military coup if the men and women in uniform feel that their interests are so threatened that the only way to protect them is actually to take over the state itself.

Typical threats to the military's welfare include cuts in the defence budget and a restriction of the army's organisational autonomy. The 1994 Gambian coup, for example, came in the wake of barrack food and accommodation problems, and pay not getting through to Gambian peace-keeping units serving in Liberia. The Gambian army's most pressing grievance, however, was the continued presence of seconded Nigerian personnel serving as commanding officers. Gambian soldiers wanted the opportunity to run their own military.[13] They achieved this goal when junior officers overthrew President Dawda Jawara's 29-year-old multi-party state in 1994. Earlier, the 1968 coup in Mali was prompted by President Modibo Keita's establishment of a separate special forces unit. Keita assembled this brigade as a personal presidential guard to specifically act as a counterweight to the regular army. As this move threatened to dramatically weaken the military's position within state structures, a *coup d'état* followed. It is possible, in this respect, to identify a corporate imperative motivating most coups.

As a final note in this examination of why Africa has experienced so many military interventions, the foreign aspect of these coups needs to be briefly acknowledged. Although African *coups d'état* were largely a product of domestic politics, international agents also occasionally played a role. British troops, for example, helped to quell army mutinies in East Africa during the early years of independence, while the US Central Intelligence Agency was also active on the continent (if not on the same scale as it was in Central and South America). It was France, however, that intervened most in African politics. Several coups were supported by Paris, while others were defeated by French influence. For example, Gabon saw the French Foreign Legion restore the government of Léon M'ba after it had been ousted in a military *coup d'état* in 1964, while, conversely, the 1979 military overthrow of Emperor Bokassa of the Central African Republic closely resembled a French invasion, rather than just a local military coup (this after previous governments in Paris had protected the Bokassa regime). France's interaction with a more recent 2010–14 spate of military coups in West Africa brought similar mixed strategies of intervention. Indeed, in the post-Cold War period, foreign condemnation of military coups has proved more vocal, and external intervention more likely. Such evidence suggests that plotters would be wise to first assess the likely reaction of key international agents before instigating a *coup d'état*. This theme of international intervention in the African political process is expanded in Chapter 8.

Problems facing military rulers

Few Africans missed their deposed governments once the military had intervened. Indeed, with their apparent discipline and sense of national purpose, the men in uniform were often welcomed. Certainly, military regimes, with their simple hierarchical structures in which officials are expected to obey orders rather than bargain over policies, had a head start in tackling problems such as bureaucratic corruption and inefficiency. The notion that soldiers can bring parade-ground precision to institutions of government, however, proved to be somewhat optimistic. In reality, the military introduced an additional set of problems to the administration of post-colonial African states.

The obvious predicament faced by all military regimes is the fact that a precedent has been set. Now, with the professional ethic of non-intervention violated, future generations of officers consider themselves to be quite within their rights to topple governments they judge to be acting against the national interest, or, indeed, against the military's own corporate interests. The threat of a counter-coup is very real, even to an existing military government. Officers leading the *junta*, therefore, have always to sate their colleagues left in barracks. Austerity drives initiated by the ruling army council to stabilise economies, for example, would not usually include army cuts (for fear of how junior officers might react). Despite this accommodation, several African countries fell victim to a succession of coups and counter-coups during the post-colonial period. Once the military has taken the initial decision to intervene in the political process, it is very difficult to keep future generations of soldiers confined to barracks.

The second basic problem that the military had in ruling was that soldiers had little training for, or experience of, government. Army organisational structures were not sufficiently sophisticated to manage an entire state. Coup leaders soon realised that it was much easier to topple a government than it was to build its successor. To endure, military governments therefore had to learn the arts of political persuasion quickly, deploying these alongside their more familiar skills of coercion. The army's natural ally, in this respect, was the civilian bureaucracy. Although the African military usurped politicians, they nearly always retained the bureaucrats who had served under the previous administration. After all, these individuals had experience of the day-to-day running of the country. Indeed, having purged *selected* politicians, coup leaders then often invited opposition figures, or even individual former cabinet ministers, into their own regime (those representing a particular ethnic group, maybe). Ultimately, the army could not cope without these professional bureaucrats and politicians. They were required as a substitute for the military's own deficiencies in the practice of politics and public administration. This is why it is often misleading to talk of post-coup governments as strictly 'military regimes'. They were more often hybrids consisting of both civilian and army personnel.

The third key dilemma faced by the military when they took power was the problem of legitimacy. Like all political leaders, these officers had to build and maintain links with civil society. Since those who seized power were usually few in number, their links to the rest of society were limited. As a result, they had to set about reviving or replacing the client–patron networks of the old regime. Again, this often involved co-opting major patrons from the previous administration. Normally, new regimes were initially popular because they ousted the former corrupt elites, but once the honeymoon period was over, legitimising links to civil society became vital for ensuring the stability of government. Yet as soon as the military started dealing with established social groups within the country, or reviving the old clientelism, the old inefficiencies of political bargaining returned.

Then there was the question of delivering promises. In their initial radio broadcasts to the nation, the military talked of curbing corruption and developing the economy. This was easier said than done. Effectively, a successful military administration had to produce more from the same resources that had been available to the previous regime. Military coups occurred in the first place because of dire socio-economic conditions, and this situation did not change simply because soldiers were now in control. Inefficient government in Africa stemmed from ethnic balancing, the servicing of a bureaucratic bourgeoisie, and client–patron networks generally. Once they occupied the presidential palace, the military soon found out why the old regime had tolerated these political relationships. Support from these social groups was required to maintain political order. Again, it is easier to overthrow a bad government than it is to create a good one.

The final key dilemma the military faced when it captured power related to what exactly the men in uniform were going to do in the future. Should they hold elections and return to barracks immediately? If they were going to form a caretaker administration, in order to build the 'right environment' for a just society, how long should they stay in power? Should the leaders of the coup resign their commissions and carry out their political duties as civilians? Alternatively, they could use the army as a support base, but recruit from wider civil society, to create a new mass participatory one-party state. Most coups were instigated in Africa without their participants first devising a clear blueprint for the future. Once they took power, however, the army had to find answers to all the above questions rapidly.

The outcomes of military rule in Africa

Just as the reasons behind each military coup are different, so are the outcomes of these events. No one type of regime results. Soldiers preside over administrations as diverse, both in nature and in success, as their civilian counterparts. Sometimes the ideals behind an original takeover, especially in the case of guardian or breakthrough coups, resulted in very distinct governments. More often, however, with the military forced to forge close links with the bureaucracy and wider civil society, these regimes came to resemble their civilian predecessors (personal rulers and client–patron networks included).

One common outcome of military rule was that, once in power, soldiers tended to increase public spending on themselves. Military budgets rose noticeably in post-coup Africa. Initially, the corporate interests that prompted the coup in the first place were addressed. Then, those in government had to look after their colleagues left in barracks, for fear of a counter-coup. Pay, conditions and the equipment of the armed forces improved markedly. Ghana's defence spending, for example, increased by 22 per cent after 1966. This was despite ongoing economic hardship that resulted in social services to the countryside being cut by 28 per cent in the same period.[14]

Using the simple typology introduced earlier, guardian coups went one of two ways in post-coup Africa: either intermediate or longer-term military rule. Immediately after taking power, the 'guardians' in both cases vowed to return to barracks when an appropriate political order had been restored. A few did this. Ghana, for example, demilitarised its government in 1969 and 1979. Nigeria, too, went through this hand-back process in 1979 and 1999. Yet the military do not abdicate political influence at this point, reaffirming their professional ethic of non-interference. They remain in the background as self-appointed 'political referees'. The military, after all, determined the rules of the game while in power, having drafted the new constitution that the civilian successor regimes have to abide by. Likewise, once the direct 'caretaker' phase is over, the military also reserve the right to retake control, via yet another coup, if civilian successors fail their probation. And apparently most do fail in the eyes of the soldiers. Several

African states were locked into a repetitive cycle of civilian and military regimes from the 1960s through to the 1990s. Military power is never far from the surface in this particular type of former guardian coup country.

Other guardian coup states endured longer-term military rule. Despite their 'guardian' pretensions, most post-colonial African military regimes simply refused to hand back power voluntarily. Caretaker governments commonly evolved into more permanent institutions, resulting in the military–civilian hybrid regimes discussed later in this chapter.

Breakthrough coups often have slightly different outcomes. The regimes that result from them abandon old political structures altogether, and attempt to create their own institutions building links between the state and civil society. More often than not, a new (single) party is established. This becomes the tool to unite the army and the masses, and, apparently, to instil a new national spirit and a society in which development will emerge from graft and discipline. People's militias and people's courts are also part of this process. The early years of Mariam Mengistu's Ethiopia are a good illustration of a military-led 'revolution' (see also Thomas Sankara and Jerry Rawlings's military-populist ideologies recounted earlier in Chapter 3). Yet even breakthrough regimes fall foul of Africa's underlying political realities. The new mass party, for example, often atrophies as its civilian counterparts did before it. After all, Africa's single parties existed more to heighten a sense of participation for civil society, rather than to provide a mechanism to allow the masses to actually become involved in the making of public policy. Given these circumstances, it is easy for these 'radical breakthrough' governments to descend into centralised personal rule, in which client–patron networks become the predominant mechanism of political exchange.

Post-colonial Africa saw the vast majority of its military coups, whether their pretensions were guardian, breakthrough or veto, result in a stalemate between civilian and military power. Armed forces felt no compulsion to keep out of the political process, yet they could not rule effectively without civilian support. The outcomes were hybrid governments. Military leaders were forced to 'civilianise' themselves to a degree, co-opting individuals from the old regime in order to maintain control, but, in Kunle Amuwo's words, as soon as the soldiers waded into the 'murky water of politics', they found themselves 'more or less submerged in the internal dynamics of civil society'.[15] Similarly, the restraints of the international economy were no less pressing simply because the president now wore a uniform. The average performance of Africa's post-colonial military regimes, in this respect, proved to be no more successful than that of their civilian counterparts.

State and civil society

In terms of this book's central theme of analysing the relationship between state and civil society, military coups did little to alter the overall balance between these two parties. On the state side of the equation, however, these *coups d'état* were dramatic. Military intervention helped to 'speed the circulation of élites and the realignment of factions'.[16] In this respect, military coups were a reflection of the internal jockeying for power among the bureaucratic bourgeoisie discussed in Chapter 5. It was simply that, since soldiers had greater access to the state's resources of violence, it was the military, the 'armed wing' of this ruling elite, which usually came to dominate. Once they had taken power, however, the ruling officers were usually forced to accommodate at least some of

Table 7.2 Chapter summary: a typology of military coups

Types of military coup	
Guardian coup	• Military intervenes with claims to rescue state from civilian mismanagement
	• Corruption and inefficiency targeted by new regime (e.g. Nigeria)
Veto coup	• Military intervenes to prevent social development from damaging its corporate interests
	• Prevents targeted social groups from taking power (e.g. Algeria)
Breakthrough coup	• Military intervenes to help oust out-of-date traditional regime
	• Results in revolutionary social change (e.g. Ethiopia)
Precipitants of coups	
Ability of the military	• Military have control of a state's resources of violence, enabling a coup
Correct political/social/ economic conditions	• Socio-political conflict and poor economic conditions create a favourable environment for a coup
Suitable political culture	• Coups occur in states where there are weak legal-rational democratic structures
Professional ethic of the military	• Military may be motivated to intervene if a government is demonstrating a lack of discipline or acting against the national interest
Self-interest	• Coups will occur when the interests of the military, or a faction of the military, are served
Outcomes of military coups	
Problems facing the military	• Precedent of military intervention set; possibility of counter-coup
	• Little experience of running government
	• Lack of legitimacy
	• Pre-coup socio-economic challenges still remain
Results of military rule	• Increase in the military budget
	• Links between military and old bureaucracy forged
	• Populist drives and policies in an attempt to build legitimacy

the factions active within the former civilian regime. It was only with the support of these powerful factions (ethnic, regional, economic, bureaucratic, etc.) that the military government could retain power. Again, this illustrates the fact that, beyond the short term, the power of coercion alone cannot underpin government.

In terms of civil society, the vast majority of military coups did little to alleviate the exploitation of groups outside the state within post-colonial Africa. In most cases, the men in uniform, just like their civilian predecessors, failed to involve the masses in the political process. 'Breakthrough' administrations came closest to doing this, but even here it was largely a state elite that retained control. And, as long as political administrations remained under the control of a bureaucratic bourgeoisie, personal rule and clientelism remained substitutes for more positive methods of generating legitimacy. Corruption and inefficiency were the consequence of this, leaving Africans under military governments no better off than those ruled by civilians. It was not until civil society itself, rather than the army, began to regulate regime change (in the 1990s, through multi-party elections) that African states became more responsive and accountable to their people.

Case study: Uganda's 1971 military coup

Uganda sits on a massive plateau in eastern Central Africa. It is a lush and fertile country, with large freshwater lakes and a number of towering mountains. This country's physical beauty, however, was not reflected by standards of political rule during the independence period. Indeed, to the outside world, one particular Ugandan regime, that of Idi Amin Dada, confirmed stereotypes of the perceived instability and brutality of Africa's post-colonial politics. This case study investigates the 1971 military *coup d'état* that brought Amin to power, plotting both its origins and its outcomes.

Immediately prior to imperial rule, this part of East Africa was home to the polity of Buganda, along with a number of other smaller kingdoms. In 1891, the British East Africa Company signed a treaty with the Kabaka (king) of Buganda, bringing the territory under European administration. When this company collapsed as a consequence of financial problems, the British government itself took over, and Buganda became a formal British protectorate in 1894. Two years later, the neighbouring kingdoms of Bunyoro, Toro, Ankole and Bugosa also gained a similar status. All these territories would later be consolidated, with Buganda, to form the inclusive state of Uganda.

The colonial authorities, however, failed to build a single nation from these separate political units during the 70 years of imperial rule. This left a pressing problem at independence. How would Buganda sit within the post-colonial Ugandan state? Bugandans saw their future as separate from the rest of Uganda. Indeed, the British exiled the Kabaka after he instigated a campaign demanding that Buganda be granted its independence as a distinct sovereign state. The removal of the Kabaka, however, did not quell the demand for Bugandan autonomy. Protests on this issue ensured that 95 per cent of Bugandans heeded the call to boycott Uganda's 1961 (pre-independence) national assembly elections.[17]

This boycott persuaded the British colonial authorities to end the Kabaka's exile, and to suggest that Buganda enjoy a semi-federal status after decolonisation. On his return, the Kabaka Yekka royalist party was established, and, in an alliance with the Uganda People's Congress (led by Milton Obote), it won a majority in the elections that paved the way to independence in 1962. This coalition formed Uganda's first post-colonial government, with the Kabaka as president and Obote serving as prime minister. This alliance, however, proved to be fragile.

Ugandan politics, in the nine-year period between independence and Amin's military coup, was marked by an ongoing power struggle among Uganda's political elite. Factional politics were the dominant feature. First, Obote wrestled power away from the Kabaka, with the help of Amin and the military. Then the military itself asserted its power, eventually toppling the Obote regime in January 1971.

Using the Office of the Prime Minister as his power base, Milton Obote followed the well-worn path of post-colonial African politics by centralising the state. One-party rule was Obote's goal, with his own Uganda People's Congress (UPC) as the 'one party'. In this respect, the Kabaka and his Kabaka Yekka movement, as rival sources of political power, had to be eliminated. This is exactly what happened. By the mid-1960s, Obote had persuaded several Bugandan politicians to defect to the UPC, with rewards of patronage. Remaining sources of opposition suffered state intimidation. Yet, in pushing through this centralisation programme, Obote alienated many in Uganda. In E.A. Brett's assessment, 'By the end of 1965 Obote was confronted by so much opposition that he would have certainly lost the next elections. He responded by building a base in the army and eliminating this opposition by force'.[18]

The power struggle between the Kabaka and Obote came to a head in 1966. Obote received intelligence that Shaban Opolot, a Kabaka loyalist and the commander of the Ugandan national army, was moving units loyal to the prime minister away from Kampala. This was interpreted as paving the way for military action on behalf of the Kabaka. Obote acted quickly. He made himself president, cancelled the forthcoming elections, and sent Amin, a colonel in the Ugandan army at this time, to arrest the Kabaka. The Kabaka's palace was overrun, which earned Amin promotion to the post of Obote's Chief of Staff.

As well as destroying the Kabaka's power base, this action also resulted in the political neutralisation of Brigadier Opolot. Obote sidelined Opolot into an advisory role, with Amin taking over the army's operational duties. A year later, constitutional amendments were added to Obote's political manoeuvrings. He used his majority in Parliament to revoke Buganda's semi-federal standing, creating a unitary state. With this act, Obote's consolidation of power was complete.

Obote's reliance on coercive force, however, proved to be his downfall. In his efforts to eliminate constitutional opposition, he had strengthened the hand of the state's agencies of violence. The military itself now became a prominent player in Ugandan politics. The result was yet another power struggle within Uganda's ruling elite, with Obote pitted against Amin's faction of the army. This struggle was settled in January 1971, when Amin led a *coup d'état*, taking advantage of Obote's absence at a Commonwealth conference in Singapore.

How, then, should Amin's putsch be accounted for? Is the theoretical analysis of African coups discussed in the main text of this chapter relevant to this specific case? Were the key factors of ability, environment, organisation and motivation present in Uganda at this time? The events of January 1971 certainly prove that the Ugandan army was capable of mounting a military coup. At independence, the small Ugandan army, with its origins in the British colonial King's African Rifles, gained symbolic importance as the defender of the state's newly won sovereignty. The Ugandan army's political significance, however, was more than just symbolic. As Obote was forced to rely heavily on the military to underpin his power, large sums of public money were invested in the army (10 per cent of the national budget, compared with 7 per cent in Kenya and 4 per cent in Tanzania). Uganda's military personnel grew in number, from 700 in 1962 to 7,000 by 1969.[19] By 1971, the Ugandan army clearly had the resources to take on other factions within Uganda's political elite. Consequently, the first prerequisite for any potential military coup was in place.

Military coups, however, as was seen above, are precipitated by far more than a well-equipped army with organisational capabilities. They also require an appropriate economic, social and political environment. Uganda experienced troubles in all three of these areas during the 1960s. As well as Buganda's demands for autonomy, for example, other ethnic groups also stressed their separate identities. Uganda, in this respect, fell far short of being a politically harmonious nation-state. This situation led to unrest. Obote's clashes with the Kabaka, and his moves to centralise the state, left few channels open for constitutional opposition. Opportunities for institutionalised dissent, operating as a 'safety valve', were thus effectively absent in Ugandan politics by the mid-1960s. Even Obote's so-called 'Move to the Left' later in the decade, by which the president attempted to gain legitimacy for his regime by introducing populist and socialist reforms, failed to win Obote the people's respect.

The scene was set. The background requirements for a coup, namely the right economic, social and political environment, and a sufficiently resourced and organised army, were in place. All that was needed now was a motive for the military, or a faction of the military, to intervene. This spur came in the form of a personal threat to Amin's position within the state. The power struggle between Obote and his chief of staff reached a climax in January 1971. One of them had to go, and Amin struck first.

After Colonel Amin had become chief of staff, he sought to consolidate his status within the military, and the state in general. He promoted personnel from his own political stronghold of the North, court-martialling rivals from the South. Obote, however, acknowledging the power that his chief of staff had accumulated, tried to reduce his reliance on Amin's faction of the army. He sought to do this by expanding his own personal special forces units. This attempt to marginalise the army, combined with Obote's order to disband a military division loyal to Amin, created a flashpoint. Amin was also under suspicion of murdering Brigadier Okoya, an Obote loyalist and Amin's potential replacement as head of the army. The investigation of Amin for this murder, ordered by the president himself, and rumours of the chief of staff's imminent sacking, forced Amin's hand. He took advantage of Obote's absence and replaced him as head of state. Having come so far, gaining high office and all the rewards that this brought, Amin was unwilling to submit to Obote's command, as this would mean suffering demotion, imprisonment, exile or worse. This personal motivation was the last element to fall into place, prompting the *coup d'état*.

Despite the initial popularity that Amin gained from ridding Uganda of Obote's rule, and the fact that, in his first broadcast to the nation, he promised to hold democratic elections within five years, Amin's regime proved catastrophic for Uganda's political, social and economic development. Amin dealt with the key dilemma that all military regimes face by simply ignoring it. He made little attempt to build institutions or links with civil society in order to legitimise his government. Instead, he relied heavily on the state's powers of coercion. The national assembly was dissolved, with Amin ruling by decree; military tribunals replaced judicial hearings; and military personnel were employed as provincial governors. In one of his more absurd acts, Amin, seeking the 'Africanisation' of Uganda, simply exiled practically the whole of the country's economically significant Asian community. British economic interests in Uganda were also nationalised. Any opposition, or even any *potential* opposition, to the regime was brutally eliminated. Amin's personal 'Public Safety Unit' was kept busy perpetrating many of the hundreds of thousands of politically motivated murders committed between 1971 and 1979.

Plate 7.2 President Idi Amin Dada of Uganda addressing his troops, 1978. Photographer: William Campbell.

Only the army itself benefited from Amin's rule. As with most military governments, the army expanded dramatically after the coup. In 1971, there were 7,680 soldiers in Uganda; by 1974 this figure had risen to 20,000.[20] The military now enjoyed immense power within Ugandan society. It appropriated what it desired, and exercised summary justice when it saw fit. Half of the wealth left by the exiled Asian community, for example, found its way into military hands.[21] Yet being a soldier was not a particularly safe occupation during the Amin years. The military was repeatedly purged of potential opposition by its commanding officers, with many soldiers of Acholi or Langi ethnic backgrounds being massacred. Military factions competed for power, and there was intense distrust between senior and junior ranks. Indeed, towards the end of Amin's rule, the country came under the control of a number of army warlords.

Eventually the factional fighting became so intense that Amin had to order an invasion of northern Tanzania in order to restore army unity. He hoped that fighting this border war would unite his military. Instead, it proved to be his downfall. The Tanzanian army responded by repelling this invasion with ease, and then marched on Kampala itself. Fighting alongside Ugandan dissidents, the Tanzanian force finally succeeded in removing Amin in 1979. Although Amin's government was always weak, having never tried to legitimise its rule through linking state and civil society, its use of the state's powers of coercion had secured for the military the reins of power for eight brutal years. It is a classic case study of how much easier it is for the military to remove a government than it is for it to govern itself.

Bringing Uganda's post-colonial history up to date, the 1980s was also a lost decade for Uganda in terms of economic and political development. Obote's UPC was returned to power through elections held on the eve of the withdrawal of the Tanzanian army. The UPC, however, once again failed to unite the country. Indeed, it is estimated that a further 100,000 Ugandans died in political violence between 1980 and a second military coup which took place in 1985.[22] The instability that this coup caused assisted Yoweri Museveni's insurgent force, the National Resistance Army, to take Kampala a year later. The National Resistance Movement (NRM) has been in power since, during which time economic stability has returned, as has a greater respect for human rights. Indeed, despite its policy of 'no-party government', and evidence of the intimidation of opposition politicians, Museveni's regime was initially held up as an example of good government by both the World Bank and Western governments. Latterly, however, this reputation has become tarnished due to constitutional manoeuvring (abolishing term limits to permit Museveni to remain in power), further intimidation of opposition groups, and alleged election irregularities perpetrated by the ruling NRM. Despite this deterioration of Museveni's reputation, however, what the NRM has achieved is the breaking of the cycle of coup and counter-coup. The military has not enjoyed power in Uganda since 1985.

Uganda[23]

Territory:	241,139 sq. km.	Independence:	1962
Colonial power:	Britain	Ethnic groups:	Baganda
Major cities:	Kampala (capital)		Basoga
	Jinja		Banyankole
	Mbale	Urban population:	15 per cent
Languages:	English	Life expectancy:	59 years
	Kiswahili	Adult literacy:	73 per cent
	Luganda	Exports:	Coffee
Infant mortality:	44 deaths/1,000 live births		Telecommunications
Religion:	Traditional		equipment
	Christian		Fish
Currency:	Ugandan shilling		Tobacco
GDP per capita:	US$598		Lime and cement
Population:	37.6 million		

Questions raised by this chapter

1. To what extent can African military coups be explained by environmental (socio-economic/political culture) factors?
2. Did the professional characteristics of the military force it to intervene in Africa's political process?
3. Can African military coups be accounted for by the personal interests of soldiers?
4. What problems do military governments face once they come to power?
5. How would you rate the performance of military regimes in post-colonial Africa?

Glossary of key terms

Breakthrough coup   A coup where the military acts in the vanguard of a revolution, replacing tradition political institutions with more radical structures of government.

Coercive power   The use or threat of violence to achieve a political or social purpose.

Coup d'état   A sudden illegal displacement of government in which members of the security forces play a prominent role.

Guardian coup   A coup where the military ousts a failing government, allegedly in the national interest.

Political authority   A psychological relationship between the governed and their governors, which engenders a belief that state personnel and institutions should be obeyed.

Political culture   Commonly held political ideas, attitudes and behaviour that permeate a society.

Veto coup   A coup where the military intervenes to arrest political transition, protecting its corporate interests.

Further reading

For those interested in the causes of military coups, Samuel Huntington (environmental causes), Morris Janowitz (organisational characteristics) and Samuel E. Finer (political culture) delimit the original debate on this issue. Samuel Decalo's book is more up to date on this subject, and confines itself to the African continent. Also worth reading are two articles: one by Arnold Hughes and Roy May, and the other by David Goldsworthy. They both take an inverted look at the military in Africa, asking why the army has *not* intervened in a large minority of African states. As to the problems that military governments face once they have taken power, and the outcomes of this rule, a good starting point once again is Samuel Decalo's book, as well as the book edited by Christopher Clapham and George Philip. For a case study, Amii Omara-Otunnu provides an excellent narrative on the role of the military in Ugandan politics.

Clapham, Christopher and George Philip, eds. *The Political Dilemmas of Military Regimes*. London: Croom Helm, 1985.

Decalo, Samuel. *Coups and Army Rule in Africa: Motivations and Constraints*. New Haven, CT: Yale University Press, 1990.

Finer, Samuel E. *The Man on Horseback: The Role of the Military in Politics*. London: Pall Mall, 1962.

Goldsworthy, David. Civilian control of the military in Black Africa. *African Affairs*. 1981, 80(318), 49–74.

Hughes, Arnold and Roy May. The politics of succession in Black Africa. *Third World Quarterly*. 1988, 10(1), 1–22.

Huntington, Samuel P. *Political Order in Changing Societies*. New Haven, CT: Yale University Press, 1968.

Janowitz, Morris. *Military Institutions and Coercion in the Developing Nations*. Chicago, IL: University of Chicago Press, 1977.

Omara-Otunnu, Amii. *Politics and the Military in Uganda, 1890–1985*. London: Macmillan, 1987.

Notes and references

1 Weber, Max. *The Theory of Social and Economic Organization* [translated by A.M. Henderson and Talcott Parsons]. New York: Free Press, 1964. 324–91.

2 McGowan, Pat and Thomas H. Johnson. African military coups d'état and underdevelopment: a quantitative historical analysis. *Journal of Modern African Studies*. 1984, 22(4), 634.

3 Ball, George W. *The Discipline of Power*. 1968. Cited in First, Ruth. *The Barrel of a Gun: Political Power in Africa and the Coup d'État*. London: The Penguin Press, 1970. 1.

4 First. *The Barrel of a Gun: Political Power in Africa and the Coup d'État*. 4.

5 See Huntington, Samuel P. *Political Order in Changing Societies*. New Haven, CT: Yale University Press, 1968. 192–263. See also Clapham, Christopher. *Third World Politics: An Introduction*. London: Routledge. 1985. 140–9.

6 Huntington. *Political Order in Changing Societies*. See also Finer, Samuel E. *The Man on Horseback: The Role of the Military in Politics*. London: Pall Mall, 1962.

7 Janowitz, Morris. *Military Institutions and Coercion in the Developing Nations*. Chicago, IL: University of Chicago Press, 1977.

8 First. *The Barrel of a Gun: Political Power in Africa and the Coup d'État*. 17.

9 Finer. *The Man on Horseback: The Role of the Military in Politics*.

10 Huntington. *Political Order in Changing Societies*. 196.

11 Janowitz. *Military Institutions and Coercion in the Developing Nations*. 104.

12 Clapham. *Third World Politics: An Introduction*. 143.

13 See Wiseman, John A. Military rule in the Gambia: an interim assessment. *Third World Quarterly*. 1996, 17(5), 917–40.

14 Decalo, Samuel. *Coups and Army Rule in Africa: Motivations and Constraints*. New Haven, CT: Yale University Press, 1990. 18.

15 Amuwo, Kunle. Military-inspired anti-bureaucratic corruption campaigns: an appraisal of Niger's experience. *Journal of Modern African Studies*. 1986, 24(2), 299.

16 Luckham, Robin. Militarism: force, class and international conflict. In: Richard Little and Michael Smith, eds. *Perspectives on World Politics*. London: Routledge, 1991. 368.

17 Grace, John and John Laffin. *Fontana Dictionary of Africa Since 1960: Events, Movements, Personalities*. London: Fontana, 1991. 363.

18 Brett, E.A. Neutralising the use of force in Uganda. *Journal of Modern African Studies*. 1995, 33(1), 135.

19 *Ibid*. 135–6.

20 *Africa South of the Sahara 1992. 21*. London: Europa Publications, 1991. 1054.

21 *Ibid*.

22 *Africa South of the Sahara 1998. 27*. London: Europa Publications, 1997. 1080.

23 Statistics taken from United Nations Conference on Trade and Development. *UNCTAD Handbook of Statistics 2014*. New York: United Nations, 2014. Tables 8.1, 8.4 and 3.2.D; World Bank data http://data.worldbank.org/indicator/SP.DYN.LE00.IN (accessed 24 July 2015) and http://data.worldbank.org/indicator/SP.DYN.IMRT.IN (accessed 24 July 2015); and UNESCO data www.uis.unesco.org/DataCentre/Pages/regions.aspx (accessed 24 July 2015).

8 Sovereignty I

External influences on African politics

Chapter outline

- Inter-African international relations
- Superpowers, the Cold War and Africa

  - The communist powers
  - The Western powers
  - Other external interests

- The impact of the Cold War on African politics
- Africa and the 'New World Order'

  - The cessation of proxy wars
  - Africa downgraded strategically
  - Political conditions tied to external aid
  - A more muted but continued French presence
  - A renewed British interest
  - China's diplomatic and economic offensive

- State, civil society and external interests
- Case study: Somalia's international relations
- Questions raised by this chapter
- Glossary of key terms
- Further reading
- Notes and references

So far, this book has concentrated on the internal relationships between state and civil society in Africa. The competition and co-operation between these two protagonists have explained a great deal about the political process on the continent. Yet the introduction of this book identified *three* parties to be considered. Alongside those of state and civil society, the influences of external interests also have to be taken into account when examining the politics of post-colonial Africa.

External interests have already come to the fore in previous chapters with the analysis of colonial rule, economic underdevelopment, and the possible influence of an 'international bourgeoisie'. It is now time, however, to investigate this third party more systematically. The current chapter will do exactly this by assessing diplomatic and political influences on the continent emanating from outside Africa. The following chapter will then continue this assessment, concentrating on the political economy of these external influences.

'Sovereignty' is the natural choice for these two chapters' underlying theme. This is because the very concept of sovereignty, despite its flaws, lubricates the machinery of international relations.[1] Sovereignty, in this respect, can be defined as *the claim of supreme political authority within a territory.* It is about governments enjoying autonomy and freedom of constraint within their own borders.

The notion of sovereignty underpinned international politics throughout the twentieth century, and is still dominant today. It is a concept that gains respect from governments around the world because it is of mutual benefit. The recognition of state B's sovereignty by state A usually implies a reciprocal recognition of state A's own sovereign status. Consequently, an international system advocating 'non-interference' in the domestic jurisdiction of other states has developed. Each sovereign state is attributed unfettered power within its own territorial borders, being recognised as the sole political authority within these frontiers. This understanding of non-interference has the effect of reducing conflict between states, and has thus been enshrined in the charter of the United Nations (UN).

Yet, despite this international respect for sovereignty and non-interference, in reality, no state enjoys unconstrained power within its domestic jurisdiction. The state's monopoly of power is challenged by two sources. There is internal opposition to this sovereignty (examined in Chapter 10), but more relevant to the present chapter are the external challenges. Like planets in a solar system, states in the international political arena all exert influence over one another. Small territories bordering larger states, for example, will often succumb to their neighbour's 'gravitational pull'. Similarly, the actions of the most powerful states within the system will have ramifications that affect the whole political universe. In this respect, governments can only hide behind their sovereignty to a certain degree. Even the United Kingdom, for example, a state that has enjoyed sovereign status for longer than most, has its domestic arena buffeted by external events. Take, for instance, the UK's gradual ceding of political sovereignty to the institutions of the European Union. Likewise, the British government has also yielded a degree of its economic sovereignty to foreign transnational corporations investing in this country. Indeed, since the end of the Cold War, respect for sovereignty seems to be declining in the world. The 1990s and the start of the twenty-first century have seen Western powers violating the sovereignty of smaller states on the grounds of 'humanitarian intervention' (the former Yugoslavia and Iraq, for example) or more recently 'the fight against terrorism' (Afghanistan and Iraq, again).

African states know the strengths and limitations of the concept of sovereignty better than most within the international community. The vast majority of African countries, after all, are direct creations of external imperial intervention. Having won its political sovereignty at independence, the continent now enjoys a greater degree of international respect and non-interference. Yet economic and political fragility still result in vulnerability to outside intervention. In short, because of their relatively weak position, African governments find it difficult to resist the attentions of other, more powerful states. Consequently, as the following paragraphs show, although the continent has always been on the margins of 'Great Power' competition, global politics have had a considerable impact on the development of this part of the world. This chapter divides its investigation of this external impact between two time periods: the 'Cold War' era, followed by the 'New World Order'.

Inter-African international relations

The bulk of this chapter concentrates on political intervention from states outside the African continent. This is in no way meant to imply that inter-African international relations are insignificant. The continent's post-colonial history has, in many instances, been shaped by interaction exclusively involving African players.

In terms of inter-African co-operation, there is much sympathy on the continent for pan-African ideals, attempting to build solidarity among African states. Consequently, in an attempt to tackle similar ex-colonial experiences, bolster continent-wide security and promote wider economic collaboration, the Organisation of African Unity (OAU) was founded in 1963. The OAU's membership subsequently expanded as each newly liberated African state joined at independence. The Organisation was certainly a powerful symbol of potential political co-operation on the continent. In reality, however, the OAU soon developed a reputation for being just a 'talking shop'. This institution's lack of resources and deference to the internal jurisdiction of member states limited its impact. Indeed, in an effort to revive the potential of pan-African co-operation, the OAU was disbanded altogether in 2002, and was replaced by a restructured African Union (AU). This more recent rebooting of inter-African international relations is discussed in more detail in the book's final chapter. All one needs to note here is the fact that multilateral African politics, on a continental scale, were not overly prominent in the bulk of the post-colonial period.

Despite an underlying sympathy for pan-African co-operation, it was actually regional co-operation that proved more dynamic after independence. Multilateral co-operation could be observed in institutions such as the Southern African Development Community (SADC) and the Economic Community of West African States (ECOWAS). SADC provided the 'Frontline States' with an institutional base for solidarity against apartheid South Africa in the 1980s, before reinventing itself in 1992 as a broader regional organisation, with the new, non-racial South Africa becoming one of its number by 1994. Similarly, ECOWAS saw initial economic co-operation later develop into accompanying political and security co-operation. ECOWAS-sponsored peacekeepers have seen service in Liberia, Guinea–Bissau and Sierra Leone, among other conflict zones.

Not all inter-African international relations, however, have been positive. As shown in previous chapters, factors such as Somalia's irredentism, Libya's adventurism and apartheid South Africa's destabilisation have all brought inter-state conflict to the continent. Additional major outbreaks of violence include the following: both South Africa and Zaire (Congo-Kinshasa) intervening in the Angolan civil war during the mid-1970s; Tanzania's invasion of Uganda in 1979; troops from Rwanda, Uganda, Angola, Namibia, the Sudan, Chad and Zimbabwe all being active in the Democratic Republic of the Congo (DRC, Congo-Kinshasa) in the late 1990s and beyond; the Eritrean/Ethiopian border war of 1998–2000; and Ethiopia's invasion of Somalia in 2008.

Despite these violent examples, however, one should not see Africa as a continent of inter-state conflict. This type of conflict has been the exception, not the norm, in the post-colonial period. A similar analysis of inter-state violence in other parts of the world would generate a much longer list of hostilities. As was noted in Chapter 3, African countries have been remarkably successful in maintaining the borders inherited from the colonial powers, which, in turn, has brought a degree of harmony to inter-continental foreign relations. Where Africa was less blessed, however, was where violence was fomented by extra-continental powers. The current chapter will now turn to this external intervention.

Superpowers, the Cold War and Africa

The vast majority of African countries gained their independence in the 20-year period between 1955 and 1975. This was a time when global politics were dominated by the Cold War. Newly created sovereign African states were therefore thrust into an international political system where the capitalist West was engaged in ideological combat with the communist East.

At first glance, it would seem that Africa had no reason to be caught up in this conflict. The continent was too poor (with few resources to protect) and geographically too peripheral (not within either superpower's immediate sphere of influence) to trouble these Cold War warriors. The Cold War, however, was truly global. With the United States and the Soviet Union locked in a nuclear stalemate in Europe, both these powers reasoned that strategic advantage could be gained elsewhere. Rivalries were therefore extended to the African continent, and, although these peripheral strategic policies may have been of only minor importance to officials in Washington DC and Moscow, their consequences had a dramatic impact within Africa itself.

The communist powers

The USSR portrayed itself as a natural ally for the new sovereign states of Africa. This was because tsarist Russia had not been involved in the colonisation of the continent, while the Soviet Union itself shared the African nationalists' anti-imperialist sentiments. Indeed, many African leaders proclaimed their countries to be socialist after independence. With these shared ideological foundations, it was only natural that officials in Moscow sustained a generally sympathetic approach towards Africa. In particular, fraternal links were forged with the more radical governments of Ghana, Guinea and Mali, and later with the Marxist–Leninist states of Angola, Mozambique and Ethiopia.

Essentially, the Soviet Union sought to promote socialism in Africa. There was no question of the USSR overwhelming African governments, trying to establish a buffer zone on the continent, as it had in Eastern Europe. Instead, Moscow reasoned that any allies it could win through diplomacy and aid would help to expand the communist world, denying opportunities to the West. The objective was therefore to reinforce the break between the ex-colonies and their ex-colonisers.

Soviet policy towards Africa in the 1950s and 1960s can be described as 'pragmatic'. Although the continent was never high on its list of priorities, Moscow was willing to intervene when opportunities emerged. For example, one of the first instances of Cold War tension on African soil was precipitated when the Soviet Union assisted Egypt in building the Aswan High Dam. This was after relations between Egypt and the West had become strained. The United States and Britain pulled out of the dam project after General Nasser's government had accepted an arms shipment from Czechoslovakia. This gave Moscow the opportunity to win friends in Africa, and in 1956 the USSR took over the Aswan construction programme and completed it. Similarly, the Soviet Union also built close ties with Guinea. Moscow became Guinea's patron after this country had defied France's wishes and opted for complete independence in 1958. Isolated from the West, Sékou Touré's government was grateful for any external assistance it could secure.

Later, in the 1970s, the Soviet Union took a more active role in African affairs. Officials in Moscow sought to profit from the political instability created by Portugal's withdrawal from Africa, as well as Emperor Haile Selassie's removal from power in

Ethiopia. They were also keen to assist liberation struggles against the white minority governments of Southern Africa. Consequently, Angola, Mozambique and Ethiopia received comparatively large amounts of aid, boosting the capacity of these new Marxist–Leninist regimes to defend themselves against 'counter-revolutionary' forces. Similarly, arms were supplied to the liberation movements of the south, namely the African National Congress of South Africa (ANC), Namibia's South West Africa People's Organization (SWAPO), and the Zimbabwe African People's Union (ZAPU). It was hoped that these states would become Soviet allies once the insurgent nationalists had defeated the incumbent white minority governments.

The expansion of socialism was the long-term objective of Soviet foreign policy. In the shorter term, however, Moscow also sought to improve its strategic position in Africa. Over time, the USSR gained access to a network of airfields and seaports right across the continent. This advanced the Soviet Union's Cold War capabilities considerably. Flights out of Conakry in West Africa, for example, enabled Moscow to monitor Western shipping in the Atlantic, while defence facilities in Somalia, and then in Ethiopia, enhanced Soviet naval operations in the Indian Ocean. As will be seen later in the chapter, this superpower attention benefited African governments through the 'rent' that they could charge for granting such strategic access.

The Soviet Union's primary method of paying this rent was through the supply of arms. Millions of tons of military equipment were shipped to Africa. This was undertaken without charge (or very cheaply). By contrast, the West was in the business of selling more sophisticated arms at a considerably higher price. Although tanks, MiG aircraft and surface-to-air missile systems were reserved for prized clients (Angola and Ethiopia), Moscow was willing to sell arms to almost any country where it considered influence could be won. Just under half of the continent's governments took up this opportunity in the post-colonial period. As a result, Soviet arm sales to Africa rose from US$150 million in the 1960s to US$2.5 billion in the 1970s.[2]

The Soviet Union was not the only communist power involved in Africa. Cuba was also heavily committed to the defence of socialism on this continent. Cuba, as a Third World country itself, empathised with Africa's position. Consequently, African regimes were less suspicious of Havana's offers of assistance than they were of Moscow's overtures. This resulted in thousands of Cuban doctors, engineers, teachers and other technical advisers serving African governments. Havana was also willing to deploy combat troops to support its allies. Up to 50,000 Cuban soldiers were dispatched to Angola and Ethiopia from the mid-1970s onwards.[3] In Angola, for example, Cuban troops, fighting alongside government forces, saw active service against invading South African regiments, who had themselves intervened to support the (US-backed) rebels of the União Nacional para a Independência Total de Angola (UNITA). Without this Cuban intervention, it is likely that the socialist government in Luanda would have been defeated.

The People's Republic of China also involved itself in African affairs during the Cold War era. Beijing, after its ideological rift with Moscow, attempted to export its own brand of socialism to the continent. As well as assisting African regimes, this intervention was aimed at blunting rival Soviet expansionism. Again, Beijing stressed its Third World credentials, something Moscow had difficulty doing, and doctors, engineers and teachers were duly dispatched to the continent. The apogee of China's Africa policy of this period came with the building of the TanZam railway, completed in 1975. This was a project that Western governments had earlier refused to undertake, considering it too difficult and too costly. It involved a formidable piece of engineering, laying 1,680 km of railway track across Central Africa, linking Zambia to the Tanzanian port of Dar es Salaam, thus giving Zambia access to the sea, avoiding the need to transport goods through white-ruled Rhodesia or South Africa. However, China was not to repeat this scale of co-operation anywhere else on the continent. Indeed, Beijing's Africa policy remained somewhat discreet during the Cold War, when compared with Soviet Union or Cuban activity.

The Western powers

The global containment of communism was the primary foreign policy goal of the United States during the years of the Cold War. Not only did this involve the United States shoring up democracies in Western Europe, with the provision of Marshall Plan aid and the deployment of US troops, but it also led Washington DC to seek out allies on other continents. Friendly governments in far-off places, it was reasoned, could act as a bulwark against potential Soviet expansion.

Although, again, African states were only of minor importance to Cold War strategists in Washington DC, no area of the world could be neglected. It was feared that any state 'going communist' had the potential to tip the overall balance of this global confrontation. Therefore, despite the United States' limited economic and strategic interests on the continent, African governments were courted. Washington considered it imperative that the continent's nationalist and anti-imperial regimes should not be converted into Soviet satellites.

US administrations selected a number of states for special attention. These countries were seen as regionally important. At various times, Zaire (now DRC), Morocco, Ethiopia, Somalia and Kenya could be identified as US clients. This resulted in economic aid flowing to these states, as well as diplomatic support when this was needed. Morocco, for example, received sympathy from Washington over its claims to the Western Sahara, while Zaire was supported in its border clashes with Angola.

The United States also sought to back 'moderate' groups, while disabling 'radical' factions, in the continent's disputed territories. In the 1960 Congo crisis, for example, which was precipitated by Katanga's secession, US power was directed against Prime Minister Patrice Lumumba. The CIA's local chief of station reported that he was unsure whether Lumumba was actually a 'Commie or just playing Commie', but 'there may be little time left in which to take the action to avoid another Cuba'. Consequently, US activity contributed both to Lumumba's assassination and to the subsequent rise of General Mobutu Sese Seko. These actions eliminated any potential gains for the Soviet Union in this particular part of the world.

The Congo crisis, and other cases, such as Angola in the 1970s and 1980s, are dramatic examples of US African intervention during the Cold War. The bulk of Washington's policy, however, revolved around the more mundane allocation of aid. Most African governments that expressed pro-Western leanings could expect favourable attention. Indeed, it often seemed as if Washington was too eager to assist some of the continent's regimes. In several instances, the United States stood accused of supplying aid to governments that readily violated their own citizens' human rights. US strategic interests, in this respect, were being put ahead of humanitarian considerations. Although US support for Zaire, for example, clearly denied the Soviet Union opportunities, the military and monetary assistance offered to Mobutu's regime allowed him to sustain a brutal and corrupt dictatorship for several decades.

Plate 8.1 President Mobutu Sese Seko successfully positioned Zaire as a US client state throughout the Cold War. Mobutu at the White House, Washington DC, meeting J.F. Kennedy in 1963.

Plate 8.2 Mobutu at the White House, Washington DC, meeting Ronald Reagan 20 years later in 1983.

Similarly, although the United States officially disapproved of white minority rule, no administration in Washington was prepared consistently to challenge South Africa over its policy of apartheid.[5] Throughout the Cold War period, US officials marginalised human rights concerns, hiding behind notions of state sovereignty and non-interference in domestic jurisdictions in order to capture the more coveted prize of global containment.

Moving on to look at other Western powers, Britain and France took very different approaches towards Africa after decolonisation. Britain, considerably less inclined to intervene than France, was content to operate a low-key Africa policy. Indeed, officials in London seemed to regard this continent as a 'source of trouble rather than opportunity'.[6] Britain did help the newly independent governments of Kenya, Tanganyika and Uganda to put down army mutinies in 1964, but these proved to be isolated incidents. Even when pushed by other Commonwealth countries to punish the white settler government of Ian Smith, when Rhodesia illegally declared unilateral independence in 1965, Britain refused to deploy troops. Instead, London was more active in quietly pursuing its not inconsiderable economic interests in the post-colonial era.

By contrast, inactivity is not a charge that could be levelled against France. Paris, after decolonisation, maintained a particularly close relationship with a number of African countries, much closer than was the case for the other ex-colonial powers or the newer Cold War patrons. Although France never managed to construct the Communauté franco-africaine, a confederal system with Paris at the centre, as envisaged by President Charles de Gaulle at independence (African nationalism was far too strong for this), France did remain the most influential foreign government on the continent.

This was because France saw itself as having a particularly rich civilisation, with a duty to spread this culture overseas. Just as the *mission civilisatrice* (civilising mission) was at the centre of France's original colonial intervention in Africa, this remained ingrained in Franco-African relations throughout the Cold War period. Indeed, France's influence was so successful in Africa during the Cold War that several states from other colonial backgrounds, such as (Belgium's) Zaire, Rwanda and Burundi, also associated themselves with *la Francophonie* (the French-speaking cultural community or 'commonwealth'). Underlining this point, more states sent representatives to the 1982 Franco-African summit in Kinshasa than attended a parallel meeting of the Organisation of African Unity in Tripoli.[7]

Christopher Clapham attributes France's success in Africa to three factors: people, money and force.[8] In terms of people, diplomatic and financial ties between Paris and the continent's capitals were much more intimate than those offered by Britain, the United States or the Soviet Union. French relationships were underwritten by bonds of mutual trust and friendship. In this respect, several Africanists have likened the Franco-African international community to a family, with Paris acting as a paternal figure, tending to its children, especially when they become disobedient.[9] These personal links stretched back prior to independence. Most of France's colonies remained loyal to General de Gaulle and the Free French during the Second World War, for example, while several African nationalist leaders, such as Félix Houphouët-Boigny of Côte d'Ivoire, served as deputies in the French parliament and ministers in the national government before going on to rule their own countries.

Later, in the Cold War period, Paris continued to pay close attention to its ex-colonies. Africa policy was given the distinction of being co-ordinated by a dedicated department within the Elysée Palace itself. Regular Franco-African summits were held, reciprocal ministerial and head-of-state visits were undertaken, and several French nationals served as high-ranking civil servants within African governments. No other state (Western or communist) came close to matching the status and personal attention that France accorded its Africa policy.

France also offered its African clients financial support. Throughout the Cold War period, Paris consistently gave twice as much aid as any other donor. In 1985, for example, France's contribution constituted 70 per cent of sub-Saharan Africa's total development assistance.[10] The French treasury also guaranteed the Communauté Financière Africaine (CFA) franc. This gave the member states of this common monetary zone a fully convertible currency tied to the value of the French franc. Although, in effect, members relinquished their financial sovereignty for this privilege, in return they received a degree of monetary stability absent elsewhere on the continent.

Then there was the factor of force. During the Cold War period, Paris negotiated military co-operation agreements with almost all of the francophone African countries. These pacts brought a good deal of security to African governments. France, with some 13,000 troops stationed on African soil (with bases in Côte d'Ivoire, Gabon, Senegal, Togo, the Central African Republic and Djibouti), intervened militarily on numerous occasions.

In 1964, for example, French troops helped restore Léon M'ba to the presidency of Gabon in the wake of a military coup. The Foreign Legion arrived in Libreville, Gabon's capital, 24 hours *before* M'ba officially requested help. Similar examples of direct French military intervention include Zaire (where incursions from Angola were thwarted), Chad (as a counter-measure to Libyan attentions), the Western Sahara (to help the Mauritanian government repel POLISARIO rebels) and the Central African Republic (protecting President Jean-Bédel Bokassa's regime). This last case proves to be particularly interesting, as French troops also contributed to Bokassa's eventual overthrow in 1979. The self-proclaimed emperor's murderous regime had simply become too embarrassing for officials in Paris to support.

Thus French patronage was an essential element in the politics of francophone Africa. Personal, economic or military support came to underwrite many of these regimes. While the more powerful Cold War patrons concentrated their efforts in the Horn and Southern Africa, Paris enjoyed a *chasse gardée* (private hunting ground) elsewhere.

Other external interests

In terms of external states intervening in African politics, the countries analysed above are certainly those that created most impact during the Cold War period. This is not to say, however, that they were the only influences. Other ex-colonial powers still retained links with their former territories; bilateral trade strengthened contacts elsewhere (most notably with Germany and Japan); Scandinavian countries, after France, led the way in providing development and humanitarian aid; Arab states offered material assistance to the continent's Islamic countries; and, as will be seen in the next chapter, international financial institutions also played a major role in Africa's post-colonial political history. So far, however, this chapter has been focusing on external foreign policies *towards* Africa; the next section attempts to assess how African states pursued their own interests in this Cold War environment.

The impact of the Cold War on African politics

The diplomacy conducted with African regimes, and the military skirmishes acted out on this continent, rarely register more than a passing mention in most histories of the Cold War. Conflicts in Korea and Vietnam, and the Cuban missile crisis, draw far more

Plate 8.3 Arrest of rebel suspect during French military intervention in Kolwezi, Zaire, 1978. Photographer: Patrick Chauvel.

attention. What was of little concern to Europeans and North Americans, however, had major ramifications in Africa itself. The Cold War brought both positive and negative challenges for regimes on this continent. With skilful manoeuvring, international patrons could be manipulated into providing much needed external resources and security for African governments. This said, it was also possible for African countries to be drawn catastrophically into the East–West conflict, notably through proxy wars.

Opportunities existed for African regimes in that the former colonial powers wished to retain their economic and strategic interests on the continent. Since they could no longer do this by the direct political subjugation of imperialism, Western states now had to work with the new sovereign governments of Africa. Consequently, an international patron–client relationship emerged. African governments, in return for granting access to economic markets or strategic sites, could demand concessions. If the patron's offer of material, diplomatic and military resources was considered inadequate, client regimes could use their sovereign authority to play one patron off against another. Given that Cold War protagonists were also now seeking access to the continent, even greater concessions could be secured. Zaire's President Mobutu Sese Seko, for example, was an expert at manipulating international patrons. During his 30-year reign, Mobutu fostered contacts, first with the CIA, and then with Belgium, France, West Germany, Saudi Arabia and even China, not to mention additional negotiations with international financial institutions. Observing these and other leaders' manoeuvrings, Tanzania's president, Julius Nyerere, considered there to be a 'second scramble for Africa' under way during the Cold War.[11]

African states welcomed the development aid, cheap loans, technical assistance and other benefits granted by international patrons. This material support made a considerable difference to the continent's regimes, given that there was often a scarcity of resources produced within their own societies. There was also military support. Direct French and Cuban interventions have been noted above. In addition to this, the majority of African states also received arms shipments from Cold War patrons. Between 1967 and 1978 alone, the USSR supplied US$2.7 billion worth of weapons to Africa, while the United States contributed US$1.6 billion.[12] Numerous other suppliers, from France and West Germany through to Israel and Czechoslovakia, also found ready takers for their military hardware. In effect, with these weapons, external interests were underwriting the power of the state in Africa. Challenges to state sovereignty could now be countered by coercive agencies armed with sophisticated weaponry.

Superpower patronage, however, did not always prove beneficial for African states. The danger was that if one side of the global divide paid an interest in a particular country, so might the other. On several occasions, rival domestic political factions came to be supported by competing Cold War patrons. This happened in Angola, for example, where the MPLA government was favoured by the Soviet Union and the UNITA rebel movement was backed by the United States. An internal conflict had become 'internationalised', and a proxy war resulted. In other words, the Cold War became a hot war, and hundreds of thousands of Angolan lives were lost.

Conflicts in Africa that became 'internationalised' by Cold War intervention were particularly difficult to quell. Whereas before, the indigenous parties might have been able to come to some agreement based on local bargaining, now a resolution to the conflict also required superpower interests to be served. In the meantime, the fighting continued at an intensity that local resources alone could not have sustained. With access to the armouries of the West or the Soviet Union, greater destruction and more deaths occurred. Indeed, external resources fuelled these wars, keeping them going where, with no external intervention, local resources would soon have been exhausted, and peace might have been sought. Angola's civil war lasted 27 years. It is true that the Cold War may not have actually caused any conflicts in Africa; it did, however, exacerbate the intensity and duration of these confrontations. As President Olusegun Obasanjo of Nigeria observed, 'even the most innocuous of conflicts in Africa became intractable and protracted, often resulting in wars of attrition'.[13]

Africa and the 'New World Order'

The early 1990s saw Moscow lose its grip on its satellites in Eastern Europe. Soon after that, the Soviet Union itself disintegrated, abandoning socialism and splitting into a number of separate sovereign states. The Cold War was at an end. US President George H.W. Bush, accepting the responsibilities his country now had as the sole superpower, declared the commencement of a 'New World Order'. This whole transitory period was symbolised in the West by the television pictures showing German citizens breaching the Berlin Wall. The end of the Cold War, however, did not just have ramifications for the people of Europe and North America; there were also major residual effects in Africa. Just as they had adapted to the demands of an international system dominated by the Cold War, African states now had to adjust to the realities of this so-called New World Order.

The cessation of proxy wars

One of the more immediate effects of the Soviet Union's demise was the ending of proxy wars. In 1990, for example, Moscow ceased its supply of weapons to Ethiopia. This removed both external interests and external resources from this particular conflict. The incumbent Mengistu regime fell to an alliance of rebel forces a year later, something that would have taken much longer, or might not have happened at all, had previous Soviet backing remained.

Similar patterns of events occurred in Southern Africa. The unwillingness of external patrons to continue funding proxy wars assisted a number of interlinked negotiated settlements in this region. With global strategic interests waning in Angola, for example, conflict resolution based on local realities now became possible. Previously, the MPLA government could rely on Soviet and Cuban support, while UNITA rebels received US and South African assistance. In a wider regional settlement, brokered by the US government and assisted by Moscow, South Africa agreed to withdraw its troops from both Angola and Namibia, in return for a simultaneous Cuban withdrawal. Now denied external backing, UNITA and the MPLA themselves sought an internal negotiated settlement in Angola. Although national reconciliation collapsed in 1992, the subsequent intermittent clashes between these two forces did not have the ferocity of those of the 1980s. This was because there was no longer access to superpower-supplied military hardware. Angola achieved a more permanent peace in 2002.

In South Africa itself, the end of the Cold War accelerated the arrival at the negotiating table of the incumbent National Party government and the rebel African National Congress (ANC). Having lost its weapons supply from Moscow, and with its rear bases under threat from improving relations between the Frontline States and Pretoria, the ANC was forced to put its negotiation strategy to the fore. Similarly, the South African government could no longer expect tacit support from the West. The days were numbered when Pretoria could rely on Western powers ignoring apartheid's human rights abuses in favour of backing a minority-ruled South Africa as a bastion against communist encroachment. With both parties' external support fading, negotiations became the favoured option. An ANC-led government of national unity emerged in 1994, ending 350 years of white rule in this country.

Africa downgraded strategically

The end of the Cold War not only extinguished a number of proxy wars, but also dramatically affected the flow of external resources to the continent's governments. With no global conflict, the West strategically downgraded Africa. There was no reason to supply African regimes with diplomatic and military aid. As Jeffery Lefebvre observed, in the New World Order, 'The days of right-wing and left-wing dictatorial regimes being lavished with aid and excused for their internal excesses were over'.[14]

For a start, there was no longer the Soviet Union to act as a patron to countries expressing socialist solidarity. And without Soviet influence on the continent, Washington's attention also declined. The United States had few other interests in Africa. US economic investment on the whole continent, for example, measured considerably less than one-third of its exposure in the single country of Brazil.[15] Apart from a general desire to spread liberal democracy and capitalism across the globe, African affairs troubled few within Washington DC's circle of foreign policy makers. Consequently, consulates were closed, assistance programmes were cut, and CIA agents packed their bags and sought more relevant hunting grounds elsewhere.

Tellingly, a number of former US clients were removed from government in the 1990s. For example, Samuel Doe in Liberia, Hissène Habré in Chad, Siad Barré in Somalia, and even Mobutu Sese Seko in Zaire, were all deposed. All these individuals would have stood a better chance of retaining power if the external-resource taps had kept flowing. Washington, however, made it clear that ex-clients in Africa now had to deal with local realities largely on their own. They could no longer rely on superpower patrons to prop up their regimes.

Initially, the United States, buoyed by its single superpower status, did consider intervening in Africa. Somalia proved to be a test case for US foreign policy in the New World Order. The events of this early 1990s 'humanitarian intervention' are discussed in more detail in the case study at the end of this chapter. It is sufficient to note, at this point, that the mission ended in UN forces becoming embroiled in the country's civil war. When a number of US soldiers were killed while attempting to arrest a militia leader, Washington withdrew its troops altogether. With this one incident, full-scale United States involvement in African humanitarian missions had ended. US troops have not returned since to African soil. Not even genocide in Rwanda could persuade Washington DC to deploy ground forces. Indeed, US overt intervention in Africa for the rest of the 1990s was confined solely to the bombing of an alleged chemical weapons factory in the Sudan. This was in direct retribution for simultaneous Islamist-inspired terrorist attacks on US embassies in Tanzania and Kenya in 1998. Covert US operations continued against Islamist 'terrorist' organisations in the Horn of Africa, but it was not until 2003 that the US was involved once again in overt military intervention. Even here the US Navy confined itself to providing logistical support for Nigerian peacekeeping troops in Liberia. Africa remains firmly on the periphery of US interests.

Africa has also been strategically downgraded by other Western states. The development of the European Union (EU), for example, became much more of a priority for the ex-colonial powers than maintaining links with their former African possessions. Although Britain and France ensured that the EU gave a preferential trading status to their ex-colonies, through the Lomé Convention, this agreement, as a result of preparations for European monetary union, became less favourable to African countries in the 1990s.[16]

Political conditions tied to external aid

Western development aid did not dry up altogether in the New World Order. Given that Africa is so dependent on external assistance, a humanitarian disaster would have occurred if aid had been severed completely. Aid, however, lost its geopolitical strategic function with the end of the Cold War. Consequently, assistance now came with political conditions attached. Whereas, previously, domestic indiscretions had been overlooked, African governments now had to do more for their money. As early as June 1990,

Douglas Hurd, the British Foreign Secretary, was talking about the need for 'good governance' in Africa. Similarly, French President François Mitterrand declared that French aid would not be forthcoming to 'regimes that have an authoritarian approach without accepting an evolution towards democracy'.[17] And the West was serious about this conditionality. Paris suspended development aid to Zaire in 1991, and to Togo in 1993. Both of these countries' ruling elites fell foul of their international patrons because they had resisted pressures for democratic reform. It was Kenya, however, that came under most scrutiny during this new era of aid conditionality.

Kenya had taken a pro-capitalist, pro-Western stance throughout the years of the Cold War. In return, the West had given generously in terms of development and military assistance. The altered environment of the New World Order, however, made more demands on Daniel arap Moi's regime. By 1990, the Kenyan opposition had become more active, and organised demonstrations nationwide. Moi's government suppressed the pro-democracy protesters violently, calling them 'hooligans and drug addicts', who would be hunted down 'like rats'.[18] This kind of behaviour may have been overlooked previously, when the containment of communism, and not human rights, was the primary goal. In the 1990s, however, material assistance was now directly exchanged for 'good governance'. Consequently, Moi came under massive donor pressure to instigate reforms. International financial institutions, the United States, the EU and Scandinavian countries, all of whom had previously helped to sustain Moi's rule, now suspended their aid programmes to Kenya. Moi eventually succumbed to this donor pressure, amending the constitution to allow the registration of opposition political parties. Kenya's 'Big Man' would finally succumb to multi-party politics, with his retirement contributing to the ruling party's defeat by an opposition coalition in 2002.

Kenya was far from being alone in having to accept external political demands in return for aid. This has been commonplace on the continent in the post-Cold War period. Good governance is the requirement, while the notion of non-interference in the domestic jurisdiction of a sovereign state is now much less in vogue.

A more muted but continued French presence

Even French policy towards Africa has not been immune to the wider strategic downgrading of the African continent. Paris has been less active in this part of the world. Indeed, France actually devalued the CFA franc in 1995, reducing by half its fiscal subsidy of *la Francophonie*. Similarly, the funeral of Félix Houphouët-Boigny, President of the Côte d'Ivoire, can be seen as symbolising this changing relationship between France and its former colonies in the New World Order. Although Houphouët-Boigny's funeral in 1994 saw the attendance of three former French presidents, and six former Prime Ministers, it is unlikely that relations between Paris and current francophone African leaders will ever be this intimate again.

France, despite its more pressing European commitments, however, did not totally abandon its idea of a *chasse gardée* in Africa. Paris still reserves the right to intervene in order to maintain its influence and interests. Pressure may have been put on clients to hold multi-party elections, but this did not prevent Paris from helping a favoured candidate to victory. French aid to Cameroon, for instance, rose from US$159 million in 1990 to US$436 million in 1992. This increase in assistance can largely be explained by the fact that the incumbent, Paul Biya, fought a presidential election in 1992. These additional funds allowed Biya's government to expand public spending as part of its election campaign.[19]

Paris has also been selective in its criticism of authoritarian behaviour. Former clients in Chad (1990) and Mali (1991) may have been left to their own fate when faced with opposition challenges, but there was little criticism when more favoured clients (in Côte d'Ivoire and Madagascar, for example) suppressed rival political movements. Similarly, Algeria continued to receive preferential treatment from French policy makers, as it did from all Western governments, despite the military in this country having annulled the 1991 national elections. The West was willing to overlook this annulment because the Front Islamique du Salut (FIS), an 'Islamist' party, had emerged as the poll's victor. External interests, in this case, were apparently only willing to promote multi-party competition if the result of this election suited their own ideas of democracy.

In terms of continued French military intervention on the continent, events in Central Africa in the 1990s proved to be something of a watershed. Failed operations in Rwanda and Zaire marked an end to Paris's trademark grandiose style of unilateral troop deployment. After licking its wounds for a period, France began a new era of military intervention that was more muted and multilateral in nature. In the mid-1990s, Paris was particularly concerned about losing its acquired influence in the former Belgian colonies. A chain reaction saw the insurgent Rwandan Patriotic Front (RPF) defeat the incumbent Kigali government, a French client, in 1994. The RPF then, in turn, assisted Zairian rebels to defeat Mobutu Sese Seko, another French client, in 1997. These events were seen as damaging to French interests. Accordingly, in familiar style, French troops mounted 'Opération Turquoise' in Rwanda. Although it was billed as a humanitarian mission, offering protection to civilians caught up in the Rwandan genocide, this operation seemed to be more interested in creating a safe haven to allow defeated government forces to regroup. Similarly, France also tried unsuccessfully to arrange a 'humanitarian mission' to Zaire. Whatever assistance may have been given here, this military force would also have served to stall the Zairian rebels' advance on Kinshasa, possibly giving Mobutu time to negotiate a future for his regime. France's effort to create this peacekeeping force was rejected by other members of the international community. Consequently, Paris lost its client regimes in Central Africa. Rwanda's decision to adopt English, alongside French, as an official language in 2008 was the final nail in the coffin for French policy in this part of the continent.

In the twenty-first century, in the light of what occurred in the 1990s, French governments have become more circumspect about deploying troops within African conflict zones. Paris has also been more careful to act in concert with the UN and the African Union when intervening. Yet France is still the external power that most regularly uses military force on the African continent. French troops saw combat in Côte d'Ivoire during 2002 and 2011, in Chad during 2006 and 2008, in the Central African Republic during 2008 and 2013, and in Mali during 2013. Genuine humanitarian and security threats were present on each occasion, but Paris's actions also sought to thwart the potential removal from government of French clients. With some 10,000 French troops stationed across several bases on African soil, and another 800 military advisers serving the continent's governments, France still retains the capacity to intervene rapidly in this part of the world.[20]

A renewed British interest

The United Kingdom has shown greater political interest in Africa during the New World Order. Moving from its previous low-key commercially led approach to the continent, Britain has became a more engaged diplomatic voice calling for change in Africa.

It was ministers in the Conservative government of John Major who first brought African debt relief to the agenda of the G8 forum of industrialised nations during the mid-1990s, but Tony Blair's 'New Labour' administration, after 1997, widened the British government's focus on Africa. Indeed, at his party's annual conference in 2001, Prime Minister Blair called Africa 'a scar on the conscience of the world'. The UK was of the view that the international community had a 'moral duty' to defend human rights in Africa, alongside an obligation to assist the continent's economic development. Blair even talked about a Marshall Plan for Africa. Britain too now sought to pursue an active African policy. As Foreign Secretary Jack Straw put it, 'Africa matters. It matters if you want to produce a stable world. You can't have four continents going forward and one going backwards.'[21]

In return for African governments committing themselves to programmes of good governance and poverty reduction, the UK undertook to increase aid and provide debt relief. As Blair himself stated, 'Our challenge is to support the good. Africa's challenge is to eliminate the bad.'[22] Importantly, London also pledged itself to persuade its fellow industrialised states to support this new partnership. British officials persistently placed Africa on the agenda of the G8 and other international organisations. Alongside moral arguments, Prime Minister Blair, and his successor Gordon Brown, underlined that it was in the rich countries' own interests to invest in Africa. Not to do so would endanger security. After all, an impoverished and unstable African continent would potentially become a platform for international terrorism, transnational crime, illegal migration and disease. The UK made its position plain: it would now be timely to support African democracy and poverty reduction.

The most obvious outcome of this new energised position was British troops intervening in Sierra Leone's civil war during 2000. After a decade of rival groups battling for control over Sierra Leone's diamond mines, the Revolutionary United Front (RUF) had finally gained the upper hand, and was threatening to topple the internationally recognised government in Freetown. It was at this point that London intervened. UK military power was used to assist government forces in repelling the rebel advance. RUF troops were routed by British trained and supported government troops, fighting alongside British units themselves. The RUF's leadership was captured and indicted for war crimes.

The UK subsequently invested heavily in programmes of reconciliation and reconstruction for Sierra Leone. This investment has been rewarded by a remarkable transition from the brutal conflict of the 1990s. Democratic advances have been consolidated, and Sierra Leone's economy has grown as a consequence. As a case study of how Western intervention can assist African conflict resolution, Sierra Leone was a significant feather in the cap for new British engagement.

Elsewhere, the United Kingdom sought to assist African states by expanding its aid regime. Programme allocations of the UK Department for International Development (DfID) rose from £3 million in the first year of Blair's government to over £1 billion by 2005–06.[23] The most notable successes for this investment programme were primary education and access to health care, particularly in Tanzania, Ghana, Rwanda and Uganda. The British government was now providing political support and a level of funding previously more associated with the foreign policies of Scandinavian countries.

The most important international agreement assisted by British activism at this time, however, was the decision to cancel significant sums of African debt. The origin of these debts is discussed in Chapter 9, but it is worth noting here that, with UK officials taking the lead, by 2009 over US$110 billion of debt had been written off globally with respect to Heavily Indebted Poor Countries (HIPCs).[24] Western creditor governments had collectively agreed to loosen the noose of debt. Potentially, all HIPCs now have 'manageable' debts, and in return these countries have agreed to policies of fiscal responsibility (negotiated with the International Monetary Fund) and developed poverty alleviation programmes (ensuring that funds released by debt relief are spent legitimately). The UK has gone beyond the multilateral HIPC agreement and pledged to write off 100 per cent of all its bilateral debts owed by HIPCs, should they meet these two criteria.

With the onset of the economic downturn in 2008, and the arrival of a Conservative-led coalition government in London during 2010, Africa was downgraded in terms of UK policy engagement. Air strikes against the crumbling Gaddafi regime in Libya during 2011 proved to be this government's high-water mark in terms of its interaction with African politics. Yet, despite opposition from within his own party, Prime Minister David Cameron did make good his predecessors' commitment to meet, by 2013, the UN target of states spending 0.7 per cent of their national income on overseas development aid. In this respect, the UK has joined a very select group of countries. Only Norway, Sweden, Denmark, Luxembourg and the United Arab Emirates could claim to honour this 0.7 per cent measurement in 2013.[25] British policy towards Africa has certainly been less evangelical since the passing of the 'New Labour' governments, but UK actions did have a significant impact across Africa in the post-Cold War era. British lobbying helped to adjust international attitudes and multilateral policies towards the continent. London, although still quietly pursuing its commercial interests, continues to have a more nuanced and animated approach than had been seen earlier.

China's diplomatic and economic offensive

Of all the major powers, it is China that has concerned itself most with African affairs in the New World Order. Beijing has expanded its engagement with the African continent dramatically. Gone are the earlier ideologically driven relations of the Cold War, which had the aim of demonstrating political solidarity. Today, China has a very different agenda: capitalism. Although notions of anti-imperial co-operation can still be found in the rhetoric of Chinese diplomats, these representatives are present on African soil to ensure that Africa plays its role in China's emergence as an economic superpower. As a consequence, the volume of trade between China and Africa rose tenfold in the decade to 2008. By 2012, over US$200 billion worth of goods were being traded annually. Beijing is now Africa's most significant commercial partner.[26]

Much of this growing trade can be explained by China's global search for raw materials. Among other commodities, Beijing is involved in extracting copper from Zambia, chrome and platinum from Zimbabwe, timber from Cameroon and the Congo Basin, iron ore from Gabon, and cotton from Tanzania. It is, however, China's thirst for oil that lies at the heart of this country's new engagement with Africa.

As a consequence of its economic expansion, China, in 1993, moved from being a net exporter to a net importer of oil. Beijing had become vulnerable. An inability to secure sufficient hydrocarbons from foreign suppliers would halt the 'economic miracle'. This reality was compounded by the fact that Middle Eastern oil production is dominated by US corporate interests. It therefore became a priority for Beijing to locate and develop previously untapped reserves of this commodity, giving China better control over the supply and price of this raw material. China has thus become a major partner in oil exploration and production on the African continent. Its corporations have major drilling operations in Angola, the Sudan, Nigeria, Gabon and Algeria, and are involved in development ventures with a wide range of states, including Niger, Congo-Brazzaville, Kenya, Equatorial Guinea, Ethiopia and Madagascar. Angola became China's single largest supplier of oil from 2006, when it surpassed imports from Saudi Arabia. Observing this reality, academic Ian Taylor is of the opinion that 'it would be difficult to overstate the importance of Africa to China's own development'.[27]

Africa is also important to China as a destination for its manufactured goods and, more recently, its service industries. A visit to even the most remote market on the continent will reveal Chinese products for sale. The bulk of these commodities are cheap household items, textiles, clothing, footwear and lower-end electrical goods. Chinese nationals have also emigrated to African countries in large numbers to establish small shops selling these items. These entrepreneurs can be found in both urban and rural communities. In 2003, Africa imported goods to the value of US$6 billion from China. By 2008, this figure had increased to US$28 billion, and in 2013 it was US$65 billion.[28] Again, it is clear that Beijing is emerging as the continent's prime economic partner.

In many ways, Africa is benefiting from this new attention. China is providing much needed foreign investment and access to cheap consumer goods. This sort of economic stimulation was not previously forthcoming from Western transnational corporations. Oil fields are being developed, mining operations have been rejuvenated, and income is being generated for African states. China has also embarked on a generous programme of infrastructure and public works projects right across the continent. This activity seeks to provide visible assets symbolising the advantages of this new co-operation. Pristine parliament buildings have been constructed (in Uganda, for example), as have national stadiums (in Sierra Leone and the Central African Republic), along with presidential palaces (in Zimbabwe and DRC). Likewise, China has built or repaired numerous schools, roads and railways. Inevitably, comparisons have been made with the less dramatic and more measured Western development programmes. Beijing's co-operation is decisive and rarely involves political conditions. As one African diplomat observed, 'China is able to build a railway before the World Bank would get round to doing a cost-benefit analysis.'[29]

Yet this economic activity does come at a price. It can be argued that China's approach to the continent is neo-colonial, while, at the same time, undermining potential liberal democratic gains. In terms of the neo-colonial charge, China portrays its relationship with Africa as one based on mutual respect and benefit. As with their Western corporate competitors, however, there is little evidence of Chinese companies attempting to stimulate economic development that will benefit domestic African economies. As before, productive capital tends to be exported, rather than invested locally. The objective is the expansion of the Chinese economy, not a strategy of developing African manufacturing instead.

With respect to the 'good-will' public works discussed above, for example, it is often the case that Chinese construction companies will import their own materials, and even their own labour force, to complete these projects. These corporations do not turn to African business partners or the local employment market. There have also been complaints that Chinese corporations have little respect for health and safety, or for the environmental impact of their drilling and mining. Such low standards are a feature of Chinese society as well, so are not 'neo-colonial' per se, but they do contribute to a growing perception among Africans that China, whatever its former socialist credentials, is just the latest in a long line of foreign resource grabbers. Has not Beijing created the same unequal exchange relationship that was endured under European colonialism?

It is China's clothing and textile exports that have done most to fuel charges of neo-colonialism. African manufacturers simply cannot compete with the flood of cheap Chinese goods entering their domestic markets. The consequence has been the devastation of what was previously one of Africa's most successful economic sectors. In recent times, for example, some 800 South African textiles factories have been forced to close, costing 60,000 jobs, while Nigeria has lost upwards of 80 per cent of its factories, putting 250,000 workers out of employment. This story has been repeated continent-wide. Indeed, by 2006 the situation had become so bad that China, concerned about the knock-on effect on its standing in Africa, voluntarily imposed a quota on textile exports to South Africa. Likewise, Beijing began to be more sensitive about the domestic economic impact of its trade. It is currently working closely with local manufacturers in Benin, Mali and Togo.[30]

Beyond 'neo-colonialism', China's renewed interest in Africa has also been accused of undermining the liberalisation objectives of Western aid regimes. Beijing is offering an alternative to Western 'conditionality', putting little emphasis on fiscal restraint and democratic reform. Whereas (as will be shown in the following chapter) this conditionality had its faults, an international environment had been created in the 1990s where African leaders understood that they would not receive external assistance unless they reformed their regimes. China has altered this understanding.

Once again, African leaders can play foreign patrons off against one another. China, for example, offered Angola a US$2 billion loan in 2005. This permitted Luanda to walk away from parallel negotiations with the International Monetary Fund (IMF). The IMF's alternative assistance package contained strict economic and political conditions. By contrast, Beijing's sole rider was the option to buy 10,000 barrels of oil a day from Angola.[31] Similarly, China is willing to sell arms to governments on the African continent, even if these regimes are subject to formal or informal Western embargoes. For example, Nigeria, one of Beijing's major oil partners, was able to purchase patrol boats in 2006 to deploy in the politically sensitive Niger Delta.[32]

Beijing is not necessarily taking an immoral position on African trade and aid. Instead, it is more of an amoral stance. Like the protagonists of the Cold War era, China believes in non-interference in the domestic jurisdiction of a state. It is up to Africans to determine how they govern themselves; this is nothing to do with China. Beijing will do business with any recognised sovereign authority representing a state. In this respect, China leaves issues of humanitarian intervention and conditionality, and hand-wringing in general, to the West.

For pariah states, China has provided a lifeline. External resource taps, originally blocked for political and moral reasons, have been turned on once again. Similarly, for more legitimate governments, but those that still have autocratic reflexes or weak democracies, Beijing represents a welcome countervailing force to the conditionality demanded by the West. Should a particular set of aid negotiations not be to the liking of these illiberal states, diplomats can turn to China instead. In both instances, external resources secured can rejuvenate patronage networks, whilst arms bought can shore up the state's coercive powers. Consequently, as will be seen in Chapter 10, enclave states are back in business. Raw materials are exchanged for external patronage, bypassing the need for a state elite to have local accountability.

The Sudan and Zimbabwe provide two good examples of African states benefiting from China's amoral approach to international relations. With the Sudan coming under criticism after 2003 for its brutality in suppressing rebel groups in Darfur,

Western aid was suspended. The Sudan, however, produces some 600,000 barrels of oil a day, with two-thirds of this output being exported to China. Indeed, Beijing invested US$15 billion in Sudanese refineries, roads and railways between 1996 and 2006 to ensure it had access to this oil. The Darfur crisis did not interrupt this co-operation. China and the Sudan engaged in US$3.9 billion of trade in 2005 alone, whilst Beijing advanced a US$3 million preferential loan to Khartoum the following year. Without this Chinese support, President Omar al-Bashir's regime would have struggled. It would have been difficult to sustain patronage networks and the state's coercive power in the face of this Western opposition. Yet China has enabled the al-Bashir government to continue, including its security operation in Darfur. Beijing has provided revenue, diplomatic protection in terms of its UN Security Council veto, and even assistance to build a light arms factory to circumvent the effects of the Western arms embargo.[33]

Zimbabwe, likewise, has received external patronage from China. With Western governments suspending aid and imposing sanctions as a consequence of the Mugabe regime's descent into authoritarianism, China has kept the resources flowing. Zimbabwe had nowhere else left to go. Even Gaddafi's Libya, previously a champion of anti-Western African governments, had reduced its association with Harare. Beijing stepped in to provide loans, transport regeneration, food aid and weapons. In return, Chinese corporations were awarded significant shares in Zimbabwe's mining operations (particularly coal, manganese and platinum), its tobacco plantations, and the opening up of the country to imports (crippling the local textile, clothing and shoe manufacturing industries as a consequence). Chinese companies even received access to land previously confiscated from white farmers during Zimbabwe's land reform programme. Just like the 'Big Men' of the Cold War era, Mugabe now owed his political survival to an external patron, and not to the democratic will of his own people. Zimbabwe's assets were sold off to ensure the regime's continued existence.

China, of course, is not alone in taking an amoral stance on Africa's economic and political plight. Western transnational corporations have worked with autocratic regimes throughout the post-colonial period. Likewise, Western governments have, from time to time, also found themselves uncomfortable bedfellows with African partners accused of anti-democratic practices. Yet, post-Cold War, Beijing's Africa policy has become unique in its willingness to ignore what governments do in their domestic jurisdiction. At a time when the West had collectively signed up to promoting values of good governance, accountability and fiscal responsibility, China was willing to deal with autocrats in order to secure its own economic advantage. Beijing does not share the West's liberal democratic vision for Africa in the New World Order. China is adhering to a different model of economic development. This reality, contradicting Western aid strategies, has thrown a lifeline to African state elites still seeking to survive on the back of patronage networks and coercion.

State, civil society and external interests

In terms of this book's central theme of the relationship between state and civil society in Africa, it can be seen that external interests had a major impact on the continent's post-colonial politics. This is because foreign powers channelled the bulk of their interaction with Africa through this continent's sovereign governments. This automatically gave state elites an advantage over their civil societies.

Table 8.1 Chapter summary: characteristics of Africa's external relations since independence

Cold War period

The Soviet Union	• Limited interests on the continent • Sympathetic to national liberation and socialist ideologies • Seeking military bases • Provides limited amount of aid • Sells/provides large amounts of weapons to allies • Large commitment to specific hot-spots (e.g. Angola, Ethiopia) • Assistance to 'national liberation' movements in southern Africa (ANC, SWAPO, ZANU) • However, no large-scale or long-term involvement on the wider continent
United States of America	• Limited strategic interests on the continent • Seeking allies on the continent who would help to contain communism • Willing to overlook authoritarianism of anti-communist allies (e.g. Zaire and South Africa) • Provision of aid to allies • Some assistance to 'client' rebel groups • Looking to expand markets and commercial interests
United Kingdom	• Relations largely confined to consolidating and expanding economic interests
France	• Continued intimate contacts with ruling elites • Underpins monetary system in ex-colonies • Intervenes militarily to defend allies • Large aid donations • Strong economic links • Expands influence in former non-French colonial countries in Central Africa
Ramifications of 'New World Order'	• End of proxy wars • Africa strategically downgraded • Political conditions attached to aid • Cold War clients lose support • USA attempts humanitarian intervention, but becomes hesitant after Somalia debacle • France becomes more multilateral-minded after its Rwanda intervention, but does continue to underwrite its influence on the continent • Britain encourages fairer aid and debt regime for Africa • China builds strong diplomatic relations to secure economic resources

If sovereignty is defined as enjoying supreme political authority within a territory, then many African countries did not meet the basic theoretical requirement of statehood. They were simply not powerful enough. This was not only because external interests violated this sovereignty relatively easily, but also because many African regimes struggled to assert their sovereignty internally. In this sense, the African state often did not have the resources, legitimacy or penetrative power to command complete control over its own territory or all of its population. As much as the centralised state attempted to monopolise political, economic and social activity within its jurisdiction, there was insufficient means to transmit power to the periphery. Just as in pre-colonial times, state power tended to wane the further one travelled from the capital city or from major economic assets (discussed further in Chapter 10). Given this failure to meet the empirical requirements of statehood, Robert Jackson regards such countries as 'quasi-states'.[34]

External interests, however, supporting the notion that international politics is conducted within a network of sovereign governments, nevertheless recognise quasi-states. They accord these territories a level of sovereignty above that of empirical reality. This explains why micro-states incapable of supporting themselves, such as the Gambia and Lesotho, survive in a competitive world, and why regimes such as the civil war MPLA government in Angola are accorded international recognition as a territory's sole legitimate authority, even when large tracts of this territory are held by rebel forces.

Given that many African countries fell into Jackson's category of quasi-statehood, such international recognition proved to be an invaluable asset for state elites during the post-colonial period. The trappings that accompanied this international sovereignty went a long way towards securing the survival of these regimes. External resources, after all, flowed to those who 'represented' a particular state, and given that African countries produced relatively little economic wealth internally, the controllers of these donated external resources gained considerable power. After elites had secured their own 'commission' on this wealth, they then used the remaining resources to bolster public services, to 'buy' legitimacy from civil society, or to expand the state's coercive capacity in order to suppress opposition. The longer-surviving regimes of post-colonial Africa, such as Mobutu Sese Seko's Zaire and Houphouët-Boigny's Côte d'Ivoire, were those that could manipulate most from their international patrons. Indeed, in several cases, it was almost as if regime survival actually relied more on securing external backing than it did on building internal legitimacy.[35]

However, the end of the Cold War saw a change in the pattern of Africa's foreign assistance. No longer driven by ideological rivalry, external interests were now more precise in how they spent their money. Whereas before, strategic imperatives had persuaded foreign donors to turn a blind eye to domestic excesses, now recipient state elites were made accountable for how they governed their domestic jurisdictions. Consequently, political conditions attached to aid programmes and trade agreements contributed to the pressures that produced political reform in the 1990s. Multi-party elections followed.

In effect, with the New World Order, civil society joined state elites in becoming a beneficiary of the attentions of external interests. Indeed, some aid projects specifically encouraged sub-state political activity in Africa. Foreign donors bypassed state elites, and engaged in assisting civil society directly. The United States, for example, funded an extensive programme of 'voter education' and 'voluntary-sector management' in Ghana during the 1990s.[36]

Conditionality, therefore, changed the nature of the political game in Africa. All the continent's governments remained reliant on external aid and patronage, yet in order to receive this aid they now had to serve their citizens', and not just their own, interests. 'Good governance' was the demand. There were certainly numerous deceptive practices adopted by rulers to ensure that the elite still benefited most from the distribution of this aid, but they could no longer hide behind Cold War interpretations of 'sovereignty' and 'non-interference in domestic jurisdictions'. With the occasional exception of China, donors no longer blindly handed over resources to state elites simply because they were the representatives of sovereign power. To conclude with Christopher Clapham's observation:

African states, certainly, have continued in most cases to survive, and some of them have a remarkable capacity to reconstitute themselves from a condition of apparently terminal decay. If they are to sustain themselves, and to gain the capacity to carry out the functions for which no effective substitute for statehood has yet been devised, they will, however, have to do so on the basis of their relations with their own citizens, rather than the support of international convention.[37]

Case study: Somalia's international relations

Occupying 3,000 kilometres of coastal territory where the Red Sea flows into the Indian Ocean, Somalia forms the 'Horn' of East Africa. It is a country of arid plains which rise to mountains in the north. Traditionally, the Somali are a nomadic people whose subsistence relies on the herding of goats, cattle, sheep and camels. Arable cultivation, however, can be found in a fertile region located between the country's two permanent rivers, the Jubba and the Shebele.

Ethnically, Somalia is one of Africa's most homogeneous countries. References to the Somali people go back as far as the fifteenth century. It was not until the arrival of colonialism, however, that these people were gathered into modern nation-states. Britain declared a protectorate over the north of this territory in 1887, while Italy completed the 'pacification' of the southern Somali people in 1927. Significantly, colonial boundaries left other Somalis outside these two main colonies. Many found themselves under French jurisdiction (in modern-day Djibouti), others were stranded in northern Kenya, and yet more were left in the Ogaden region of the Ethiopian empire. This problem of a divided people was only partly solved by decolonisation.

In 1960, the former British and Italian territories merged by mutual agreement, within days of independence, to form the Somali Democratic Republic. Nationalists of both north and south united behind the leadership of the Somali Youth League. Most Somalis, however, saw this instance of unification as only the beginning. They desired a greater Somaliland which would include all of their people. Consequently, the new government supplied arms to insurgent movements in both northern Kenya and the Ogaden region of Ethiopia. That the Republic also rejected the OAU's 1964 declaration on acceptance of the colonial boundaries clearly identified Somalia as an irredentist state (see Chapter 2).

The Somali Republic was dependent upon external actors at independence, and remained so throughout the post-colonial period. Decolonisation may have left Somalia with the political trappings of a modern state, but it bequeathed it very little by way of a modern economy. With a large proportion of the population engaged in subsistence herding, and no industrial base or mineral reserves to speak of, the government had to attract capital from abroad, both to develop the economy, and to enhance the capacity of the state itself. Somali leaders proved to be quite adept at this.

With respect to military assistance, for example, the government tapped into a number of external sources. Although wary of Somalia's irredentist ambitions, the superpowers jostled for influence in the Horn of Africa. Initially, for example,

Western powers offered a small military programme amounting to US$10 million. The Soviet Union responded by outbidding this offer with a US$30 million package.[38] Paradoxically, Cold War competition resulted in a situation where the USSR supplied and trained the army during the 1960s, while the West did the same for the country's police force.

Economic assistance was also sought from equally diverse sources. Having very little domestic capital to invest itself, most of the costs of Somalia's development projects were met by foreign donors. Italy provided US$190 million of aid between 1953 and 1975, the Soviet Union made available US$152 million, China gave US$133 million, the United States bestowed US$75 million, and other Western countries contributed a total of US$64 million.[39]

After 1969, however, the diverse nature of these external patrons came to an end. This was prompted by a military coup led by Major General Siad Barré. Seizing power, the military responded to the fragmented nature of Somali politics. Although Somalia can be described as an ethnically homogeneous state, its people are divided into five major clan families, and can be further divided into numerous sub-clans. Between 1960 and 1969, Somalia had resisted the trend elsewhere in Africa to form a one-party state. Consequently, pluralist competition mobilised along ethnic lines. In the 1969 election, for example, 1,002 candidates representing 62 parties competed for 123 seats in the national assembly.[40] Barré justified his *coup d'état* on the grounds that this inter-clan competition wasted scarce resources and bred corruption. Indeed, the military simply took advantage of the fact that it had become the most organised force in Somalia's fragmented society. External aid, after all, had made it the fourth biggest army on the African continent, after those of Ethiopia, Nigeria and Ghana.

The range of external patrons shrank in post-coup Somalia because Barré's regime adopted scientific socialism as its ideological guide. Domestic and foreign businesses were nationalised, land became strictly controlled by the state, political pluralism was suppressed, and a single Somali Revolutionary Socialist Party was established. Although the banana plantations, Somalia's biggest cash crop, remained in private hands, Barré's experiments in Marxism–Leninism won the backing of the Soviet Union. This alliance was confirmed with the signing of a Treaty of Friendship and Co-operation in 1974, whereby, in return for external resources, the USSR gained access to the Indian Ocean port of Berbera and several Somali airfields. Moscow considered its presence in the Horn of Africa to be a vital counter-balance to the US arming of Emperor Haile Selassie's regime across the border in Ethiopia.

It was the army itself that benefited most from Soviet patronage. Military aid flowed into Somalia during the first half of the 1970s. The army, for example, increased in size from 12,000 soldiers in 1970 to 30,000 by 1977. These personnel had at their disposal Soviet-built tanks, as well as surface-to-air missiles, coastal patrol vessels and MiG aircraft. Similarly, over 1,000 Soviet military advisers were dispatched to Somalia during this period, while 2,400 Somalis travelled in the opposite direction to be trained in the USSR. Although Moscow concentrated on giving military aid to Somalia, as it did with most of its African clients, economic assistance was also forthcoming. Soviet aid helped to build meat-canning plants, irrigation systems and fisheries.[41]

Although Somalia now relied heavily on the Soviet Union as its primary patron, the government in Mogadishu was careful to keep its options open. External resources, after all, were invaluable whatever their ideological origin. For this reason, Barré made efforts to court fellow Islamic countries, joining the Arab League in 1974. Somalia also had profitable relations with China and North Korea.

In hindsight, it was fortunate that these alternative diplomatic and aid channels remained open, because, by 1978, Soviet assistance had ceased. The break with Moscow came as a response to Somalia's invasion of Ethiopia. The border between these two states had never been precisely defined, and, under colonial rule, nomadic Somalis had retained grazing rights across the frontier. The irredentist government in Mogadishu had consequently always claimed the Ogaden to be an integral part of a greater Somaliland. In 1977, Barré, taking advantage of the political instability created by a revolution in Ethiopia, decided to strike. The Somali regular army, trained and equipped by the Soviet Union, crossed the border in large numbers to fight alongside the insurgent (ethnic Somali) Western Somali Liberation Front.

These events posed something of a dilemma for officials in Moscow. The ousting of Haile Selassie by a Marxist–Leninist-oriented regime, led by Mariam Mengistu, had made Ethiopia a potentially valuable ally to the Soviet Union. In effect, Moscow was now forced to choose between Barré in Somalia (a country in which the USSR had invested heavily since 1969), and Mengistu in Ethiopia (a new client state with more revolutionary potential). The USSR attempted to defuse the conflict by persuading all parties to abandon their nationalist claims and build, instead, a socialist federation in the Horn of Africa. Barré, however, refused Moscow's advances, and responded by unilaterally breaking the Treaty of Friendship and Co-operation, revoking the USSR's access to Berbera, and expelling all Soviet advisors from Somalia.

At first glance, Barré's decision to abandon the patronage of the Soviet Union seems odd. How could Somalia afford to lose these external resources? It would have seemed more prudent for Mogadishu to reel in its irredentist ambitions in favour of retaining Moscow's assistance. There was, however, a strategy behind Barré's actions.

Somalia was seeking to switch Cold War patrons. In April 1977, the United States had suspended its military aid to Ethiopia. Although Washington had continued to court the government in Addis Ababa after the revolution, US officials soon faced ideological incompatibilities. This left the United States with no clients in this strategically important region. Barré's plan was to offer the services of Somalia in this role. If Washington accepted these advances, Somalia, he gambled, could both still receive external (now US) backing, and also be able to prosecute its irredentist war in Ethiopia. This, however, proved to be one gamble too many.

Initially, it looked as if Barré had succeeded in his diplomatic volte-face. A deal involving US$460 million of US arms was negotiated between the two countries in June 1977, with Saudi Arabia acting as mediator.[42] This was the breakthrough that prompted Barré's expulsion of the Soviet Union from Somalia. Yet, back in Washington DC, the administration of President Carter placed a good deal of emphasis on human rights in its foreign policy. As part of this arms deal, the United States insisted that Somalia should withdraw its army from the Ogaden. This, however, Barré refused to do. From having almost succeeded in manipulating historical events and Cold War competition to Somalia's advantage, Barré was now left with no major external backers. Consequently, although the Somali army had made impressive progress in its invasion of the Ogaden, it was now no match for Soviet-supplied Ethiopian forces, reinforced by Cuban combat troops. The Somalis, outnumbered and outgunned, finally withdrew from the Ogaden in March 1978.

Defeat in Ethiopia threatened the very future of Siad Barré's regime. His government's overriding concern became the need to secure external patronage once more. Foreign assistance, in this respect, represented the regime's best hope of restoring vital legitimacy and prestige. Resources were needed to feed Barré's client–patron networks. Mogadishu sought help from Saudi Arabia, Iran, Egypt, China, France, the United Kingdom, West Germany, Italy and the United States, and reconciliatory advances were even made towards the Soviet Union.[43] Although economic assistance was forthcoming from some of these countries, none was prepared to re-arm the irredentist Somali army. For Barré, however, military aid was essential. Arms were required not only to keep any idea of a greater Somaliland alive; they were also now desperately needed to maintain domestic order and protect the regime itself.

Barré's government spent two years in the wilderness. In 1980, however, Mogadishu came to an agreement with the United States whereby US forces gained access to the military facilities of Berbera in return for military aid. Washington was persuaded to extend this assistance in the light of Cold War developments, where the United States had lost a client state in Iran, and the Soviet Union had invaded Afghanistan. Barré's softer rhetoric, talking about creating a greater Somaliland only by peaceful means, clinched the deal. And once the United States was back in Somalia, other donors followed suit. Alongside Washington's US$51 million of military assistance and US$53 million of development aid, Italy gave US$9 million for irrigation and hydroelectric projects, while European Community institutions gave a further US$53 million.[44] In terms of external resources, the state of Somalia was now back in business.

Barré's regime, however, was never able to secure the levels of patronage it had enjoyed in the 1970s. Western donors were too aware of the government's deteriorating human rights record, and the ever present threat of irredentist adventurism. Eventually, with the Cold War waning, the United States suspended its aid to Mogadishu in 1988, and, in 1991, reacting to the collapse of Barré's regime, despatched naval vessels to evacuate its citizens and diplomats. As T. Frank Crigler, a former US ambassador to Somalia, put it, the United States 'turned out the lights, closed the door, and forgot about the place'.[45] With the imperatives of world politics having changed in the absence of a Soviet threat, Western governments were now no longer particularly interested in Somalia's fate.

Without these external resources, the regime in Mogadishu could no longer assert its authority over the entire territory of Somalia. Since the Ogaden defeat, Barré had attempted to retain power by arming 'loyal' sub-clans, and encouraging them to 'pacify' other factions. Sources of opposition in rival clan lines were thus destroyed via harassment, exile, assassination and, towards the end, even the bombing of whole villages.[46] Barré's forces were pitted against the secessionist Somali National Movement in the north, the Majetein Somali Salvation Democratic Front in the north-east, the Somali Patriotic Movement in the south and west, and the United Somali Congress around Mogadishu. Essentially, as power in the centre faded, local factions based on clan allegiances carved up Somalia. Civil war was the result, and, defeated, Siad Barré finally fled the country in 1991.

Somalia's former patrons had few remaining interests in this state, and had no wish to be embroiled in the civil war. Global strategic factors that previously might have fuelled a proxy war were now absent. As a result, clan warlords were left to fight among themselves. The world looked on as the state of Somalia disintegrated.

This position did briefly change in 1992. With non-government organisations (NGOs) reporting the deaths of some 50,000 Somalis, and a further 4.5 million at risk through famine, the United Nations decided to act on humanitarian grounds. UN emergency aid, and troops to protect it, was subsequently dispatched. Significantly, this operation coincided with the declaration of the 'New World Order' envisaged by US President George H.W. Bush. Wanting to show the potential for conflict resolution that this new international order offered, Bush agreed to bolster the UN operation with up to 30,000 US troops. The 'peace enforcement' of Operation Restore Hope commenced in December 1992.

Initially, this humanitarian intervention went well. Emergency aid reached the needy, ceasefires came into force among the clans, and there was even progress made at a conference of 'national reconciliation'. The United Nations, the United States in particular, however, overstretched itself in terms of peace *enforcement*. Rather than mediating between factions, the UN operation suffered from 'mission creep', and began to dictate terms to the parties involved. For example, US officials tried to marginalise a militia led by General Mohammed Farrah Aidid, who was seen as an obstacle to negotiations. When 23 Pakistani peacekeepers were killed trying to disarm Aidid's supporters, the UN sought to arrest the general. Months of raids against militia strongholds followed. US special forces, ferried by helicopter gunships across the skies of Mogadishu, exacted a high death toll on the city's population. The UN had lost its neutrality in the conflict.

Then, in October 1993, the tables were turned. During yet another raid against Aidid's militia, a US 'Black Hawk' helicopter was shot down. In the ensuing firefight, 18 US Rangers were killed (alongside some 300 Somalis). The television pictures of dead US troops being paraded in the streets of Mogadishu proved too much for the American public. Washington DC's brief appetite for New World Order 'humanitarian' peace enforcement was at an end in Africa. By March 1994, US forces had withdrawn from Somalia, as did most of the UN mission.

The state collapsed. No government was able to generate sufficient legitimacy either internally (among all Somalis) or externally (benefiting from international patronage). Protracted negotiations to build a government of national unity were constantly stymied by competing factional interests. Other groups attempting to use Islamist values as a unifying force also failed to gain sufficient popular support. Violence and instability were the result as these groups resorted to military power in an effort to assert their authority. Hundreds of thousands of people died as a consequence of this anarchy, either directly in political violence or as victims of famine. International terrorist and criminal groups also came to use Somalia as a safe haven from state power. Likewise, it is no coincidence that piracy has become one of Somalia's most productive industries. Having had its fingers burnt during the failed humanitarian intervention in 1994, the international community came to realise that there is also a price to pay for non-intervention.

Two decades later, Somalia is only just getting back on its feet. A government of national unity has brought a degree of respite since 2010. This authority appears to be making some headway in restoring a sovereign state, but Somalia is still an atomised society vulnerable to warlords mobilising on the basis of clan and religious loyalty. In the north, clan alliances have sought to build an alternative state, founding a smaller secessionist Republic of Somalia. This proto-state follows the borders of the old colonial British Somaliland. This new republic, however, has not received external recognition. The international community, protecting the traditional sovereign state system of international relations, prefers to recognise only the original 'space-that-is-Somalia'.[47] External powers favour the Mogadishu national unity administration, as a government of reconciliation that seeks to rule the whole space of Somalia drawn on existing maps. With the help of military interventions from Ethiopia in 2006, Kenya in 2011, and, more recently, with the boosting of an African Union peacekeeping force, this national unity administration is gaining in authority. Western governments have played their part, too, in recent years by supplying aid approaching US$1 billion annually.[48] As before, it would seem that a government in Mogadishu needs assistance from external backers to compensate for sovereignty that it cannot itself generate across its territory and society.

Somalia[49]

Territory:	637,635 sq. km.	Population:	10.5 million
Colonial power:	Britain/Italy	Independence:	1960
Major cities:	Mogadishu (capital)	Ethnic groups:	Somali
	Hargeysa	Infant mortality:	90 deaths/1,000 live births
	Kismayu	Religion:	Islam
Languages:	Somali	Urban population:	39 per cent
	Italian	Life expectancy:	55 years
	English	Adult literacy:	24.1 per cent
Currency:	Somali shilling	Exports:	Livestock
GDP per capita:	US$128		Vegetable oil
			Fuel wood and charcoal

Questions raised by this chapter

1. Did African states benefit from the international political environment of the Cold War?
2. To what extent have external patrons differed in their policies towards African states?
3. Would you describe the 'New World Order' as a positive development for Africa?
4. Has the intervention of external interests merely served to underwrite the power of the African state in the post-colonial period?
5. Are external interests ever justified in violating a state's sovereignty?

Glossary of key terms

Chasse gardée	A term (meaning 'private hunting ground') used to convey the freedom and extent of France's diplomatic, economic and military activities within francophone Africa.
Containment of communism	The primary goal of US foreign policy during the Cold War, which aimed to restrict opportunities for communist expansion globally.
Humanitarian intervention	Diplomatic and military activity, more common from the 1990s onwards, where state sovereignty may be violated in order to protect a population's human rights.
La Francophonie	A reference to the French-speaking group of states or 'commonwealth'.
Non-interference in domestic jurisdictions	The respect of state sovereignty among states where it is agreed that no state has the right to interfere in the internal affairs of another.
Political conditionality	The demands of 'good governance' to which aid donors required recipient states to conform.

Proxy war	A local conflict which has been 'internationalised', effectively making the protagonists surrogates of competing 'superpowers'.
Quasi-state	A state that is too weak to meet the empirical demands of a sovereign territory, but is still recognised as a full member of the international system of sovereign states.
Sovereignty	The claim of supreme political authority within a territory.

Further reading

For a comprehensive outline of Africa's place in the global political system, Christopher Clapham's book is an excellent place to start. His focus on international relations from the African side of the fence is both enlightening and accessible. An alternative broad perspective is provided by Edmond Keller and Donald Rothchild. After digesting these two overviews, readers could seek out articles and books that are more geospecific. Two good case studies on the Cold War era are Marina Ottaway's work on the Horn of Africa, and John Stockwell's memoirs of being the CIA's task-force leader in Angola. Moving into the 'New World Order', Tom Porteous provides an analysis of UK policy, Guy Martin and Tony Chafer attend to France's adventurism, Gorm Rye Olsen studies European actors in general, F. Ugboaja Ohaegbulam is enlightening on the United States, and Chris Alden and Ian Taylor assess China's impact.

Alden, Chris. *China in Africa*. London: Zed, 2007.

Chafer, Tony. Franco-African relations: no longer so exceptional? *African Affairs*. 2002, 101(404), 343–63.

Clapham, Christopher. *Africa and the International System: The Politics of State Survival*. Cambridge: Cambridge University Press, 1996.

Keller, Edmond J. and Donald Rothchild, eds. *Africa in the New International Order: Rethinking State Sovereignty and Regional Security*. Boulder, CO: Lynne Rienner, 1996.

Martin, Guy. Continuity and change in Franco-African relations. *Journal of Modern African Studies*. 1995, 33(1), 1–20.

Ohaegbulam, F. Ugboaja. The United States and Africa after the Cold War. *Africa Today*. 1992, 39(4), 19–34.

Olsen, Gorm Rye. Western Europe's relations with Africa since the end of the Cold War. *Journal of Modern African Studies*. 1997, 35(2), 299–319.

Olsen, Gorm Rye. Europe and the promotion of democracy in post Cold War Africa: how serious is Europe and for what reason? *African Affairs*. 1998, 97(388), 343–67.

Ottaway, Marina. *Soviet and American Influence in the Horn of Africa*. New York: Praeger, 1982.

Porteous, Tom. *Britain in Africa*. London: Zed, 2008.

Stockwell, John. *In Search of Enemies: A CIA Story*. London: Andre Deutsch, 1978.

Taylor, Ian. *China's New Role in Africa*. Boulder, CO: Lynne Rienner, 2009.

Notes and references

1 See Hoffman, John. *Sovereignty*. Buckingham: Open University Press, 1998.

2 See Clapham, Christopher. *Africa and the International System: The Politics of State Survival*. Cambridge: Cambridge University Press, 1996. 153. See also Grey, Robert D. The Soviet presence in Africa: an analysis of goals. *Journal of Modern African Studies*. 1984, 22(3), 518.

3   Sarris, Louis George. Soviet military policy and arms activities in Sub-Saharan Africa. In: William J. Foltz and Henry S. Bienen. eds. *Arms and the African: Military Influences on Africa's International Relations*. New Haven, CT: Yale University Press, 1985. 35.

4   Gavshon, Arthur. *Crisis in Africa: Battleground of East and West*. Harmondsworth: Penguin, 1981. 70.

5   See, for example, Thomson, Alex. *Conflict of Interests: US Foreign Policy Towards Apartheid South Africa, 1948–1994*. New York: Palgrave Macmillan, 2008.

6   Clapham. *Africa and the International System: The Politics of State Survival*. 88.

7   Young, Crawford. African relations with the major powers. In: Gwendolen M. Carter and Patrick O'Meara, eds. *African Independence: The First Twenty-Five Years*. Bloomington, IN: Indiana University Press, 1985. 221.

8   Clapham. *Africa and the International System: The Politics of State Survival*. 88.

9   See, for example, Golan, Tamar. A certain mystery: how can France do everything that it does in Africa—and get away with it? *African Affairs*. 1981, 80(318), 3–11.

10 Clapham. *Africa and the International System: The Politics of State Survival*. 95. See also Martin, Guy. Continuity and change in Franco-African relations. *Journal of Modern African Studies*. 1995, 33(1), 11.

11 Cited in Campbell, Kurt M. *Southern Africa in Soviet Foreign Policy* [Adelphi Paper 227]. London: International Institute for Strategic Studies, 1987. 8.

12 Gavshon. *Crisis in Africa: Battleground of East and West*. 79.

13 Obasanjo, Olusegun. A balance sheet of the African region and the Cold War. In: Edmond J. Keller and Donald Rothchild, eds. *Africa in the New International Order: Rethinking State Sovereignty and Regional Security*. Boulder, CO: Lynne Rienner, 1996. 16–17.

14 Lefebvre, Jeffery A. Moscow's Cold War and post-Cold War policies in Africa. In: Edmond J. Keller and Donald Rothchild, eds. *Africa in the New International Order: Rethinking State Sovereignty and Regional Security*. Boulder, CO: Lynne Rienner, 1996. 215.

15 United States Department of Commerce, Bureau of the Census. *Statistical Abstract of the United States: 1997*. Washington, DC: Hoover's Business Press, 1997. Table 1302.

16 Olsen, Gorm Rye. Western Europe's relations with Africa since the end of the Cold War. *Journal of Modern African Studies*. 1997, 35(2), 299–319.

17 *Ibid*. 306.

18 Volman, Daniel. Africa and the New World Order. *Journal of Modern African Studies*. 1993, 31(1), 16.

19 Schraeder, Peter J. France and the great game in Africa. *Current History*. 1997, 96(610), 207.

20 Cumming, Gordon. French development assistance to Africa: towards a new agenda? *African Affairs*. 1995, 94(376), 392.

21 MacAskill, Ewen. Blair braced for a long haul in Africa. *The Guardian* (London). 24 January 2002. 17.

22 Address by Tony Blair, Johannesburg, South Africa, 30 May 2007. http://news.bbc.co.uk/1/hi/uk_politics/6708917.stm (accessed 17 November 2015).

23 Porteous, Tom. *Britain in Africa*. London: Zed, 2008. 105.

24 www.dfid.gov.uk/Global-Issues/Millennium-Development-Goals/8-Develop-a-global-partnership-for-development/ (accessed 2 July 2009).

25 United Kingdom Department for International Development. *Annual Report 2008: Making it Happen*. London: The Stationery Office, 2008. Annex 3.

26 'Africa–China Trade' Special Report. *Financial Times* (London). 24 January 2008. 1.

27 Taylor, Ian. *China's New Role in Africa*. Boulder, CO: Lynne Rienner, 2009. 15.

28 Wang, Jian-Ye and Abdoulaye Bio-Tchané. Africa's burgeoning ties with China. *Finance and Development*. 2008, 45(1). www.imf.org/external/pubs/ft/fandd/2008/03/wang.htm (accessed 9 July 2009). See also Broadman, Harry G. Connecting Africa and Asia. *Finance and Development*. 2007, 44(2). www.imf.org/external/pubs/ft/fandd/2007/06/broadman.htm (accessed 9 July 2009).

29 Taylor. *China's New Role in Africa*. 42.

30 Alden, Chris. *China in Africa*. London: Zed, 2007. 49, 80–81.

31 Lee, Don. China barrels ahead in oil market. *Los Angeles Times*. 14 November 2004. http://articles.latimes.com/2004/nov/14/business/fi-chinaoil14?pg=2 (accessed 9 July 2009).

32 Mahtani, Dino. Nigeria shifts to China arms. *Financial Times* (London). 28 February 2006. www.ft.com/cms/s/0/331fcea0-a800-11da-85bc-0000779e2340.html?nclick_check=1 (accessed 9 July 2009).

33 Harman, Danna. In Sudan, China focuses on oil wells, not local needs. *Christian Science Monitor*. 25 June 2007. www.csmonitor.com/2007/0625/p11s01-woaf.html (accessed 9 July 2009). See also Alden. *China in Africa*. 61–2.

34 Jackson, Robert H. *Quasi-States: Sovereignty, International Relations and the Third World*. Cambridge: Cambridge University Press, 1990.

35 This section draws on Christopher Clapham's work, *Africa and the International System*.

36 See Hearn, Julie. The US democratic experiment in Ghana. In: Alfred Zack-Williams, Diane Frost and Alex Thomson, eds. *Africa in Crisis: New Challenges and Possibilities*. London: Pluto, 2002. 97–108.

37 Clapham. *Africa and the International System*. 272.

38 Ottaway, Marina. *Soviet and American Influence in the Horn of Africa*. New York: Praeger, 1982. 25.

39 Yohannes, Okbazghi. *The United States and the Horn of Africa: An Analytical Study of Pattern and Process*. Boulder, CO: Westview, 1997. 225.

40 Simons, Anna. Somalia: the structure of dissolution. In: Leonardo A. Villalón and Phillip A. Huxtable, eds. *The African State at a Critical Juncture: Between Disintegration and Reconfiguration*. Boulder, CO: Lynne Rienner, 1998. 59.

41 Ottaway, Marina. *Soviet and American Influence in the Horn of Africa*. 67. See also Gavshon. *Crisis in Africa: Battleground of East and West*. 267.

42 Yohannes. *The United States and the Horn of Africa: An Analytical Study of Pattern and Process*. 241–2.

43 Ottaway, Marina. *Soviet and American Influence in the Horn of Africa*. 124.

44 *Ibid*. 126. See also Yohannes. *The United States and the Horn of Africa: An Analytical Study of Pattern and Process*. 244.

45 Cited in Volman. Africa and the New World Order. *Journal of Modern African Studies*. 1993, 31(1), 7.

46 Adam, Hussein. Somalia. In: William I. Zartman, ed. *Collapsed States: The Disintegration and Restoration of Legitimate Authority*. Boulder, CO: Lynne Rienner, 1995. 74.

47 Simons. In: Villalón and Huxtable, eds. *The African State at a Critical Juncture: Between Disintegration and Reconfiguration*. 70.

48 World Bank. Data. Net official development assistance and official aid received (current US$). http://data.worldbank.org/indicator/DT.ODA.ALLD.CD (accessed 10 July 2015).

49 Statistics taken from United Nations Conference on Trade and Development. *UNCTAD Handbook of Statistics 2014*. New York: United Nations, 2014. Tables 8.1, 8.4 and 3.2.D (accessed 24 July 2015); World Bank data http://data.worldbank.org/indicator/SP.DYN.LE00.IN (accessed 24 July 2015) and http://data.worldbank.org/indicator/SP.DYN.IMRT.IN (accessed 24 July 2015); and UNESCO. Institute for Statistics. *Global Education Digest 2009: Comparing Educational Statistics Across the World*. UNESCO, 2009. Table 15 (no data available since 2010).

9 Sovereignty II

Neo-colonialism, structural adjustment and Africa's political economy

Chapter outline

- Burdens of the international economy
- The African debt crisis
- The era of structural adjustment
- The consequences of structural adjustment

  - The economic impact
  - The social impact
  - The political impact

- Debt relief and continued conditionality
- State, civil society and external interests
- Case study: Ghana's structural adjustment
- Questions raised by this chapter
- Glossary of key terms
- Further reading
- Notes and references

For most of the post-colonial period, economic poverty has been a key concern for African governments. The sustained economic growth predicted at independence failed to emerge, while the last two decades of the twentieth century saw many parts of the continent come close to financial collapse. In terms of gross national product (GNP), this region clearly produced less wealth for its people than other parts of the world. This meant, for instance, that an average African economy in 2000, such as that of Mauritania, generated only US$478 for each of its citizens. The United States, by comparison, enjoyed US$35,906 per person. Somalia, Africa's poorest country at this time, was even more disadvantaged. It had to make do with a per-capita GNP of just US$111. There has been a remarkable upsurge in the continent's economic fortune since the millennium (discussed in the final chapter of this book), but the relative statistics are still damning (see Table 9.1). The per-capita gross domestic product (GDP) of sub-Saharan Africa in 2007 was still 56 times smaller than that of the United States, with this statistic only narrowing to 27 times smaller (for the whole of Africa) by 2012. The economies of East Africa (78 times smaller than the US economy) and West Africa (41 times smaller) lagged behind this continent-wide average.[1]

Macro economic indicators such as GDP and GNP, however, fail to convey what this poverty actually means for individuals in Africa. When a country fails to develop its

Table 9.1 Per-capita gross domestic product (US dollars), 1960–2013

	1960	1970	1980	1990	2000	2010	2013
Developing economies – Africa	—	—	909	787	743	1,698	1,881
United Kingdom	1,308	2,346	9,592	17,751	25,239	36,840	39,969
United States	3,007	5,247	12,329	23,290	35,906	47,644	52,220
Eastern Africa	—	—	363	339	279	515	686
Middle Africa	—	—	637	620	380	1,391	1,814
Northern Africa	—	—	1,221	1,265	1,483	3,167	3,637
Southern Africa	—	—	2,574	2,855	2,817	6,702	6,382
Western Africa	—	—	925	460	377	1,137	1,320
Algeria	242	331	2,174	2,359	1,727	4,365	5,357
Angola	—	—	706	996	636	4,221	5,904
Benin	93	115	370	369	339	690	798
Botswana	58	139	855	2,689	3,297	6,980	7,515
Burkina Faso	68	81	283	356	227	579	702
Burundi	70	70	225	200	104	226	239
Cameroon	115	171	993	981	583	1,145	1,295
Cape Verde	—	—	536	995	1,386	3,413	4,236
Central African Republic	75	103	489	495	251	457	503
Chad	104	129	254	271	167	761	837
Comoros	—	—	394	591	382	777	923
Congo, DRC (Kinshasa)	130	206	374	268	112	212	309
Congo (Brazzaville)	220	244	950	1,174	1,030	2,987	3,376
Côte d'Ivoire	157	278	1,231	982	662	1,208	1,365
Djibouti	—	—	838	775	769	1,353	1,675
Egypt	—	211	448	638	1,447	2,749	3,026
Equatorial Guinea	—	228	244	356	2,272	17,792	20,247
Eritrea	—	—	—	—	179	369	566
Ethiopia	—	—	156	227	122	302	469
Gabon	284	550	7,214	6,167	4,478	12,062	15,629
The Gambia	—	117	834	772	637	566	492
Ghana	183	258	482	682	424	1,326	1,744
Guinea	—	—	331	485	365	481	580
Guinea–Bissau	—	115	627	598	292	533	522
Kenya	98	142	563	471	403	787	1,016
Lesotho	41	67	269	341	415	1,097	1,120
Liberia	170	228	404	232	183	271	385
Libya	—	—	12,405	7,298	7,432	13,400	15,622
Madagascar	132	169	373	267	246	415	472
Malawi	46	64	338	316	262	450	313
Mali	—	63	225	315	259	672	724
Mauritania	108	182	975	802	478	874	1,046
Mauritius	—	—	1,201	2,481	3,935	7,897	9,622
Morocco	165	247	1,062	1,169	1,290	2,869	3,157
Mozambique	—	—	397	219	236	387	601
Namibia	—	—	2,500	1,893	2,059	5,063	5,256
Niger	135	147	462	340	157	360	429
Nigeria	93	224	1,264	366	378	1,437	1,638
Rwanda	41	59	273	357	211	519	644

Table 9.1 Per-capita gross domestic product (US dollars), 1960–2013 (Continued)

	1960	1970	1980	1990	2000	2010	2013
São Tomé and Principe	—	—	818	966	520	1,216	1,590
Senegal	249	243	584	826	475	995	1,069
Seychelles	288	344	2,711	6,410	9,362	10,672	13,753
Sierra Leone	149	172	419	218	208	448	874
Somalia	65	92	94	157	278	111	128[a]
South Africa	423	811	2,770	3,044	2,963	7,060	6,679
South Sudan	—	—	—	—	—	—	1,044
Sudan	107	151	333	491	381	1,528	1,753
Swaziland	100	252	1,100	1,257	1,433	3,262	2,850
Tanzania	—	—	391	215	306	524	679
Togo	77	120	416	472	266	503	634
Tunisia	—	281	1,522	1,662	2,248	4,169	4,311
Uganda	62	133	237	222	251	506	623
Zambia	227	427	738	484	321	1,225	1,621
Zimbabwe	281	362	981	1,122	604	568	714

[a]= 2012 figure.

Source: Assembled from World Bank and UNCTAD data. 1960 and 1970 statistics: World Development Indicators database. http://databank.worldbank.org/data/views/variableselection/selectvariables.aspx?source= world-development-indicators (accessed 20 June 2015). 1980–2013 statistics: United Nations Conference on Trade and Development. *UNCTAD Handbook of Statistics 2014*. New York: United Nations, 2014. Table 8.1. http://data.worldbank.org/country/sudan (accessed 20 June 2015) and http://data.worldbank.org/country/ south-sudan (accessed 20 June 2015).

economy, hardship inevitably results. A quick survey of contemporary social statistics illustrates this point. Sub-Saharan Africans die, on average, in their fifties. Europeans and North Americans, on the other hand, have a life expectancy that extends into their eighties. At the other end of life, babies in Africa are over 20 times more likely to die before their fifth birthday than are those born in the West. Even in the field of Africa's post-colonial success story, namely education, the comparisons remain distressing. Approximately 40 per cent of Africans remain illiterate (with women particularly disadvantaged). In the West, literacy is almost taken for granted.[2]

Africa is poor due to a combination of factors both internal and external to the continent. A neo-liberal school of thought tends to internalise the problem, focusing blame on corrupt and inefficient African governments. Others disagree. They claim that Africa's problems can be more accurately explained by the nature of the international economy. These scholars consider the underdevelopment discussed in Chapter 2 to have continued into the post-colonial era, with the West still exploiting African economies through unfavourable terms of trade and unequal exchange.

Both of these schools make valid points. Consequently, both sides of the debate need to be explored. This chapter, however, will focus solely on the external factors hindering African development, as the internal constraints are discussed in the next chapter.

Given this focus on 'external factors', it is useful to continue to use *sovereignty* as our guiding concept for this chapter. Two central questions will be posed. The first of these explores the extent to which external powers have influenced the economic development of Africa in the post-colonial era. Has African sovereignty continued to be violated in this economic sphere? The second question then considers what has been the political impact of this external input.

In answering these two questions, the chapter is divided into six sections. The first of these will examine how underdevelopment adapted itself to the post-colonial era. Is it true that, after independence, the West merely substituted imperial rule with neo-colonial exploitation? Then the continent's debt crisis will come under scrutiny. Why did African states come to owe the West such colossal sums of capital? The third section of the chapter brings the continent's post-colonial economic history up to date by exploring the phenomena of 'structural adjustment' and 'conditionality'. Again, is this a case of foreign political agencies dictating terms to African governments? Is this intervention warranted? The fourth section assesses the economic, social and political impact of this foreign intervention. The fifth section then explores the recent readjustment of this relationship, in the form of a debt relief programme. This is followed by the final section, which will put this debate in the context of the book's ongoing theme of the interaction between state, civil society and external interests. Taken together, these six components of the chapter will provide a good overview of the external impact on post-colonial African political economies.

Burdens of the international economy

The imperial inheritance, as documented in Chapter 2, left Africa somewhat disadvantaged in the modern international economy. During the colonial years, limited development based on the continent's primary sector had been undertaken (in agriculture and mining), and a basic infrastructure was built to support this. Yet the actual level of economic growth enjoyed in Africa was scant reward for this activity. Profits, on the whole, were exported to the West, rather than being invested locally. This left independent Africa with highly specialised export economies, a minute manufacturing base, a lack of access to technology, and populations in which few were trained in the ways of modern business, social services or public administration. In short, Europe had indeed underdeveloped Africa. As Walter Rodney put it, 'the vast majority of Africans went into colonialism with a hoe and came out with a hoe'.[3]

Exploitation of African economies did not end, however, with the flag-lowering ceremonies at independence. Decisions made in the West still continued to have a considerable influence over Africa's potential to develop. Indeed, Kwame Nkrumah, Ghana's first president, argued that colonialism had merely made way for a type of *neo*-colonialism. He explained: 'The essence of neo-colonialism is that the State which is subject to it is, in theory, independent and has all the trappings of international sovereignty. In reality its economic system and thus its political system is directed from outside'.[4] Hence, although formal political control had now ended, Africa still had to contend with the old colonial inequalities.

One of the major structural problems of this international economy, in African eyes, was 'unequal exchange'. Colonial rule left almost all African states with highly specialised 'monocrop' economies, usually producing just one, two or three commodities for export. The Rwandan economy, for example, was dominated by coffee, while Malawi concentrated almost exclusively on tobacco and tea (see Table 9.2). These countries had no other sources of major economic activity with which to generate additional income, nor was there a substitute export available to mitigate against a bad harvest or a slump in a particular commodity market. Moreover, given that there was little local demand for merchandise such as tea and coffee on the African continent, all of this produce had to be exported. Africa, as a result, was totally dependent on the West to buy its products.

Table 9.2 African export concentration, 1982–86 (countries in which one, two, three or four primary products account for over 75 per cent of a state's total export earnings)

One product (15 countries)

Algeria: *oil and gas*	Angola: *oil*	Botswana: *diamonds*
Burundi: *coffee*	Congo: *oil*	Gabon: *oil*
Guinea: *bauxite*	Libya: *oil*	Niger: *uranium*
Nigeria: *oil*	Rwanda: *coffee*	São Tomé: *cocoa*
Somalia: *livestock*	Uganda: *coffee*	Zambia: *copper*

Two products: (14 countries)

Cape Verde: *fish, fruit*	Chad: *cotton, livestock*	Comoros: *vanilla, cloves*
Congo-Kinshasa: *copper, coffee*	Egypt: *oil, cotton*	Equatorial Guinea: *cocoa, timber*
Ethiopia: *coffee, hides*	Ghana: *cocoa, bauxite*	Liberia: *iron ore, rubber*
Malawi: *tobacco, tea*	Mali: *livestock, cotton*	Mauritania: *iron ore, fish*
Réunion: *sugar, fish*	Seychelles: *oil, fish*	

Three products: (8 countries)

Benin: *oil, coffee, cocoa*	Burkina Faso: *cotton, vegetable oil, livestock*
Cameroon: *oil, coffee, cocoa*	Central African Republic: *coffee, diamonds, timber*
Guinea–Bissau: *cashews, groundnuts, palm oil*	Kenya: *coffee, refined oil, tea*
Senegal: *fish, groundnuts, phosphates*	Sudan: *cotton, vegetable oil, livestock*

Four products: (4 countries)

Côte d'Ivoire: *cocoa, coffee, refined oil, timber*	Madagascar: *coffee, cotton, cloves, fish*
Sierra Leone: *diamonds, cocoa, coffee, bauxite*	Togo: *phosphates, cocoa, cotton, coffee*

More diverse export economies (11 countries)
Djibouti, Gambia, Lesotho, Mauritius, Morocco, Mozambique, South Africa, Swaziland, Tanzania, Tunisia, Zimbabwe

Source: Brown, Michael Barratt. *Africa's Choices: After Thirty Years of the World Bank*. London: Penguin, 1995. 28.

This put Western buyers at a considerable advantage. They operated so-called 'closed markets', which were used to depress prices. In 1988, for example, the French transnational corporation, SucDen, bought Côte d'Ivoire's entire cocoa harvest.[5] Given that the GNP of Côte d'Ivoire was almost totally dependent on this sale, and that there were few alternative companies to sell to, SucDen was always going to obtain this cocoa at a bargain price. This helps to explain why the value of Africa's exports fell on average by 20 per cent between 1980 and 2000 (see Table 9.3), a situation that only exacerbated Africa's problem of a lack of access to investment capital.

This structural inequity meant that the continent had to buy expensive Western-manufactured goods with the income generated by the export of these cheaper primary products. In effect, Africans had to buy back their own raw materials, in a manufactured form, at an inflated rate. A United Nations report estimated that 85 per cent of the value of manufactured goods was kept in the West. Only 15 per cent of this capital found its way back to the country that had provided the raw materials.[6] This disadvantage was compounded by the fact that, over time, prices paid for primary commodities fell, while

Table 9.3 Index of international trade, 1960–2000 (1980 = 100)

	1960	*1970*	*1980*	*1990*	*2000*
Volume of exports:					
Developed countries	24	54	100	155	191
South and South-East Asia	46	51	100	276	523
Developing Africa	45	132	100	102	105
Unit value of exports:					
Developed countries	28	33	100	127	136
South and South-East Asia	21	20	100	95	94
Developing Africa	12	10	100	81	84
Terms of trade:					
Developed countries	117	122	100	110	113
South and South-East Asia	92	79	100	85	79
Developing Africa	49	36	100	70	64

Source: Assembled from data from United Nations Conference on Trade and Development. *Handbook of International Trade and Development Statistics, 1995.* New York: United Nations, 1997. Tables 2.1, 2.3 and 2.5.

the price of manufactured imports increased. Consequently, the West's terms of trade improved, while those of the developing world declined (see Table 9.3).

Until Africa is able to diversify its economies and manufacture its own raw materials, it will be difficult for it to escape this trap of unequal exchange. It is not, however, an impossible task. The so-called 'Asian Tigers' have made considerable economic progress since independence. Starting, apparently, with similar imperial legacies, economic diversification has occurred, and wealth has been generated (compare, for example, the figures for sub-Saharan Africa and East Asia in Table 9.3). This would seem to point to the importance of additional factors, both external and internal, not just unequal exchange, when explaining the African continent's poor economic performance in the second half of the twentieth century.

The African debt crisis

African states were not passive victims of unequal exchange. Independence gave governments a degree of political autonomy with which they attempted to diversify their economies and break the continent's dependence on problematic primary exports. Each state drew up its own development plan, striving to build on what it could salvage from its colonial inheritance. For example, many states adopted policies of import substitution. They tried to establish local manufacturing plants to produce goods previously imported from the West. African states also invested heavily in infrastructure (for example, roads and power generation), as well as human resources (education and health).

Development requires investment capital, however, and since little economic surplus was generated within Africa itself, governments took the decision to borrow from the West in order to kick-start their economies. Unfortunately, this strategy backfired. By the 1990s, Africa was crippled by these debts. In the 20 years to 1994, sub-Saharan

Africa's total indebtedness had increased from the equivalent of 15 per cent to 90 per cent of its GNP. Just paying the interest on these loans had a debilitating effect on local economies. The service on the US$221 billion continent-wide debt cost Africa the equivalent of 21 per cent of its export income each year. With so much capital being drained from the continent, further development was almost impossible.[7]

But how did the continent get into such a precarious financial position? Why was Africa so indebted to the West? The answers to these questions again lie in a combination of internal and external factors. The internal issues are addressed in the next chapter. Externally, this debt was a result of the continent's declining terms of trade, the massive increases in oil prices during the 1970s, and a rise in interest rates in the early 1980s.

Initially, African governments borrowed investment capital that they thought could be repaid through future sales of primary produce. In effect, they mortgaged future harvests and mining output for funds to launch Africa's development process. They did not, however, bank on the international prices paid for these commodities declining as they did (see Table 9.3). Take the case of Ghana. Income from this country's 1981 cocoa exports measured just one quarter of their 1973–74 value. A decade later, the price for cocoa had fallen by half again.[8] Given that Africa's monocrop economies had no alternative sources of income, declining commodity prices made it difficult for the governments to repay their loans.

In 1973, and then again at the end of the 1970s, the Organisation of Petroleum Exporting Countries (OPEC) increased oil prices dramatically. Economic shock waves hit the entire world. The West sank into recession, but Africa was pushed even further towards the brink. Where the continent had spent just 1 per cent of its GDP on fuel imports in 1970, 10 years later this had risen to 6 per cent.[9] Put another way, in 1960, a ton of African sugar bought 6.3 tons of oil. By 1982, this same ton of sugar could be exchanged for only 0.7 tons of oil.[10] Consequently, Africa's declining terms of trade sank even further.

The OPEC oil-price hikes also had further repercussions. The newly enriched oil-producing countries invested large amounts of their new-found wealth in the Western banking system. This gave these financial institutions a surplus of 'petrodollars', which they then offered to African countries in the form of cheap loans. Starved of foreign exchange by the very same oil price rises, African governments gladly accepted these loans. By the time these liabilities matured, however, they were no longer inexpensive debts. The second oil shock of 1979, combined with the reaction to a rising budget deficit in the United States, saw interest rates soar. What were initially attractive loans had now become impossible burdens on African economies. External factors not of Africa's making, then, had transformed the relatively responsible borrowing of the 1970s into the debt crisis of the 1980s and 1990s.

Zambia was one of the countries hit hardest by these economic trends.[11] After decolonisation in 1964, the country's economy was relatively prosperous. The first eight years of independence saw per-capita GNP grow annually at an average rate of 2.4 per cent. The government used this revenue to invest in human resources, building up welfare provision. Education and health improved rapidly, while poverty was alleviated through state food subsidies. A strategy of import substitution was also implemented, with relative success, and Zambia's manufacturing sector grew at a rate of 9.8 per cent per annum.

In 1973, however, Zambia, as a fuel importer, was hit by the OPEC oil rises. This was compounded by a fall in the price of copper on the international commodity markets.[12]

Copper was Zambia's monocrop. Previously, copper (along with cobalt) had accounted for 97 per cent of Zambia's export income, and 58 per cent of government revenue. With no alternative economic activity to fall back on, Zambia was forced to seek loans from the West. The country's debt spiralled upwards. By the millennium, Zambia owed US$6.3 billion, more than double its annual GDP.[13] The drain of capital created by servicing this debt reduced a previously impressive public welfare service to almost nothing.

In 1993, Susan George asked, 'What logic can there be for grinding down a whole continent?'[14] By that time, it was obvious that Africa, in all probability, was never going to be able to repay its accumulated debts. Despite the vast sums of capital leaving the continent in debt service, little impact was made on the total owed. The more the West demanded its 'pound of flesh', the less chance Africa had of developing and generating income to clear these debts. In the meantime, there was a human cost. UNICEF calculated that the debt crisis was responsible for the deaths of half a million children annually.[15]

The era of structural adjustment

With African economies struggling against an international economy based on unequal exchange, running balance of payments deficits, and then imploding as a consequence of their debt burden, something had to give in the 1980s and 1990s. The continent's governments were finding it increasingly difficult to raise new loans to service their previous borrowing. In most cases, the International Monetary Fund and the World Bank had become the only sources of credit left. It was at this point that these international financial institutions (IFIs) introduced Structural Adjustment Programmes (SAPs).

SAPs were programmes of conditional lending. In return for further loans, recipients were obliged to make changes to their economic policy. IFIs required African countries to liberalise their economies, opening them to international and domestic private capital, while at the same time reducing the role of the state in economic governance. African governments had very little choice but to go along with this structural adjustment, as there were no alternative sources of credit available.

Kenya, Malawi and Mauritius were the first states to introduce SAP reforms, at the start of the 1980s, and by the mid-1990s almost all other African countries had followed suit. Several states initially defied this external intervention. Zambia and Tanzania, for example, sought to continue their African socialism development strategies. Nonetheless, the will and economic influence of the IFIs proved irresistible. Despite there being no strong African constituency for structural adjustment, Western financial institutions were now dictating the basics of the continent's public policy.

After independence, African governments adopted statist development strategies. With only very small indigenous *private* sectors, governments decided that *public* institutions should be constructed to drive the development process forward. SAPs, however, were about dismantling these developmental states. IFI officials sought to introduce free-market discipline to African economies, mimicking the neo-liberal reforms of the Western economies at this time. Placing the blame for Africa's previously poor performance squarely on inefficient state-centred development strategies, IFIs decreed that the continent should change tack. Now the market, not the state, would determine the pattern of Africa's economic progress.

Each SAP was specifically tailored to the individual country concerned, but there were three universal pillars at the heart of all these programmes. Lending was conditional on the following: first, that development strategies should favour agricultural production; second, that governments should operate more 'realistic' trade and exchange-rate policies; and third, that the public sector should be made more efficient.[16] Given the impact that these SAPs had on African politics during the 1980s and 1990s, it is well worth exploring these three conditions in more detail.

The key concern of the IFIs was that the continent's development strategies prior to the 1980s had resulted in a significant state bias. Despite rural areas being the most productive sector of the economy, and African governments relying on this agricultural income to fund the bulk of their spending, it was urban constituencies that had benefited most from the state's allocation of public resources. Effectively, capital was being drained from the countryside to subsidise the activities of town and city life. The state, dominating the marketing of agricultural produce, for example, consciously paid farmers below market prices for their harvests. They then used the difference between this low price and the income they received for these crops on the international market to bolster the state and its public policy. Import substitution industries, other state enterprises (known as parastatals) and bloated bureaucracies all benefited from this investment. An urban coalition of bureaucrats, industrial workers, business people, and the politicians themselves (in effect, all the most powerful social groups within African society) came to take this privileged position for granted.

The consequence of rural areas losing out in this manner was that agricultural production performed badly in the post-colonial period. Farmers, given the low prices paid, had little incentive to increase their output. This situation eventually resulted in Africa importing, rather than growing, the majority of its food. It was this neglect of agricultural production, as well as the inefficient state investment in itself, that the structural adjustment programmes sought to address.

SAPs demanded that farmers be paid the full market price for their crops. This rise in price would have the effect, it was predicted, of encouraging greater agricultural output, which, in turn, would increase African export revenues. In effect, IFIs were directing African countries to concentrate on exporting agricultural goods, and to abandon their inefficient investments in state development enterprises such as import substitution (see below).

The second pillar of structural adjustment was the reform of trade and exchange-rate policies. A neo-liberal approach requires no state restrictions on imports and exports. The IFIs argued that administrative command over Africa's international trade proved costly. Not only was the system of issuing import and export licences too bureaucratic, but it was also open to corruption.

Similarly, SAP directives also required governments to remove tariffs protecting import substitution industries. The World Bank's 1981 Berg Report considered African manufacturers who had previously enjoyed this state protection to be, on the whole, wasteful. These state corporations were portrayed as parasitic, bleeding the economy of capital, rather than being able to pay their own way. Despite years of protection, a competitive indigenous manufacturing sector had not emerged in African states. IFIs therefore reasoned that, if these organisations were not competitive, they should be liquidated, as Africans would benefit more from having access to cheaper foreign imports instead.[17]

The third, and final, SAP condition related to making the public sector more efficient. The Berg Report argued that previous African development strategies had resulted in too much state intervention. Instead, the IFIs required that state influence be 'rolled back', and economies opened up to more efficient private-sector investment.[18] A primary goal of the SAP reforms, therefore, was a significant reduction in government spending. Administrative budgets were to be cut, and services, where appropriate, handed over to the private sector. Again, it was a case of subjecting as much economic (and social) activity as possible to the discipline of the free market, as opposed to central planning. In short, whereas African states had previously enjoyed a virtual monopoly over economic activity, structural adjustment was about eliminating this monopoly.

The consequences of structural adjustment

Structural adjustment had widespread repercussions across the African continent, and these were not solely confined to the economic field. The West's requirement that African states change their economic policies had major knock-on effects on the continent's social and political processes as well.

The economic impact

Research on the economic results of structural adjustment has produced a variety of opinions. Back in 1994, the World Bank suggested that, as a consequence of its own interventions, 'African countries have made great strides in improving policies and restoring growth'. Using six countries that had fully implemented their SAPs as case studies, the bank showed how these states succeeded in transforming previous negative economic growth into positive growth (2 per cent annually over the 1987–91 period).[19] Other researchers are more sceptical. The United Nations Economic Commission on Africa, for example, considered the results of structural adjustment to be dubious, at best. Its report suggested that non-adjusting African economies had performed just as well as, if not better than, their SAP counterparts.[20]

The reality of the situation is that some countries experienced modest improvements under the SAP regime, achieving a degree of economic stability, while others continued to decline. No economy returned any outstanding improvement or degeneration as a result of structural adjustment. As a World Bank report itself concedes, of all the sub-Saharan countries monitored, six enjoyed obvious improvement, nine experienced small improvements and eleven showed deterioration.[21] Even here, opinions are mixed. Is it true, for example, that decline continued in some countries because of the ill-conceived nature of the SAPs? Or did this decline merely result from poor implementation of these programmes by host governments? Similarly, could it be that, although economies continue to deteriorate, this would have been far worse without the implementation of structural adjustment? No clear pattern emerged.

Structural adjustment's envisaged strategy for raising much needed foreign capital was also questioned. The Berg Report clearly suggested that Africa should concentrate its efforts on increasing income from the export of primary produce. As the World Bank's 1995 report confirmed, SAPs are about 'putting exporters first'.[22] Yet the problem with pushing export-led growth is that this simply reproduces the disadvantages of unequal exchange experienced before. Also, where African countries succeeded in increasing output this was often offset by other SAP countries doing likewise. IFIs, after all, were encouraging a multitude of SAP countries worldwide to expand primary production. Since all these states had devalued their currencies and increased production, there was little relative advantage to be gained. International markets reacted to the increased availability of primary goods by lowering commodity prices. Consequently, increased production did not realise greater income. Africa was running in order to stand still, still plagued by falling commodity prices and unequal exchange. Percy Mistry, a former senior manager at the World Bank, commented: 'To the extent that [Africa] continues to rely on primary commodities to generate further export earnings, it is cutting its own throat'.[23]

A more prosperous Africa will always be predicated on the success of both the export of primary goods *and* the development of secondary manufacturing industry, for both the export and domestic markets. This, however, requires capital, most likely in the form of foreign investment, and a fairer world market. SAPs were meant to attract this external capital. This simply did not happen. Transnational corporations (TNCs) will not invest in fragile economies, whose governments, partly due to the impact of SAPs, cannot guarantee a stable currency, the maintenance of infrastructure, public order or administrative continuity. TNCs were therefore more attracted to Latin American and Asian operations.[24]

Similarly, despite structural adjustment calling for the liberalisation of African economies, Western states remained protectionist in vital areas of their own trade. Even if Africa was to loosen its reliance on tropical cash crops (tea, coffee, cocoa, etc.), in order to diversify its agriculture into more generic foodstuffs (vegetables, meat, cereals), it would come up against the Western states' prohibitive tariffs and subsidies in this sector of the economy. The West protects its own agriculture, preventing cheaper foreign exports, at the expense of free trade and opportunities for the Third World. Continued unequal exchange is writ large if you consider that the United States government pays its farmers a subsidy of US$1,057 per cow, yet the average income of Ethiopia is just US$100 per capita.[25] The Western states that dominate the governance policies of the IFIs are not prepared to implement the same policies that are demanded of their African counterparts.

In terms of a development strategy, then, structural adjustment was flawed. As the World Bank pointed out, 'development cannot proceed when inflation is high, the exchange rate overvalued, farmers overtaxed, vital imports in short supply, prices and productivity heavily regulated, key public services in disrepair, and basic financial services unavailable'.[26] SAPs, in this respect, at least started to address constraints on growth, such as the urban bias and the inefficient bloated state. They did not, however, provide a strong enough foundation. Export-led growth through traditional primary products was misguided, while there was little investment available to develop non-traditional economic activity (especially given the continued drain of debt service). Africa received little that was positive, by way of long-term development, in return for its loss of economic sovereignty. This sad reality is all the more apparent when the social and political consequences of structural adjustment are considered.

The social impact

If the economic impact of structural adjustment in Africa was somewhat uncertain, the social outcomes were very apparent. Reforms of the public sector resulted in widespread increases in unemployment and cuts in public services. In Zambia, for example, the SAP-required reduction of state protection for the country's (import substitution) textile industry resulted in 8,500 workers losing their jobs. In Livingstone alone, 47 clothing manufacturers ceased production. The remaining factories operated at between 15 and 20 per cent of capacity. Similarly, many of Zambia's loss-making parastatals were also liquidated under the SAP regime. Among the casualties were Zambia Airways, the United Bus Company of Zambia, the National Hotels Development Corporation, Manza Batteries, and the National Import and Export Corporation. Over 25,000 redundancies resulted. This, combined with 60,000 job losses in the civil service between 1991 and 1995, increased the country's already swollen ranks of unemployed.[27]

Structural adjustment also required government spending to be curtailed. Zimbabwe, for example, halved its budget deficit between 1989 and 1995. In order to do this, public services were hit hard. For instance, expenditure on medical staff and drugs was cut significantly. Similarly, education budgets were reduced. Fees for all secondary schools and urban primary schools were introduced, where previously education had been free.[28] This reduction of services brought the greatest disadvantage to the most vulnerable.

Perhaps the most contentious social consequence of structural adjustment, however, was the removal of state food subsidies. The urban poor, in particular, had come to rely

Plate 9.1 SAPs required reduced government spending on education, resulting in the withdrawal of free schooling for many Africans. Zimbabwean school children, Mahwanke, Zimbabwe, 1994. Photographer: Gideon Mendel.

on these subsidies in order to simply survive. They had few other sources of food (unlike their rural compatriots, who could grow their own). In Zambia during 1977, the maize subsidy amounted to 71 per cent of the market value for this staple. By 1983, Zambians were expected to pay the full price themselves.[29] Such subsidies were revoked right across the continent, making the SAP reforms deeply unpopular.

By the mid-1990s, even the World Bank was forced to admit that 'More could have been done, should have been done, to reduce poverty in the context of structural adjustment programs'.[30] When the extent of this suffering became apparent in the late 1980s, the IFIs began to build 'poverty alleviation programmes' into their SAPs. These were designed to combat the worst excesses that the switch towards neo-liberal economics brought. By this time, however, it was too late for many. Millions of Africans had experienced hardship or worse. Consequently, the social impact of structural adjustment had already begun to have major repercussions on Africa's political process.

The political impact

An IMF condition for a SAP loan to Sierra Leone in the mid-1980s demanded that the government cut its rice subsidies. President Siaka Stevens warned the IMF that it was asking his administration 'to commit political suicide'.[31] He felt that his government's already strained legitimacy would collapse altogether if it was forced to raise prices on this chief staple. In this respect, Stevens' comment highlights that what may be rational in terms of economic change is not necessarily rational politically. Most African governments had great difficulty building constituencies in favour of the SAP reforms among their people. Indeed, many failed miserably in this task, and the price of failure was their removal from office.

The problem was that structural adjustment directly attacked Africa's political status quo. The political process on this continent, more so than in other parts of the world, revolved around the state. Government institutions were recognised as the key providers of employment, services and resources. In effect, the state was the gatekeeper to opportunities for social mobility and welfare. This is how a political system based on client–patron relationships emerged in the post-colonial period (discussed in Chapter 6). Clients would offer their support to governments in return for benefits such as jobs in the public sector, administrative 'favours', new schools for their region, a well for their village, the metalling of a local road, and so on. It was this client–patron interdependence that provided the societal 'glue' that bound the whole political system together, thus generating a degree of stability. SAPs consciously aimed to break these client–patron relationships, as they were judged to be economically (if not politically) inefficient.

A key element of structural adjustment, in this respect, was 'rolling back' the state. It aimed to keep the state's intervention in the economy to a minimum, promoting civil society activity instead. Consequently, government budgets were cut, parastatals liquidated or privatised, and public services reduced.

The political consequences of this 'rolling back' were nothing short of traumatic. The shrunken state simply could not command the resources it had enjoyed previously. Patronage, as a consequence, also shrank. Clients lost their jobs in the liquidated parastatals and diminished civil services; 'favours' could no longer be given to importers and exporters, as international trade was now less controlled by state administrators; and governments did not have budgets from which they could offer new schools or wells to supporters. In short, SAP reforms resulted in the state elite being able to look after fewer of its existing clients, and having less flexibility to recruit new supporters. The result was declining government legitimacy, and growing political instability.

This instability was most apparent in the urban areas. It was here, after all, where most of the disaffected resided. These included unemployed industrial labourers (who had been laid off when their import substitution factories closed), redundant civil servants and parastatal workers, students (protesting at reduced education funding), doctors, teachers and other professionals (hit by scaled-down public service provision), and, most threatening of all, the urban poor (whose standard of living had been dramatically affected by the removal of food subsidies). These urban groups operated in a confined area, which made mobilisation simpler, and in close proximity to the actual apparatus of government (parliament buildings and ministries). This made it all the easier for them to challenge their former patrons, calling for a change of government.

The consequences of this political instability were unique in each of the countries concerned. Common manifestations, however, included sustained strikes by public-sector workers, ethnic tensions (as states often did not now have the resources to commit to 'ethnic arithmetic'), and, more violently, 'food riots', with the urban poor in particular registering their distress at the removal of state subsidies. In more extreme cases, SAPs contributed to an environment where the military or armed rebel groups were encouraged to topple the struggling incumbent governments (in Sudan and Liberia, for example). Elsewhere, elites continued in their exploitative ways in a scaled-down state, risking complete state collapse (in Zaire and Somalia; see Chapter 10). More frequently, however, this instability assisted campaigns which sought a transition to multi-party democracy (Zambia and Malawi; see Chapter 11). Whatever the outcome, the external structural adjustment intervention left state elites struggling to plug the gap created by declining legitimacy. IFIs had seriously undermined the old political status quo of centralised states based on clientelism.

Debt relief and continued conditionality

Agreements made at the 31st G8 summit, convened in Gleneagles during 2005, profoundly changed the nature of sovereign debt within the international economy. At this conference, the G8 states recognised that it was no longer sustainable to insist that the poorest African economies should structurally adjust while simultaneously continuing to service their debts. Likewise, there had been a growing acknowledgement among Western governments that the neo-liberal excesses of the SAPs had caused considerable social hardship in the developing world. The era of structural adjustment, in its crudest form, had come to an end.

At Gleneagles, G8 members pledged to cancel the external debts of the world's most 'Heavily Indebted Poor Countries' (HIPCs). More than US$37 billion owed to the World Bank, the International Monetary Fund (IMF) and the African Development Fund were written off.[32] The summit also undertook to consider additional debt forgiveness for the remaining HIPCs, and by 2014 a total of US$96 billion of debt had been 'forgiven'.[33] As a consequence, state debt on the continent has largely returned to manageable levels (see Table 9.4).

Table 9.4 Debt service payments of African HIPC countries (expressed as US$ million, and as a percentage of GDP), 2001–14

	2001	2002	2003	2004	2005	2006	2007	2008	2009	2010	2011	2012	2013	2014
Benin														
Debt service paid	56.7	62.3	66.3	58.1	38	63	88.1	29.4	37.4	48.3	54.8	70.5	79.5	103.6
Service as % of GDP	2.3	2.2	1.9	1.4	0.9	1.3	1.6	0.4	0.6	0.7	0.8	0.9	1.0	1.1
Burkina Faso														
Debt service paid	35.1	33.5	48.9	45.7	44.5	41.3	45.9	46.4	51.1	52.4	62.8	79.3	89.8	112.8
Service as % of GDP	1.2	1.0	1.2	0.9	0.8	0.7	0.7	0.6	0.6	0.6	0.6	0.7	0.8	0.9
Burundi														
Debt service paid	14.2	28.5	23.6	64.8	31.7	10.9	5.7	3.4	1.7	2.7	5.2	15.8	24.7	22.6
Service as % of GDP	1.7	4.0	3.0	7.1	2.6	0.8	0.4	0.2	0.1	0.1	0.2	0.7	0.9	0.7
Cameroon														
Debt service paid	260.9	240.4	284.8	259.1	406.2	418.3	146.9	59.9	70.2	52.4	80.9	122.8	147.9	234.6
Service as % of GDP	2.8	2.2	2.1	1.6	2.4	2.3	0.7	0.3	0.3	0.2	0.3	0.5	0.5	0.7
Central African Republic														
Debt service paid	32.3	43.3	45.9	46.6	27.7	40.9	36.4	43.7	23.4	10.7	11	24.8	20	22.3
Service as % of GDP	3.6	4.5	4.1	3.7	2.1	2.8	2.1	2.2	1.2	0.5	0.5	1.1	1.3	1.3
Chad														
Debt service paid	19.9	36.4	52.4	45.5	57.2	69.8	61.6	136.5	65.3	62.1	109.2	152.6	297.2	526.2
Service as % of GDP	1.2	1.8	1.9	1.0	0.9	0.9	0.7	1.3	0.7	0.6	0.9	1.2	2.2	3.3
Comoros														
Debt service paid	2.5	2.4	2.6	4.4	4.1	3.5	6	9.1	8.4	5.9	1.6	9.5	2.1	3.0
Service as % of GDP	1.1	0.9	0.8	1.2	1.1	0.9	1.3	1.7	1.6	1.1	0.3	1.6	0.3	0.4

(Continued)

Table 9.4 Debt service payments of African HIPC countries (expressed as US$ million, and as a percentage of GDP), 2001–14 (Continued)

	2001	2002	2003	2004	2005	2006	2007	2008	2009	2010	2011	2012	2013	2014
Congo, Democratic Republic of														
Debt service paid	—	34.2	363.8	175.4	373	213.1	170.7	254.4	187.9	177	160	181.7	194.6	189.3
Service as % of GDP	—	0.6	6.4	2.7	5.2	2.4	1.7	2.2	1.7	1.3	1.0	1.1	1.0	0.9
Congo, Republic of														
Debt service paid	183.6	230.6	158.4	222.7	607.8	563.5	389.2	217.7	539.1	145.3	139.3	137.1	305.1	366.7
Service as % of GDP	6.6	7.6	4.5	4.8	10	7.3	4.6	1.8	5.6	1.2	1.0	1.0	2.3	2.6
Côte d'Ivoire														
Debt service paid	—	1.9	274.5	189.5	118	72	240.8	318.6	286.3	288.4	114.5	255.2	492.7	684.7
Service as % of GDP	—	0.0	1.6	1.1	0.7	0.4	1.1	1.4	1.2	1.2	0.5	0.9	1.5	1.9
Ethiopia														
Debt service paid	572.3	521.1	191.3	160	165.6	168.2	182.2	89.2	79.5	130.7	229.7	393.6	502.8	755.6
Service as % of GDP	7.1	6.8	2.3	1.6	1.4	1.1	0.9	0.3	0.2	0.4	0.7	0.9	1.1	1.5
The Gambia														
Debt service paid	20.8	34.3	16.8	15.6	24.4	25.3	26.5	20.9	19.3	19.9	21.5	24.1	23.4	24.3
Service as % of GDP	3.4	6.4	3.2	2.7	3.9	3.9	3.3	2.2	2.1	2.1	2.4	2.7	2.8	2.6
Ghana														
Debt service paid	463.9	446.1	442	532.4	573.6	601.6	225.9	358.5	316.1	370.5	462.7	632.7	732.9	962
Service as % of GDP	6.2	4.7	4.0	3.7	3.3	2.9	0.9	1.3	1.2	1.2	1.2	1.5	1.5	2.6
Guinea														
Debt service paid	103.7	108.6	102.5	98.2	143.5	149.1	145	138.9	80.2	57.6	138.8	147.8	55.6	81.4
Service as % of GDP	3.7	3.7	3.0	2.7	4.9	5.1	3.5	3.1	1.7	1.2	2.7	2.6	0.9	1.2
Guinea–Bissau														
Debt service paid	1.4	2.6	5.7	6.2	4.2	5.1	5.6	4.1	11.3	3.8	1.2	1.7	2.9	10.5
Service as % of GDP	0.4	0.6	1.1	1.1	0.7	0.8	0.8	0.5	1.3	0.5	0.1	0.2	0.3	1.0

Liberia														
Debt service paid	0.6	—	—	0.6	0.6	1.2	0.2	0.7	0.5	4.2	6.2	6.9	7.3	9.6
Service as % of GDP	0.1	—	—	0.1	0.1	0.2	0.0	0.1	0	0.3	0.4	0.4	0.4	0.5
Madagascar														
Debt service paid	42.2	47	56.6	77.2	66.6	51.7	22.1	27.7	53.9	41	51.1	49	70.9	95.4
Service as % of GDP	0.9	1.1	1.0	1.8	1.3	0.9	0.3	0.3	0.6	0.5	0.5	0.5	0.7	0.8
Malawi														
Debt service paid	93.7	78.7	94.8	102.7	103.1	86.3	16.1	12.8	13.3	17.5	22.9	33	40.8	65.8
Service as % of GDP	5.5	3.0	3.9	3.9	3.7	2.8	0.4	0.3	0.3	0.3	0.4	0.8	1.1	1.5
Mali														
Debt service paid	68.3	89.9	97.8	107.7	102.1	121.3	94.5	86.4	124.5	91.5	129.2	112.4	124.3	130.7
Service as % of GDP	2.3	2.6	2.1	2.0	2.0	1.9	1.2	1.1	1.3	1.0	1.3	1.1	1.1	1.2
Mauritania														
Debt service paid	33.8	28.9	28.9	22	30.4	26.4	57.9	85.9	112.4	64	84.5	71.4	72.5	92.8
Service as % of GDP	3.0	2.5	2.2	1.5	1.6	1.0	2.1	2.4	3.7	1.8	2.1	1.8	1.7	2.1
Mozambique														
Debt service paid	27.1	62	71.8	58.1	66.6	23.3	35.1	81.1	46.2	56.6	75.0	129.9	196.2	244.8
Service as % of GDP	0.7	1.5	1.5	1.0	1.0	0.3	0.4	0.8	0.5	0.6	0.6	0.9	1.3	1.5
Niger														
Debt service paid	32.6	48.8	45.3	43.1	31.6	13.8	30.7	28	24.3	30.4	54.7	11.7	42.7	381.4
Service as % of GDP	1.8	2.4	1.7	1.5	0.9	0.4	0.7	0.5	0.4	0.5	0.9	0.2	0.6	4.6
Rwanda														
Debt service paid	39.8	38.5	38.4	42.4	47.2	32.6	12.6	14.3	15.3	17.6	23.1	26.5	233	71.4
Service as % of GDP	2.4	2.3	2.1	2.1	1.9	1.0	0.3	0.3	0.3	0.3	0.4	0.4	3.2	0.9

(Continued)

Table 9.4 Debt service payments of African HIPC countries (expressed as US$ million, and as a percentage of GDP), 2001–14 (Continued)

	2001	2002	2003	2004	2005	2006	2007	2008	2009	2010	2011	2012	2013	2014
São Tomé and Príncipe														
Debt service paid	2.7	2.2	2.8	3.3	7.0	25.1	3.3	1.9	1.6	1.6	2.4	2.4	4.6	5.9
Service as % of GDP	3.5	2.6	2.7	2.9	5.7	18.6	2.3	1.0	0.8	0.8	0.9	0.9	1.5	1.6
Senegal														
Debt service paid	168.6	213.1	264.1	799.7	299.3	178.2	163.6	151.7	155.3	185.1	501.4	276.1	274.2	430.7
Service as % of GDP	3.5	4.0	3.8	9.9	3.4	1.9	1.4	1.1	1.2	1.4	3.5	2.0	1.9	2.7
Sierra Leone														
Debt service paid	94.2	14.3	14.3	24.5	25.9	18.6	15.0	41.1	15.1	16	19.9	29.2	43.6	45.6
Service as % of GDP	8.7	1.1	1.0	1.7	1.6	1.0	0.7	1.6	0.6	0.6	0.7	0.8	0.9	0.8
Tanzania														
Debt service paid	120.9	165.9	125.4	128.7	114.9	98	42.5	53	46.4	39	74.7	114	162.5	221.1
Service as % of GDP	1.2	1.6	1.1	1.1	0.8	0.7	0.3	0.3	0.2	0.2	0.3	0.4	0.5	0.6
Togo														
Debt service paid	17.8	1.4	2.7	2.3	2.5	3.5	8.7	39.6	53.7	60.4	31.7	38.2	69.4	71.9
Service as % of GDP	1.3	0.1	0.2	0.1	0.1	0.2	0.3	1.2	1.7	1.9	0.8	1.0	1.6	1.5
Uganda														
Debt service paid	168.8	169.2	152	167.5	185.5	135.2	80.8	73.9	89.9	94.4	98.1	110.9	116.2	132.3
Service as % of GDP	2.9	2.7	2.3	2.3	2.0	1.4	0.7	0.5	0.6	0.5	0.6	0.6	0.5	0.5
Zambia														
Debt service paid	146.9	172.3	135.7	131.2	130	56.9	13.3	54.1	131.2	39.8	44.8	74.1	94.7	167.3
Service as % of GDP	3.6	4.1	2.8	2.1	1.6	0.4	0.1	0.3	0.9	0.2	0.2	0.3	0.4	0.7

Source: Assembled from IMF data. International Monetary Fund. *Heavily Indebted Poor Countries (HIPC) Initiative and Multilateral Debt Relief Initiative (MDRI): Statistical Update*. Washington, DC: IMF, 2014. Table AIII2. www.imf.org/external/np/pp/eng/2014/121214.pdf (accessed 19 June 2015).

Yet political conditionality did not cease with this 2005 summit. African governments, in return for debt forgiveness, are still required to operate economic and governance policies approved by the IFIs. IFI intervention on the continent has certainly become less intrusive since the SAPs ended, with the IMF and World Bank making a conscious effort to consult more with the HIPC governments and their populations, but conditionality does remain. The performance of HIPC states is measured against a number of criteria which favour liberal approaches to macroeconomic, fiscal and trade policies, alongside tight public spending.[34] Countries that wish to receive continued debt relief, or remain on the right side of the international donor community generally, are expected to operate within this IFI-determined framework. The reality is that, in order to receive the full benefit of bilateral and multilateral debt relief initiatives, African

Table 9.5 Chapter summary: Africa's recent political economy

Economic decline

Disadvantages in the international economy	• 'Neo-colonialism' compounding the underdevelopment of colonialism • Unequal exchange • Monocrop economies
Debt crisis	• African states borrow to kick-start economic development • Repayment hampered by interest rate rises and two oil crises • Crippling debt service requirements mount on African states

IFI-imposed remedies

Structural adjustment (1980s and 1990s)	• Neo-liberal economic reforms imposed by IFIs on African (and other Third World) states • African states accept SAP conditions, as IFIs are the only remaining source of credit left • States required to increase producer prices to farmers, end food subsidies, reduce tariffs, privatise parastatals and reduce public spending
Economic impact of structural adjustment	• Stabilisation of economies, but little growth
Social impact of structural adjustment	• Cuts in public services (e.g. education and health) • Mass unemployment created by job cut backs in the public sector • User charges imposed on citizens for basic services • Increased poverty
Political impact of structural adjustment	• State cannot now patronise its urban constituency (i.e. removal of food subsidies and public services) • State has fewer opportunities to bestow patronage to clients within the bureaucracy • SAPs prompt 'food riots' and industrial strikes which, in turn, lead to campaigns for multi-party democracy
Debt relief for Heavily Indebted Poor Countries (2005 onwards)	• Recipient states receive relief in return for meeting economic criteria, good governance goals and delivering poverty alleviation

states have mortgaged their sovereignty with respect to key public policy decisions for several decades to come.

State, civil society and external interests

The continent's debt crisis, and the structural adjustment and IFI conditionality that followed this, had a considerable impact on the three-way relationship between state, civil society and external interests in post-colonial Africa. The 1980s and 1990s saw external interests become more influential, and civil society expand, while the state lost a significant amount of power.

The debt crisis allowed the Western interests to annex a good deal of economic sovereignty from African states. With the continent's governments forced to accept conditional lending, IFIs succeeded in imposing their preferred neo-liberal economic order on African economies. Consequently, African politicians lost considerable control over setting their own exchange rates, establishing price controls, organising budgets, and determining what services should be offered to citizens. Decisions on public policy now had to be made in consultation with IFI officials back in Washington DC.

Civil society was one of the main beneficiaries of this external intervention. Where once the state was truly a leviathan, now it no longer had the resources to maintain all the political space it had once occupied. This enforced roll back of the state allowed civil society to expand. Rival sources of power, for example, emerged in the private sector. Private businesses replaced disbanded parastatals. Similarly, local associations and non-governmental organisations took on some of the public services terminated by the state. Even in the political field, civil society organisations became more active. The apparatus of the one party no longer held a monopoly on political expression. Sustained pro-democracy campaigns precipitated the holding of multi-party elections in most of the continent's territories during the 1990s.

As for the state elite itself, the last 30 years have proved to be difficult times to navigate. The lack of economic development during this period always meant that resources available for political bargaining were scarce. The conditions imposed by the SAPs and the MDRI, however, severely compounded this problem. 'Empires' once commanded by state patrons were now under direct attack from the neo-liberal demands of the IFIs. Parastatals and civil services were 'downsized' (to use the parlance of the day), and budgets and public services were cut. Patronage opportunities diminished as a result. To remain in power, elites had to adapt to these new conditions. Some successfully managed this by manipulating the move towards multi-party competition, while others, such as those in Zaire and Somalia, lost control, and their states spiralled towards complete collapse.

It would be wrong to think, however, that state elites were completely emasculated by IFI conditionality. Even today, state institutions remain the best opportunity for social advancement on the African continent, and the state itself continues to be the main prize of political competition. Given these facts, those in power have not given up their privileged position lightly. They have sought, instead, to tame the intrusion of external interests into their domain. The results of this elite 'survival strategy' are discussed in the following chapter.

Case study: Ghana's structural adjustment

The year 1957 saw the end of imperial rule in Ghana, when the former British Gold Coast Colony and British Togoland merged to form sub-Saharan Africa's first independent 'black' state. As one of the wealthier colonial possessions, Ghana's economic future seemed secured. It was the largest producer of cocoa beans in the world, it had considerable reserves of minerals, vast timber supplies grew in its tropical forests, there was a relatively good transport infrastructure, and the potential existed to generate hydroelectric power. Twenty-five years later, however, Ghana's economy had virtually collapsed. Food production failed to keep pace with population growth, cocoa and timber output had fallen, a solid manufacturing sector was yet to emerge, and the country's health, education and transport services were in disarray.[35] This case study examines the reasons behind this economic decline, as well as chronicling the attempts to reverse this deterioration with structural adjustment and debt relief reforms implemented from 1983 onwards.

Ghana's post-colonial political history mimics that of many other African countries. Once in power, the nationalist government centralised the state, and the political process became personalised around the chief executive (in this case President Kwame Nkrumah). Nkrumah was ousted from government in 1966 by a military coup, and during the next 15 years Ghana underwent further coups and counter-coups, interspersed by transfers to civilian rule. A greater degree of stability entered Ghanaian politics, however, with the arrival of the military government of Flight Lieutenant Jerry Rawlings. Coming to power in 1981, it was this regime that oversaw the country's structural adjustment. Rawlings went on to remain at the helm of the Ghanaian state until he retired in 2000, having successfully won multi-party elections in 1992 and 1996.

As ever, both external and internal factors conspired to limit Ghana's economic development prior to structural adjustment. Despite being one of Africa's wealthiest colonies, Ghana still inherited a monocrop economy distorted towards the export of primary produce. The country was locked into selling cocoa, timber and minerals to the West, and importing manufactured goods in return. As a result, regular economic crises arose when the cocoa harvest failed or international prices dropped. Even in good years, primary produce still had to be bartered for manufactured goods on the international market of 'unequal exchange'. With relatively little capital to invest in economic diversification, Ghana found it difficult to loosen this dependency on primary exports.

Ghana's decline, however, cannot be attributed solely to an exploitative international market. There were also internal constraints on development. Most of these arose from an 'urban bias' created by the government's chosen strategy of import substitution. Understandably, Ghana wished to rely less on the international market and more on domestic manufacturing. It therefore invested heavily in forging a fledgling manufacturing base, largely managed by parastatals and protected from outside competition by import tariffs. Foreign assets were also nationalised as part of this show of defiance against neo-colonialism.

State-led development, however, like all development, needs investment, and Ghana's only ready source of domestic capital was its cocoa crop. Profits were therefore squeezed from this sector of the economy in order to foot the bill for Ghana's welfare programmes, its import substitution investment, its food subsidies, its general administration, and indeed almost all state activity. Consequently, state marketing boards, which enjoyed a monopoly, paid cocoa producers below the market value for their harvests. The government then pocketed the difference between this low price and the higher international market price, once it had sold this produce on. Effectively, rural producers were being forced to subsidise the state and its development strategy, as well as the elite's expansive and expensive client–patron networks.

Market forces, however, were not completely subdued by state intervention. Given the marketing boards' refusal to pay realistic prices, the incentive for rural Ghanaians to expand production was minimal. In the case of cocoa, many farmers refused to sell to the state marketing boards, choosing illegal parallel markets ('black markets') instead. Cocoa was smuggled across the border to Côte d'Ivoire, where higher prices could be obtained. Other farmers chose to cease production of cocoa altogether. In 1965, Ghana had exported 560,000 tonnes of cocoa; by 1981, the (official) yield was down to 150,000 tonnes.[36] Similar declines in output also occurred in the timber, diamond and bauxite industries.

In effect, the government had squeezed its only productive sector too hard, and this had resulted in the collapse of the entire economy. There was no incentive to produce when the state retained so much of the profit for itself. Yet, despite this reality of economic contraction, the state still attempted to expand. There were now over 235 parastatals, and the civil service was growing annually by 17 per cent.[37] The supply of capital from the rural areas may have been exhausted, but the state elite was still intent on building its patronage networks.

It was at this point (in December 1981) that Jerry Rawlings intervened. 'Fellow citizens of Ghana, as you would have noticed we are not playing the National Anthem. In other words, this is not a coup. I ask nothing less than a revolution.'[38] This was the message of Rawlings' first radio broadcast. His Provisional National Defence Council (PNDC) aimed to build a people's democracy in Ghana.

In terms of economic policy, Rawlings, like his predecessors, initially blamed his country's poor position on external factors. His revolution therefore attempted to achieve 'total economic independence by ensuring a fundamental break from the existing neo-colonial relations'.[39] This meant trying to isolate Ghana from the influence of the international market. Under the threat of further nationalisation, for example, Rawlings negotiated more favourable contracts with transnational corporations operating in his country. Similarly, in an effort to stem inflation, the PNDC tightened its control of domestic prices. The cost of maize, for example, was reduced by 37 per cent, and that of cooking oil by 69 per cent. At the same time, while exhorting Ghanaians to produce more for the revolution, Rawlings also cut the producer price of cocoa by half.[40]

These measures did little for the economy. Indeed, compounded by a drought, the situation worsened. Rawlings' lower producer prices resulted in few wanting to sell their produce in the formal market. Consequently, production declined further, while parallel markets and smuggling grew. Ironically, this slump in output occurred at the very time when international cocoa prices reached a historic high. The government, however, could not take advantage of these increased commodity rates, as its own low producer prices had already chased too many farmers out of the formal, state-controlled market. By the end of 1982, attempted coups against the Rawlings regime had become commonplace, foreign investors were threatening to disinvest, and the country had become dependent on food aid from Western relief agencies. Reading the signs, the PNDC changed tack. Rawlings now began to endorse a strategy of structural adjustment.

The PNDC, in its 1983 budget, introduced sweeping measures to liberalise Ghana's economy. It portrayed these reforms not as a U-turn, but as a continuation of its revolution. Rawlings implored Ghanaians to produce for their country, and he promised that producers would be justly rewarded for their toil. It was a case of the PNDC embarking on a neo-liberal policy programme, with a populist spin.

Encouraged by the World Bank, one of the first SAP measures to be implemented was a 67 per cent increase in producer prices paid for cocoa.[41] Cash incentives were also offered for the planting of new cocoa trees, and pesticides were made more readily available. Given that they were now being offered competitive rates in the formal economy, farmers were prepared to produce for the official market. Similar liberalisation reforms were applied to Ghana's trading sector and national currency. Price controls, for example, had been abolished by the government on all but five products by mid-1985, while the Ghanaian Cedi had devalued, by 1988, to just 2 per cent of its 1982 value.

Major changes also occurred in the public sector. Eighty parastatals were immediately earmarked for privatisation, and the government let it be known that it would consider bids from the private sector for all other state enterprises (apart from 18 that were deemed to be too strategic). By 1995, a total of 195 parastatals had been removed from the public sector.[42] Many had been sold to transnational corporations. Indeed, the Rawlings regime now actively encouraged TNC investment in its economy. Finance Secretary Kwesi Botchway went out of his way to assure a 1984 audience of international financiers that they would 'not be frustrated when the time comes to transfer their profits and dividends to their shareholders overseas'.[43]

The extent to which Ghana adopted these neo-liberal reforms made this country a flagship for the IFIs' programme of structural adjustment. Although the Rawlings regime initially dragged its feet a little with the proposed privatisation schedule, due to patronage concerns, the World Bank and the IMF regularly implored other African countries to follow Ghana's example. The result was that the PNDC enjoyed a good-credit rating in the West, and development loans were forthcoming on a regular basis. The key question, however, is whether this structural adjustment had actually improved Ghana's economic position.

There is little doubt that SAP reforms did much to stabilise Ghana's economy, and pulling the country away from the financial nadir of 1982 was no mean feat. Responding to increased producer prices, the output of primary goods increased dramatically. The cocoa harvest, for example, increased by 65 per cent between 1983 and 1990. Timber, bauxite, manganese and diamond production saw similar improvements. Consequently, export earnings rose year on year throughout the SAP period, and Ghana's budget deficit benefited as a result.[44]

Yet it is arguable that structural adjustment did little beyond stabilising the economy. There was certainly no 'take-off' into sustained development. The country's economy was still dominated by cocoa, timber and minerals, and international commodity prices remained volatile. The price of cocoa, for example, fell during the SAP period, due to an increase in production and currency devaluations, not only in Ghana, but also in other adjusting countries around the world. Consequently, Ghana had to increase production each year merely to retain the same income. There were also concerns that this increase in primary produce for export was damaging the domestic food market. Should not farmers be concentrating on growing crops for home consumption? And, all the time, Ghana's debts grew. In 1998, Ghana's external public debt was the equivalent of 76 per cent of its GDP, while the country ran a balance of payments deficit of US$806 million.[45]

One way to kick-start the economy, of course, would have been an influx of foreign direct investment. International capital, however, remained largely uninterested in the Ghanaian economy because of its continued fragility and lack of long-term growth prospects.[46] The SAP reforms had not made Africa more attractive to the TNCs. In short, structural adjustment may have turned the Ghanaian economy around, but it still had to find a way to precipitate growth on shaky foundations.

Structural adjustment also had a remarkable impact on Ghana's political system. The SAP reforms hit the PNDC's former clients hard. Forty per cent of the state cocoa board's employees, for example, were dismissed, as were 3,600 civil servants and numerous other public employees.[47] Industrial workers also fared badly as a result of import substitution investments being cut, and the removal of tariff protection. Similarly, the professional and managerial classes (doctors, nurses, teachers and university staff, for example) had to cope with the scaling down of public services by the state. Those who had previously benefited from these services also suffered. Numerous students, for example, could no longer afford to continue their higher education, while the introduction of user charges excluded many Ghanaians from schooling and basic health care. The removal of food and other subsidies added to the hardship. The belated Programme of Action to Mitigate the Social Costs of Adjustment (PAMSCAD) convinced few Ghanaians of the merits of the SAP reforms.

The PNDC faced considerable opposition from these disadvantaged groups. Former clients of the state elite, who previously could be relied upon to support the government, now voiced their opposition. Initially, the state was able to contain these groups through suppression and harassment. Pressure for political change, however, continued to mount. The more organised opposition movements channelled this discontent into calls for multi-party democracy, in line with a continent-wide move towards pluralism. Eventually the Rawlings regime succumbed to this pressure, and contested open elections. The PNDC calculated that it could rely on its rural support, winning any poll, while at the same time this would defuse pressure emanating from the urban opposition. Rawlings was indeed victorious in 1992, capturing 58 per cent of the vote. With renewed legitimacy for the regime, and praise from the West for returning Ghana to democracy, the flight lieutenant exchanged his airforce overalls for an immaculate civilian suit. Securing re-election in 1996, Rawlings remained head of state until his retirement in 2000.[48] The former leader of a military coup 20 years earlier was now a model democrat, honouring the presidential two-term limit enshrined in the new Ghanaian constitution. Indeed, with the 'Big Man' gone, democracy was the beneficiary. The opposition was finally able to defeat the PNDC and take office. Structural adjustment had precipitated major political change.

Since the millennium, Ghana has kept to the IFI prescription. The government in Accra has maintained an externally approved macroeconomic environment, and has undertaken key structural reforms in the areas of governance, education and health. Given this co-operation, it is not surprising that Ghana was one of the first African countries to benefit from international debt relief. In terms of the 2005 Gleneagles Summit, for example, Ghana's initial reward was US$4.2 billion of debt 'forgiveness' which represented a sizeable chunk of the country's total debt of US$6 billion. This IFI support helped the country's export industries. Buoyed by high commodity prices, and oil production coming on stream in commercial volumes during 2011, Ghana's economy grew annually by an average of 5 per cent between 2000 and 2015. This is a marked contrast to the dark days of the 1980s. Yet debt is still an issue for Ghana. By 2014, the country's external debt stock had risen to US$14.6 billion.[49] Although it is now in a much better position to service its debts, Ghana is still vulnerable to the vagaries of the international market and the demands of its creditors.

Stability has also been a feature of Ghanaian politics since the millennium. Following Rawlings' retirement, John Kufuor served two terms as president, and then retired himself, observing the Ghanaian constitution's term limits. In both cases, and in subsequent presidential elections, there have been relatively democratic and peaceful transfers of power, despite narrow margins of electoral victory.

Again, this has to been seen as a positive development, especially when compared with the coups and counter-coups of the 1970s and early 1980s.

However, despite this much needed economic and political stability, it still has to be recognised that Ghana has a long way to go before it will produce sustainable wealth generation. An externally facing export economy may satisfy IFI criteria, but this should not hide the fact that Ghana is vulnerable to the vagaries of commodity prices, and that exports remain locked into an international system based on unequal exchange. What is more, although Accra had little choice with regard to adopting structural adjustment and the conditions of its debt relief, it should be noted that, by doing so, Ghana has relinquished sovereignty over its development strategy. Standard and Poor's assessment of the Ghanaian economy sums up the situation well. Analysts at this US financial corporation are of the view that:

> ratings on the Republic of Ghana (B+/Stable/B) are constrained by a narrow economic base, low development, and a widening of fiscal and current account balances, despite the considerable support of donors. The ratings are supported, however, by a comparatively stable political system, and the easing of external and fiscal balance-sheet pressures following various phases of debt relief.[50]

It is to be hoped that an alternative source of internal wealth generation, maybe from the new oil production, will emerge. This would enable Ghana to break its dependence on conditional assistance and the export of cash crops. Only in this manner will the key underlying impediment to Ghana's economic growth, its 'narrow economic base', be addressed.

Ghana[51]

Territory:	238,305 sq. km.	Population:	25.9 million
Colonial power:	Britain	Independence:	1957
Major cities:	Accra (capital)	Ethnic groups:	Akan
	Kumasi		Ga
	Tamale		Ewe
Languages:	English		Guan
	Twi		Moshi-Dagomba
	Fante	Urban population:	53 per cent
	Ga	Life expectancy:	61 years
	Ewe	Adult literacy:	72 per cent
Infant mortality:	52 deaths/1,000 live births	Exports:	Oil
Religion:	Traditional		Cocoa
	Islam		Gold
Currency:	Cedi		Fruit
GDP per capita:	US$1,605		Base metals

Questions raised by this chapter

1. To what extent has the international economy hindered Africa's post-colonial economic development?
2. How did African states become so indebted to the West?
3. What are the key reforms associated with structural adjustment programmes?
4. Have structural adjustment programmes produced economic growth on the African continent?
5. What has been the political and social impact of structural adjustment and debt relief?

Glossary of key terms

Debt service	Interest due on loan repayments.
Import substitution	An economic strategy that seeks to reduce a state's dependence on imported foreign goods, substituting these with domestically manufactured produce.
International financial	Non-governmental bodies that help to regulate institutions, the international economy, such as the International Monetary Fund and the World Bank.
Marketing boards	State institutions charged with buying goods from producers, and then selling these on to the international market.
Monocrop economies	Economies that rely heavily on a small number of (primary) exports for the bulk of their national income.
Neo-colonialism	Economic control and exploitation that Western powers still retain over the ex-colonies even after political independence.
Parastatals	Public sector companies or agencies, such as state marketing boards, state manufacturing industries or state transport companies.
Primary sector	Economic activity (largely mining and agriculture) other than secondary manufacturing industry or the service sector.
Producer price	The price paid by state agencies to primary producers for their harvests/output.
Structural adjustment	Neo-liberal economic reform strategies promoted by international financial institutions during the 1980s and 1990s.
Terms of trade	The relationship between a state's income gained from exports, measured against the cost of its imports.
Unequal exchange	A problem where the international economy purchases (Third World) primary produce relatively cheaply, compared with the greater costs of (Western) manufactured products in the same market.
Urban bias	The result of state policies exploiting production, and revenues raised, from the rural sector, used to subsidise government and economic activities in urban regions.
User charges	Fees paid by citizens, at the point of use, in order to access public services (prompted by SAP reforms).

Further reading

Kwame Nkrumah's original manifesto on neo-colonialism is well worth a read. This brings the underdevelopment debate into the post-independence era. For those interested in structural adjustment, the best place to start is with two World Bank reports, both of which are surprisingly accessible, and give an understanding of why the IFIs considered the SAPs necessary. The 1981 Berg Report laid the framework for structural adjustment, while the 1994 report makes a preliminary assessment of this economic strategy. A more critical examination of the SAPs is provided by Michael Barratt Brown's work. With regard to the political impact, two articles, one by Jeffrey Herbst and the other by Christopher Clapham, raise some interesting issues.

Brown, Michael Barratt. *Africa's Choices: After Thirty Years of the World Bank*. London: Penguin, 1995.

Clapham, Christopher. Governmentality and economic policy in Sub-Saharan Africa. *Third World Quarterly*. 1996, 17(4), 809–24.

Herbst, Jeffrey. The structural adjustment of politics in Africa. *World Development*. 1990, 18(7), 949–58.

Nkrumah, Kwame. *Neo-Colonialism: the Last Stage of Imperialism*. London: Thomas Nelson and Sons, 1965.

World Bank. *Accelerated Development in Sub-Saharan Africa: An Agenda for Action* [The Berg Report]. Washington, DC: World Bank, 1981.

World Bank. *Adjustment in Africa: Reforms, Results and the Road Ahead*. New York: Oxford University Press, 1994.

Notes and references

1   World Bank. *Development Report 1997*. Oxford: Oxford University Press, 1997. Table 1. See also United Nations Conference on Trade and Development. *UNCTAD Handbook of Statistics 2008*. New York: United Nations, 2008. Table 8.1. Sub-Saharan figure for 2007 excludes South Africa. See also United Nations Conference on Trade and Development. *UNCTAD Handbook of Statistics 2014*. New York: United Nations, 2014. Table 8.1.

2   World Health Organization. *World Heath Statistics 2014*. III. Tables 1 and 9. Geneva: World Health Organization, 2014. www.who.int/gho/publications/world_health_statistics/2014/en/ (accessed 2 June 2015).

3   Rodney, Walter. *How Europe Underdeveloped Africa*. Nairobi: East African Educational Publishers, 1972. 239.

4   Nkrumah, Kwame. *Neo-Colonialism: The Last Stage of Imperialism*. London: Panaf, 1965. ix.

5   Brown, Michael Barratt and Pauline Tiffin. *Short Changed: Africa and World Trade*. London: Pluto, 1992. 100.

6   *Ibid*. 97–8.

7   United Nations Conference on Trade and Development. *Handbook of International Trade and Development Statistics. 1994*. New York: United Nations, 1995. Table 5.7. See also United Nations Conference on Trade and Development. *Handbook of International Trade and Development Statistics. 1995*. New York: United Nations, 1997. Table 5.7.

8   Haynes, Jeff, Trevor W. Parfitt and Stephen Riley. Debt in Sub-Saharan Africa: the local politics of stabilisation. *African Affairs*. 1987, 86(344), 352. See also United Nations Conference on Trade and Development. *Handbook of International Trade and Development Statistics, 1994*. Table 2.7.

9   World Bank. *Accelerated Development in Sub-Saharan Africa: An Agenda for Action* [The Berg Report]. Washington, DC: World Bank, 1981. 18.

10 Cheru, Fantu. *The Silent Revolution in Africa: Debt, Development and Democracy*. Harare: Anvil, 1989. 28.

11 The data on Zambia has been drawn from Jones, Stephen. Structural adjustment in Zambia. In: Willem van der Geest, ed. *Negotiating Structural Adjustment in Africa*. London: James Currey, 1994. 25–46.

12 Makgelta, Neva Seidman. Theoretical and practical implications of IMF conditionality in Zambia. *Journal of Modern African Studies*. 1986, 24(3), 396.

13 Organisation for Economic Co-operation and Development (OECD). African Development Bank. *African Economic Outlook Report 2003/2003*. Paris: OECD, 2003. 344. See also *UNCTAD Handbook of Statistics 2008*. Table 8.1.

14 George, Susan. Uses and abuses of African debt. In: Adebayo Adedeji, ed. *Africa Within the World: Beyond Dispossession and Dependence*. London: Zed, 1993. 60.

15 Cited in Susan George's foreword to Brown and Tiffin. *Short Changed: Africa and World Trade*. xvi.

16 World Bank. *Accelerated Development in Sub-Saharan Africa* [The Berg Report]. 99.

17 *Ibid*. 27.

18 *Ibid*. 99.

19 World Bank. *Adjustment in Africa: Reforms, Results and the Road Ahead*. New York: Oxford University Press, 1994. *Passim*.

20 United Nations Economic Commission on Africa (UNECA). *African Alternative Framework to Structural Adjustment Programmes for Socio-Economic Recovery and Transformation*. Addis Ababa: UNECA, 1989. 9–10.

21 World Bank. *Adjustment in Africa: Reforms, Results and the Road Ahead*. 3.

22 World Bank. *Adjustment in Africa: Reforms, Results and the Road Ahead*. 11.

23 Mistry, Percy. *The Present Role of the World Bank in Africa*. 1998. Cited in Brown and Tiffin. *Short Changed: Africa and World Trade*. 25.

24 United Nations. *Handbook of International Trade and Development Statistics, 1995*. Table 5.3.

25 Denny, Charlotte and Larry Elliot. Farming's double standards will be laid bare at Cancun. *The Guardian* (London). Trade Supplement. 8 September 2003. 18.

26 World Bank. *Adjustment in Africa*. 2.

27 Simutanyi, Neo. The politics of structural adjustment in Zambia. *Third World Quarterly*. 1996, 17(4), 831–7.

28 Tevera, Dan. The medicine that might kill the patient: structural adjustment and urban poverty in Zimbabwe. In: David Simon, Wim Van Spengen, Chris Dixon and Anders Närman, eds. *Structurally Adjusted Africa*. London: Pluto, 1995. 79–90.

29 Jones, Stephen. Structural adjustment in Zambia. In: Geest. *Negotiating Structural Adjustment*. 46.

30 World Bank. *Adjustment in Africa: Reforms, Results and the Road Ahead*. 14.

31 Stevens, Siaka. The people will decide. *West Africa*. 1985, 3523, 404.

32 See World Bank press release: 2006/327/PREM *World Bank Approves US$37 Billion for Multilateral Debt Relief Initiative*. http://web.worldbank.org/WBSITE/EXTERNAL/NEWS/0,,contentMDK:20867307~menuPK:34463~pagePK:34370~piPK:34424~theSitePK:4607,00.html (accessed 14 July 2009).

33 World Bank. *Brief: Heavily Indebted Poor Country (HIPC) Initiative*. 10 October 2014. www.worldbank.org/en/topic/debt/brief/hipc (accessed 18 June 2015).

34 See for example, World Bank's *Country Policy and Institution Assessments*. http://siteresources.worldbank.org/IDA/Resources/73153-1181752621336/CPIA08CriteriaB.pdf (accessed 15 July 2009).

35 See Price, Robert. Neo-colonialism and Ghana's economic decline: a critical assessment. *Canadian Journal of African Studies*. 1984, 18(1), 163–93.

36 *Africa South of the Sahara 1997*. 26. London: Europa, 1996, 449.

37 Gyimah-Boadi, E. Ghana: adjustment, state rehabilitation and democratisation. In: Thandika Mkandawire and Adebayo Olukoshi, eds. *Between Liberalisation and Oppression: The Politics*

of Structural Adjustment in Africa. Dakar: Council for the Development of Social Science Research in Africa (CODESRIA), 1995. 218.

38 Jerry Rawlings' radio broadcast of 31 January 1981. Quoted in Nugent, Paul. *Big Men, Small Boys and Politics in Ghana*. London: Pinter, 1995. 15.

39 PNDC policy statement. Quoted in Ahiakpor, James C.W. The success and failure of dependency theory: the experience of Ghana. *International Organisation*. 1985, 39(3), 542.

40 Ahiakpor. The success and failure of dependency theory. 546.

41 *Africa South of the Sahara 1997*. 26. London: Europa, 1996. 451.

42 *Ibid*. 449.

43 Cited in Eshun, Isaac. Investment priorities. *West Africa*. 1984, 3485, 1155.

44 Gyimah-Boadi E. In: Mkandawire and Olukoshi. *Between Liberalisation and Oppression: The Politics of Structural Adjustment in Africa*. 220.

45 US Department of State, Bureau of Economic and Business Affairs. *2000 Country Reports on Economic Policy and Trade Practices*. March 2001. www.state.gov/documents/organization/1598. pdf (accessed 16 July 2009).

46 Gyimah-Boadi E. In: Mkandawire and Olukoshi. *Between Liberalisation and Oppression: The Politics of Structural Adjustment in Africa*. 220.

47 *Ibid*. 223.

48 Nugent. *Big Men, Small Boys and Politics in Ghana*. 268.

49 Okudzeto, Eline, Wilberforce Aminiel Mariki, Radhika Lal and Sylvia Sefakor Senu. *Ghana 2015*. African Economic Outlook (AfDB, OECD, UNDP), 2015. 3. www. africaneconomicoutlook.org/fileadmin/uploads/aeo/2015/CN_data/CN_Long_EN/ Ghana_GB_2015.pdf (accessed 18 June 2015). See also Government of Ghana, Ministry of Finance. *Ghana's Public Debt Report*. Accra: 2015. www.mofep.gov.gh/?q=news251013/ ghana%E2%80%99s-public-debt-report (accessed 19 June 2015).

50 Standard and Poor's. *Summary: Ghana (Republic of)*. 19 August 2008. www.alacrastore.com/ research/s-and-p-credit-research-Summary_Ghana_Republic_of-666016 (accessed 16 July 2009).

51 Statistics taken from United Nations Conference on Trade and Development. *UNCTAD Handbook of Statistics 2014*. New York: United Nations, 2014. Tables 8.1, 8.4 and 3.2.D; World Bank data http://data.worldbank.org/indicator/SP.DYN.LE00.IN (accessed 24 July 2015) and http://data.worldbank.org/indicator/SP.DYN.IMRT.IN (accessed 24 July 2015); and UNESCO data www.uis.unesco.org/DataCentre/Pages/regions.aspx (accessed 24 July 2015).

10 Authority

The crises of accumulation, governance and state collapse

Chapter outline

- The growing crisis of state legitimacy

  - The crisis of accumulation
  - The crisis of governance

- The loss of state authority

  - Disengagement and 'exit strategies'
  - A new wave of insurgency
  - The road to state collapse

- The state's own survival strategies

  - Re-legitimisation of the state
  - State inversion
  - Tapping into foreign patronage
  - Exploiting parallel markets
  - The 'warlord state'

- State and civil society
- Case study: Zaire – Mobutu's vampire state
- Questions raised by this chapter
- Glossary of key terms
- Further reading
- Notes and references

That fuck? is moribund?

During the 1980s and 1990s, several African countries experienced state collapse. Many others could be described as moribund. Security was not guaranteed, political institutions had decayed, and public services declined rapidly. In short, a majority of African governments were struggling to administer even the most basic functions of a modern state.

Previous chapters help to explain the *external* reasons why this point of crisis had been reached. The colonial inheritance had hindered governments since independence; the continent was disadvantaged by its position in the international economy; and the end of the Cold War restricted opportunities for foreign patronage. These external factors, however, only partly explain this evolving crisis of the post-colonial state. The current chapter is designed to investigate the other side of the coin: the *internal* contributions to Africa's malaise.

Initially, the chapter will concentrate on two crises, namely those of accumulation and governance. State elites simultaneously failed to oversee successful economic development while neglecting to represent society adequately. These crises of accumulation and governance prompted, in turn, a third crisis, that of legitimacy. Each of these predicaments will be considered individually.

The second half of the chapter then moves on to chart how this loss of legitimacy encouraged elements within civil society to 'disengage' from the state. Africans attempted to distance themselves from their exploitative rulers, and the result of this disengagement was a decline of state capacity and control.

Given this situation, the political concept of *authority* has been selected as the underlying theme for this chapter. State authority can be defined as *a psychological relationship between the governed and their governors, which engenders a belief that state personnel and institutions should be obeyed*. Such authority, as discussed in previous chapters, can be generated from two sources: legitimacy and coercion. Legitimate authority is built by governors commanding the approval of their people through the provision of security, economic and social welfare, and good governance. Legitimate rulers are obeyed because citizens believe they receive reciprocal benefits for doing this. Coercive authority, on the other hand, is secured through the threat of violence. Citizens comply with state demands for fear of what may happen if they do not.

All governments around the world use a mixture of both persuasion and force (legitimacy and coercion) to maintain their authority over society. A combination of these two powers helps to underwrite political stability. When the state's legitimacy declines, however, and rulers no longer command sufficient resources of coercion, authority is threatened. This is exactly what happened in many parts of Africa in the 1980s and 1990s.

The growing crisis of state legitimacy

The crisis of accumulation

Even a rudimentary glance at comparative economic figures shows Africa to be the poorest continent in the world.[1] Yet Africa is not short of natural resources. In terms of power generation, for example, the continent houses 40 per cent of the world's hydroelectric potential. It also has 12 per cent of global natural gas reserves, and 8 per cent of the world's oil extraction. Similarly, Africa produces 70 per cent of the world's cocoa beans and 60 per cent of its coffee. Its earth is rich in minerals, and many regions have fertile soils.[2] Why, then, given these resources, did African economies perform so poorly in the post-colonial period? An answer to this question can be found in the continent's crisis of accumulation.[3]

To develop, all economies initially have to accumulate capital. This surplus capital is then invested back into the economy to produce further profits, which, in turn, can themselves be reinvested. The key to development, therefore, is the accumulation of surplus capital, followed by its productive investment. If this cycle of economic surplus and productive investment continues, prosperity is generated.

Africa's economic problems stemmed from the fact that surpluses were scarce, and productive investments rare. Chapter 9 examined external factors that hindered this process of capital accumulation. Monocrop export economies, unequal exchange and declining commodity prices all hampered Africa's prospects for development. Yet disadvantage in the international economy cannot be offered as a comprehensive explanation of the continent's position. Even if Africa did not receive its 'fair' share of world profits, at least some income was generated from the cash crops and minerals sold, and these funds, together with loan capital, were invested in development projects. The problem was that much of this investment proved to be unproductive.

Capital was wasted because post-colonial state investments were largely founded on erroneous policy choices. In retrospect, two misguided development strategies stand out. First, many African governments concentrated too heavily on overambitious import substitution, and, second, they spent too much revenue expanding institutions of the state. Fatally, this strategy of industrial and public sector investment came at the expense of developing agricultural production.

Import substitution became the centrepiece of most African development plans. The idea was to diversify economies away from existing primary production, expanding them into the secondary manufacturing sector. This would assist economic self-reliance, reducing the continent's dependence on imported manufactured goods. After all, had not the West itself developed by diversifying its agricultural economies into industrial production? Economists in both the developed and the developing worlds agreed that this was the most appropriate path to modernity.

The problem was that many of these import substitution projects were inefficient. They could only survive with state protection. Large, prestigious production units often became 'white elephants', not sustainable given the underdeveloped nature of their host economies. State-of-the-art assembly plants, for example, were of little use when Africans could not afford to buy the goods they produced. Indeed, ironically, most of the technology and materials needed to run these operations had to be imported from the West, given that the local manufacturing base was unable to supply these needs. With little demand locally, and their goods uncompetitive in international markets, many of these import substitution industries became a burden on African economies, rather than being their saviours. Political leaders needed to be much more selective with regard to the type and scale of the industries they sought to stimulate. Instead, sectors where genuine competitive advantage could have been built were swamped by projects based more on ambition and prestige.

The capital invested in import substitution would have been more profitably invested in the agricultural sector. This, after all, was where most Africans earned their living. Diversifying farms away from export crops into the production of goods demanded locally (such as food) might have generated more wealth for a greater number of people. Instead, the agricultural sector was taxed heavily, bearing the brunt of the whole industrialisation project. State marketing boards, for example, which usually enjoyed a monopoly over selling the country's cash crops, often appropriated harvests from farmers at below market prices. They used the difference between the sum they paid the farmers and the income they raised on the international markets to underwrite the bulk of government expenditure (including the import substitution projects). Yet, with state marketing boards offering such low producer prices, farmers had little incentive to increase agricultural output. Consequently, in many parts of Africa, crop yields actually declined in the post-colonial period. State managers, in their desperation to accumulate capital for development, had overburdened the agricultural sector. Year after year, they siphoned away too much of the farmers' profits, effectively strangling the most productive area of their domestic economies.

The agricultural sector, however, was not just squeezed to produce investment capital for import substitution. Rural capital was also used to expand the public sector. By the

1980s, African state institutions had clearly become 'overdeveloped'. Bureaucracies simply became too large to be supported by their own economies. In Congo-Brazzaville, for example, by 1985, the wages of the civil service alone accounted for 50 per cent of state expenditure.[4] Even in Kenya, which prided itself on private, as well as public, sector initiatives, the state extended its tentacles into almost all areas of economic activity. Richard Sandbrook, for example, found that; → (KRAKEN)

> In 1980, statutory boards and corporations operated all the conventional public utilities (telephones, electricity, water, ports, etc.) as well as transport services (for instance, Kenya Airways and Kenya Railway Corporation). Public corporations were also engaged in productive activities: agriculture (Kenya Meat Commission, Kenya Co-operative Creameries, National Cereals and Produce Board), finance (Agricultural Financial Corporation), commerce (Kenya National Trading Corporation) and industry (Industrial and Commercial Development Corporation).[5]

Parastatals of this nature came to dominate almost all large-scale economic activity across the continent. In doing this, they absorbed colossal amounts of public finance. This capital could have been more productively invested elsewhere.

From an ideological point of view there is nothing necessarily wrong with public enterprise. Those on the Left argue that state-controlled economic activity can produce wealth and equity in the workplace, leading to greater social justice, while public services, rather than private enterprise, are better at targeting the needy within society. This was not entirely the case in Africa, however, where the public sector expanded more to meet *political* demands, rather than social or economic imperatives. Patronage was again the driving force.

As was seen in Chapters 5 and 6, access to state institutions became the main conduit of power and wealth in post-colonial African countries. Employment in the civil service, the military or parastatals was used by the state elite to reward clients. In effect, whole bureaucracies were built to service client–patron networks, rather than to manage and deliver public services efficiently. Long-term productive investment was being sacrificed for short-term political gain.

Given a post within the state, clients used this office to 'rent-seek'. Income was generated by receiving gratuities for ensuring a favourable or prompt service. Clients effectively added their own private levy to governmental transactions such as providing a driving licence, raising an export certificate or permitting a loan from the national bank. Rent-seeking also includes simply using or selling off state assets for private gain. Official government vehicles, for example, could be used for private taxi services, or office equipment requisitioned and sold on the black market. And with clients able to seek rent from their position of employment within the state, political support was guaranteed for the patron.

Thus, with political considerations overriding administrative or economic needs in these neo-patrimonial institutions, efficiency inevitably suffered. Public servants were often employed because of their loyalty, or faction or ethnic links, not for their skills, experience or ability to do the job. Indeed, the need to provide patronage often left these institutions considerably overstaffed. In this respect, African bureaucracies were far removed from the legal-rational institutions of Western civil services. Over developed bureaucracies may have represented a good *political* investment for ruling elites, but in *economic* terms the investment of scarce resources in this manner was clearly unproductive.

These bureaucracies accounted for considerable sums of public finance, yet generated few profits. No capital was accumulated, and no surplus was available for reinvestment. Instead, throughout Africa, bloated bureaucracies became burdens on fragile economies.

Max Weber's requirement of a legal-rational bureaucracy is that 'Public monies and equipment are divorced from the private property of the official'.[6] Again, this was not the case. Corruption became the norm.

Corruption is a relative term. It occurs all over the world, and what may be regarded as corrupt in one society may be acceptable, or even expected, behaviour in another. There can be little doubt, however, that corruption in Africa was endemic. Officials required bribes before they reached favourable decisions; public resources were misappropriated for private use; and individuals were employed and promoted on the basis of clientelism rather than merit. In many cases, ordinary people who used public services came to recognise only a minimal difference between bribes, gifts and official fees.[7] Chabal and Daloz, in this respect, talk of African corruption not being a case of 'a few "rotten apples" or of a venal "class", ... On the contrary, it is a habitual part of everyday life, an expected element of every social transaction'.[8] After all, in the absence of a legal-rational order, it would have been irrational for individuals not to work the system like those around them.

Corruption could be found at all levels within state institutions. An investigation of the Rural Electricity Board of Nigeria, for example, revealed 'a whole range of malpractices'. Board officials

> acquired privileged access to electricity for their own private concerns. They extracted kickbacks from equipment suppliers. They consolidated their patron–client networks by the preferential allocation of electricity supplies to individuals, firms and communities who were political supporters. And some of the top officers channelled Board revenues to their own enterprises and acquisitions. Indeed, a popular state governor used illegally acquired funds from the Board to buy no fewer than 22 farms and several retail businesses.[9]

Corruption could even be found at the pinnacle of the client–patron network. In 1980, for instance, Kenya's president, Daniel arap Moi, sought to purchase 12 jet fighters for his air force. His first call was British Aerospace. No deal could be struck here, however, because British Aerospace refused to pay Moi's agent a 'personal fee' (they did, however, offer a £100,000 contribution to assist Kenya's anti-poaching campaign). Instead, the jets were bought from the French firm Marcel Dassault Preguet, even though the French aeroplanes would cost the Kenyan taxpayer considerably more money. More forthcoming, Dassault were prepared to offer Moi a free presidential jet as part of the deal.[10] This private 'incentive' secured the contract, despite the extra public cost. Elsewhere, numerous state presidents spent years siphoning off public money into their own Swiss bank accounts. Perhaps the finest exponent of this 'creative accountancy' was Zaire's Mobutu Sese Seko (the subject of the case study at the end of this chapter). It was common practice for leaders right across the continent to make self-authorised withdrawals of foreign exchange from their central banks. The impressive National Reserve building in Harare, Zimbabwe, for example, is locally known as 'Big Bob's Takeaway', referring to President Robert Mugabe's regular personal use of the bank.

Whether the source was a prestigious but loss-making import substitution industry, a bloated bureaucracy, or money wasted through the demands of patronage and corrupt public officials, there can be little doubt that Africa contributed considerably to its own economic problems in the post-colonial period. Added to the restraints of the international economy, the continent's process of capital accumulation largely failed. With leaner bureaucracies, more appropriate development strategies, and fewer resources 'disappearing' into bureaucratic black holes, African economies would have fared better. This is important in terms of the authority states commanded. With a healthy economy, the distributive powers of a government are improved. They can tap into the economy, redistributing far more resources and services to citizens. This, in turn, generates legitimacy in the eyes of people, reinforcing state authority. An ailing economy, on the other hand, presents problems for those in power. They have fewer resources to convert into legitimacy. They also have fewer funds to invest in coercive actions, and with less legitimacy and less coercion, authority diminishes. The consequences of this loss of authority are explored in more detail later in the chapter.

The crisis of governance

'We have two problems: rats and the government'.[11] This comment, from a rural community leader in Lesotho, hints that there was not just a crisis of accumulation during the 1980s and 1990s. State authority was also being undermined by a crisis of governance. African elites were not representing their citizens adequately.

Chapter 6 explored the centralisation of the post-colonial African state. It was shown how, after independence, neo-patrimonialism led to the atrophy of legal-rational political institutions. Without this legal-rational order, African leaders came to rely instead on extensive client–patron networks to generate legitimacy. This was the main mechanism through which the political leadership represented their people.

The problem during the 1980s and 1990s, however, was that there were no longer enough resources to sustain these networks. Economic decline, and the changing nature of external support (due to structural adjustment and the loss of Cold War patronage), meant that governments now had less to pass down to their clients. Indeed, the shrinking distributive capacity of these states resulted in public services breaking down generally. Health centres experienced shortages of staff and drugs; textbooks were scarce in schools; trains did not run because of a lack of foreign exchange to buy spare parts; road systems fell into disrepair, as did electricity-generating plants. Consequently, legitimacy declined.

This crisis of legitimacy became a crisis of governance because constitutional means of replacing these failing regimes were no longer available. During the earlier centralisation period, formal opposition organisations had been systematically neutralised, and political parties other than the one in power had been co-opted, harassed or banned. In many cases, representative local government, and independent parliaments, had also disappeared. Formal political activity was now confined to the core executive, or institutions that were closely controlled by the 'presidential monarch'.

All governments, wherever they are in the world, will eventually lose the support of their citizens. In liberal democracies, however, this rarely precipitates a crisis of governance. This is because constitutional mechanisms exist which ensure that unpopular administrations can be removed from office in a peaceful and timely manner. Elections are held, the ailing ruling party is exchanged for an opposition party, and legitimacy is renewed. Orderly political succession occurs, with the authority of state institutions remaining intact.

In post-colonial Africa, this was not the case. The centralisation of the state meant that incumbent governments could only be removed by force. Consequently, unless the military intervened with a *coup d'état*, or a mass rebellion occurred, the same party, and usually the same president, remained in power, however unpopular they became. This obstacle to political succession lay at the heart of the crisis of governance. Simply put, there was no constitutional method of re-legitimising governments through the removal of unpopular incumbents.

The pincer effect of these crises of governance and accumulation meant that Africans were effectively living in 'vampire states' (also known as 'kleptocratic states', 'predatory states' or 'pirate states'). Resources were 'sucked out' of society by the government, yet the government offered little in return. Neither economic improvement nor political representation was forthcoming. Indeed, in many cases it seemed as if political elites were simply ignoring their duties of government. Many officials were too busy taking care of their own interests. Public money was being invested unproductively, with development projects designed to return political profits (for the elite themselves) rather than economic profits (for the wider national interest).

This is not to say, however, that civil society passively accepted the vampire state. After all, constitutional means are not the only channel through which citizens can challenge and remove their rulers. During the 1980s and 1990s, many Africans registered their discontent by effectively disengaging themselves from the state. And by removing many of their activities from government control, civil society seriously undermined the state's authority. Indeed, several states were so weakened by this disengagement that they approached a condition of complete collapse. In effect, civil society was taking its revenge upon the vampire state.

The loss of state authority

In political environments where governments lacked legitimacy, and where powers of coercion were diminished, Africans did indeed begin to challenge the authority of their states. In some cases, this resulted in outright rebellion. Urban riots and guerrilla campaigns became common on the continent during the 1980s and 1990s (as discussed below). Violent outbursts of this nature, however, were only the more spectacular examples of civil society confronting the state. More frequently, collections of more insidious individual acts achieved greater success in weakening a regime's political authority. Rather than being destroyed by one explosive act of violence, states were slowly ground into submission.[12] It is these less obvious, but still powerful, acts of disengagement that will be addressed first.

Disengagement and 'exit strategies'

In extreme cases, Africans evaded exploitative vampire states by disengaging totally, through emigration. There is no better way to escape the clutches of an abusive government than simply to leave its territory. In reality, however, only a small minority chose to exercise this ultimate form of disengagement. Ties to the local area proved strong, and obstacles to emigration were often significant. This is not to say, however, that those who chose to stay gave up exit strategies entirely.

Confronted by predatory states, Africans combined both engagement and disengagement. They tended to work with the state when it was in their interests to do this, but avoided doing so when it was not. Individuals, to use Eric Hobsbawm's phrase, were 'working the system…to their minimum disadvantage'.[13] Opportunities could certainly arise from interacting with state officials and institutions, but often this contact merely led to exploitation. The key, therefore, was to carefully control the level of engagement. If, for example, the government concentrated on extracting revenue from tobacco crops, farmers would switch production to less taxed commodities, such as maize. If the state decided to tap into the revenue created by a city's bus companies, entrepreneurs moved into the taxi business instead. In the event of all commercial activity being prohibitively exploited, an extreme exit strategy was to revert to subsistence farming (only producing for the needs of the immediate family). It was about insulating oneself from the excesses of government predation, and removing economic activity to the margins of state control.

Declining state capacity also required civil society to increase its self-sufficiency. People could now rely even less on public services for their welfare than they did before. This self-sufficiency, too, should be seen as part of the disengagement process. Africans came to rely on family, kinship, village, community and professional relationships in place of state provision. As Naomi Chazan observed, 'The most noticeable changes took place at the local level, where the multiplication of communal associations was everywhere in evidence. Entrepreneurial, credit, banking, and barter groups were established alongside new welfare associations, mutual aid societies, educational initiatives, and self-defense groups'.[14] Where formal state institutions had decayed, civil society itself stepped into the breach. Communities built and ran their own schools, for example, and organised tax collections to pay for this.[15] They even formed their own militias to compensate for the state's declining ability to maintain law and order. Even in extreme cases of total state collapse, associational life continued. As Virginia Luling wrote of Somalia in the mid-1990s, 'The centre of Mogadishu may be bombed out, but the markets on the outskirts are busy; there may be no banks but there are plenty of money-changers; [and] with a well-functioning, privately run satellite service it is far easier to telephone Somalia than it was before the war'.[16] States are certainly the most efficient way of organising and administering a society, but civil societies can survive without them.

The above cases of switching markets, withdrawal from the formal economy, and establishing alternative public services within civil society are all examples of 'legal' disengagement. None of these 'exit' or 'coping' strategies involve a direct challenge to state laws. Most Africans, however, also acted illegally in their efforts to survive the hostile political and economic environment of the 1980s and 1990s. They dealt with atrophy and exploitation by simply ignoring some of the state's regulations. After all, if African leaders were not subject to the rule of law, why should the people they governed be? The following paragraphs highlight some of the most popular illegal disengagement strategies found on the continent.

The most widespread challenges to state authority were 'parallel markets'. Instead of buying and selling produce in the formal (state-controlled) economy, Africans took to operating in the informal sector instead (also termed the second economy, the shadow economy, parallel markets, black markets, and *magendo* in East Africa and *kalabule* in West Africa). Throughout the post-colonial period, governments had sought to manipulate economic production for their own ends. Producers, particularly those in rural areas, suffered accordingly. Consequently, many within civil society attempted to avoid the formal economy. Instead, farmers (illegally) sold their crops in the unregulated second economy, and not to the state marketing boards. Similarly, street hawkers sold their wares without a government licence or reference to state laws, landlords rented out property without government authorisation, and entrepreneurs (such as illicit brewers) operated largely in the informal sector.

By the 1980s, most African countries had considerable second economies. *Magendo*, for example, accounted for up to two-thirds of Uganda's GDP, while more than 90 per cent of Tanzania's grain production was sold through parallel markets.[17] Large-scale economic avoidance of the state reached equivalent levels in other areas of the continent. Smuggling, in particular, was a mainstay of this shadow economy.

African borders, given their artificial nature, had always been relatively porous. The (illegal) flow of people and goods across state boundaries, however, grew considerably in response to the crises of accumulation and governance. For example, instead of submitting to painfully low state-determined producer prices, farmers sought opportunities to sell their crops in neighbouring countries instead. Again, the figures are revealing. Two-thirds of Ghana's cocoa crop was smuggled out of the country in 1982. Legally, the Ghanaian state was entitled to all the income from this harvest. Similarly, one-third of Guinea's coffee harvest was sold in parallel markets.[18]

The illegal sale of foreign exchange was another example of individuals undermining the authority of the state. Most African governments operated financial policies to keep the value of their national currency artificially high. This was a method of reducing the cost of imports. Parallel money markets developed, however, responding to this artificial price. Instead of exchanging their currency at official state-determined rates, Africans conducted their business with street traders instead. In several cases, official currencies became virtually worthless, as states could no longer maintain their authority. US dollars often became the dominant means of exchange instead. In wartorn Angola, cans of beer were the preferred currency (with the value of these cans accurately reflecting the fluctuating strength of the United States dollar).[19]

Other survival strategies included resorting to petty crime and banditry. Noting the state's declining coercive powers, criminal activity became more widespread. Again, it was a case of individuals taking matters into their own hands when the formal economy had failed them. In the worst cases, districts of cities, and even large tracts of rural areas, became virtual 'no-go' areas for the state's law-enforcement agencies. Organised crime prospered in this environment.

A new wave of insurgency

With disengagement both contributing to, and compounding, a decline of state capacity in the 1980s and 1990s, central authority was severely weakened. Sometimes civil associations and parallel markets filled this institutional vacuum, bringing a degree of economic and political order. In other cases, Africans had to take their chances living in areas of insecurity and banditry. A third scenario developed during the 1990s in a smaller, but still significant, number of cases. This involved a new wave of insurgency campaigns.

Insurgency or guerrilla movements differ from bandit groups in that, although they operate outside the law, they are politically driven. They seek to overthrow the existing state, and replace it with a new political order. In this sense, although these rebels have disengaged from the state, they are actively attempting to build an alternative political authority.

Guerrilla armies had earlier helped to defeat colonialism in several countries on the continent (most notably in Kenya, Algeria, Guinea–Bissau and the Southern African states of Angola, Mozambique, Zimbabwe, Namibia and South Africa). Rebel groups had also challenged several ruling elites after independence. The governments of Angola, Mozambique, Chad, the Sudan, Uganda and Ethiopia, for example, all lost territory to rebel groups during this period. In the 1990s, however, guerrilla politics came to the fore once more, this time continent-wide.

In Uganda, Yoweri Museveni's National Resistance Army started the trend by taking Kampala in 1986. The Ethiopian People's Revolutionary Democratic Front and the Eritrean People's Liberation Front followed suit in 1991, forming governments in Addis Ababa and Asmara, respectively. Three years later the Rwandan Patriotic Front took Kigali, and three years after that an Alliance of Democratic Forces for the Liberation of Congo-Zaire ousted Mobutu from the Congo. Added to these insurgency-induced regime transitions were the defeat of incumbent governments in Somalia, Liberia and Sierra Leone. Armed rebellion was back in fashion in Africa.

The reasons for this rise in insurgency, again, go back to the crises of accumulation and governance. Guerrilla warfare can only be conducted successfully in regions where incumbent governments have lost their authority. With the state unable to project power over the whole of its territory, alternative sources of authority emerge. And given that the centralisation of the African state offered few constitutional channels of political regeneration, these alternative centres of authority were often sustained by violent rebellion. Whether insurgents were separatist movements seeking independence for just one region, or they were attempting to capture the state as a whole, they stood more chance of succeeding in the 1990s than they had in previous decades.[20]

The road to state collapse

African states had survived in the post-colonial period because they were able to appropriate resources both domestically (minerals and cash crops) and internationally (trade and aid). These resources were then used to sustain institutions of the state, to boost officials' private incomes, and also to 'buy' legitimacy through the provision of patronage and public services. By the 1980s, however, the crises of accumulation and governance had badly damaged the ability of ruling elites to appropriate these resources. Many African territories were on the road to state collapse.

Some post-colonial governments had experienced difficulty in controlling their territories prior to the 1980s. Angola had won its independence from Portugal in 1975, yet, from day one, UNITA insurgents ensured that the MPLA government would not enjoy total sovereignty within this country for the following quarter of a century. Similarly, northern (Muslim) administrations in the Sudan always failed to assert complete authority over the southern (Christian) region of their jurisdiction. The 1980s, however, saw a wider loss of state capacity across the continent. The government of Mozambique lacked control in rural areas when confronted by apartheid South Africa-funded bandits/guerrillas; Ethiopia's leaders lost their authority over parts of Eritrea and Tigray; and the state collapsed completely in Uganda and Chad. Later in the 1990s, several more states withered away. Central authority disappeared in Liberia, Sierra Leone, Somalia, Rwanda and Zaire/DRC.

The phenomenon of state collapse occurs where national institutions of enforcement, execution and decision making fail. As a result, basic functions of the state are no longer guaranteed. There is no rule of law, no security from external aggression, and few public services. Moreover, any power remaining at the centre can no longer be projected into all the regions of the territory.

Plate 10.1 Collapsed states. Militias competing for power in Mogadishu, Somalia, 1993. Photographer: Chris Rainier.

Plate 10.2 Refugees returning to Rwanda having earlier been displaced by genocide, 1996. Photographer: Howard Davies.

Often, collapse occurs when opposition forces have been successful in ousting the incumbent elite, thereby destroying its authority, but then themselves fail to generate the necessary authority to reconstruct the state. Uganda's President Museveni does not fall into this category; he successfully converted his insurgency movement into a central government that now commands authority over most of what geographically is Uganda. Somalia, however, is a good example of state collapse. Although Somali clans were sufficiently united to bring down Siad Barré's corrupt regime in 1991, these disparate groups collectively failed to reconstitute a national government in its place. Somalia, as a consequence, did not have an effective central authority for a quarter of a century.

Frequently, collapsed states split into enclaves ruled by militias and charismatic warlords. These private governments survive through the coercive power that they command, and through their access to resources. It is no coincidence that three of the most intractable failures of the state in post-colonial Africa have occurred in Angola, Liberia and DRC. In all three cases, the rebel militias have had access to diamonds, diamonds being a guerrilla's best friend.[21] Such resources allow 'conflict entrepreneurs' within these private governments to enrich themselves personally and to sustain their authority. More weapons can be purchased, and local legitimacy can be bought if necessary. A criminal, rather than political, regime emerges, which is often difficult to dislodge. It is not in these warlords' interests to relinquish power to a reconstituted central government, especially when you consider the example of one militia in DRC which alone exported some US$12 million of coltan (a mineral used in the manufacture of mobile phones) and US$30 million of gold and diamonds in the single year of 2000.[22] With this sort of income, why would any militia want to advance national reconciliation?

The experiences of DRC, Angola, Liberia and other African states that remain in a state of collapse or semi-collapse continue to serve as beacons to all other territories on the continent, warning them of the consequences of failing to address ongoing crises of legitimacy and governance.

The state's own survival strategies

The end of the twentieth century saw a partial eclipse of state power in Africa. In a few cases, central authority collapsed altogether. This was inevitable given the long list of problems facing incumbent regimes. Yet, to paraphrase Mark Twain, the death of the African state has been widely exaggerated.

Geographically, for example, maps of the continent still show the same number of states, in the same positions, that were found in 1980 (with the exception of the addition of Eritrea and South Sudan). Territorially, all of these states survived. There was no case of neighbours taking advantage of state collapse, and moving in to annexe territory. The 'political-space-that-is-Somalia', for instance, still remains.[23]

Similarly, although several states did collapse in the 1980s and 1990s, many of these are now enjoying a successful afterlife. Central institutions that were destroyed by insurgent (and invading) forces in Rwanda and Uganda, for example, were subsequently replaced. Authority was generated by a new set of institutions, built from the rubble of the old state. Indeed, in the 1990s, Western governments regarded Yoweri Museveni's Uganda as one of Africa's more successful governments.

Elsewhere, central authority may have been undermined, but African leaders demonstrated considerable skill in maintaining their grip on state power. Just like civil society, state elites had their own survival strategies during these hard times, and the success of these strategies explains why there was a good deal of political continuity throughout these troubled years. States may have had to adapt, but few went the way of Somalia into total oblivion. The following paragraphs highlight the most common survival strategies employed by political elites.

Re-legitimisation of the state

In the long term, the most effective way to guarantee the state's survival was through the re-legitimisation of its institutions. If trust was maintained or restored, authority would be regained. The holding of multi-party elections, as will be seen in Chapter 11, proved the best way of achieving this. Indeed, by the end of the twentieth century, most African elites had taken this option.

Yet multi-party elections risked everything. Given the ongoing crises of accumulation and governance, it was very possible that incumbent elites would be defeated at these polls. Consequently, democracy was not the initial survival strategy to be enacted. In the short term, more exploitative behaviour was dominant.

State inversion

The first reaction of state elites to their predicament was to scale down operations. Like a balloon losing altitude, political leaders jettisoned parts of the state in an effort to keep the remaining structure airborne. It was a case of prioritising productive or strategic areas, and abandoning the rest. Consequently, scarce resources would now only be invested in the most important conduits of power: valuable economic activity, for example, key clients, agencies of coercion, and critical tracts of territory. Unproductive areas, such as weaker clients or poorer regions, were simply discarded. State managers could no longer afford to uphold the pretence that they controlled all the territory within their national boundaries, nor did they try to serve all their citizens.

This scaling down of the state came at the expense of wider civil society. Many public services were abandoned, and the whole nationalist economic development project was put on hold. Health care, welfare and education provision, in particular, suffered. As Victor Azarya and Naomi Chazan point out, the aim was to reduce 'state responsibility' without relinquishing the 'benefits of state power'.[24] It was almost as if the state, to use Joshua Forrest's term, had become 'inverted'.[25] Institutions turned in on themselves, supporting areas of the state that served elite interests, but discarding their wider duties. A natural gas production plant, for example, would be maintained, as this generated considerable and scarce income for the elite. By contrast, demands for hospital funding would be ignored, as such an investment would bring no direct short-term benefits to the elite.

Tapping into foreign patronage

The scaling down of their domestic operations also required elites to maximise resources and legitimacy that could be raised externally. In this respect, although diminished since the end of the Cold War, the international convention of state sovereignty was still an advantage. State managers continued to pose as 'representatives of their people', enabling them to win aid and preferential trade agreements from the outside world. These resources could then be used to shore up remaining institutions of the state (and not necessarily for wider economic development, as the donors had intended). Given the even greater lack of resources now being produced locally, this international lifeline was essential for the survival of the elite and their state.

Exploiting parallel markets

Elites, however, could not just make do with consolidating their position within the state and the international community. Opportunities in both these areas had shrunk considerably. If they were to maintain their privileged existence, hard-pressed officials now had to find additional sources of power and wealth to exploit. The most obvious target for them was the most dynamic and productive area of their territory: the second economy.

Throughout the continent, public officials turned a blind eye to *magendo*. Indeed it is doubtful that the second economy could have survived without a degree of state collusion. The whole foundation of the informal sector, after all, was based on bribes, embezzlement, fraud and official theft. Consequently, state managers could maintain their incomes by facilitating these parallel markets. They received money when they chose not to prosecute illegal traders or smugglers; they could divert public goods (food aid, perhaps) into these parallel markets; and they could also issue official documents to illegitimate operations. Again, it was a case of holders of public office being able to extract rent by using their position within the state. Indeed, in many cases, it was actually the officers of the state who were leading these illegal entrepreneurial projects. Just as many KGB operatives moved in to run organised crime in Russia following the collapse of the Soviet Union, African holders of political office also found a home in the strategic niches of the criminal underworld. It is no coincidence that, in the 1990s, African countries such as Nigeria became prime staging posts for drugs smuggled into Western Europe and North America. Jean-François Bayart, Stephen Ellis and Béatrice Hibou refer to this development as the 'criminalisation of the African state'.[26]

The 'warlord state'

In some cases, these self-serving state survival strategies became the sole focus of a regime. Having lost, almost entirely, their bureaucratic power base through state collapse, leaders sought to convert their remaining influence into material gains through commercial activity. William Reno calls these extreme cases 'warlord states'.[27]

Warlord politics results in rulers abandoning the whole idea of administrating a state for the collective good. Instead, institutions now merely serve the elites' private interests. Opportunism replaces ideology, legal-rational motivations are even harder to find, and governments are no longer in the business of trying to generate legitimacy. In this respect, even client–patron networks are scaled down to a minimum. A warlord state is an inverted, predatory or vampire state taken to its most exploitative conclusion.

Given that public responsibilities have vanished in warlord states, private syndicates tend to replace the previously more inclusive patronage networks. Political leaders are also much more in touch with market opportunities, and do not just rely on rent raised from political office. For example, warlord governments often enter into partnerships with transnational corporations (TNCs), concentrating their remaining authority on the most productive natural resource that their country has to offer. Loyal remnants of the national army, for example, will be deployed to guarantee the security of this particular region. They then grant concessions to TNCs to extract minerals or agricultural produce.

Profits are shared between political leaders, the military and the TNC, with little of this revenue filtering down into civil society. *Where, specifically? Examples...*

Naturally enough, warlord states generate little legitimacy, and, as such, citizens have few incentives to support such governments (apart from the fear of any remaining coercive powers). Consequently, instability is a hallmark of this kind of state. Often, rebel or bandit groups wrestle vast tracts of territory away from central political control. Yet the ruling elite is always careful to ensure that those parts of the country that do contain strategic resources remain in government hands. In several cases, elites have even hired mercenaries to guarantee this control, as they were no longer able to rely on their own military. The South African-based private company Executive Outcomes (EO), for example, helped the besieged government of Sierra Leone to protect its TNC partnerships based on diamond production. As William Reno observes, 'EO and its partners give politicians the option to jettison old, inefficient, but more inclusive patronage networks for efficient, powerful, and profitable commercial networks to boost their personal power'.[28] No longer able to control the rest of the country, elites simply give up the pretence that they can serve all the citizens of the state.

In the 1990s, Zaire, Liberia and Sierra Leone came closest to meeting this notion of a warlord state. Central power all but evaporated in these countries, and rebel groups exercised alternative political authority in regions outside government control. Yet these states did retain enough power to look after the elite's private interests. Major cities remained in government hands, as did outlying economic installations (even if mercenaries had to be deployed). The elite was skilful enough in its survival strategies to ensure that political power continued to be converted into economic wealth. In these cases, the state was just as adept at disengaging from civil society as (as seen above) civil society was at disengaging from the state. *✗ MUTUAL DISENGAGEMENT*

State and civil society

This chapter has charted how the post-colonial African state reached something of a watershed in the 1980s and 1990s. The crises of accumulation and governance had gnawed away at the capacity of central institutions to rule society. Legitimacy had declined, and since it is difficult for states to maintain their authority by coercion alone, the political environment was ripe for radical change.

The problem was that often no replacement government was available for these ailing regimes. Due to shrinking client–patron networks, scope for the circulation of elites was limited. Similarly, few states harboured an opposition strong enough to topple the political incumbents. Ruling elites therefore limped on, withdrawing into their inverted states. This resulted in many citizens being more or less abandoned.

Civil society's response to this turn of events was to disengage. By taking their activities to the margins of state control, citizens avoided the worst excesses of the predatory bureaucratic elite. Parallel markets, smuggling and other illegal activities became well established during the 1980s and 1990s.

Some commentators regarded this disengagement as a positive phenomenon. Naomi Chazan, for example, considered that 'the centre of political gravity' had shifted on the continent. 'Viewed from above', she continued,

> institutional mechanisms have been undergoing a process of contraction and disaggregation. But from below, social and economic niches have been carved out and are

Table 10.1 Chapter summary: the crisis of political authority in Africa

Crisis of legitimacy

Crisis of accumulation	• Import substitution economic strategies usually inefficient
	• Agricultural sector taxed too hard in order to raise income for state spending
	• Little surplus capital generated for reinvestment
Crisis of governance	• Short-term political imperatives (patronage) override long-term economic investment
	• Bureaucracies become bloated
	• Corruption thrives in this client–patron environment
	• Centralisation of the state leaves no avenue open for constitutional regime change

The loss of state authority

Civil society disengagement	• Citizens distance themselves from the predatory state (via emigration, the second economy, tax avoidance and ignoring state regulations)
Insurgency	• Growth of insurgency movements challenges the state from the 1980s onwards (e.g. Ethiopia, Uganda, Rwanda and DRC)
State collapse	• Central institutions can no longer project authority into the hinterland of the state
	• No rule of law, no public services
	• State no longer has monopoly over resources of coercion
	• Armed militias step into the power vacuum

State survival strategies

Re-legitimisation of the state	• Renewal of government usually through multi-party elections
State inversion	• The state limits its activities, primarily looking after elite interests
	• Strategic resources are still protected, but public services and representation are cut
	• Shrinking client–patron networks
Exploiting parallel markets	• State officials collude with second economy activities for private gain
The 'warlord state'	• No pretence of public service and representation
	• Coercive resources used to protect key strategic installations for the elite's private gain

beginning to interact and adhere in new ways.... From this perspective, political rhythms may lack cohesion; they are not, however, incoherent.... As local arrangements come into play, political spaces are being reorganised and diverse links between government structures, specific social groups, and resource bases are being devised. A more diffuse and variegated, but perhaps more viable, pattern of political realignment is slowly taking shape.[29]

In other words, civil society was learning to look after itself, and potentially a new political order could be built on these foundations.

Yet disengagement was only *relatively* positive. It may have reduced citizen exploitation, but in achieving this, civil society had to relinquish the benefits of the modern state. History has shown, after all, that legitimate states give individuals an advantage in realising security, economic gain and improved welfare generally. As Robert Fatton puts it, 'the phenomenon of exit should not evoke the utopian image of a brave new world of unalien-ated villagers discovering within African authenticity a miraculous cure for poverty, exploi-tation and tyranny'.[30] Life in such an environment may be better than that in a vampire state, but it is certainly no substitute for a well-managed society based on the rule of law, legal-rational institutions and participatory democracy. Disengaged civil societies could only, at best, provide their members with informal imitations of these political benefits.

And here lies the true crisis of the post-colonial African state. Civil society was adept at taking its revenge on the predatory state, helping to destroy its capacity and legiti-macy. Yet it was often unable to replace this central authority. Consequently, weak but still exploitative state structures remained. In the ebb and flow of political power, when the inverted state gained the upper hand, coercion increased. When civil society was in the ascendancy, the state moved closer to disintegration and total collapse. Few on the continent gained any long-term benefits from this stalemate between state and civil society. It was costly in terms of both economic production and public service provision. As such, the last two decades of the twentieth century proved to be difficult times for most Africans to live through. As the millennium approached, however, a new hope emerged in the form of multi-party elections. The African state was indeed recon-structed. Whether these elections created an advantageous balance between state and civil society is the subject of the next chapter.

Case study: Zaire – Mobutu's vampire state

In 1990, Chris Simpson wrote that 'Zaire under Mobutu has become almost a caricature of an African dictatorship', it is 'autocratic to a fault' and 'its resources are shamelessly squandered'.[31] In his 32-year rule as president (1965–1997), Mobutu Sese Seko oversaw a kleptocracy of the highest order. Once the ruling elite, and their TNC allies, had taken their cut of Zaire's mineral wealth, little profit found its way back into civil society. In Mobutu's pirate state, self-interested extraction among politicians and bureaucrats became both an art form and an end in itself.

It did not have to be this way. Zaire, formerly the Belgian Congo, and renamed the Democratic Republic of the Congo (DRC) in 1997, is blessed with many natu-ral resources. Straddling the Equator in western Central Africa, DRC has an abun-dance of land, and agriculture should flourish, given the good soils and plentiful rains. The country also has excellent mining and hydroelectric potential. Yet the twentieth century was not kind to the inhabitants of this part of Africa. Economic development was not only hampered by the vagaries of the international market, but it was also fatally restricted by the actions of domestic political leaders.

Post-colonial Congo-Kinshasa got off to an inauspicious start in 1960. Within five days of independence, the army, led by Colonel Joseph Désiré Mobutu, had mutinied, taking and holding power for a number of months. In the confusion, the mineral-rich province of Katanga seceded. It took a costly civil war, and the mili-tary intervention of the United Nations, to restore Congo-Kinshasa's territorial integrity. Political unity, however, was not restored. Constitutional deadlock was complete after the 1965 parliamentary elections, when the state president failed to secure a majority in the national assembly. Mobutu took his opportunity to intervene in the political process for a second time, this time refusing to relinquish power.

Initially, Mobutu's rule proved successful. With the state territorially reunited, and a military 'strong man' replacing the squabbling politicians, Congo-Kinshasa could get on with the business of economic development. Good relations with external powers, and the high price of copper on the international commodity markets, also helped. Yet, within ten years, Zaire (as it was renamed in 1971) had started its journey to state collapse. Like so many other African leaders, Mobutu's political decisions precipitated both a crisis of accumulation and a crisis of governance.

Zaire's crisis of accumulation, in classic fashion, was created by a combination of wrong policy choices and naked corruption. In terms of inappropriate public policy, import substitution was pursued at the expense of developing agricultural production. A case in point was the Maluku steel mill (completed by Italian and German contractors in 1975). Unable to find foreign investors for this project, the US$250 million bill for this state-of-the-art factory was met entirely by government funds. Zaire, however, did not have enough capital to develop its own iron ore deposits to actually supply the smelting plant. Maluku therefore relied on imported scrap metal. This added to the production costs, resulting in its steel being uncompetitively priced on the international market. Indeed, even domestically, the steel produced in this mill cost eight times more than foreign imports. Consequently, Maluku never ran at more than 10 per cent capacity. The whole project was an expensive and ill-conceived white elephant.[32]

Similar development mistakes were made throughout the Mobutu years. Take, for instance, the Inga–Shaba power scheme. The idea was to transport electricity, generated by the Inga hydroelectric plant, a distance of 1,800 kilometres to Shaba province, where there was a concentration of mining activity. Despite the technical ingenuity displayed to achieve this, the reality was that it would have been cheaper for Shaba factories to generate their own electricity regionally. Other industrialisation measures also failed. Locally assembled cars and locally produced tyres and textiles, for example, cost between 20 and 40 per cent more than their imported equivalents.[33] Ultimately, since these projects brought little capital accumulation, the outcome was unproductive investment of public funds.

Agriculture was potentially Zaire's most profitable sector of the economy. Government policy, however, consistently squeezed the rural areas excessively. Marketing boards, year after year, bought farmers' harvests at below market prices. The result was a lack of incentive for these farmers to produce. Cotton yields, for example, fell from 60,000 tons of lint at independence to just 8,500 tons by 1976. Similarly, whereas the Belgian Congo had exported a small surplus of food, independent Zaire was forced to import its basic staples. Farmers were simply not prepared to supply the formal economy at the low prices set by the state. Since Zaire has such a conducive climate for agriculture, this was a criminal waste of resources.

Unproductive investment in ill-conceived development projects, and the misuse of the country's agricultural potential, however, pale into insignificance alongside the level of corruption found in Mobutu's Zaire. At times it seemed that there was no limit to the greed of this country's public servants.

At the pinnacle of government, and of the corruption therein, was Mobutu himself. During his time in office, the president amassed between US$5 and US$8 billion worth of assets, much of it deposited in Swiss bank accounts.[34] It is difficult to see how Mobutu's 'legitimate' businesses could have generated so much wealth. Regular confusion between the president's public and private spending helps to explain this discrepancy. Lower down the political hierarchy was General Eluki, secretary of state for national defence. His spouse was allegedly once stopped at a roadblock and found to be in possession of 17 suitcases of money. A subsequent search of Eluki's home found US$2 million stashed away. Eluki was convicted of corruption, but his 20-year sentence was set aside and he returned as the military commander of Shaba province.[35]

Mobutu and Eluki, however, were just two of the more high-profile abusers of public office. From the state president down to the humblest government clerk, from generals through to privates operating roadblocks, corruption was an everyday part of life in Zaire. It became a case of citizens having to buy public services through private negotiations with the official concerned.[36] As Archbishop Kabanga of Lubumbashi wrote in a 1976 pastoral letter,

> We bear daily witness to agonizing situations.... How many children and adults die without medical care because they are unable to bribe the medical personnel who are supposed to care for them? Why are there no medical supplies in the hospitals, while they are found in the marketplace? How did they get there? Why is it that in our courts justice can only be obtained by fat bribes to the judge?...Why do our government officers force people to come back day after day to obtain services to which they are entitled? If the clerks are not paid off, they will not be served. Why, at the opening of school, must parents go into debt to bribe the school principal? Children who are unable to pay will have no school.... Whoever holds a morsel of authority, or means of pressure, profits from it to impose on people and exploit them.[37]

As well as ruling over a state that failed to accumulate capital, Mobutu's Zaire also suffered from a crisis of governance.

Zaire followed a familiar path to other African countries in the post-colonial period, with Mobutu overseeing the centralisation of the state and a personalisation of power. Spurred on by the failure of political parties to stabilise the country in the First Republic, the president abandoned multi-party democracy altogether. This was replaced by a one-party structure, and Mobutu himself came to dominate the legislative and judicial as well as the executive roles of the state. Sources of opposition were systematically eliminated by co-option, harassment, imprisonment, exile and assassination. It was also made plain to those members of the ruling party itself that they owed their position specifically to Mobutu's patronage. As one reporter commented, the number of significant political players in Zaire was kept to just 80 or so individuals. Among these, at any one time, '20 of them are ministers, 20 are exiles, 20 are in jail and 20 ambassadors. Every three months, the music stops and Mobutu forces everyone to change chairs'.[38] No one, friend or foe, was left in any doubt about who held supreme power in Zaire. To challenge Mobutu was to risk losing everything, including one's life.

Whereas the political elite enjoyed the wealth that access to state institutions brought, most individuals within Zaire gained little from their government. Members of civil society were the victims of a declining economy, public services were shrinking, and they were often on the wrong end of demanding corrupt officials. Yet there was no constitutional way of ridding Zaire of this kleptocratic elite. No opposition parties existed, and any political challenge that Mobutu perceived to threaten his regime was brutally crushed. Mobutu, until the final resource-diminished days of this regime, maintained agencies of violence that were more than a match for civil society.

Lacking the ability to change the incumbent government directly, Zairians opted for the next best option. They sought to distance themselves as far as possible from the state. The scale of this disengagement is perhaps best illustrated by the growth of Zaire's parallel economy during the 1980s and 1990s. By this time, official statistics showed Mobutu's economy to be a disaster. There was a massive trade deficit, production was declining in all sectors, annual inflation stood at over 1,000 per cent, the national debt was colossal, and wages were at starvation levels. In short, in terms of economics, nothing worked as it should.[39] Yet 35 million Zairians did get on with their lives. It may be true that the formal economy could no longer meet even the most basic needs of the Zairian people, but this was just the formal economy. Indeed, by the late 1980s, it is estimated that the second economy sector measured up to three times that of Zaire's official GDP.[40]

A few statistics serve to show the extent of this economic disengagement. From the 1970s onwards, up to 60 per cent of Zaire's coffee crop annually bypassed state marketing boards and was smuggled into neighbouring countries. By 1985, farmers could sell their coffee to smugglers for 42 cents per kilogram, while the state only offered 7 cents.[41] The second economy set about supplying what the official economy could not. Low state-determined prices and transport problems, due to collapsing infrastructure, saw few willing to supply the official market with even the most basic of commodities. Yet in parallel markets, where higher prices could be charged, it was profitable to trade in staple goods.[42]

Disengagement, however, did not bring down the Zairian state immediately. Mobutu's regime limped on until the mid-1990s. Indeed, those members of the elite who were able to adapt to the shrinking state were still able to prosper. It was almost as if these individuals welcomed the disengagement of civil society. The growing gulf between the governed and their governors allowed state managers greater political space to operate their own personal survival strategies. They were free now from even the most notional responsibility of government. These survival strategies included the scaling down of patronage networks, the nurturing of foreign rather than domestic resources, and tapping into the productive activity within the second economy. Each of these strategies will now be examined in turn.

The crisis of accumulation began to bite during the late 1970s, grew considerably throughout the 1980s, and then reached a critical mass in the early 1990s. Reacting to this developing crisis, the state elite scaled down its patronage networks accordingly. Naturally enough, to maintain their privileged position, certain stronger clients still had to be placated. State managers, however, no longer had resources to distribute to weaker citizens. Consequently, public services such as health care, education and policing virtually disappeared. Education provision, for example, slumped from 17.5 per cent of the national budget in 1972 to just 2.1 per cent in 1990. Similarly, rural communities were also abandoned. Agriculture's share of the budget fell from 29.3 per cent to just 4 per cent over the same period. Investment in infrastructure was another casualty. Only 15 per cent of roads inherited from the colonial authorities still remained passable by the mid-1980s. Even in the cities, the Mobutu regime was only offering minimal government. Kinshasa itself had only intermittent water and electricity supplies, and even the sickest people refused to attend its hospitals. All this was because state patronage had dwindled to a bare minimum.[43]

The disintegration of these client–patron networks, of course, had major ramifications for the government's legitimacy. The state now served fewer people, and those former clients who had been jettisoned were naturally aggrieved. Yet Mobutu and his lieutenants were very careful to retain those that they needed for their own personal political survival. For example, whereas much of the army had been abandoned to its own devices by 1990, Mobutu made sure that his own 5,000-strong presidential guard still continued to be paid regularly. The president could lose legitimacy in the eyes of his people, but he could not afford to lose the support of his most reliable agency of coercion.

Once the Zairian state abandoned its welfare and infrastructure responsibilities, as well as much of its rural territory, it was almost as if Kinshasa was content to rule only strategic enclaves within the country. The regime sought to maintain its authority in major cities, important trading centres and sites of extraction (such as mines and plantations), that is, in all the key areas that could still deliver a profit for the benefit of state managers. It did not matter too much that the government's authority could rarely now be found elsewhere, in the non-profitable regions of the country. Mobutu's regime certainly did not conform to Weber's idea that the state should be able to exercise sovereignty over all its territory.

Ironically, however, one of the regime's most successful survival strategies relied directly on this Weberian notion of sovereignty. It required that the international community and TNCs should still recognise Mobutu as Zaire's head of state, and thus the chief representative of his people. If this was the case, the general could still gain access to international resources. And this is exactly what happened. There was still an external demand for Zaire's minerals and coffee. Mobutu granted foreign TNCs concessions to extract these commodities, in return for a share of the profits. Even in 1991, when state collapse was imminent and the Mobutu government exercised authority over only the most strategic enclaves within the country, these exports earned the regime US$2.1 billion. International aid brought in another US$494 million.[44] Given that the government was now spending very little on public services, these sums went a considerable way towards allowing the state elite to maintain its privileged position. It was able to shore up its profitable enclave operations, and run (albeit reduced) agencies of coercion. And there was also enough money left for Mobutu to employ foreign mercenaries to bolster his own presidential guard.

Nor was the international community the only source of wealth into which the state elite could tap. With public-sector wages falling behind inflation, and many instances of state employees not being paid at all, officials could not now rely solely on the formal economy to secure their living. They, too, came to need the second economy. State employees used their positions of political power to extract rent from parallel markets. Their largest source of income, in this respect, consisted of the bribes received for turning a blind eye to illegal operations. Customs officers at Zaire's border with Zambia, for instance, regularly agreed only to charge excise duty on part of a lorry driver's cargo. The official and the driver would then share the remaining unpaid duty between them, and as they were now travelling with false documents, drivers would have to bribe personnel at subsequent military and police roadblocks between the border and their destination.[45]

Benefits, however, were not confined merely to an indirect association with the second economy. Many of the elite also played a more central role in these informal activities. With their *bureaucratic* power base disintegrating, state managers had been forced to switch to additional *economic* entrepreneurial projects in order to maintain their social position.

Jean-François Bayart gives a good illustration of how one arm of the bureaucracy, the Zairian air force (FAZA), adapted to the conditions of a collapsing state. No longer enjoying regular pay, FAZA cargo pilots turned the air force into an unofficial transport company during the 1980s. Taking advantage of Zaire's ailing road network, they were able to take goods into the interior and sell them at a profit. FAZA ground crews, however, were angered that they did not share these profits. Consequently, they took less care in maintaining the cargo planes, which resulted in a number of crashes. This persuaded the cargo pilots, now that they had started an additional unofficial passenger service, to bring the ground crews into their operations. Not wanting to be left out, fighter pilots also began using their position within the state to supplement their wages. They stole aircraft parts to sell in parallel markets. Eventually, the whole air force was grounded due to a lack of spare parts. Undeterred, FAZA personnel then went on to sell the air force's fuel supplies. By the 1990s, Zaire had an air force in name only.[46]

The demise of FAZA reflects, in microcosm, the wider collapse of the Zairian state. By the mid-1990s, the game was up for the whole Mobutu regime. The state had exhausted its power and the formal economy had totally collapsed, as had the regime's bureaucratic structures. As a result, TNCs were now reluctant to risk investing in Zaire, while IFIs and foreign governments, especially now that the Cold War was over, were no longer prepared to stomach Mobutu's excesses and the country's massive external debt.

Mobutu attempted to cling to power, despite the growing strength of opposition groups. Forced to liberalise the constitution, he still managed to stall his opponents with a series of political manoeuvres, including constitutional conventions, the postponement of multi-party elections, the funding of numerous bogus opposition parties, and simply buying off opposition leaders. In the end, the country was left in constitutional deadlock, just as it had been at the start of Mobutu's 32-year reign. The president refused to relinquish control of what remained of the executive and the army, while opposition leaders in parliament failed to command the political strength to remove him.

Eventually, Mobutu would be ousted by force of arms. This came in the form of the Alliance des Forces Démocratiques pour la Libération du Congo-Zaire (AFDL), led by Laurent Désiré Kabila. The rebellion was precipitated by the influx of two million refugees into eastern Zaire after the Rwandan genocide of 1994. When the forces of the former Rwandan government began using these refugee camps as a base from which to attack ethnic Tutsis in Zaire itself, these communities retaliated. They then, with the new Rwandan government's support, began to march on Kinshasa to topple Mobutu himself. The AFDL reached Kinshasa in May 1997, and Kabila took on the presidency of the renamed Democratic Republic of the Congo. Mobutu's own death from cancer a few months later symbolised the demise of one of the most predatory states Africa has ever known.

Yet the suffering of DRC's citizens did not end with Mobutu's demise. The east of this country has become a classic example of rebel groups being able to topple an incumbent government, but then not being able to rebuild an alternative state. Today, DRC is still in a condition of partial collapse. It is ruled by a regime in Kinshasa that is unable to project its authority in the country's massive hinterland. In the east, to use Filip Reyntjens' words, 'all functions of sovereignty are thus privatised'.[47]

Rival militias control this territory, who themselves enjoy considerable support from outside powers. DRC's vast mineral wealth, combined with this power vacuum, has precipitated continued insurgency involving most of Congo-Kinshasa's neighbours. Militias and their backers vie for control over the mines that can bring vast individual riches to those that can export their contents.

A United Nations (UN) report published in 2001, for example, estimated that one of the protagonists, the Rwandan National Army, which was theoretically in the process of withdrawing from DRC at this time, netted US$250 million by extracting gold, diamonds and coltan over an 18-month period. Ugandan military leaders similarly benefited from their army's presence across the border. The UN panel concluded that the war in the DRC had become 'a very lucrative business'.[48]

A lasting peace has therefore been difficult to broker. Ceasefires and elections have occurred, but the restoration of a single state authority in the east of the country is not in the interests of any of the militias or their external sponsors. As a consequence, violence continues to flare up regularly and the death toll rises. Competition between conflict entrepreneurs in DRC has cost the lives of 5.4 million people since 1998.[49] Most of these casualties were civilian non-combatants trying to survive in this dangerous stateless environment. In this respect, these 5.4 million individuals have become the ultimate victims of Mobutu's crises of accumulation and governance.

Democratic Republic of the Congo (DRC)[50]

Territory:	2,344,885 sq. km.	Population:	67.5 million
Colonial power:	Belgium	Independence:	1960
Major cities:	Kinshasa (capital)	Ethnic groups:	Over 200
	Lubumbashi	Currency:	Congolese franc
	Mbuji-Mayi	Urban population:	42 per cent
Languages:	French	Life expectancy:	50 years
	Kiswahili	Adult literacy:	61 per cent
	Tshiluba	Infant mortality:	86 deaths/1,000 live births
Religion:	Traditional	Exports:	Copper
	Christian		Oil
GDP per capita:	US$286		Base metals

Questions raised by this chapter

1. Why had the post-colonial African state reached a point of crisis by the 1980s?
2. How successful was civil society in countering the power of the vampire state?
3. To what extent have African states collapsed over the last two decades?
4. Did elites associated with the state or, alternatively, civil society groups benefit most from the politics of the 1980s and 1990s?
5. Assess the performance of the state's own survival strategies.

Glossary of key terms

Authority   A psychological relationship between the governed and their governors, which engenders a belief that state personnel and institutions should be obeyed.

Corruption	The abandonment of legal-rational practices by officials in order to secure personal gain.
Crisis of accumulation	The failure to create wealth through the productive investment of surplus capital.
Crisis of governance	The failure of states to provide political structures that are able to represent civil society.
Disengagement, exit and survival strategies	The act of distancing civil society activities from the state, bypassing state authority (for instance, by the use of parallel markets).
Insurgency	An 'ideological' challenge to state authority from within civil society, using violence.
Unproductive investment	Economic activity that fails to produce a profit or a surplus of capital.
Warlord state	A state, usually unstable, that seeks to serve the private interests of its leaders, and does not seek to generate legitimacy among its 'citizens' or provide public service.

Further reading

There are several excellent books that cover the issues raised in this chapter. Robert Bates's work is informative for those who wish to read more about how the African developmental states failed the agricultural sector; Sahr Kpundeh's book, likewise, is revealing on corruption; and the volume edited by I. William Zartman investigates the phenomenon of state collapse. Much has been written about civil society's disengagement from the state. Victor Azarya and Naomi Chazan's article is the pick of the crop, while Michael Bratton's review article gives a flavour of additional research in this area. Janet MacGaffey's book on Zaire's second economy is also well worth investigating, as is Denis Tull's article on what happened in the absence of central state authority in the Democratic Republic of the Congo. Those interested in state survival strategies should refer to Patrick Chabal and Jean-Pascal Daloz's volume, as well as William Reno's book.

Azarya, Victor and Naomi Chazan. Disengagement from the state in Africa: reflections on the experience of Ghana and Guinea. *Comparative Studies in Society and History*. 1987, 19(1), 106–31.

Bates, Robert H. *Markets and States in Tropical Africa: The Political Basis of Agricultural Policies*. Berkeley, CA: University of California Press, 1981.

Bratton, Michael. Beyond the state: civil society and associational life in Africa. *World Politics*. 1989, 41(3), 407–30.

Chabal, Patrick and Jean-Pascal Daloz. *Africa Works: Disorder as Political Instrument*. Oxford: James Currey, 1999.

Kpundeh, Sahr John. *Politics and Corruption in Africa: A Case Study of Sierra Leone*. Lanham, MD: University Press of America, 1995.

MacGaffey, Janet, ed. *The Real Economy of Zaire: The Contribution of Smuggling and Other Unofficial Activities to National Wealth*. London: James Currey, 1991.

Reno, William. *Warlord Politics and African States*. Boulder, CO: Lynne Rienner, 1998.

Tull, Denis M. A reconfiguration of political order? The state of the state in North Kivu (DR Congo). *African Affairs*. 2003, 102(408), 429–46.

Zartman, I. William, ed. *Collapsed States: The Disintegration and Restoration of Legitimate Authority*. Boulder, CO: Lynne Rienne, 1995.

Notes and references

1   World Bank. *World Development Report 1997*. New York: Oxford University Press, 1997. Table 1.
2   Ayittey, George B.N. *Africa Betrayed*. New York: St Martin's Press, 1993. 2–3.
3   Chabal, Patrick. *Power in Africa: An Essay in Political Interpretation*. Basingstoke: Macmillan, 1992. 150.
4   Decalo, Samuel. *Coups and Army Rule in Africa: Motivations and Constraints*. New Haven, CT: Yale University Press, 1990. 49–50.
5   Sandbrook, Richard, with Judith Barker. *The Politics of Africa's Economic Stagnation*. Cambridge: Cambridge University Press, 1985. 124.
6   Weber, Max. The distribution of power within the political community: class, status, party [1914]. In: H.H. Gerth and C. Wright Mills, eds. *From Max Weber: Essays in Society*. London: Routledge and Kegan Paul, 1948. 197.
7   Kpundeh, Sahr John. *Politics and Corruption in Africa: A Case Study of Sierra Leone*. Lanham, MD: University Press of America, 1995. 44.
8   Chabal, Patrick and Jean-Pascal Daloz. *Africa Works: Disorder as Political Instrument*. Oxford: James Currey, 1999. 99.
9   Sandbrook. *The Politics of Africa's Economic Stagnation*. 126–7.
10   Ayittey. *Africa Betrayed*. 245.
11   Cited in *Ibid*. 306.
12   Monga, Célestin. *The Anthropology of Anger: Civil Society and Democracy in Africa*. Boulder, CO: Lynne Rienner, 1998. 6.
13   Cited in *Ibid*. 6–7.
14   Chazan, Naomi. Engaging the state: associational life in Sub-Saharan Africa. In: Joel S. Migdal, Atul Kohli and Vivienne Shue, eds. *State Power and Social Forces: Domination and Transformation in the Third World*. Cambridge: Cambridge University Press, 1994. 269.
15   Rothchild, Donald and Letitia Lawson. The interactions between state and civil society in Africa: from deadlock to new routines. In: John W. Harbeson, Donald Rothchild and Naomi Chazan, eds. *Civil Society and the State in Africa*. Boulder, CO: Lynne Rienner, 1994. 270.
16   Luling, Virginia. Come back Somalia? Questioning a collapsed state. *Third World Quarterly*. 1997, 18(2), 288.
17   Cited in Lofchie, Michael F. *The Policy Factor: Agricultural Performance in Kenya and Tanzania*. Boulder, CO: Lynne Rienner, 1989. 113.
18   Azarya, Victor and Naomi Chazan. Disengagement from the state in Africa: reflections on the experience of Ghana and Guinea. *Comparative Studies in Society and History*. 1987, 19(1), 121. The situation was the same elsewhere: in 1985 more than half of Senegal's groundnut harvest was smuggled over borders, while US$60 million worth of goods escaped formal state scrutiny when they passed from Nigeria to Benin in the same year.
19   Birmingham, David. Images and themes in the nineties. In: David Birmingham and Phillis M. Martin, eds. *History of Central Africa: The Contemporary Years*. London: Longman, 1998. 270.
20   See Clapham, Christopher, ed. *African Guerrillas*. Oxford: James Currey, 1998.
21   Malaquias, Assis. Diamonds are a guerrilla's best friend: the impact of illicit wealth on insurgency strategy. *Third World Studies*. 2001, 22(3), 311–25.
22   Tull, Denis M. A reconfiguration of political order? The state of the state in Northern Kivu (Congo). *African Affairs*. 2003, 102(408), 435.
23   Simons, Anna. Somalia: the structure of dissolution. In: Leonardo A. Villalón and Phillip A. Huxtable, eds. *The African State at a Critical Juncture: Between Disintegration and Reconfiguration*. Boulder, CO: Lynne Rienner, 1998. 70.
24   Azarya and Chazan. Disengagement from the state in Africa: reflections on the experience of Ghana and Guinea. 130.

25 Forrest, Joshua Bernard. State inversion and nonstate politics. In: Villalón and Huxtable. *The African State at a Critical Juncture: Between Disintegration and Reconfiguration*. 45.

26 Bayart, Jean-François, Stephen Ellis and Béatrice Hibou. *The Criminalization of the State in Africa*. Oxford: James Currey, 1999. 48.

27 Reno, William. *Warlord Politics and African States*. Boulder, CO: Lynne Rienner, 1998.

28 Reno, William. Privatizing war in Sierra Leone. *Current History*. 1997, 96(610), 230.

29 Chazan, Naomi. State and society in Africa: images and challenges. In: Donald Rothchild and Naomi Chazan, eds. *The Precarious Balance: State and Society in Africa*. Boulder, CO: Westview, 1988. 337.

30 Fatton, Robert. *Predatory Rule: State and Civil Society in Africa*. Boulder, CO: Lynne Rienner, 1992. 80.

31 Simpson, Chris. Africa's absolutist. *West Africa*. 1990, 3793, 752.

32 Young, Crawford and Thomas Turner. *The Rise and Decline of the Zairian State*. Madison, WI: University of Wisconsin Press, 1985. 296–9.

33 *Ibid*. 300 and 305.

34 Clark, John F. Zaire: the bankruptcy of the extractive state. In: Villalón and Huxtable. *The African State at a Critical Juncture: Between Disintegration and Reconfiguration*. 118.

35 Ayittey. *Africa Betrayed*. 152 and 254.

36 Clark. In: Villalón and Huxtable. *The African State at a Critical Juncture: Between Disintegration and Reconfiguration*. 119.

37 Cited in Young and Turner. *The Rise and Decline of the Zairian State*. 73.

38 Cited in Askin, Steve. Zaire's den of thieves. *New Internationalist*. 1990, 208, 18.

39 MacGaffey, Janet. Issues and methods in the study of African economics. In: Janet MacGaffey, ed. *The Real Economy of Zaire: The Contribution of Smuggling and Other Unofficial Activities to National Wealth*. London: James Currey, 1991. 7.

40 *Ibid*. 11.

41 *Ibid*. 18.

42 Reno. *Warlord Politics and African States*. 153.

43 Mukohya, Vwakyanakazi. Import and export in the second economy in north Kivu. In: MacGaffey. *The Real Economy of Zaire: The Contribution of Smuggling and Other Unofficial Activities to National Wealth*. 57.

44 *Ibid*. 156.

45 Nkera, Rukarangira Wa and Brooke Grundfest Schoepf. Unrecorded trade in Southeast Shaba. In: MacGaffey. *The Real Economy of Zaire: The Contribution of Smuggling and Other Unofficial Activities to National Wealth*. 1991. 82–3.

46 Bayart, Jean-François. *The State in Africa: The Politics of the Belly*. London: Longman. 1993. 235–6.

47 Reyntjens, Filip. The privatisation and criminalisation of public space in the geopolitics of the Great Lakes region. *The Journal of Modern African Studies*. 2005, 43(4), 587–607.

48 United Nations Security Council. *Report of the Panel of Experts on the Illegal Exploitation of Natural Resources and Other Forms of Wealth of the Democratic Republic of the Congo* [S/2001/357]. April 2001. 29 and 6. www.unhchr.ch/Huridocda/Huridoca.nsf/0/5e423385c10ae294c125 6b1100505218/$FILE/N0132354.pdf (accessed 18 July 2009).

49 International Rescue Committee estimate. Polgreen, Lydia. Congo's death rate unchanged since war ended. *New York Times*. 23 January 2008. www.nytimes.com/2008/01/23/world/africa/23congo.html?_r=1 (accessed 18 July 2009).

50 United Nations Conference on Trade and Development. *UNCTAD Handbook of Statistics 2014*. New York: United Nations, 2014. Tables 8.1, 8.4 and 3.2.D; World Bank data http://data.worldbank.org/indicator/SP.DYN.LE00.IN (accessed 24 July 2015) and http://data.worldbank.org/indicator/SP.DYN.IMRT.IN (accessed 24 July 2015); and UNESCO data www.uis.unesco.org/DataCentre/Pages/regions.aspx (accessed 24 July 2015).

11 Democracy

Re-legitimising the African state?

Chapter outline

- Democracy
- Explaining the emergence of multi-party democracy

  - The state's loss of authority
  - The changing international political arena
  - A rejuvenated civil society
  - Precedent

- The obstacles to democratic consolidation

  - The need for a credible opposition
  - The need for a strong civil society
  - The need for stronger economies
  - The need to separate the state and ruling party
  - The unleashing of ethnic mobilisation?
  - The threat of the military
  - Political culture

- State and civil society
- Case study: Zimbabwe's fall from democratic grace
- Questions raised by this chapter
- Glossary of key terms
- Further reading
- Notes and references

The last decade of the twentieth century brought dramatic political changes to Africa. The whole continent was swept by a wave of democratisation. From Tunisia to Mozambique, from Mauritania to Madagascar, government after government was forced to compete in multi-party elections against new or revitalised opposition movements. To use South African President Thabo Mbeki's words, the continent was experiencing a political 'renaissance'.[1]

Prior to 1990, opposition parties had been outlawed in most African countries. As Chapter 6 highlighted, the political norm was for a highly personalised executive to govern through tightly controlled one-party structures. There was little room for dissent or legal challenges to this ruling elite. Only in Botswana, since 1966, has political pluralism been maintained throughout the post-colonial period. The Gambia, Senegal and Mauritius sustained multi-party competition for significant lengths of time, but not for the entire independence period. These four states were the exception. Elsewhere, the democratic picture was bleak. Africa had become a continent where governments were removed by force, not by elections.

By contrast, competitive democracy bloomed in the 1990s. As late as 1988, one-party states and military governments were dominant (see Table 11.1), and Africa was still in an era of 'one leader, one ideology, and one political party'.[2] Reasonably free and fair elections did occasionally occur in these countries (when the military returned to barracks, for example, Nigeria and Ghana being good cases in point), but these elections never amounted to an ongoing commitment to democracy. Follow-up elections were rarely held. Yet by 1999, the number of multi-party constitutions on the continent had risen from 9 to 45. Granted, several of these 'multi-party democracies' amounted to paper exercises only, but many more proved to be fruitful. Momentous occasions such as

Table 11.1 Comparative African political systems, 1988 and 1999

African political systems, 1988

One-party systems (number = 29)

Algeria, Angola, Benin, Burundi, Cameroon, Cape Verde, Central African Republic, Comoros, Congo-Brazzaville, Côte d'Ivoire, Djibouti, Equatorial Guinea, Ethiopia, Gabon, Guinea–Bissau, Kenya, Madagascar, Malawi, Mali, Mozambique, Rwanda, São Tomé and Principe, Seychelles, Sierra Leone, Somalia, Tanzania, Togo, Zaire, Zambia

Military oligarchies (number = 10)

Burkina Faso, Chad, Ghana, Guinea, Lesotho, Libya, Mauritania, Niger, Nigeria, Uganda

Multi-party constitutions (number = 9)

Botswana, Egypt, The Gambia, Liberia, Mauritius, Senegal, Sudan, Tunisia, Zimbabwe

Monarchies (number = 2)

Morocco, Swaziland

Racial oligarchies (number = 2)

Namibia, South Africa

African political systems, 1999

Multi-party constitutions (number = 45)

Algeria, Angola, Benin, Botswana, Burkina Faso, Cameroon, Cape Verde, Central African Republic, Chad, Comoros, Congo-Brazzaville, Côte d'Ivoire, Djibouti, Egypt, Equatorial Guinea, Ethiopia, Gabon, The Gambia, Ghana, Guinea, Guinea–Bissau, Kenya, Lesotho, Liberia, Madagascar, Malawi, Mali, Mauritania, Mauritius, Mozambique, Namibia, Niger, Nigeria, Rwanda, São Tomé and Principe, Senegal, Seychelles, Sierra Leone, South Africa, Sudan, Tanzania, Togo, Tunisia, Zambia, Zimbabwe

Military oligarchies (number = 3)

Burundi, Libya, Zaire

Monarchies (number = 2)

Morocco, Swaziland

No central government (number = 1)

Somalia

'No party government' (number = 1)

Uganda

One-party systems (number = 1)

Eritrea

that when Kenneth Kaunda, President of Zambia for 27 years, respectfully bowed to the will of the people in 1991, or Nelson Mandela's 1994 victory in South Africa's first non-racial elections, demonstrated that multi-party democracy had gained a foothold, however precariously, on the African continent.

Democracy

Democracy literally means 'rule by the people'. It is the idea of popular sovereignty, where individuals participate in their society's government. At its most efficient, this will involve the whole community meeting regularly to make decisions, with each citizen's vote having an equal weighting. The city-states of ancient Greece are the most frequently used examples of this *direct* form of democracy (give or take the exclusion of women and slaves from the franchise). Yet the democracy enjoyed in the Western world today differs considerably from that of classical Greece.

The institutions of modern states are far too complex to be governed directly by the people. Citizens, on average, are too busy living their own lives to become involved with the minutiae of government. This is why they empower politicians to rule on their behalf. In any form of democracy, however, the governors must remain accountable to the governed, and in the case of representative democracy this is principally achieved through regular elections. Each citizen should have an equal opportunity to vote for the candidate they feel will best serve their interests. What is more, laws should be in place, and adhered to, allowing free competition between individuals to win these votes. Freedom of speech, association and assembly are all of paramount importance, as is the right to stand for office, a free press and a secret ballot. With these guarantees, citizens can collectively select representatives of their choice, and, perhaps more importantly, have the opportunity to remove those officials who have disappointed. Abraham Lincoln's ideal of 'government of the people, by the people, for the people' sums up the concept of representative democracy.[3]

In the West, multi-party competition has become the accepted mechanism for delivering this type of democracy. Parties assist the aggregation of differing views and interests found within society, and they also offer the electorate alternative public policy choices. Should the incumbent ruling party be perceived as not serving the people's interests, they can be voted out of office and replaced by a more popular party. Historically, it has been this multi-party competition that has fostered the most productive examples of open, representative and accountable government.

This model of liberal democracy, however, was largely rejected in Africa in the first three decades of independence. As Chapter 6 demonstrated, the continent's political leaders considered pluralist competition to be destructive. They favoured more unified and centralised mechanisms of government. The argument ran that multi-party politics would serve to deepen ethnic divisions, as well as to deflect the new states from their primary task of nation-building and economic development. Consequently, one-party states became the most common form of political representation.

Some of these ruling parties, such as TANU in Nyerere's Tanzania and KANU in Kenyatta's Kenya, did manage, to a degree, to link the governed and the governors. It was more common, however, for African political parties to atrophy, isolating presidential monarchs from their people. The absence of a legal opposition left the continent's political systems too open to abuse by ruling elites. Nor could Africa's leaders claim that their governments were benign 'developmental dictatorships', where economic benefits were provided as compensation for absent political rights. Economic advancement did not materialise. Consequently, by the mid-1980s, even Nyerere conceded that the one-party experiment had failed Africa. Always a sincere believer in popular representation, Nyerere called upon his party to open up Tanzania to multi-party competition.[4]

And Tanzania was not alone. After 1990, the whole of Africa was immersed in political reform. The pattern was familiar. First, isolated demonstrations would break out in urban areas, with protesters targeting structural adjustment austerity measures. These demonstrations would then become more sustained and organised, with demands moving from the economic sphere to more general political reform. Before long, full-scale multi-party democracy became the rallying cry of these protesters.

Eventually, the ruling elite grudgingly conceded to this political pressure. Constitutional changes were made to permit the registration of opposition groups, and this opened the floodgates for further political concessions. Governments were soon drafting plans for a return to full pluralist competition. In most of francophone Africa, for example, this involved constitutional conferences, followed by referenda of the people. By 1995, most countries on the continent had met the initial demand of multi-party democracy, namely the holding of reasonably free and fair elections.

There can be no doubt that these momentous events spectacularly changed Africa's political environment. Africanists were left reeling at the speed of this democratisation process, but what had prompted this swift return to multi-party democracy? An answer to this question is offered in the first section of the chapter. There is another question, however, that is more difficult to answer. What are the chances of political pluralism being consolidated on the continent? Twenty-five years after the initial round of

Plate 11.1 Voting in South Africa's first non-racial elections, De Aar, 1994. Photographer: Gideon Mendel.

multi-party elections, Africa is still far from being a bastion of democracy. Cynicism has returned to many Africanists who initially considered the events of the 1990s to be nothing short of a pluralist revolution. Today, a typical African state still has authoritarian reflexes and veers towards patronage as a method of generating legitimacy. Competitive elections continue to have an impact, but they feature alongside illiberal forms of governance. The second half of the chapter will therefore consider a series of obstacles hindering the consolidation of democracy on the continent.

Yet one should not be too cynical. Africa has not reverted to the earlier era of one-party states and presidential monarchs. Meaningful elections are being held on the continent, and regime change is occurring as a consequence. Opposition parties, intermittently, do replace incumbents. Pluralism has now become part of the political system, albeit a form of pluralism that exists within a flawed legal-rational environment. The impact of this contradictory electoral authoritarianism on the relationship between state and civil society in Africa is discussed at the end of the main body of the chapter. A case study then follows, charting Zimbabwe's fall from democratic grace. Note even here, however, the contradiction. Pluralism was not extinguished altogether in Zimbabwe, despite President Robert Mugabe's steadfast authoritarianism. Multi-party competition survived. This would not have been the case in the earlier one-party era.

Explaining the emergence of multi-party democracy

Simply put, Africa's re-embrace of multi-party democracy during the 1990s can be explained by an agreement among all of the players involved. State elites, who for so long were ideologically committed to more authoritarian forms of government, were now converted to pluralism. Similarly, civil society expanded its campaign for the same goal. It was also a period where the international community backed these political trends.

This agreement between state, civil society and international agencies, however, seems remarkable given their divergent interests just a few years, or even months, earlier. Why were all three now citing multi-party democracy as the way forward? What had changed? An explanation can be formulated via four interlinked phenomena: the state's loss of authority, a new international political environment, the rejuvenation of civil society, and precedent. Each of these factors will now be considered in turn.

The state's loss of authority

By the 1990s, Africa's political environment was ripe for change. The previous chapter highlighted the problems now faced by state institutions. Starved of resources due to the crisis of accumulation, and lacking legitimacy due to the crisis of governance, state authority was in terminal decline. The old governing formulae where presidential monarchs could skilfully combine a mixture of accommodation and coercion were no longer effective. Elements of civil society were in a process of disengagement, or, in some cases, actually violently rebelling against the ruling elite. For many African countries the prospect of total state collapse was a serious possibility.

Several ruling elites chose to ignore, as best they could, this crisis of authority. Their states became more and more inverted, with governments abandoning their public obligations. These polities were well on the way to becoming warlord states, Liberia and Zaire/Democratic Republic of the Congo (DRC) being good cases in point. By contrast, other African leaders heeded the warning signs, and attempted to steer their regimes out of danger.

The game was up. Faced by anti-government protests, the only thing the presidential monarchs could now do was to 'utter pious, self-serving calls to discipline and order'.[5] In previous years, the full weight of the state would have been directed at these malcontents, and the protests crushed. Now, the state had few replies. Its powers of coercion were diminished, and its abilities of co-option starved by a lack of resources. Previous state survival strategies were no longer enough to ensure that the regime would endure, and a different, more effective set of tactics had to be employed.

The reinvention of multi-party democracy in Africa can therefore be seen as a reaction to this crisis of authority. State elites considered the dissolution of their monopoly over political activity to be the only survival strategy left. After all, what better antidote to a crisis of authority is there than a 're-legitimisation' of the state through multi-party elections?

It was not that presidential monarchs had suddenly been converted to pluralism. In most cases, this was a concession forced upon them, and given grudgingly. It was a case of leaders weighing up the impossible costs of delaying these reforms, against the short-term benefits that could be gained.[6] Indeed, many ruling parties thought they could control the pace of this reform, remaining in power indefinitely. When the incumbent National Party, for example, decided to engage the African National Congress of South Africa (ANC) in negotiations, few of its members would have envisaged full multi-party democracy arriving just five years later. Similarly, when the presidents of most francophone countries established constitutional conferences, many thought that they could manipulate proceedings, steering these towards their own interests. Few expected the far-reaching reforms that actually emerged from these political assemblies.

To some extent, the gambles undertaken by ruling elites with this ultimate survival strategy paid off. As will be seen, a considerable number of incumbents managed to stay in power, even after free and fair elections took place. There can be no doubt, however, that these state elites' search for legitimacy, and subsequent partial abandonment of authoritarian structures, lay at the very heart of Africa's conversion to multi-party democracy in the 1990s.

The changing international political arena

Embattled leaders were not only experiencing internal pressures for reform. The international environment also now favoured a move towards political pluralism. Whereas, before, state elites had come to rely on external patronage to prop up their regimes (even when internal legitimacy was lacking), in the 1990s this source of support had largely dried up.

A change of emphasis in how foreign governments and IFIs gave aid to Africa came with the end of the Cold War. As was seen in Chapter 8, state managers had previously been able to market their countries in terms of ideological allegiance and strategic importance. The United States supported its allies in Africa as an investment against communist encroachment, backing such governments as Kenya, Morocco and Zaire, while the Soviet Union assisted states with socialist leanings, such as Ethiopia and Angola. Concentrating on their Cold War priorities, neither Washington nor Moscow seemed too concerned that these countries were largely autocratic and had poor human rights records.

The collapse of the Soviet Union, however, had massive implications for African state elites. The writing was on the Berlin Wall.[7] Soviet clients now had no external patron to turn to, whereas allies of the United States received less unconditional support, given Washington's strategic interests had diminished dramatically. 'The winds from the East', as President Omar Bongo of Gabon lyrically stated, were truly 'shaking the coconut trees'.[8]

Indeed, those international agencies that were still interested in providing aid to Africa only did so with significant conditions attached. In terms of economics, for example, aid recipients were required to undertake structural adjustment reforms (see Chapter 9). It was these reforms that provided the catalyst for embryonic pro-democracy movements. Political conditions were also attached to aid packages. Assistance would be suspended or resumed as a direct consequence of a regime's human rights record and its commitment to democratic reforms. For example, international aid to Kenya was suspended in 1991, when President Daniel arap Moi halted his country's transition to pluralism. Hastings Banda, in Malawi, came under similar donor pressure in 1993. Speaking for all of the continent's leaders, President André Kolingba of the Central African Republic stated, 'We have to accept the fact that those who lend us money for development want us to provide a choice of political parties'.[9] And given that state managers still relied heavily on the patronage of the international community, the West eventually got what it wanted.

A rejuvenated civil society

The most significant pressure for democratic reform came from African civil society itself. Churches, trade unions, ethnic associations, women's organisations, professional bodies, farming co-operatives, community groups, and eventually political parties, had all at some time played a key role in the fight against colonial rule. These same associational organisations would also contribute significantly to Africa's 'second liberation' of the late 1980s and early 1990s.

Once political space had been created by the decline of state authority, opposition forces took their chances and began to challenge the state elite. There was a feeling that anything was now possible. The façade of government was visibly crumbling, and the 'emperor' was 'indeed naked'.[10]

The transition process was initiated by the reaction to structural adjustment's austerity measures. Thousands of urban Africans took to the streets. Such 'bread riots' had always been a feature of the post-colonial period. Previously, they were usually short-lived, quickly put down by the state's coercive agencies, and a conciliatory adjustment to public policy made. This time, however, the state was less able to quell the demonstrations or provide token gestures, and consequently the protests became more sustained. Before long, these gatherings took on a more political nature. Zairian protesters, for example, were now openly chanting '*Mobutu, voleur!*' ('Mobutu, thief!').[11]

It was at this point that the leading institutions of civil society took on the organisation of this popular protest. New groups formed specifically to campaign for multi-party democracy, while older associations, previously co-opted by the state, began to de-link themselves from the ruling elite. Politicians, sensing the changing political mood, similarly entered the battle. Those in exile attempted to return to their countries, others came out of retirement, and yet more defected from the ruling party to join the growing opposition.

As was seen in Chapter 4, churches and mosques were often a significant force within the anti-authoritarian campaign. Difficult to ban, and very probably more legitimate than the government itself, religious organisations offered national opportunities for people to assemble. Consequently, church and mosque pulpits were used to hold governments to account. Archbishop Desmond Tutu, for example, with black opposition parties having been outlawed in South Africa, proved to be one of the most effective advocates against apartheid, both nationally and internationally. And in Malawi, no one had dared to criticise the rule of Hastings Banda for decades, yet in March 1992, Archbishop James Chiona and the country's Catholic bishops did just that. Banda's own denomination, the Church of Scotland, likewise called upon its congregation to 'pray for this profoundly lonely man who is locked in the prison house of power'. After these brave opening salvos, others within Malawian civil society amplified these calls for multi-party democracy.[12]

Trade unions also played a major role in the transition to pluralist elections. In Niger, for instance, the largest labour federation, the Union des Syndicats des Travailleurs du Niger (USTN), put immense pressure on the ruling elite to concede democratic reforms. Previously this organisation had been largely controlled by state co-option. By the late 1980s, however, the USTN was at the heart of the opposition movement, co-ordinating strikes in support of protests elsewhere. This action successfully brought Niger's formal economy to a standstill, and multi-party elections followed in 1993.[13]

Zambia, however, is perhaps the best example of trade union activity securing pluralist democracy. Frederick Chiluba, as the leader of the Zambian Congress of Trade Unions (ZCTU), had for a long time been an irritant to Kenneth Kaunda's UNIP one-party state. The government tried on numerous occasions to co-opt ZCTU, without success. When UNIP's tolerance ran out, Chiluba was briefly imprisoned. This had little effect, as, on his release, he again rejected a place on UNIP's central committee. Thus, when the opportunity arose in 1990 to challenge Kaunda's political monopoly, ZCTU proved to be an ideal popular and organisational base for the Movement for Multi-Party Democracy (MMD). The MMD subsequently defeated UNIP in elections in 1991, and Chiluba himself became the new president of Zambia.[14]

Church groups and trade unions, along with other associations including human rights activists, students, legal professionals, medical practitioners and academics, provided leadership for a rejuvenated civil society. Through this leadership, mass discontent was channelled into a call for multi-party democracy. It proved to be a political demand that enfeebled state managers found difficult to resist.

Precedent

In accounting for Africa's democratic transition, the issue of precedent should also be considered. African leaders, within both government and civil society institutions, were well aware of parallel events in Eastern Europe. As the power of the Soviet Union waned, there had been a chain reaction of civil society risings in Moscow's satellite states. 'People power' had overthrown communist governments across the east, from Czechoslovakia to Romania, and eventually even in East Germany and Russia itself. Protestors had successfully taken to the streets. African leaders also observed what was happening on their own continent. Nelson Mandela's release from jail in 1989, for example, and the subsequent dismantling of apartheid, demonstrated to all that even the most powerful state elites were vulnerable to pressure from below. One by one, African regimes were opened to pluralism. With one-party states toppling like dominoes, the way forward seemed inevitable to most. It would take a brave, or foolhardy, leader to try to stem this tide of history. Most eventually committed themselves to try to ride this wave of democratisation.

The same would also hold true subsequent to this 1990s watershed. People power, harnessed by civil society groups, continued to feature as a political force in the new multi-party era. If a regime lost its way and returned to authoritarian habits, mass protest became a more common response. A precedent had now been set. Demonstrators more readily took to the streets to oppose autocracy. In 2011, for example, political groups emerging from civil society toppled several ruling parties across north Africa (and beyond), in the so-called 'Arab Spring'. Regime change occurred as a result in Tunisia, Egypt and Libya, while simultaneous mass protests also wrung concessions from the governments of Algeria, Mauritania and Djibouti. In effect, rulers were being reminded of democratic pledges made in the 1990s.

In short, whether it was in the 1990s or later, there was now a more vociferous demand for multi-party democracy driven by civil society. Ruling elites, if they were to survive, had to accommodate this demand, and move away from the centralised one-party states that had typified the earlier post-colonial era.

The obstacles to democratic consolidation

By 1999, most African states had constitutions in place that encouraged political pluralism. Reflecting this, more than 140 multi-party elections were held in the last decade of the twentieth century (compared with less than 70 competitive polls held in the three decades prior to this).[15] Some of these polls were flawed, but others represented a reasonable reflection of voters' wishes. Given these facts, there can be little doubt that post-colonial African politics had reached a critical juncture.

The holding of elections, however, is not the sole prerequisite for democracy. A mature democratic order requires that the rules of the political game endure between elections. Continued accountability and representation are far more important than the simple mechanics of conducting a poll. In this sense, the danger is that the 1990s wave of pluralism was simply a one-off response to a particular set of political circumstances. It may be that, just like the multi-party polls at independence, or those following the military's return to barracks, these 1990s events were isolated elections, merely serving (temporarily) to re-legitimise the state. It could be, to use Christopher Clapham's phrase, a case of 'one man, one vote, once'.[16] Richard Sandbrook highlights exactly this point when he states that 'Africa's hostile conditions encumber not so much *transitions* to democracy as the *consolidation* of enduring democracies'.[17] The need for Tunisians to return to the streets during the 2011 Arab Spring, some 20 years after winning the right to multi-party competition in their country, underscores Sandbrook's point.

Yet, despite post-colonial Africa's overall poor democratic record, the large number of multi-party elections held at the end of the twentieth century, and subsequently, has generated a glimmer of hope. Amid the fall of presidential monarchs and, in several cases, near state collapse, pluralist competition represented a way forward. Importantly, this democratic momentum has endured. Events since the turn of the century suggest that political pluralism, although compromised, has survived. Although not ubiquitous, meaningful elections continue to occur in Africa, and several significant regime changes have transpired as a result. These elections exist, however, alongside persistent autocratic behaviour. Consolidation, and a secure democratic future, are by no means guaranteed. Major obstacles still need to be overcome before Africa can even start to contemplate a new political order based on pluralism. Several of these obstacles will now be considered in turn.

The need for a credible opposition

To state the obvious, multi-party democracies need multiple parties. If the electorate is unhappy with its government's policies or conduct, it needs an alternative political force which it can vote into power. Credible opposition choices, however, are not always guaranteed. At the opposite ends of this particular problem, pre-1999 Zimbabwe provides an example where there was an absence of an alternative party, while Côte d'Ivoire and Kenya demonstrate the converse impediment, namely too many parties.

The 1995 general election in Zimbabwe was remarkably free from instances of intimidation and malpractice. Yet, as Liisa Laakso writes, 'Unfortunately, the progress in the practical arrangements of the polling [was] accompanied by a lack of any alternatives or even counterforces to the ruling party'.[18] Robert Mugabe's regime was unpopular, procedural democracy was in place, yet the Zimbabwe African National Union Patriotic Front (ZANU-PF) faced no serious opposition. This had also been the case in the general elections of 1985 and 1990. It was easy for Mugabe to claim to be at the head of a multi-party democracy when there was little by way of an organised opposition. Yet, as will be seen in the case study at the end of this chapter, when such an opposition did emerge at the end of the 1990s, Mugabe ditched his democratic credentials and used political violence to ensure continued ZANU-PF victories.

Given this Zimbabwe precedent, one has to ask whether others among the continent's more established democracies are in danger. Botswana, South Africa and Namibia, for example, have all consistently held free and fair elections since independence/liberation. Yet the results of these elections have always been predictable. In each case, the ruling party has repeatedly enjoyed a landslide victory. Consequently, these political systems have yet to be truly tested by genuinely competitive polls. Would these contests remain free and fair if there was a chance of the incumbent party actually being defeated, and losing its control of state power? The mark of a true democracy is where the rules of the electoral game continue to be observed, even under pressure.

Indeed, political scientist Samuel Huntington goes further. He considers that free and fair elections have to result in two turnovers of government before a state can be properly classified as a democracy. This, he argues, is the only proof that pluralism is truly working.[19] It shows that both incumbents and opposition are committed to the rules of the political game, and, above all, that they are willing to concede defeat if that is the people's wish. For two turnovers of government to occur, of course, a state requires more than one party with a realistic chance of being elected. Botswana, South Africa and Namibia are not yet in that position.

Elsewhere in Africa there has been the opposite problem: too many parties. Political reforms have led to hundreds, maybe thousands, of parties mobilising across the continent. When Chad moved to pluralist competition, for example, over 60 movements registered with the state authorities.[20] Democracy, however, cannot be measured by the quantity of competitors alone. The quality of these parties is also important. Rivals should be able to offer alternative leadership and policy choices to the electorate.

Yet John Wiseman describes many of the organisations that have emerged in the new pluralist era as merely 'vanity parties'.[21] They serve more as a vehicle for party bosses than as a genuine aggregation of ideological or policy demands. Often these movements consist of just one charismatic leader, supported only by a handful of acolytes. Even the larger parties, with wider support, often revolve around a 'Big Man'. Election campaigns therefore become competitions between personalities rather than ideas. Wiseman, pointing to this absence of issue-driven politics, notes that opposition platforms are usually remarkably similar in Africa. They are based on 'support for multi-party democracy, a defence of human rights, criticisms of government corruption, and an attack on statist approaches to economic policy. None of these elements are negligible or unworthy but they hardly add up to an ideological masterplan for reconstructing society'.[22]

The concentration on the politics of personality has often led to factionalism within Africa's opposition movements. This partly explains why such a remarkable number of incumbent leaders and their parties survived the transition from one-party to multi-party politics. Where pro-democracy forces remained coherent, successful campaigns against the presidential monarchs were mounted. For example, the unified MMD in Zambia defeated Kaunda, the Alliance pour la Democratie au Mali helped to oust Traoré, and the Alliance for Democracy in Malawi saw off Banda. Divided oppositions, however, fared less well.

In many cases, the various opposition factions ended up competing more with each other than they did against the incumbent. Côte d'Ivoire proves to be a case in point. Here, 26 parties registered after the constitution was amended. Of these, 17 fielded candidates in the 1990 elections. Only the Front Populaire Ivoirien (FPI) could make any impression on Houphouët-Boigny's status and his incumbent party's well-oiled electoral machine. Even the FPI, however, led by history professor Laurent Gbagbo, had little appeal beyond the educated urban classes.[23] Consequently, Houphouët-Boigny won by a landslide.

Kenyan politics also suffered from a divided opposition. Moi, detested in many areas of the country, still won two presidential polls during the 1990s. On both occasions he emerged victorious, despite winning less than 40 per cent of the vote. More coherence and co-operation among the opposition parties would almost certainly have defeated this autocratic president in 1992 or 1997, bringing a new lease of life to Kenyan politics. Yet this was not to happen until 2002, after Moi had retired and a united opposition coalition finally managed to break KANU's 40-year monopoly of power.

This brief examination of opposition groups indicates that the consolidation of multi-party democracy is still a long way off in Africa. Elections are not about charismatic leaders espousing little by way of a policy platform. Nor should democratic polls merely require voters to select one ambitious political clique from another. Likewise, electoral contests cannot just be about a population offering predictable loyalty to the movement that historically won liberation for their society. Until Africans are offered a genuine choice between competing policy programmes, 'true' multi-party democracy remains a distant goal.

The need for a strong civil society

A second prerequisite for democratic consolidation is a strong civil society. Healthy associational activity can act as a powerful independent counter-force to prevent the state from monopolising the political process. In a multi-party democracy it is essential that civil society is present both to co-operate with, and to challenge, the government. This helps to ensure that the public interest is always paramount, and that governments continue to respect the rules of the democratic process.

In the past, African civil societies have defeated imperialism and brought post-colonial predatory states to their knees through disengagement. The question now, however, is whether contemporary associational life is strong enough on the continent to help preserve newly won multi-party democracies.

This preservation will require the growth of Africa's middle classes. After all, there cannot be a liberal, or bourgeois, democracy without a bourgeoisie.[24] It is the middle classes that have the wealth, the time and the education to organise groups that can monitor and influence the state. Professionals can provide an intellectual challenge to the ruling party; church, mosque and human rights groups can provide moral advice; women's associations can keep issues of gender to the fore; and an independent media can assess the government's dissemination of information. Without this independent associational activity there is a grave danger that the state will become too dominant and abuse its power.

Yet, as was seen in Chapter 5, few African countries have a powerful and independent middle class. The state itself has been the focus of class formation. In this respect, it could be that multi-party elections, rather than opening up the political process to all Africans, have instead just initiated new personnel into the state elite. Indeed, there is no guarantee that civil society leaders who defeat the 'old guard' and set up a new government will act in the wider interests of the population. It may be that, just like their predecessors, once in power they will be more content to pursue just their own, or their narrow constituency's, interests. Frederick Chiluba, the hero of Zambia's transition to multi-party democracy, for example, was charged with 168 counts of theft after leaving office in 2001, and, in a separate 2007 case, found guilty by a British court of fraud to the value of US$46 million.[25] Chiluba is not the only president of the new political age to face corruption charges.

The key is whether this new (or amended) political elite is more committed to the ideals of democracy and representation than the old guard. The sincerity of most who campaigned for pluralism cannot be doubted. Now that they are in power, however, the commitment to multi-party democracy may diminish, or become merely instrumental. Only an active civil society, continuing its independence from the state, will be able to check new ruling elites, ensuring that they keep to their original pluralistic promises.

The need for stronger economies

The maintenance of multi-party democracy also relies on governments looking after the economic and social welfare of their citizens. If a ruling party fails to provide what the electorate expects, they will soon be voted out of office. Accountable governments have therefore to meet many demands. As well as a sound economic environment in which one can prosper, health care, education, social provision and transport infrastructure are just a few of the basic services that are expected by citizens. This is why, in Western Europe, multi-party democracy developed alongside the construction of the welfare state.

Resources in Africa, however, remain scarce. It may be that newly elected governments will have trouble meeting the demands of their citizens. However representative these regimes may be, many simply do not have the means to service the politics of the 'pork barrel' that democratic systems demand. Consequently, severe economic problems could lead to a loss of legitimacy, and even to the collapse of pluralism itself. In Nazi Germany, for example, many citizens were willing to abandon liberal democracy altogether in favour of national socialism. Nationalist socialism, it was considered, would be a more efficient form of rule, given Weimar Germany's political and economic failings. In the light of this example from history, political leaders should always heed Afrifa Gitonga's advice that 'democracy is founded on full bellies and peaceful minds'.[26] In Africa, only an improved economic performance can guarantee this.

The need to separate the state and ruling party

Multi-party democracy also needs a neutral state whose institutions provide a 'level playing field' on which political parties can compete fairly. By winning an election, a party has the right to rule through these institutions, in the national interest. Political leaders should not use the power and resources of the state to specifically bolster the position of themselves or their own party. This would give the incumbents an unfair advantage at the next election. Democratic consolidation thus needs a new political environment across Africa in which there is a clear distinction between state institutions and those of the ruling party.

This clear distinction has yet to emerge in many African countries. Although multiple parties are now allowed to compete, opposition groups often do so at a clear disadvantage. In more serious cases of state-sponsored electoral fraud, official registers may 'inadvertently' be incomplete in opposition areas of the country, constituency boundaries will be gerrymandered, ballot boxes will either be 'lost' or be stuffed with pre-prepared voting slips, and, if all these methods fail, the state's electoral commission could always simply declare a fictitious result. These illegal practices are only available to the ruling party that controls the institutions of the state.

Electoral rules can also be manipulated in a more subtle manner. Referring to Zambia again, Chiluba's MMD may have defeated Kaunda's UNIP in 1991, yet UNIP was not spent as a political force. It took its place as the loyal opposition in parliament, and successfully rebuilt support among the electorate. Fearing UNIP's revival as the 1996 elections approached, Chiluba moved to defeat Kaunda's presidential campaign, not through winning more votes in an open election, but by using the power of the state. The MMD majority in parliament was ordered to amend the constitution to prevent 'first-generation' Zambians from running for president. All concerned knew that Kaunda's parents were born in present-day Malawi, and with Kaunda out of the race, Chiluba successfully secured his second term of office.

Ruling parties have also manipulated presidential term limits to favour themselves. At the advent of multi-party democracy, a majority of African states adopted new constitutions which stipulated that individuals could only serve a maximum of two terms as president. Yet, in practice, after this prescribed time period had elapsed, 8, 10 or 12 years later, many incumbents wished to stay in power. As a consequence, ruling parties used their majorities in state legislatures to amend their respective constitutions.

President Nujoma of Namibia was the first to successfully compete for a third term of office in 1999. Following his lead, Conté of Guinea (2001), Eyadéma of Togo (2002), Bongo of Gabon (2003), Compaoré of Burkina Faso (2005), Déby of Chad (2005), Museveni of Uganda (2005), and Biya of Cameroon (2008) all mounted successful bids to scrap or otherwise circumvent a two-term limit. Although these constitutional amendments were lawful, this manipulation of electoral rules to suit incumbents clearly disadvantaged opposition parties. It sent the message that those in power have the right to dictate the rules of the political game.

One should note, however, that not all African states have been willing to follow this route of blatant constitutional manipulation. Sounding a more positive note for Africa's potential democratic consolidation, President Obasanjo of Nigeria was forced to suspend his bid for re-election in 2006 when it became evident that he did not have the votes in parliament to secure the required amendment. This echoes similar failed attempts for third terms by Muluzi of Malawi and Chiluba in Zambia. Indeed, President Blaise Compaoré of Burkina Faso was removed from office by a popular uprising sparked by his attempts to circumvent the limits of his state's constitution during 2014, while in Burundi, President Pierre Nkurunziza had to climb down and hold constitutional talks in 2015 as a consequence of his attempt to cling to power. Furthermore, there are other African leaders who have bucked this trend altogether. Individuals such as Mandela of South Africa (who only served one term), Konaré of Mali, Kerekou of Benin, Rawlings of Ghana, Moi of Kenya, Trovoada of São Tomé and Principe, Nyerere, Mwinyi and Mkapa of Tanzania, Monteiro of Cape Verde, René of Seychelles, Chissano of Mozambique, Kabbah of Sierra Leone, Pires of Cape Verde, Mogae of Botswana, and Pohamba of Namibia have all voluntarily stepped down from office after two terms, in compliance with their national constitutions.[27]

Returning to Africa's more autocratic regimes, ruling parties have not just used their power to constitutionally improve their chances of re-election. The illiberal among their number also appropriate public resources to boost their power. With access to the national treasury, for example, incumbent parties can mount extensive and elaborate election campaigns. Opposition groups, starved of funds, cannot compete with this 'public' spending. President Daniel arap Moi, for example, took full advantage of his privileged position during Kenya's 1997 campaign. Government spending was augmented by US$100 million prior to the elections, increasing the country's money circulation by 35 per cent.[28] Moi effectively bought the votes he needed for victory.

Other resources that incumbents readily utilise are the state-owned media and the security forces. Almost all state newspapers, radio and television on the continent provide a pro-government outlook in their reporting. By contrast, opposition groups find it hard to get their views and policies expressed through these media. One study of the 1996 election in the Gambia, for example, found that President Yaya Jammeh commanded 83 per cent of radio and television airtime dedicated to the campaign, leaving the opposition parties at a distinct disadvantage.[29] It should come as no surprise that Jammeh succeeded in winning the subsequent multi-party elections.

Agencies of coercion are also at the ruling party's disposal. The police and the army can be used to disrupt anti-government rallies and harass opposition leaders. This is of particular advantage during election campaigns. Few Africans are surprised, for example, when they hear that the police have banned an opposition election rally for 'health and safety' reasons, or that an opposition leader's entourage has been held up at a 'routine' police roadblock immediately prior to a meeting. In Uganda, for example, ahead of the 2006 elections, President Museveni deployed the Police Force of Uganda against his competitors. Opposition campaigning was disrupted, while Museveni's main rival, Kizza Besigye, was arrested and detained, accused of treason, concealment of treason, and rape. Although none of these charges were upheld, nor the specific timing of this action explained, Besigye was denied a full opportunity to win the office of the president. Museveni was returned to power.

Indeed, state intimidation can be even less subtle than that deployed in Uganda. Voters at one polling station in Equatorial Guinea, for instance, were apparently told that any person wanting to vote for an opposition candidate could do so in a separate ballot box to be found behind the building. A soldier would show them the way.[30]

All of the above cases are extreme examples of the way governments use state institutions to manipulate elections. A majority of the multi-party polls held in the last two decades have been declared *reasonably* free and fair. Yet the fact remains that incumbent parties have a major advantage over their rivals. Until there is a clear separation between state and ruling party institutions, there will not be a 'level playing field', and democracy will not be consolidated. A shadow is cast over the whole multi-party experiment when many incumbents still share the views of President Pascal Lissouba of Congo-Brazzaville, who reasoned that 'You don't arrange elections if you are going to lose them'.[31]

The unleashing of ethnic mobilisation?

A fifth potential problem that democratic consolidation will have to overcome is the perennial issue of ethnicity. The fact remains that imposed colonial borders have caged different ethnic groups within a single state. Competition between these groups was previously restricted by the one-party state and centralised structures. Multi-party democracy, however, opens up the possibility of full-scale ethnic mobilisation. After all, as Claude Ake points out, 'Liberal democracy assumes individualism, but there is little individualism in Africa'.[32] Africans interact on a more communal basis. In this respect, there is a possibility that African political parties will come to mirror the ethno-regional divisions within their societies. The recent revival of ethnic tensions in Congo-Brazzaville, Kenya, Malawi, Zambia and South Sudan, among other countries, certainly suggests this.

The danger with competition based on ethno-regional identities is that a victory for one group may be seen as a total defeat for another. One 'tribe' is to rule over the rest. Under these circumstances, it may be difficult for the losing ethnic group to accept the election results. Indeed, if an ethnic group feels that its interests will not be served within a nation ruled by its rival, outright secession may be sought. The consequence of this could be dismemberment of the state, just as occurred in the fledgling democracies of Yugoslavia and Czechoslovakia, and within the former Soviet Union.

Yet, so far, secession has not been a popular demand on the continent. Most Africans are still committed to the project of nation-building and accommodation within inherited nation-state structures. Indeed, ethnicity may be a positive contribution to democratic behaviour, offering an aggregation of demands. Pluralism, after all, revolves around the competition of interests. It is a way of resolving such conflicts peacefully. As long as all respect the rules of the game, democracy will survive. Harvey Glickman's conclusion seems to be sound: 'while democratization trends provide opportunities for expansion of ethnic conflict, they also allow opportunities for controlling such conflict through institutional mechanisms'.[33]

The threat of the military

Along with the need for a strong opposition, civil society and economy, the requirement that state institutions and the ruling party be separated, and that ethnic conflict be successfully managed, the behaviour of the military is also critical in a period of democratic consolidation.

Chapter 7 has already examined how the coercive agencies of the state have previously intervened in African politics. Time after time, the military usurped civilian politicians. However, for democracy to survive, the men in uniform will now have to adopt an apolitical role, leaving issues of regime change to the electorate.

A universal end to military intervention in African politics will not materialise immediately. The 1990s saw several instances in which security forces vetoed election results, installing their own governments instead (in Algeria, Nigeria, Burundi, Congo-Brazzaville and the Central African Republic). Even when some of these countries subsequently returned to multi-party competition, there was often a tacit understanding that candidates must first have the approval of the army. In Nigeria's case, the 1999 return to pluralist competition saw Olusegun Obasanjo elected as president. Previously, General Obasanjo had run Nigeria's 1976–79 military government. Did this handback to civilian rule represent the army endorsing the electorate's choice, or was it the people endorsing the military's nominee?

Electoral victories for successive (military-approved) presidential candidates in Algeria beg the same question. The Algerian army has effectively vetoed the possibility of an Islamist party coming to power. This is something that this state's electorate apparently wanted in 1990, before this poll was annulled prior to a second round of voting. The military in Egypt acted in a similar manner in 2013, underwriting popular protests that removed the elected Muslim Brotherhood from power. Elsewhere, in Madagascar, the military was closely associated with regime change in 2009. After a sustained period of rioting, and under intensifying pressure from mutinous soldiers and large crowds of protestors, the incumbent president Marc Ravalomanana resigned and handed power to a military council. The military, in turn, transferred authority to opposition politician Andry Rajoelina. Once again there can be little doubt that, behind the scenes, the military enjoys a veto over any political outcome which it considers undesirable.

It is a sobering thought that even the Gambia suffered a military coup in the last decade of the twentieth century. This brought to an end 29 consecutive years of multi-party democracy. Going by this evidence, consolidation will take several generations to complete.

Political culture

All of the above considerations can be drawn into the idea of political culture, which can be defined as *the shared political ideas, attitudes and beliefs that underlie a society*. Naturally enough, all individuals have their own views and interests, but more stable societies usually have some general political principles held in common. Ideas of liberal democracy, for example, permeate the whole of society in Britain and the United States. Most individuals, whether they are politicians or lay persons, respect and defend the rules of the political game. Consequently, democracy as a method of conflict resolution is valued in institutions throughout both the state and civil society. African polities have to replicate this political culture if multi-party democracy is to survive.

Normally, one would look to political leaders to be at the forefront of defending their society's political culture. It could be argued, however, that many of the political elites in Africa, both incumbents and opposition, are only using multi-party democracy instrumentally. In other words, they support pluralism because it is a method of retaining or gaining power, not because they inherently believe in its moral value. Consider

Zaire's politicians Etienne Tshisekedi and Nguza Karl-i-Bond, for example. Both formed political parties attempting to benefit from the new era of multi-party competition. They also made late bids to join Laurent Kabila's rebellion against Mobutu Sese Seko. Earlier, however, they had both been quite happy to serve Mobutu. Such political chameleons, or political entrepreneurs, cannot be trusted as the guardians of democracy. As Robert Fatton observes, 'When the old guard, the "dinosaurs", abruptly discover that they are after all good democrats, a country's release from authoritarianism may be facilitated, but its future as a democratic society can only be endangered'.[34] A drift back into personal rule and neo-patrimonialism is highly likely unless other political forces can check authoritarian tendencies.

The 'masses' could be one obvious source to keep notions of representation and accountability foremost in politicians' minds. Yet there is no real evidence to suggest that a multi-party political culture is ingrained in the African 'masses' either. Botswana, for example, has enjoyed pluralist competition since independence in 1966, but, despite this, an opinion poll conducted in the 1980s found that only 47 per cent of a representative sample considered multi-party democracy essential. The study concluded that 'among those with less than a secondary school education there is not yet a significant majority in favour of the idea that the public should have a voice in who should rule and for what purpose'.[35] The majority of Batswana were content for the political elite to rule on their behalf, and expected to participate only minimally in the political process. If this is the case in Botswana, then it would not be unreasonable to expect there to be even more deference to politicians in other African countries, and deference is not an effective check against potential authoritarianism.

Pluralism also requires a political culture where democrats wear victory or defeat gracefully. Africa's weak democratic environment, however, has resulted in a reality whereby fewer parties have accepted the results of multi-party elections than have been willing to participate in them. Certainly there *have* been numerous cases of grace in defeat, but there have also been a worrying number of contested, ignored or manipulated results.

Earlier in the chapter it was seen how ruling parties have the ability to control polling outcomes, but opposition challengers also abuse the democratic process. If their party does not poll well, a common reaction of opposition leaders is for them to declare the whole electoral contest a fraud. The results are rejected, parliamentary seats are boycotted, legal action is initiated, and appeals are made to the international community. In several instances, these actions have been warranted. The opposition was not permitted to compete on level terms with the incumbent ruling party. Yet, more often than not, African elections are reasonably free and fair, with any irregularities unlikely to affect the overall results. To make accusations of fraud in these cases is to damage a country's democratic culture. It can even lead to violence. In Angola during 1992, for example, multi-party elections were held after 17 years of civil war. The MPLA government defeated UNITA in free and fair elections, yet UNITA's response was not to form a loyal opposition, but simply to return to the bush and carry on its insurgency campaign. What UNITA could not win by the ballot box, it continued to seek by force of arms.

In too many cases, African elections fail to be a definitive mechanism for determining who governs. Instead, they are increasingly becoming merely a starting point for negotiations over who gains what amount of power. Elections in Kenya during 2007, for instance, ended in clashes between supporters of the two main political parties. Serious violence was precipitated by allegations that the state had rigged the poll in favour of the incumbent president, Mwai Kibaki. Eventually, the conflict was quelled, and a 'Grand Coalition' government formed, served by a cabinet of 41 ministers. Peace negotiations had ended the violence, and politicians from both parties had gained the access to the state they sought, but one has to question to what extent the electorate's choices were satisfied by this outcome. The coalition government decided not to hold new elections, leaving Kenya's leaders with a compromised democratic mandate. The government in Nairobi was a product of agreement among only an elite political class, not the people. As will be seen below, a similar negotiated power-sharing arrangement also emerged in Zimbabwe, in the wake of that country's 2008 election.

If, after electoral defeat, the first reaction of a losing party, government or opposition is to make unsubstantiated charges of fraud, rig the result, negotiate a better outcome under the threat of violence, or actually take up arms, then democratic consolidation is still a long way off. This is a political culture that cannot sustain pluralism.

Table 11.2 Chapter summary: obstacles to democratic consolidation in Africa

Lack of a credible opposition	• Alternative personnel and policy programme choices required by electorate
	• Coherent opposition parties needed, not numerous 'vanity parties' with limited support
Weak civil society	• Civil society to act as a counterbalance to state hegemony
	• Civil society groups to avoid co-optation by state, and instead to provide a permanent independent check on state power
	• Stronger African middle classes needed to sustain civil society activity
Weak economies	• Productive economy needed to allow state to supply goods and services to electorate
	• Scarce resources could persuade electorate to abandon democratic processes
No separation between state and ruling party	• Ruling party to guarantee free and fair polls, avoiding manipulation of the electoral process
	• Constitutions not to be amended solely to suit the interests of the ruling party
	• State resources not to be used to bolster ruling party electoral campaigns
	• All parties to have equal access to state-owned media
	• State security forces to underpin democracy, and not be used to intimidate the opposition
Potential of uncontrolled ethnic conflict	• Ethnic competition reinvigorated by freedom of democratic competition
	• Need to ensure ethnic competition is confined within democratic processes
Potential of military intervention	• Military may seek to vet candidates, holding a veto over electoral process
Weak democratic political culture	• Respect for democracy needed among ruling elite – no abandoning of pluralism once in power
	• Respect for democracy needed by opposition – no abandoning the democratic process if there is a failure to win power
	• Respect for democracy needed in civil society – no deferral to a state that abandons the democratic process
	• Education and experience of democracy needed on the continent to ensure its longevity

State and civil society

Success and failure with the considerations discussed above have left African countries at various stages of democratic transition. A few countries never started the reform process (where incumbents were able to resist the pressures for liberalisation); others have stumbled along the way (with authoritarian practices resuming, military intervention occurring, or a descent into state collapse); more have made hesitant progress (involving genuine liberalisation of the political arena, but with authoritarian practices still in vogue); while a number have displayed more positive signs of a democratic culture. It should be recognised, however, that none of this last category is free from the danger of retrogression. Newly won democratic concessions are easily reversed, and several more countries are bound to fall back into old habits.

Conversely, no state on the continent is incapable of making further progress. Even those that have collapsed completely may wish to start the rebuilding process with multi-party elections. Consequently, after an amazing period of change in Africa, the continent today is certainly more democratic than it was two decades ago. Progress, however, is inevitably slow. In terms of democratic consolidation, Africa can be characterised as taking a metaphoric one step back for every two steps forward. But where does this leave Africa's shifting relationship between state and civil society?

Both state and civil society have benefited from the move to multi-party democracy. In terms of the state, the previous chapter saw most African governments in a pincer movement between the crisis of accumulation and the crisis of governance. Legitimacy was declining rapidly, states were inverting, and, for many, a complete collapse beckoned. In this respect, the transition to multi-party constitutions has to be seen as the deployment of yet another state survival strategy. The presidential monarchs set about mounting a tactical retreat through the offer of democratic reforms. It was their last hope to re-legitimise the state, and thus to retain a degree of power for themselves and their clients.

The price paid for using this particular survival strategy was the liberalisation of African political systems. Political space that previously was deliberately restricted by the elite became liberated. Civil society could now openly and legally challenge the ruling party. To survive, incumbents had first to win elections and then to cope with an official opposition within state legislatures. Indeed, many of the old guard failed in their attempts to do just this. They did not possess the skills of manipulation, resources or public support to survive the transition to the new system. Others did make it into the new era, however, and although these politicians may well still possess their old authoritarian reflexes, they are all aware that they now have new responsibilities towards the electorate. Both democracy and the state can only be strengthened by this recognition.

Civil society, or at least parts of it, was also strengthened by the transition to multi-party competition. Churches, trade unions, human rights groups and professional associations have all gained confidence and experience with respect to participating in the political process. Having forced the old regimes to concede democratic reforms, they are now in a position to help to ensure that pluralist competition survives. In many cases, civil society activists and organisations have actually replaced the old guard. Again, this rejuvenation of pluralism in Africa has had positive results.

The depth to which this democratic culture has permeated society, however, has to be questioned. Leaders within these social institutions may be fully committed to the new era of pluralism, but to what extent has the peasantry in Africa been converted? Does this form of politics offer them anything but an occasional chance to vote?

Indeed, it may be that multi-party democracy has only served to expand the political class on the continent, with circulating elites now encompassing leaders of both the state *and* civil society. Government, under these circumstances, would only be account-able and representative to these higher echelons of society. If this is the case, the vast majority of Africans will still be left with few benefits from government. The links between the governors and the governed remain weak. Only a consolidated democracy together with economic development will produce a political system that is truly rele-vant to all. In this respect, more successful democracies 'arise from popular demands for a share in a going concern'. They are less effective if they emerge as a 'last-gasp attempt' to hold together a concern that is 'on its way down'.[36]

There is no doubt that the political environment in Africa has improved dramatically since the 1990s. There is a possibility that these reforms mark the start of a positive political journey that will benefit many over the coming decades. It would be remiss, however, to be over-optimistic about Africa's political future. This would be relying too heavily on hope, and ignoring the hard evidence presented above. Currently, Africa is dominated by hybrid electoral autocracies. It is painfully plain to see that the consolida-tion of future widespread multi-party democracy in Africa is possible, but by no means guaranteed.

Case study: Zimbabwe's fall from democratic grace

Zimbabwe, formerly Southern Rhodesia, is a landlocked country located in central southern Africa. Like its neighbours South Africa and Namibia, Zimbabwe emerged from the colonial era later than most states on the continent. This was because, as well as having to persuade a distant imperial power (the United Kingdom) to relinquish sovereignty, nationalist forces also had to defeat a locally entrenched white-minority government. The intransigence of Rhodesia's settler population stalled the decolonisation process. Indeed, white settlers refusing to share political power in 'the country they had built' dragged the country into a 25-year civil war that cost an estimated 40,000 lives. This bush war of attrition fought by the 'Patriotic Front' (PF), an uneasy nationalist alliance of the Zimbabwe African National Union (ZANU) and the Zimbabwe African People's Union (ZAPU), eventually forced the white-minority Rhodesian Front government to the negotiating table, and an agreement signed at Lancaster House, London brought independence to Zimbabwe in 1980.

Aside from a number of 'sunset clauses' that temporarily guaranteed limited white representation, Zimbabwe's first constitution sought to underwrite a non-racial multi-party democracy. Accordingly, at independence, a competitive poll took place, with ZANU-PF victorious, and its leader, Robert Mugabe, being installed as Zimbabwe's first prime minister (see Table 11.3). ZAPU representatives,

Table 11.3 Results of House of Assembly elections, Zimbabwe, 1980–2008

Party	1980	1985	1990	1995	2000	2005	2008	2013
Zimbabwe African National Union – Patriotic Front (ZANU-PF)	57	64	117	118	62	78	97	197
Zimbabwe African People's Union (ZAPU)	20	15	—	—	—	—	—	—
Rhodesia Front (RF)	20	—	—	—	—	—	—	—
United African National Council	3	—	—	—	—	—	—	—
Conservative Alliance of Zimbabwe	—	15	—	—	—	—	—	—
Independent Zimbabwe Group	—	4	—	—	—	—	—	—
Independent	—	1	—	—	—	1	1	1
Zimbabwe African National Union – Ndonga	—	1	1	2	1	—	—	—
Zimbabwe Unity Movement	—	—	2	0	—	—	—	—
Movement for Democratic Change (MDC)	—	—	—	—	57	41	—	—
MDC – Tsvangirai	—	—	—	—	—	—	99	70
MDC – Mutambara/Ncube	—	—	—	—	—	—	10	2
ZANU-PF majority/minority	*14*	*28*	*114*	*116*	*4*	*36*	*22*	*124*

as ZANU's comrades in arms, joined Mugabe's government, while Members of Parliament from the Rhodesian Front (with their guaranteed 'sunset' seats) formed an official opposition alongside the United African National Council. Zimbabwe had thus followed the path of most African states at independence. A new liberal democratic constitution had been agreed, political parties had competed relatively freely and fairly (against the odds), and a new regime had emerged corresponding to the will of the people. Unfortunately, the 1980 elections represented the high tide of Zimbabwe's democratic history.

Despite experiencing decolonisation later than most African states, the pattern of Zimbabwe's post-colonial political development was familiar. Mugabe and ZANU-PF oversaw both a centralisation of the state and a personalisation of power. Mugabe's primary objective, in this respect, was to neutralise sources of opposition. Initially, although there were differences between the two constituent parts of the Patriotic Front, ZAPU had agreed to serve as a junior partner in Mugabe's ZANU-PF government. ZAPU's leader, Joshua Nkomo, was invited to be a member of Zimbabwe's first cabinet, along with three of his party colleagues. Mugabe, however, was to terminate this coalition within two years. The prime minister was wary of ZAPU's legitimacy, generated by its role in the liberation struggle, and its solid support among the country's largest minority ethnic group, the amaNdebele of the Matabele region.

Plate 11.2 Robert Mugabe addressing journalists prior to becoming Zimbabwe's first president, 1979.

When a cache of arms was discovered on a property associated with ZAPU, in February 1982, Mugabe struck. The prime minister dismissed Nkomo, accusing him of plotting a coup. Other ZAPU leaders were detained and accused of treason. Mugabe explained his actions as follows: 'ZAPU and its leader, Dr Joshua Nkomo, were like a cobra in a house. The only way to deal effectively with a snake is to strike and destroy its head'.[37] Nkomo's dismissal and his colleagues' treason trial, however, ignited civil unrest in Matabeleland, which, in turn, prompted thousands of former ZAPU combatants to desert the national army. Mugabe's response to this deteriorating security situation was brutal. The prime minister's loyal Fifth Brigade, recently trained by North Korean advisers, was deployed in Matabeleland with a view to neutralising all opposition.

Approximately 20,000 to 30,000 people lost their lives as a consequence of this security action. ZAPU, although still able to muster considerable ethnic support in the 1985 elections, was effectively broken. Sporadic violence continued until a weakened ZAPU leadership agreed to sign a unity accord with ZANU-PF in 1987. The two parties theoretically 'merged' at this point, but the fact that the 'new' party retained the name ZANU-PF, with Mugabe very much at its head, alludes to where the power remained. With the defeat and co-optation of Zimbabwe's most prominent source of opposition, Mugabe had come closer to realising his overall objective of creating a one-party state.

With ZAPU disabled, Mugabe turned his attention to consolidating his own powers. Using ZANU-PF's majority in parliament, the constitution of Zimbabwe was amended to abolish the office of prime minister in favour of a new executive president. Mugabe assumed this position in December 1987. The new president's location as head of state and commander in chief, with powers to dissolve Parliament and declare martial law, left few doubting Mugabe's intentions to place his residence of Zimbabwe House at the apex of political power. Likewise, the president's dominant role in appointing military and police officers, senior civil servants, and the managers of Zimbabwe's parastatal corporations put Mugabe firmly in command of the country's patron–client network.

Further constitutional reforms also confirmed ZANU-PF's ascendancy over the legislative branch. The 20 seats temporarily reserved for white MPs by the Lancaster House agreement were abolished in 1987, while, three years later, Parliament was expanded to a total of 150 members. This extension permitted the president to personally appoint 30 MPs. The success of these reforms in creating a de facto one-party state can be measured by the absence of opposition representatives elected to Parliament. ZANU-PF's political dominance in the period between the ZANU/ZAPU unity agreement of 1987 and the poll of 2000 was overwhelming (see Table 11.3). Zimbabwe had arrived at a position, discussed in the main text of this chapter, where its elections failed to offer any meaningful choice between parties or policies. The country's democratic institutions were only procedural.

Robert Mugabe, however, never enjoyed the unfettered power of earlier generations of African presidential monarchs. His hold over Zimbabwean politics came close to this goal during the 1980s and 1990s, but the longevity of ZANU-PF's iron rule was challenged more effectively in the twenty-first century. Economics and the wider democratisation of the African continent conspired against the president's ongoing programme of political centralisation. By the end of the 1990s, Zimbabwe's de facto one-party state had resulted in a crisis of legitimacy.

The Zimbabwean economy in the decade after independence had fared reasonably well. Good rains and a return to peace produced an average of 3.6 per cent growth during the 1980s. Yet this growth had slowed dramatically by the mid-1990s, and the economy had entered recession by 2000.[38] This turn of fortunes can be accounted for by Zimbabwe's debilitating levels of debt service, the high running costs of its inefficient parastatal corporations, and drought. Put simply, Harare was having difficulty raising enough foreign exchange to pay its international creditors, and to maintain its bloated state industries. Consequently, in 1990, Zimbabwe negotiated a home-grown package of structural adjustment measures with the World Bank. Abandoning its more socialist-oriented policies, ZANU-PF now oversaw reforms that removed price and wage constraints, reduced government expenditure (particularly in the areas of health and education), devalued the Zimbabwean dollar, shrank subsidies on basic consumer staples, relaxed protective measures on non-productive import substituting industries, and radically restructured several parastatals and other public enterprises.

The social and political effects of this structural adjustment programme (SAP) were far-reaching. Provision for mass education and health had been ZANU-PF's success story. In 1980, Zimbabwe had just 177 secondary schools teaching 66,215 pupils. Four years later, there were 1,206 such establishments with 422,583 children enrolled.[39] Likewise, Zimbabwe's primary health care services expanded rapidly after independence.[40] With the implementation of structural adjustment, however, 'user fees' were introduced. In order to reduce public spending via 'recovery measures', Zimbabweans were now expected to meet, or contribute towards, the cost of their welfare provision at the point of access. Consequently, the social achievements of the 1980s suffered. For instance, after fees were introduced in 1992, the number of rural women who attended state clinics to give birth fell by 20 per cent. Maternal mortality rose from less than 80 to over 110 deaths per 100,000 births between 1990 and 1993.[41] New school fees, although limited to urban children, likewise added to citizens' budgets at a time of hardship.

Unemployment was also rising. In urban areas, between 1986 and 1991, the number of job seekers rose from 18 to 26 per cent of the potential working population. Adults under 25 years of age were particularly harshly affected. Up to half of this demographic were out of work.[42] The prospect of 40,000 to 50,000 SAP retrenchments among civil servants and parastatal workers added to the gloom, as did the removal of state food subsidies. Average prices for basic consumer goods rose by 250 per cent between 1990 and 1994.[43]

Certainly, in hindsight, much has been made of the impact of this SAP on Zimbabwe's subsequent political and economic development. President Mugabe himself blamed IMF-imposed policies for most of the economic ills that later beset his country. In truth, however, it is much harder to disentangle cause and effect. A long list of woes account for Zimbabwe's continued economic turndown during the 1990s. These include drought, ZANU-PF's non-implementation and mismanagement of the SAP, steadfast protection of parastatals, and a refusal to cut the military budget as part of an overall retrenchment of public spending.

What is important for this particular case study, however, is the effect on political legitimacy that the SAP policies and the economic recession precipitated. As a consequence of financial hardship, there was now a growing perception, particularly among urban Zimbabweans, that ZANU-PF could no longer provide. Mugabe's popularity, born of his part played in the liberation struggle, and the social improvements of the 1980s, was beginning to wane. This in turn put the focus on opposition politics. Like many urban dwellers across the continent, politically aware Zimbabweans were now demanding alternative sources of policy choices and leadership. The call was for a functioning pluralist democracy.

One of the first groups within civil society to challenge the ZANU-PF regime was one of its closest allies. Prompted by the harsher economic climate, former Patriotic Front guerrillas lobbied for financial recognition, in terms of pensions. The so-called 'war veterans' demands were met. Mugabe, realising that he needed the continued support of this client group, agreed to pay a one-off sum for each of these ex-combatants (US$5000), and a monthly salary of US$210 thereafter.

The fact that over 50,000 individuals qualified for these payments, when there were fewer than 30,000 Patriotic Front soldiers demobilised in 1980, says a great deal about the unsustainable financial demands of ZANU-PF's patronage networks.[44]

Hit hardest by the SAP reforms, urban workers also began to mobilise in the later 1990s. Initially, as a direct response to retrenchments and cuts in services, professional groups, such as civil servants, teachers, doctors, nurses and lawyers, took sporadic strike action. Eventually, however, the Zimbabwe Congress of Trade Unions (ZCTU) got involved. ZCTU, led by Morgan Tsvangirai, was persuaded to break its ties with ZANU-PF, and campaign independently. General strikes were called in 1997 and 1998, protesting against increased taxes levied to pay for the war veterans' pensions, and against deteriorating labour conditions generally. As was the case with other African countries, this labour-led opposition, which initially focused on specific hardships, soon evolved into a broader call for multi-party democracy. As a consequence, the Movement for Democratic Change (MDC) was formed in 1999, with Tsvangirai at its head.

Reacting to this challenge, and the potential loss of the de facto one-party state, Robert Mugabe embarked on a radical strategy to re-legitimise his government. A policy of land redistribution was proposed.

Land reform had always been one of ZANU-PF's goals. Colonial rule left half of Zimbabwe's arable land in the hands of just 1 per cent of the population (white commercial farmers). As part of the Lancaster House agreement, the United Kingdom had pledged to help to fund land resettlement. Yet the 1980–2000 period had seen slow progress in redressing this inequality. The momentum of redistribution had been hampered by the Zimbabwean government not having sufficient funds to compensate white farmers for their loss of livelihood, at market prices, while the government in London was unwilling to bankroll any settlement unless the outcome would genuinely relieve poverty. The UK government sought a programme that was properly planned, transparent, and would actually deliver land to the landless poor, rather than to Mugabe loyalists. The United Kingdom did authorise payments totalling £44 million during this period, which saw the land still held by white commercial farmers fall from 50 to 29 per cent of total arable land, but Mugabe now needed a quicker pace of redistribution to shore up his party's legitimacy.[45]

The issue of land reform was written into a proposed new constitution presented to the Zimbabwean people in 2000. Impatient with the British insistence on conditions, and desperate to regain popular support, ZANU-PF was serving notice that its previous 'willing buyer, willing seller' policy was to be abandoned. Mugabe now planned to go ahead with compulsory land redistribution, without compensation.

The president's 'land for legitimacy' strategy got off to a bad start. Generating widespread surprise, the 'Yes' campaign, pressing for the new constitution, lost the February 2000 referendum by 45 per cent of the poll to 55 per cent. Civil society groups ran a well-organised 'No' campaign, which capitalised on fuel shortages and the crippled economy, to defeat a complacent ZANU-PF. The fact that civil society was becoming politically active once again boded well for any future democratic reforms.

The biggest beneficiaries of this defeat, however, were the MDC. Although taking a back seat with respect to the referendum itself, the MDC returned 43 per cent of the vote four months later, in parliamentary elections. Urban voters, by withdrawing their allegiance from ZANU-PF, had made Zimbabwe a competitive multi-party democracy. ZANU-PF, however, which had campaigned under the slogan 'land is the economy, the economy is the land', still clung on to its overall majority in the House of Assembly (see Table 11.3).

Despite the setbacks of 2000, the Zimbabwean government continued with its land-based re-legitimisation strategy. Ignoring the referendum defeat, ZANU-PF, using its majority in Parliament, amended the constitution anyway, announcing that it would repossess 1,471 commercial farms totalling more than 11 million hectares. In order to implement this policy, the government turned to its ally, the war veterans' association. In a series of land invasions, the veterans (whose ranks had swelled to include many younger 'veterans') evicted white landowners and occupied the country's commercial farms. An intimidation campaign left several farm owners and workers dead, with many abandoning their property as a result. By 2009, only 500 of the original 4,500 commercial farmers still remained on their land. The beneficiaries were 127,000 peasant households and 8,000 new (African) commercial farmers. Alongside the allocation of land plots to the war veterans and peasant farmers, ZANU-PF officials made sure that they exercised their bureaucratic power to allot a small proportion of this land, but some of the most valuable, to themselves and their clients.[46] After all, patronage networks had to be rejuvenated, in addition to generating popular support.

As a re-legitimising strategy, however, the land redistribution programme fell short. Although 135,000 households had directly benefited from the seizure of the commercial farms, the economy did not. Compounding earlier problems, the colossal disruption to agricultural output sent the Zimbabwean economy into freefall. A list of indicators tell their own tale. The national economy shrank by a third after 1999: average per-capita purchasing power returned to 1953 levels; 35 per cent of the population lived below the poverty line in 1996, but this share grew to an estimated 80 per cent by 2003; the commercial production of maize, the national staple, dropped by 86 per cent between 2000 and 2005; and the volume of tobacco exports, once the country's leading foreign exchange earner, fell by more than 60 per cent after 2000. An indicator of the scale of the economic collapse was that Zimbabwe, once a food exporter, and the so-called 'breadbasket' of Southern Africa, became food insecure. More than one-third of the population became reliant on imported food aid. With inflation running at 500 billion per cent in 2008, and the Zimbabwean dollar becoming worthless, even those who had received land through the redistribution programme must have questioned ZANU-PF's competence to rule.[47]

Having failed to replenish its legitimacy, the Mugabe regime resorted to coercion in order to retain power in the twenty-first century. Assessing Zimbabwe's prospects for recovery, Moss and Patrick, in a 2006 report, came to the conclusion that:

> Zimbabwean society has undergone intense stress stemming from organized violence and intimidation by the state. The security forces, intelligence services, and an array of government-backed militias have terrorized civilians, committed gross human rights violations, and been deployed to infiltrate and disrupt the opposition. In some cases, tactics from the guerrilla war—including re-education camps, propaganda bombardment, and all-night pungwes [clandestine political meetings]—have been revived. Hundreds of thousands of citizens have been forcibly relocated. These conditions have produced high levels of suspicion, low levels of trust, and a steep deterioration of social capital.[48]

Between April and June 2008 alone, the MDC reported the assassination of 85 of its members, with 1,734 more being beaten.[49] Morgan Tsvangirai himself suffered a severe assault, alongside four arrests.

To a large extent, the coercion campaign succeeded, albeit temporarily. ZANU-PF remained in power. Robert Mugabe won the presidential election of 2002, and the ruling party increased its parliamentary majority in 2005, amid accusations of vote rigging. The incessant intimidation even manufactured a split of the MDC. By contrast, the ruling elite was very much intact.

Its legitimacy, however, was not. By 2008, the game was up. Coercion alone could not keep Mugabe in power, especially given the ongoing economic catastrophe. A political watershed was reached during the presidential and parliamentary elections of that year. Despite the murder of opposition candidates, widespread violence and vote rigging, Tsvangirai's branch of the MDC won a majority in the House of Assembly, and Tsvangirai himself took a lead in the first round of the presidential poll. Mugabe, however, remained head of state, emerging victorious after a delayed second round of voting. Tsvangirai had withdrawn his candidacy on the eve of this presidential run-off, amid intense violence. The MDC leader stated that he did not wish to continue to risk the lives of his supporters by asking them to vote for him a second time.

This political stalemate, with the MDC controlling Parliament and Mugabe entrenched in Zimbabwe House, together with continued economic strife, prompted negotiations. ZANU-PF's survival strategy was to manufacture a power-sharing arrangement with the MDC. It would try to reassert its legitimacy by governing alongside the opposition. Negotiations between the two parties eventually agreed that Mugabe would remain president, while Tsvangirai would serve as prime minister. Cabinet seats were split evenly between the parties.

In a similar manner to the Kenyan case discussed above, after an election, violence and negotiations, Zimbabwe ended up with a 'government of national unity'. In this respect, Zimbabwe's democratic evolution had stalled. Political leaders were not chosen, nor was public policy selected, by the electorate. The political elite negotiated among themselves to allocate power. No doubt ZANU-PF thought it could out manoeuvre the MDC within this coalition government, retaining de facto power and patronage, while the MDC hoped that they could press home their more legitimate claim to govern relatively free from intimidation and violence. Consequently, the power-sharing deal brought a degree of much needed peace and stability to Zimbabwe. It did not, however, advance democracy.

In the end, it was ZANU-PF that emerged victorious from this spell of coalition government. After elections in 2013, ZANU-PF reclaimed its majority in Parliament (see Table 11.3), and Mugabe himself remained resident in State House, capturing 61 per cent of the presidential vote (against Tsvangirai's 34 per cent). Reports of electoral irregularities and intimidation were widespread, but there is no doubt that however tarnished this victory was, ZANU-PF had succeeded in re-legitimising itself in the eyes of many voters. Rural Zimbabweans, in particular, responded to ZANU-PF's efforts to mobilise their vote. The 'party of liberation' did not take its most loyal constituency for granted this time, as it had in 2008. This activism contrasted strongly with opposition campaigning. Complacency and a lack of political direction, combined with splits and internal wrangling within the MDC, helped ZANU-PF back to its familiar position as Zimbabwe's sole ruling party.

In many respects, this case study provides a good example of the broader challenges for democratic consolidation found on the African continent. On a positive note, there have been regular elections in Zimbabwe since 1980. Likewise, opposition parties and voices have existed, and continue to do so, in this country. Indeed, this political 'tolerance' has occasionally been key to keeping the Zimbabwean state itself functioning, the 2008 Government of National Unity being a case in point. Yet the odds are stacked against opposition activists. All too often the coercive forces of the Zimbabwean state have been used to intimidate and eliminate any serious challenge to the ruling party. ZANU-PF has likewise used its position of power to manipulate the constitution, disrupt opposition campaigning and finesse electoral results. There is little separation of party and state when it comes to winning votes. The opposition itself has also lacked consistency. Although powerful enough to emerge as a serious challenger, survive intimidation and even win a place in a coalition government, the MDC has been too divided and self-interested to oust the ruling party. The overall consequence for the role of democracy in Zimbabwe has been this concept being an important force, but not the dominant arbiter within this political system. As with most African states, democracy has had to compete with authoritarianism, patronage, corruption and violence in post-colonial Zimbabwe.

Zimbabwe[50]

Territory:	390,757 sq. km.	Independence:	1980
Colonial power:	Britain	Ethnic groups:	amaNdebele
Major cities:	Harare (capital)		maShona
	Bulawayo		White Zimbabweans
	Mutare	Currency:	Zimbabwean dollar (replaced
Languages:	English		by the US dollar in 2009)
	chiShona		
	isiNdebele	Life expectancy:	60 years
		Adult literacy:	84 per cent
Urban population:	33 per cent	Infant mortality:	55 deaths/1,000 live births
Religion:	Traditional	Exports:	Tobacco
	Christian		Coke
GDP per capita:	US$714		Cotton
Population:	14.2 million		

Questions raised by this chapter

1. Why were so many multi-party elections contested in Africa during the 1990s?
2. Will multi-party democracy be consolidated on the African continent?
3. Are Africa's political cultures a suitable host for multi-party democracy?
4. To what extent did the move to multi-party democracy alter the relationship between state and civil society in Africa?
5. Did the 1990s democratisation process re-legitimise the African state?

Glossary of key terms

Consolidation of democracy Ensuring that the democratic process endures beyond the first multi-party election. This will be assisted by a favourable political culture, a strong civil society and a supportive economy.

Democracy A form of government where sovereignty rests with the people.

Double turnover criteria The view that the democratic process has not been proven until elections have removed two regimes fairly and peacefully from office (S. Huntington).

Military veto The instigation of a *coup d'état* by the military in order to block the civilian political process.

Political culture The shared political ideas, attitudes and beliefs that underlie a society.

Rejuvenation of civil society A reference to the revitalisation of African associational life in the 1980s and 1990s, caused by organisations de-linking themselves from government co-option, and by civil society moving into the political space vacated by the state.

Further reading

Those interested in learning more about multi-party democracy in Africa during the 1990s could start with John Wiseman's own book (1996), and then go on to his edited collection (1995) for some detailed case studies. Michael Bratton and Nicolas van de Walle's volume is also worth a look, as it offers a comprehensive, more statistical approach to the subject. In terms of journal articles, three papers stand out: Patrick Molutsi and John Holm provide a fascinating study of Botswana, where democracy has been in place since 1966; Claude Ake looks at how traditional democratic values have been incorporated into modern African states; and Christopher Clapham puts the 1990s wave of democratisation into its historical context, and offers hopes and fears for the future.

Ake, Claude. The unique case of African democracy. *International Affairs*. 1993, 69(2), 239–44.

Bratton, Michael and Nicolas van de Walle. *Democratic Experiments in Africa: Regime Transitions in Comparative Perspective*. Cambridge: Cambridge University Press, 1997.

Clapham, Christopher. Democratisation in Africa: obstacles and prospects. *Third World Quarterly*. 1993, 14(3), 423–38.

Molutsi, Patrick P. and John D. Holm. Developing democracy when civil society is weak: the case of Botswana. *African Affairs*. 1990, 89(356), 323–40.

Wiseman, John A., ed. *Democracy and Political Change in Sub-Saharan Africa*. London: Routledge, 1995.

Wiseman, John A. *The New Struggle for Democracy in Africa*. Aldershot: Avebury, 1996.

Notes and references

1 Thabo Mbeki's address to the Corporate Council on Africa, April 1997, Chantilly, Virginia, USA.

2 Hyden, Goran and Michael Bratton, eds. *Governance and Politics in Africa*. Boulder, CO: Lynne Rienner, 1992. ix.

3 Abraham Lincoln's Gettysburg Address, 1863.

4 See Kweka, A.N. One-party democracy and the multi-party state. In: Colin Legum and Geoffrey Mmari, eds. *Mwalimu: The Influence of Nyerere*. London: James Currey, 1995. 74.

5 Fatton, Robert. *Predatory Rule: State and Civil Society in Africa*. Boulder, CO: Lynne Rienner, 1992. 107.

6 See Sandbrook, Richard. *The Politics of Africa's Economic Recovery*. Cambridge: Cambridge University Press, 1993. 88.

7 Bratton, Michael and Nicolas van de Walle. *Democratic Experiments in Africa: Regime Transitions in Comparative Perspective*. Cambridge: Cambridge University Press, 1997. 182.

8 Cited in Wiseman, John A. *The New Struggle for Democracy in Africa*. Aldershot: Avebury, 1996. 70.

9 Cited in Toulabor, Comi. 'Paristroika' and the one-party system. In: Anthony Kirk-Greene and Daniel Bach, eds. *State and Society in Francophone Africa Since Independence*. Basingstoke: Macmillan, 1995. 115.

10 Fatton. *Predatory Rule: State and Civil Society in Africa*. 107.

11 Bratton and van de Walle. *Democratic Experiments in Africa: Regime Transitions in Comparative Perspective*. 105.

12 Wiseman. *The New Struggle for Democracy in Africa*. 38–40.

13 *Ibid*. 46.

14 *Ibid*. 44–5.

15 Statistics compiled from *Africa Confidential*; *Africa South of the Sahara*; and Nohlen, Dieter, Michael Krennerich, and Bernhard Thibaut, eds. *Elections in Africa: A Data Handbook*. Oxford: Oxford University Press, 1999.

16 Clapham, Christopher. Democratisation in Africa: obstacles and prospects. *Third World Quarterly*. 1993, 14(3), 425.

17 Sandbrook. *The Politics of Africa's Economic Recovery*. 91. Original emphasis.

18 Laakso, Liisa. Relationship between the state and civil society in the Zimbabwean elections 1995. *Journal of Commonwealth and Comparative Politics*. 1996, 34(3), 218.

19 Huntington, Samuel P. *The Third Wave: Democratization in the Late Twentieth Century*. Norman, OK: University of Oklahoma Press, 1991. 267.

20 Buijtenhuijs, Robert. Chad in the age of the warlords. In: David Birmingham and Phillis M. Martin, eds. *History of Central Africa: The Contemporary Years*. London: Longman, 1998. 36.

21 Wiseman. *The New Struggle for Democracy in Africa*. 107.

22 *Ibid.* 111.

23 Bratton and van de Walle. *Democratic Experiments in Africa: Regime Transitions in Comparative Perspective*. 200.

24 Beckman, Björn. Whose democracy? Bourgeois versus popular democracy. *Review of African Political Economy*. 1989, 16(45-46), 84.

25 Pallister, David. UK lawyers helped Zambia ex-president launder £23m. *The Guardian* (London). 5 May 2007. 9.

26 Gitonga, Afrifa K. The meaning and foundations of democracy. In: Walter O. Oyugi, E.S. Atieno Odhiambo, Michael Chege and Afrifa K. Gitonga, eds. *Democratic Theory and Practice in Africa*. Portsmouth, NH: Heinemann, 1988. 19.

27 Data taken from McKie, Kristin. The Politics of Adopting Term Limits in Sub-Saharan Africa. Paper prepared for delivery at the Annual Meeting of the American Political Science Association, Boston, MA, 29 August 2008.

28 Bratton and van de Walle. *Democratic Experiments in Africa: Regime Transitions in Comparative Perspective*. 204.

29 Adejumobi, Said. Elections in Africa: a fading shadow of democracy. *International Political Science Review*. 2000, 21(1), 68.

30 McGreal, Chris. Tourist deaths cap a loss. *The Guardian* (London). 6 March 1999. 4.

31 *Ibid.*

32 Ake, Claude. The unique case of African democracy. *International Affairs*. 1993, 69(2), 243.

33 Glickman, Harvey, with Peter Furia. Issues in the analysis of ethnic conflict and the democratization processes in Africa today. In: Harvey Glickman, ed. *Ethnic Conflict and Democratization in Africa*. Atlanta, GA: African Studies Association Press, 1995. 4.

34 Fatton. *Predatory Rule: State and Civil Society in Africa*. 110.

35 Molutsi, Patrick P. and John D. Holm. Developing democracy when civil society is weak: the case of Botswana. *African Affairs*. 1990, 89(356), 330.

36 Clapham. Democratisation in Africa: obstacles and prospects. 434 and 435.

37 Nkomo, Joshua. *Nkomo: The Story of My Life*. London: Methuen, 1984. 2.

38 United Nations Conference on Trade and Development. *UNCTAD Handbook of Statistics 2008*. New York: United Nations, 2008. Tables 8.2 and 8.3.

39 Cited in Maravanyika, O.E. *Implementing Educational Policies in Zimbabwe*. [World Bank Africa Technical Department discussion paper]. Washington, DC: World Bank, 1990. 16.

40 Nkrumah, F.K. and K.J. Nathoo. Recent trends in child health and survival in Zimbabwe. *Journal of Tropical Pediatrics*. 1987, 33(3), 153–5. See also Dugbatey, Kwesi. National health policies: sub-Saharan African case studies (1980–1990). *Social Science & Medicine*. 1990, 49, 230.

41 Marquette, Catherine M. Current poverty, structural adjustment, and drought in Zimbabwe. *World Development*. 1997, 25(7), 1144.

42 Knight, John. Labour market policies and outcomes in post-independence Zimbabwe: lessons for South Africa. In: Lennart Petersson, ed. *Post-Apartheid Southern Africa: Economic Challenges and Policies for the Future*. London: Routledge, 1998. 213.

43 Gibbon, Peter. *Structural Adjustment and the Working Poor in Zimbabwe: Studies on Labour, Women, Informal Sector Workers and Health*. Uppsala: Nordic Africa Institute, 1995. 16.

44 Blair, David. *Degrees in Violence: Robert Mugabe and the Struggle for Power in Zimbabwe*. London: Continuum, 2002. 39.

45 See Moyo, Sam. *The Land Question in Zimbabwe*. Harare: SAPES Books, 1995.

46 Moyo, Sam and Paris Yeros. Land occupations and land reform in Zimbabwe: towards the national democratic revolution. In: Sam Moyo and Paris Yeros, eds. *Reclaiming the Land: The Resurgence of Rural Movements in Africa, Asia and Latin America*. London: Zed, 2005. 188.

47 See Moss, Todd and Stewart Patrick. After Mugabe: applying post-conflict recovery lessons to Zimbabwe. *Africa Policy Journal*. 2006, 1. www.zimbabwesituation.com/old/apr26_2007.html#Z8 (accessed 24 November 2015).

48 Moss and Patrick. After Mugabe: applying post-conflict recovery lessons to Zimbabwe.

49 Peta, Basildon, Anne Penketh and Daniel Howden. Zimbabwe death toll reaches 85 as militias step up killings and torture. *The Independent* (London). 20 June 2008. www.independent.co.uk/news/world/africa/zimbabwe-death-toll-reaches-85-as-militias-step-up-killings-and-torture-851042.html (accessed 4 August 2009).

50 United Nations Conference on Trade and Development. *UNCTAD Handbook of Statistics 2014*. New York: United Nations, 2014. Tables 8.1, 8.4 and 3.2.D; World Bank data http://data.worldbank.org/indicator/SP.DYN.LE00.IN (accessed 24 July 2015) and http://data.worldbank.org/indicator/SP.DYN.IMRT.IN (accessed 24 July 2015); and UNESCO data www.uis.unesco.org/DataCentre/Pages/regions.aspx (accessed 24 July 2015).

12 Conclusions

The changing relationship between state, civil society and external interests in the post-colonial era

Chapter outline

- Independent Africa's political and economic decline
- 'Africa Rising'?
- Further reading
- Notes and references

The relationship between state, civil society and external interests should be of considerable interest to political scientists, whichever country or countries they choose to study. It is a conceptual approach that helps to place basic political events into some kind of historical and social context. Isolated political incidents gain greater meaning, and political outcomes are easier to explain. Indeed, for Africanists, this technique is invaluable as it allows a sense of order to be imposed on the last 60 years of post-colonial political history. This concluding chapter will sum up previous pages by constructing an overarching view of this period. How did shifts in the relationship between state, civil society and external interests influence the political journey from the heady days of independence, through the experiments of the one-party state era, into today's more liberal governance?

The first half of this conclusion will chart the continent's pre-millennium political development. These were the decades when the state took a stranglehold on African politics. Civil societies were marginalised. Yet states could not maintain this level of control over the people they governed. Transformations in governance, starting with the multi-party elections and external conditionality of the 1990s, combined with an upturn in economic fortunes since the turn of the century, have led to contemporary commentators talking about 'Africa Rising' or 'Africa Emerging'. Such rhetoric is in stark contrast to the literature analysing Africa that was penned 20 years ago. The second half of this conclusion will therefore investigate the idea of 'Africa Rising'. Is the continent on the cusp of reversing previous post-colonial political and economic failures?

Independent Africa's political and economic decline

Africa, from independence to the millennium, had to endure an uneasy relationship between state and civil society. Each party clearly needed the other, but there was considerable inefficacy in their engagement. It was a case of states trying to dominate civil society, yet failing to command enough power to complete their hegemonic ambitions. Civil society, for its part, mastered various techniques of distancing itself from state exploitation, but it was never in a position to rid itself entirely of predatory regimes. As the balance of power ebbed and flowed, it became clear that, in the long term, few Africans would actually benefit from this political stalemate. The continent, quite rightly, may not have wanted simply to mimic the systems of government found in Europe and North America, but the political institutions that did emerge after independence comprehensively failed to maximise the continent's economic welfare and political freedom. Africans were left somewhat enviously comparing their own position with the material wealth and liberty being generated in the West. It is no coincidence that these more prosperous countries enjoyed a generally positive, though by no means perfect, relationship between state and civil society.

At the start of the post-colonial period, African civil societies were in the ascendant. Indeed, they were much more vibrant than their host states. Ethnic ties, for example, were perhaps the strongest social bonds to be found on the continent. These had become more coherent during the colonial era, and would be powerful conduits of political mobilisation throughout the independence years. Similarly, it had been civil society that had actually overthrown the colonial state. Associational activity among ethno-regional groups, trades unions, professional societies and community organisations had all combined to make the nationalist movements the powerful forces that they were. Decolonisation was largely a case of Africans acting collectively to topple the mighty European empires that had ruled over them for the previous 70 years or so.

African states, by contrast, were relatively weak at independence. Most obviously, the colonial inheritance had left them with arbitrary boundaries. Ruler-straight borders, reflecting European rather than African interests, divided some traditional communities between different nation-states, while others found themselves caged together with potential domestic rivals. Virtually nothing had been done by the imperial authorities to build a collective consciousness among these people, so now, after independence, it was up to the new governments to build nations within these artificial state territories.

Similarly, the nationalist governments also had to develop economies rapidly. Colonial policy had resulted in underdevelopment. This produced an urgency to increase these countries' productive capabilities, for only in this manner could investment capital be raised, enabling diverse modern economies to be created. Without economic success, African states would be unable to command the resources needed to provide the social welfare that civil society now demanded. After all, a significant element of political legitimacy is the ability of governors to supply adequate public services to the governed.

Yet African political managers had been left with neither suitable state capacity, nor established institutional tools, to do this job. This made the provision of effective government problematic. The departing colonial powers may have bequeathed to their successors liberal democratic constitutions, but these hastily erected pluralist institutions had been built on woefully weak political foundations. European imperial rule had usually consisted of seven or eight decades of bureaucratic authoritarianism. No political culture of democracy had been nurtured, and no tradition of political pluralism established. The inherited mechanisms of power were as unfamiliar to the new state leaders as they were to members of civil society.

In hindsight, then, it is not surprising that African countries abandoned liberal democracy soon after independence. Faced by complex, economically disadvantaged and divided societies, and encumbered by untested and weak governmental structures, the continent's political leaders chose to rule through more centralised institutions instead. This, it was argued, would help states create both unity among their people and strategies to produce economic development. As a result, Africa entered the age of the one-party state.

In this era of centralised rule, political pluralism was curtailed, with any formal representation now being channelled through one-party structures; remaining civil society institutions were co-opted, harassed or banned; local government became local administration directed from the centre; economic activity was discouraged in the private sector, while public corporations dominated; and parliaments and the judicial functions of government were usurped by the executive. Indeed, with even the 'one-parties' soon experiencing atrophy, African core executives now had a monopoly over formal political activity within their territories. At the apex of this highly centralised state there usually resided a 'presidential monarch' enjoying the power of 'personal rule'.

These autocrats had little to fear by way of formal political challenges to their leadership. No constitutional mechanisms remained to unseat them, and civil society had all but been excluded from the political process. Indeed, political competition within postcolonial Africa was now limited to the infighting found within the state elite itself. In this environment, factional politics dominated, with various 'wings' of the bureaucratic bourgeoisie manoeuvring in their attempts to gain, consolidate or to increase power. Often it was the military that benefited most from this internecine conflict. Using its access to the resources of violence to stage *coups d'état*, on numerous occasions the army captured the state for itself. Civil society, now largely detached from the formal political arena, stood on the sidelines and was forced to accept the leadership of whichever faction of the state elite was in the ascendant.

Skilful manipulation of his (rarely her) lieutenants, however, often resulted in presidential monarchs being able to lift themselves above this factional infighting. Indeed, they could use internal competition to their advantage. Presidents made sure that potential challengers were too busy fending off their own rivals, and thus too distracted to mount any threat to the president himself. Consequently, political leadership was often remarkably stable in post-colonial Africa. 'Big Men', such as Mobutu, Gaddafi, Kaunda, Moi and Houphouët-Boigny, for example, became almost permanent features on this continent's political landscape.

All of these leaders, however, had to deal with the central paradox of the African state. The continent's post-colonial regimes were 'lame leviathans'.[1] Despite having accumulated a monopoly of formal political activity within the country, these states still did not have enough power to project their authority into all areas of their territory or society. Similarly, they were 'overdeveloped'. In order to maintain a hegemonic position, states had accumulated virtually all the formal economic and political functions of a society, draining civil society of considerable potential in the process. Yet, even with these massive powers, states still failed to deliver. Africans were left with little by way of welfare services or political representation. Legitimacy, as a consequence, was compromised.

State elites had, however, to offer civil society something. They could not survive by coercion alone. And since centralisation had seriously undermined the state's legal-rational credentials, other sources of legitimacy had to be found. It was client–patron networks that formed the main links between state and civil society for most of the postcolonial period. These patronage chains allowed presidential monarchs to 'buy' legitimacy from their people, in return for distributing goods and services. The president looked after his lieutenants, the lieutenants attended to their own clients, and intermediaries could be found all the way down to the local patrons operating at village level.

In this manner, (unequal) exchange took place between the governed and the governors, and a degree of legitimacy was generated.

State elites, however, could not rely solely on these domestic networks to secure their position. There were rarely enough resources generated internally to keep such patronage mechanisms 'oiled' and functioning at the required efficiency. This is why Africa's international links were of major importance in the post-colonial period. The concept of international sovereignty ensured that state elites gained access to resources available from the external environment. As 'representatives' of their people, government officials could appropriate capital from foreign trade and aid. During the Cold War, when foreign powers were not especially concerned about their African clients' democratic or human rights records, these external resources proved to be a massive asset to elite power. It was almost as if the continent's rulers gained greater rewards for servicing the interests of the international community than they did for representing their own people.

The end of the Cold War, however, saw a withering of indiscriminate international aid. In the 'New World Order' and the era of structural adjustment, donors now gave funds for specific purposes, with stringent conditions attached. At the same time, domestic economic problems reduced the availability of the already limited internal resources. Client–patron networks were consequently starved and began to contract. Africa had reached a political turning point. State legitimacy began to fail, and with no constitutional mechanisms present to enable a formal re-legitimisation of political systems, something had to give.

In a few cases, the state's agencies of coercion were still strong enough to mount a *coup d'état*. Elsewhere, state authority was so diminished that elements of civil society could mount a direct and violent challenge to government authority, usually via insurgency campaigns. In most cases, however, there was a further period of stalemate. Although states were now critically weak, and had difficulty controlling both citizens and territory, civil society itself still did not possess enough power to overthrow the ruling elite. Under these conditions, Africans opted for a less dramatic challenge to state authority. This came in the form of disengagement.

Through withdrawing from formal markets and operating instead in the second economy, Africans slowly undermined their rulers. In most cases, this prompted inverted states (that scaled down their public services); in other instances, warlord states emerged (where no pretence of legitimacy was maintained); and on a few extreme occasions, total state collapse occurred.

Most regimes, however, managed to steer their countries away from this extreme of total collapse. Africa's state managers of the 1990s attempted to re-legitimise their rule by submitting their governments to multi-party competition. Leaders were willing to take the risk of losing control of this democratisation process, and consequently being ousted from power, because many considered this to be their only remaining chance of securing a political future. The last decade of the twentieth century, therefore, brought a tidal wave of multi-party elections to the continent. Some of the 'Big Men' perished in this exercise, but many more survived, either by consolidating genuine popularity among the voters, or by manipulating the electoral process itself. Although a considerable number of these political contests were far from free and fair, many more were true reflections of the people's wishes. Consequently these polls did indeed go a long way towards re-legitimising the African state. Civil society had been brought back into the constitutional political process, and the relationship between state and civil society had become more productive.

'Africa Rising'?

Is it fair to say, then, that Africans have rid themselves of their centralised 'vampire' states? Have the predatory governments that so dominated the first three decades of the post-colonial period now been defeated, just like their colonial predecessors? Is the continent on its way to economic prosperity?

Some academics argue that this could be the case. Cautious optimism permeates certain sections of the literature addressing current African politics. Jean-Michel Severino and Olivier Ray, for example, in their book *Africa's Moment*, state: 'History continues.... Though structural vulnerability and new risks exist, the continent has genuinely entered a new era'.[2] Elsewhere, George Ayittey writes about Africa being 'unchained'.[3] These authors call upon scholars to recognise a new age of African politics. The continent is emerging from decades of poverty, poor governance and disadvantage in the world economy into a position where it can potentially carve out a more beneficial situation for itself.

Statistics back these authors' optimism. There has been a remarkable upturn in the continent's economic fortunes (see Table 12.1). As a 2014 African Development Bank report observed, 'Since the start of the new millennium, Africa's economic pulse has quickened: real gross domestic product (GDP) has been rising by 5 per cent a year and real income per capita has increased by 2.1 per cent a year. African growth has outperformed both Latin America and developed economies over the last 5 years, successfully weathering the global financial crisis of 2008/9'.[4] The much sought after economic 'take-off' predicted in the 1960s could now be a reality.

This new wealth creation has also had a social impact. Africa's distressing welfare statistics of the 1980s and 1990s are now significantly improved, if still far short of Western expectations (see Table 12.2). Infant mortality on the continent has fallen by

Table 12.1 African economic indicators, 2000–13

	Year	Africa	Eastern Africa	Middle Africa	Northern Africa	Southern Africa	Western Africa
GDP	2000	743	279	380	1,483	2,817	377
(US$ per capita)	2005	1,110	344	800	1,936	4,861	697
	2010	1,698	515	1,391	3,167	6,702	1,137
	2013	1,881	686	1,814	3,637	6,382	1,320
Imports	2000	129,967	16,938	7,589	49,135	35,187	21,118
(US$ million)	2005	256,561	31,493	19,038	89,609	71,353	45,068
	2010	479,039	61,127	41,295	178,712	112,322	85,582
	2013	628,163	88,731	57,382	219,597	145,449	117,004
Exports	2000	147,903	9,870	17,092	55,121	35,113	30,707
(US$ million)	2005	311,127	16,599	49,463	116,780	60,542	67,744
	2010	512,402	32,412	91,610	177,764	102,744	116,871
	2013	602,544	42,784	117,490	182,935	110,950	148,385
Inward direct	2000	9,621	1,468	1,503	3,250	1,269	2,131
foreign investment	2005	31,013	2,579	1,703	12,233	7,335	7,163
(US$ million)	2010	47,034	7,564	6,119	16,576	4,751	12,024
	2013	57,239	14,592	3,763	15,494	9,186	14,203

Source: Assembled from UNCTAD data. United Nations Conference on Trade and Development. *UNCTAD Handbook of Statistics 2014*. New York: United Nations, 2014. Tables 1.1, 7.2 and 8.1.

Table 12.2 African social indicators, 1990 and 2012

Africa	1990	2012
Life expectancy at birth (years)	50	58
Neonatal mortality rate (per 1,000 live births)	44	32
Access to improved drinking-water sources (percentage)	50	66
Access to improved sanitation (percentage)	27	33
Measles, immunisation coverage among 1-year-olds (percentage)	58	73
Children underweight, aged less than 5 years (percentage)[a]	34	25
Sub-Saharan Africa		
Pupil net enrolment rate, primary (percentage)	52	77
Adult literacy rate (≥ 15 years, percentage)	53	59

[a]1990–95 and 2006–12 statistics.
Source: World Health Organization. *World Health Statistics 2014*. Geneva: World Health Organization, 2014. Tables 1, 4, 5; also World Bank 'EdStats' data, http://data.worldbank.org/data-catalog/ed-stats (accessed 2 August 2015).

around one-third over the past 20 years, while average life expectancy has increased by eight years. Access to clean water has likewise improved. There has also been unprecedented progress in the development of education. Sixty million more children were enrolled in sub-Saharan Africa's primary schools in 2011 than had been in 1990. Overall, using African Development Bank data and definitions, the proportion of people living in poverty has fallen from over 50 per cent in 1981 to less than 45 per cent in 2012.[5] Although a 5 per cent improvement may be modest, this does represent over 50 million Africans who are now spared the daily grind of securing a livelihood from dangerously insufficient resources.

At the heart of this economic uplift has been the international demand for Africa's primary exports. With other developing states, India, Indonesia and Brazil, for example, joining China in the global hunt for raw materials, commodity prices have risen sharply. Africa's minerals and its newly developed oil and gas reserves are in demand. Consequently, the continent's exports have expanded fourfold since the millennium (see Table 12.1). This has been a significant boon to states in terms of their balance of payments.

African economies are also now much more in harmony with the international economy, able to benefit from this demand for raw materials. This has come about as a consequence of two decades of structural adjustment. Although this 'conditionality' brought much hardship to the continent, creating levels of suffering that even the World Bank conceded were too harsh, economies have been modified. African governments had no choice but to liberalise. Today, African currency exchange rates, inflation levels, international trade policies and support for the private sector are in line with the demands of international capitalist markets. It is now easier, and much less risky, for external interests to deal with African states.

This has stimulated foreign investment on the continent. Attracted by profits that can be made on the back of high commodity prices, transnational corporations are doing business on the continent in growing numbers. Africa's direct inward foreign investment measured just US$400 million in 1980. This had risen to US$57 billion by 2013.[6] Indeed, private lending to sub-Saharan Africa overtook bilateral aid payments for the first time in 2006.[7] This was despite foreign governments continuing to give aid to the continent at robust levels, rewarding conditionality compliance.

Another factor explaining the economic upturn is debt relief. African economies are now in a position to benefit from the improved global economy, as they are less burdened by the crippling debts of the past. The 'debt forgiveness' prompted by the 2005 Gleneagles Agreement resulted in sovereign debt among sub-Saharan African countries falling from 55 per cent of GDP in 2000 to 23 per cent by 2013.[8] Whereas before there was unsustainable debt, holding back economic growth, now the public debt of most African states is manageable.

Combined with these economic growth and welfare improvements is a social change that also bodes well for Africa's future. Africa now has a growing middle class. If the World Bank's definition is used (those earning between US$2 and US$20 per day), the continent's middle class has grown to some 350 million people (34 per cent of Africa's population), an increase from 126 million in 1980 (27 per cent of the population).[9] As discussed in the preceding chapter, a strong middle class strengthens the prospects for the consolidation of liberal democracy. These are the individuals most likely to demand the rule of law, freedom of speech and association, government transparency and political accountability.

In such numbers, this 'bourgeoisie' represents a critical mass that is able to defend itself against a predatory state. This is because, importantly, this new middle class is not the bureaucratic bourgeoisie of old. It is a new productive entrepreneurial class. It is a source of power embedded within civil society that does not rely directly on the state for its wealth creation. Africa now has a generation of business people who are versed in international norms of commerce, being politically assertive and technologically astute. They are thriving in liberalised economies, benefiting from the continent's youthful demographic and urbanising societies. Africa's home-grown, and now massive, mobile phone industry is just one example of where this class has excelled. Regarding themselves as stakeholders in the state, and not just passive recipients of government, this civil-society middle class is beginning to keep state elites in check. They demand effective and efficient public policy, not just populist politics. The bureaucratic bourgeoisie has had to adapt to, and accommodate, this new commercial bourgeoisie, and African democracy is stronger as a consequence.

Yet the economic upturn and the growth of the middle class is not a panacea correcting all that is wrong with Africa's political economy. Although the above post-millennium developments are exciting, progress towards levels of economic wealth and standards of democratic politics found in the West is by no means enviable. Africa, after all, has been in this position before. Immediately after independence, commodity prices were high and growth was recorded across the continent. There was, however, no economic take-off at this point, and liberal democracy atrophied. Could history repeat itself? Will there be an economic downturn when commodity prices fall? Will the state become overdeveloped again? Will debt re-emerge?

African states have had previous opportunities to make productive investments utilising income gained from mineral and agricultural exports. Previous chapters in this book have charted how these opportunities were lost. Will the new oil states, such as Ghana, Kenya and Uganda, repeat the mistakes of Nigeria? The danger is that the export of primary produce, not broader manufacturing and service industries, still dominates African economies. Mining and oil industries are outward facing, provide limited local employment, and rely heavily on state intermediaries to regulate foreign intervention.

African economies are diversifying, but most wealth creation is still tied to unpredictable international commodity prices.

The key to whether there will be permanent political and economic benefits as a consequence of this economic upturn largely rests on whether this injection of wealth will improve the quality of state institutions. In this respect, increased efficiency, rather than great strides in political accountability or representation, may be a realistic first goal. Radical democratic gains are unlikely at this juncture. As Asian states, most obviously China, have demonstrated, capitalist expansion can happen within an efficient, but authoritarian, state. Economic progress does not automatically bring simultaneous political benefits. US President Barak Obama, addressing the Ghanaian Parliament in 2009, stated that 'development depends on good governance'.[10] This is an oversimplification. In many cases, political liberalism may follow several decades after economic liberalism (if at all).

A more efficient and less predatory African state, combined with steady (if ultimately unsatisfactorily slow) democratic improvement, may be the best case scenario for the time being. This efficiency, at a minimum, would protect and sustain economic growth. In the past, as previous chapters have shown, most African governments failed to provide basic public goods: political stability, human security and a clear economic direction. There is now an opportunity for the continent's states to reverse this record. The economic upturn has provided politicians with resources that could be invested in political stability. The state could share resources with groups within civil society to create greater social and political cohesion. Such partnerships would also lead to more dynamic economies. Given the history of Africa's overdeveloped states, this distribution of wealth is likely to remain iniquitous, and the state is likely to retain too many resources for itself, but there is an opportunity here to create a more profitable relationship between state and civil society.

The above scenario would not radically alter day-to-day life for most Africans. The impact of these changes for the majority would be conservative. Today, most Africans have comparatively little say in how the state governs in their name. This reality is unlikely to change soon. The scenario described above would be of most benefit to the urban middle classes (both commercial and bureaucratic in nature). This is where any new economic or political dynamism would play itself out, and the fresh relationship between state and civil society would be forged. Yet there would be 'trickle-down' benefits. At a most basic level, the social statistics above show that a rise in GNP does bring better life chances for all. This wealth creation, combined with a less predatory state providing tentative improvements in political representation and accountability, would itself create a degree of political legitimacy.

However, even this modest 'less predatory' scenario may be wishful thinking. Africa's post-colonial history is littered with moments of optimism that failed to bear fruit. Today's talk of 'Africa Rising' may just be a preamble to hopes being dashed once again. For states to become more efficient and less predatory, four key changes need to come about: the continent's politicians do need to deliver at least moderate levels of representation and accountability; the practice of state institutions being used for 'rent seeking' needs to be curbed; there needs to be a greater respect for the electoral processes, protecting channels of constitutional re-legitimisation; and, ultimately, the state needs to deliver its key function of political stability. None of these changes are guaranteed. Given the importance of these necessities for the political future of the continent, it is worth ending this book by considering these four factors in more detail.

Most politicians around the world speak of representing, and being accountable to, their constituents. All states claim to protect their citizens' interests. Yet, in reality, levels of actual representation and accountability often fall far short of assertions made in public speeches. Africa, in particular, has a poor track record in this regard. What, then, are the chances of the continent's political leaders accepting greater levels of accountability and representation in this era of 'Africa Rising'? A brief look at recent intra-African foreign relations provides an illuminating case study that addresses this question. Despite 'good governance' being a key underwriting theme of the continent's international institutions, Africa's leaders have mostly shied away from enforcing these ideals.

The Organisation of African Unity was wound up in 2002 among charges that it was nothing but a talking shop, a gravy train for the diplomats and politicians who attended its conferences. Its successor institutions, the African Union (AU) and the New Partnership for Africa's Development (NEPAD), now attract similar commentary. The AU was meant to be more radical than its predecessor. Its charter makes provision for intervention, against a member state's wishes, 'in respect of grave circumstances'. In other words, should the AU judge one of its number to be abusing human rights, or failing to provide good governance, members will act collectively to rectify the situation. Likewise, the AU seeks to subject member states to peer review, monitoring accountability and representation on the continent. Again, collective sanctions are meant to be triggered should an African state descend into dictatorship.

At the same time as the AU's inauguration, a parallel initiative, the New Partnership for Africa's Development (NEPAD), was launched by key states on the continent. NEPAD aims to bring African states and external partners together to improve the continent's economic and political performance. In an effort to manage their own development strategies, the NEPAD states have pledged to work towards good governance, attempting to attract development aid and foreign investment as a result.

Despite keeping the ideal of pan-African co-operation alive, these two international institutions have yet to deliver consistently. The AU did successfully put pressure on both Laurent Gbagbo in Côte d'Ivoire (in 2010) and Mamadou Tandja in Niger (in 2012), stymieing their (unconstitutional) attempts to cling to power. This organisation also refused to recognise regime change via military coups in Guinea–Bissau and Mali during 2012, and Burkina Faso in 2015. Yet the AU is more often judged by its failure to intervene decisively elsewhere on the continent (with respect to the Darfur conflict in the Sudan, for example, or in post-Gaddafi Libya). Likewise, the AU's charter is contradicted by this organisation's unwillingness to rein in the authoritarian excesses of Robert Mugabe in Zimbabwe, or those of Isaias Afewerki in Eritrea. Nor has the AU been able to disentangle warring factions in the Democratic Republic of the Congo, despite some of these parties being closely associated with its member states.

This does not bode well for a new era of African security and democratic self-regulation. African leaders remain reluctant to hold each other to account. Similarly, the NEPAD project has been criticised for failing to consult sufficiently with civil society, whilst also lacking transparency regarding its secretariat's day-to-day functioning. The 'talking shop' and 'vested interests' criticisms of the Organisation of African Unity (OAU) era have still to be shaken. President Thabo Mbeki of South Africa talked about these institutions heralding an 'African renaissance'.[11] Two decades later, the evidence points more to 'business as usual', with state leaders prioritising their own elite interests on the international stage.

The AU and NEPAD, in microcosm, demonstrate the challenge that lies ahead if accountability and representation are to be taken seriously by African politicians. Whether at home or abroad, state elites need to embrace these norms of liberal democracy. Only with this embrace will the potential of civil society be unlocked. The individual price that politicians may pay for increased accountability is the loss of personal power. Yet with accountability comes efficiency. Sustained economic and political improvement in Africa requires that political leaders listen to their constituents, and meet their collective needs. Political stability rests on civil society working in partnership with the state. The most efficient way for politicians to facilitate this co-operation is for them to represent and be accountable to their constituents. Essentially, the 'Big Man', chief patron, leadership style of old needs to be replaced by more skilled management of civil society's needs and expectations. This is how political cohesion and legitimacy are generated. The best-case 'less predatory' scenario outlined above may not require a full transition to democratic best practice immediately, but it does require that African political leaders improve their performance with respect to these basic tenants of good governance.

One of the reasons why representation and accountability have been in short supply in Africa is because they hinder the ability of individuals to 'rent seek' from their position within the state. Despite years of external conditionality and a more liberal political environment, corruption remains endemic. Officials use state power to promote private interests. The collective public interest is often ignored. In short, the state remains predatory, and its institutions are inefficient as a consequence. Rent seeking, then, is the second factor that may stall economic and political progress in the 'Africa Rising' era.

Since the millennium, there may have been growth of a commercial middle class that is not reliant on the state for its wealth, but this alternative power source has only challenged the bureaucratic bourgeoisie, it has not tamed it. Consequently, only Botswana, Cape Verde, Mauritius and the Seychelles register in the better half of Transparency International's Corruption Perceptions Index.[12] Most Africans still live in states where corruption is part of everyday life. The new state of South Sudan provides a good illustration of this reality. Within a year of gaining its sovereignty, President Salva Kiir had written a letter to 75 of his top officials. In this letter, Kiir accused his colleagues of using their position in the state to steal public assets worth US$4 billion. 'We fought for freedom, justice and equality', the letter reads, 'Yet, once we got to power, we forgot what we fought for and began to enrich ourselves at the expense of our people'.[13] Even a new state, emerging in 2011 into the post-millennium political economy, is burdened by the traditional predatory nature of the African state.

This corruption is a serious threat to, and at odds with, the 'Africa Rising' scenario. The continent's newly found wealth, rather than being diverted into private bank accounts, needs to be of public benefit. Surpluses need to be reinvested in productive assets if economies are to diversify and grow. Likewise, resources can be distributed to civil society groups to promote social and political cohesion. The danger is that state elites will simply see the increased resources as an opportunity to further overdevelop the state and enhance personal wealth. The bloated bureaucracies, inefficient client–patron networks and naked corruption of old need to be avoided this time around. Again, the prerequisite is for the state to make investments in stability and legitimacy.

The third area of institutional efficiency required to consolidate the 'Africa Rising' phenomenon relates to the continent's electoral systems. The fact that most African states have held regular multi-party elections in the last two decades is remarkable. This embracing of electoral politics was swift, and in many cases has been sustained. Although far from mirroring (relatively) efficient elections in the West, these polls are politically meaningful. Foreign observers usually declare these elections to be problematic but 'relatively free and fair'. As a consequence, constitutional regime change has become more regular on the continent. Civil societies periodically have the opportunity to re-legitimise or replace state elites. In addition, these elections provide a method of 'rebooting' politics should the system run into trouble.

When judged against levels of political expression and participation permitted by the state in the 1970s and 1980s, the number and quality of these multi-party polls held on the continent is genuinely impressive. This democratic activity can rightly be considered part of the 'Africa Rising' phenomenon. Yet Africa's democratic gains are brittle. All too often the cycle of electoral politics breaks down. A couple of polls are held, and then a government may find an excuse not to hold the next election, or state power is used to abuse the electoral process. Likewise, opposition groups may become impatient with losing. Starved of power, these politicians may not accept the outcome of a fair poll, and seek to unseat the government by other means.

It is no coincidence that Freedom House, a non-governmental organisation that monitors political rights and civil liberties across the globe, identifies Africa as the continent where democratic gains and setbacks fluctuate the most.[14] There is little consistency. Tunisia, Senegal, Ghana, Benin, Namibia, Botswana, South Africa and Lesotho all registered in Freedom House's top 'free' category of political activity in 2015, yet past events on the continent suggest that any of these countries could fall from democratic grace very quickly. The Central African Republic, Congo (Brazzaville), Côte d'Ivoire, Djibouti, Egypt, Ethiopia, Gabon, The Gambia, Liberia, Libya, Mali, Mauritania, Sierra Leone, Togo and Uganda have all slipped down at least one Freedom House category since the millennium, while the more spectacular political unravelling of Mali (2013), Kenya (2007–08) and Zimbabwe (2000 to the present) demonstrates that representative political systems are vulnerable across the continent (see Table 12.3). For many Africans, it is a case of two steps forward and one step back. Political stability is lost, and economic development is deferred as a consequence. The progressive scenario painted above, even in its limited form, will only occur when the first ports of call for conflict

Table 12.3 Freedom House's categorisation of political rights and civil liberties in sub-Saharan Africa, 1989–2015

	Free		*Partly free*		*Not free*	
	Number of countries	*Percentage*	*Number of countries*	*Percentage*	*Number of countries*	*Percentage*
2015	10	20	18	37	21	43
2010	9	19	23	48	16	33
2005	11	23	21	44	16	33
2000–01	9	19	24	50	15	31
1995–96	9	19	19	39	20	42
1989–90	3	6	11	24	33	70

Source: Freedom House data available at https://freedomhouse.org/report-types/freedom-world#.VeQX-V6FPcs (accessed 31 August 2015).

resolution are democratic institutions. If these institutions are only considered to be one weapon in a wider political armoury available to those competing for power, with resort to unconstitutional measures being just as viable, then even this modest 'less predatory' future will prove unattainable.

The fourth factor required to sustain the 'Africa Rising' era is political stability itself. Today, Africa is generating unprecedented wealth, but peace in many states remains fragile. Inefficient institutions are often not providing the basic public good of security. Sources of conflict are multiple. There is frequently a complex combination of inter-state, ethno-regional, religious and criminal motivations at the heart of this violence, but the common denominator is the state's inability to manage these conflicts. More efficient state institutions and more inclusive politics would go a long way towards pro-viding peaceful channels of conflict resolution, addressing grievances at source. Again, it is a case of states needing to offer their civil societies levels of legitimacy that make citizens stakeholders in government, not its enemies. The episodic violence experienced during the last 15 years in Burundi, the Central African Republic, Chad, Comoros, Côte d'Ivoire, the Democratic Republic of the Congo, Djibouti, Egypt, Guinea, Kenya, Libya, Mali, Niger, Mozambique, Nigeria, Somalia, South Sudan, the Sudan and Zimbabwe all demonstrate that violence is still part and parcel of political interaction in too many parts of the continent. No state will prosper if it is at war with itself or others.

It can be seen, then, that since the millennium, Africa's economic successes have been running ahead of the continent's political development. The global demand for raw materi-als has provided considerable wealth for many in Africa's middle classes. Increased resources have created economic and political space for both a bureaucratic and a commercial bour-geoisie to prosper. The co-operation and competition between these two groups have given a new dynamism to the continent's politics. Yet the four factors outlined above demon-strate that political stability on the continent remains fragile. The state, despite its new wealth, is still struggling to perform its basic tasks of representation, underwriting the rule of law and projecting political authority into all parts of its territory. The pursuit of private interest and, ultimately, criminal and political violence is all too often the consequence of this inefficiency. In this respect, now as before, the primary relationship explored through-out this book remains key. The maximisation of the continent's economic and political potential will only be realised when state and civil society are engaged productively.

Further reading

The following two books are good examples of the new, more optimistic literature exploring the African continent's prospects. Both of these volumes predict a better African political economy for the future, but all of the authors concerned are careful to highlight the associated challenges that lie ahead.

Severino, Jean-Michel and Olivier Ray. *Africa's Moment*. Cambridge: Polity, 2011.
Rotberg, Robert I. *Africa Emerges*. Cambridge: Polity, 2013.

Notes and references

1 Callaghy, Thomas M. Politics and vision in Africa: the interplay of equality and liberty. In: Patrick Chabal, ed. *Political Domination in Africa*. Cambridge: Cambridge University Press, 1986. 36.

2 Severino, Jean-Michel and Olivier Ray. *Africa's Moment*. Cambridge: Polity, 2011. 77.
3 Ayittey, George. *Africa Unchained: The Blueprint for Africa's Future*. New York: Palgrave Macmillan, 2006.
4 African Development Bank. *Tracking Africa's Progress in Figures*. Tunis: African Development Bank, 2014. 21.
5 *Ibid*. 2.
6 United Nations Conference on Trade and Development. *UNCTAD Handbook of Statistics 2014*. New York: United Nations, 2014. Table 7.2.
7 Severino and Ray. *Africa's Moment*. 95.
8 External debt, total (percent of GDP). International Monetary Fund. *World Economic Outlook Database April 2015*. www.imf.org/external/pubs/ft/weo/2015/01/weodata/weorept. aspx?sy=1995&ey=2013&scsm=1&ssd=1&sort=country&ds=.&br=1&c=603&s=D_ NGDPD&grp=1&a=1&pr.x=53&pr.y=13 (accessed 17 August 2015).
9 African Development Bank. *Tracking Africa's Progress in Figures*. 2014. 24.
10 President Barak Obama's address before the Ghanaian Parliament, Accra, 11 July 2009. www.whitehouse.gov/the-press-office/remarks-president-ghanaian-parliament (accessed 30 July 2015).
11 Thabo Mbeki first popularised the phrase 'African renaissance' in a public statement, as deputy president, broadcast by the South African Broadcasting Corporation on 13 August 1998.
12 Transparency International. *Corruption Perceptions Index 2014*. Berlin: Transparency International, 2014.
13 Smith, David. South Sudan president accuses officials of stealing $4bn of public money. *The Guardian* (London). 5 June 2012. www.theguardian.com/world/2012/jun/05/south-sudan-president-accuses-officials-stealing (accessed 13 August 2015).
14 Freedom House. *Freedom in the World 2015*. Washington, DC: Freedom House, 2015. 5.

Index

Page numbers in **bold** refer to tables

Abiola, Moshood 78
accumulation, crisis of 214–218, 219, 221,
   222, 227, 244; definition of 237; in Zaire
   230–33
Afewerki, Isaias 280
AFDL (Alliance des Forces Démocratiques
   pour la Liberation du Congo-Zaire) 235
AFRC (Armed Forces Ruling Council),
   Nigeria 77–8
Africa Contemporary Record 123
African National Congress of South Africa
   (ANC) 94, 155, 162, 171, 245
African socialism *see* socialism, African
African Union (AU) 153, 165, 178, 280–1
'Africa renaissance' 280
'Africa Rising' 276–283; and 'debt
   forgiveness' 278; and economic growth
   276; and foreign investment 277–8;
   social impact of 276–277; and political
   accountability 281–3
agriculture: decline in crop yields 53, 193,
   203, 203–4, 204–205, 215, 230–1, 265;
   and structural adjustment programmes
   191, 193, 205, 206; *see also* monocrop
aid: to Botswana 102; from China 169;
   decline of at end of Cold War 169–70;
   275; from France 159, 164–5; and
   NEPAD 280; political conditions tied
   to external 162–4, 172, 177–8, 246;
   and Scandinavian countries 159, 164; to
   Somalia 174–5, 176; from Soviet Union
   154–5, 161; from the United Kingdom
   164, 165–7; from United States 156,
   164; to Zaire 234; *see also* debt; structural
   adjustment programmes
Aidid, Mohammed Farrah 177
Ake, Claude 254, 269
Alagiah, George 2

al-Bashir, Omar 170
Al-Qaeda 71
Al-Qaida au Maghreb Islamique 71
Algeria 14, 19, 32, 46, 165, 168, 221–2,
   248, 255; Islamist politics in 70–1, 72,
   135–6, 255
Alliance for Democracy, Malawi 250
Alliance des Forces Démocratiques pour a
   Liberation du Congo-Zaire (AFDL) 235
Alliance pour la Democratic au Mali 250
Al-Shabab 71
Amin Dada, Idi 46, 118; military coup and
   regime of 143–8; *see also* Uganda
Amuwo, Kunle 141
ANC (African National Congress of South
   Africa) 94, 155, 162, 171, 245
Anderson, Benedict 35
Angola 11, 47, 153, 156, 159, 168, 172,
   221, 222, 224; Cabinda 13; civil war in
   153, 161, 162; and China 168, 169; and
   Cuba 155, 162; independence of 32, 39;
   multi-party elections (1992) in 256; and
   Soviet Union 154–5, 155
Aouzou Strip 46
Armed Forces Ruling Council (AFRC),
   Nigeria 77–8
arms, shipments of 162, 169; during Cold
   War to Africa, 154–5, 155, 161, 176,
Arusha Declaration (1967) 51, 52
Ashanti 8, 110
'Asian Tigers' 188
Aswan High Dam 154
AU (African Union) 153, 165, 178, 280–1
Ayittey, George 276
Azarya, Victor 225

Babangida, Ibrahim 77–8
Bakary, Tessilimi 124

Ball, George 134
Banda, Hastings 37, 69, 116, 246, 247, 250; *see also* Malawi
banditry 221, 222, 227
Barré, Mohamed Siad 39, 163, 174–7, 224; *see also* Somalia
Bates, Robert 63, 74
Bayart, Jean-François 98, 99, 226, 234
BDP (Botswana Democratic Party) 101, 103
Bechuanaland 100, 102
Bèdié, Henri Konan 125–6
Belgian Congo 11, 13, 46, 90, 229, 230
Benin 40, 132, 169, 238n, 253, 282; ancient 8
Berg Report (1981) 191, 192
Berlin Conference (1884–5) 11, 13
Biafra 46, 76
Biya, Paul 116, 164, 252
black market *see* parallel markets
Blair, Tony 166
Bokassa, Jean-Bédel 117, 118, 138
Boko Haram 71, 79–80
Bongo, Omar 117, 246, 252
borders 9, 10, 254, 273; acceptance and endurance of colonial 36, 45–6; arbitrary nature of 12–14; consequences of colonial 13–14; drawing of colonial 12–13, 23; and irredentism 14, 46, 153; Kenya's 23; and nationalist ideology 36, 46–7; 'porous' nature of 221; OAU's agreement on (1964) 45–6, 152; and sovereignty 152, 153
Botchway, Kwesi 205
Botswana 3, 100–4; democratic government in 102, 240, 249, 253, 256, 281, 282; economic growth of 100; labour market in 102; 'peasantariat' in 102; public opinion on multi-party democracy 256; and social class 100–4; and wealth, distribution of 103
Botswana Democratic Party (BDP) 101, 103
boundaries *see* borders
bourgeoisie 38, 85–6, 88, 96, 98, 112–3, 251, 274, 278; bureaucratic 16, 25, 52, 92–4, 99, 101–3, 137–8, 140, 141, 142, 278, 281, 283; commercial 91–2, 283; international 95–6, 151
Bourguiba, Habib 116
breakthrough coups 136, 141, 142
Brett, E.A. 144
Britain *see* United Kingdom
British Aerospace 217
British East Africa Company 23, 143
Brown, Gordon 166

Buganda 8, 143–5
Buhari, Muhammadu 77
bureaucratic authoritarianism 21, 26, 27, 273; *see also* bureaucratic autocracy
bureaucratic autocracy 27; definition of 28; *see also* bureaucratic authoritarianism
bureaucratic bourgeoisie 16, 25, 52, 92–4, 99, 101–3, 137–8, 140, 141, 142, 278, 281, 283
Burkina Faso 14, 42, 43, 252, 253, 280
Burundi 14, 158, 253, 255, 283
Bush (Snr.), George 161, 177

Cabinda 13
Cabral, Amílcar 48
Cameron, David 167
Cameroon 11, 43, 110, 116, 252; Boko Haram in 71, 80; bureaucratic bourgeoisie in 93; ethnic groups in 62; French aid to 164; trade with China 167
Cape Town 11
Cape Verde 132, 253, 281
Caprivi, Count von 13
Caprivi Strip 13
Carter, Jimmy 176
cash crops 18, 24, 43, 90–1, 193, 208, 215, 222; definition of 28
Central African Republic 283; Bokassa's regime 115, 117, 118, 138; and China 168; and donor pressure 246; and France 138, 159, 165; Freedom House categorisation 282; military coups in 138, 159, 255
Central Intelligence Agency (CIA) 138, 161, 163
centralisation of the state 39, 109–115, 274; and civil society–state relationship 48, 121; in Côte d'Ivoire 122–5; and crisis of legitimacy 219; definition of 126; in Ghana 111, 204 ; and one-party state 111–13; in Kenya 25–7; and populist regimes 42–3; and 'quasi-states' 172; and subordination of 'peripheral' state institutions to the core executive 113–15; in Uganda 143–4, in Zaire 231–2; Zimbabwe 260–2
Ceuta 11, 32
CFA (Communauté Financiére Africaine) franc 159, 164
Chabal, Patrick 217
Chad 13, 47, 71, 153, 163, 222, 252, 283; and France 159, 165; and Aouzou Strip 46; opposition movements in 249

charisma, and political legitimacy 108–9, 118
Chazan, Naomi 220, 225, 227
chiefs *see* traditional leaders
Chiluba, Frederick: leading campaigner for
    multi-party democracy 247; corruption
    charges 251; manipulation of Zambia's
    constitution 252; *see also* Zambia
China 90, 161; Africa policy during 'New
    World Order' 167–70; Africa policy
    during Cold War 155–6; amoral stance on
    aid 168, 170; 'neo-colonialism', charges
    of 169; resource driven policy 167–8; and
    Somalia 174, 176; and Sudan 169–70; and
    Zimbabwe 170
Chiona, James 247
Christianity 3, 47; in Ethiopia 12, 67;
    spread of in Africa 11, 67
Churches 4, 66; force within anti-authoritarian
    campaigns 68–9, 247, 251; political
    influence in Malawi 69, 247; political
    influence in South Africa 68–9, 247
CIA (Central Intelligence Agency) 138,
    161, 163
civil society: and clientelism 121; and
    consolidation of multi-party democracy
    246–7, 263; co-optation by state 37,
    110; competition with African state 4–5,
    21, 73, 109–11, 112–5, 121, 172, 202,
    222–5, 232–3, 246–7, 250–1; 258–9,
    272–283; definition of 6; definition of
    4–5, 6; disengagement of 219–224,
    227–9, 232–3; ethnic groups within, and
    their relative power 64–6; force behind
    wave of multi-party elections 247–8,
    250–1, 258–9; and military governments
    42–3, 139–40, 141–2; and nationalism
    48; and populist governments 42–3; late
    1980s and 1990s rejuvenation of 246–7;
    religious groups within, and their relative
    freedom 66–9; and state centralisation
    109–11, 112–3; and structural
    adjustment programmes 202; weak links
    to colonial state 14–15; within client–
    patron networks 119, 120–1
Clapham, Christopher 116, 119, 137–8, 158
class, social 84–107; Botswana case study
    100–4; bureaucratic bourgeoisie 15–16,
    25, 52, 92–4, 99, 101, 138, 142, 274,
    278, 281; commercial bourgeoisie
    91–2; *compradors* 95–6, 101; informal
    sector entrepreneurs 94–5; international
    bourgeoisie 95–6; lumpenproletariat

94–5; Marx on 85–6; modes of production
    85–6, 87–8, 90; 'peasantariat' 90–1,
    102, 103; peasantry 18, 25, 41, 49–50,
    52–4, 87, 89–91, 265; problems with
    Marx's interpretation of in Africa 41,
    86–7; proletariat 38, 85–6, 91, 102;
    and relationship between state and civil
    society 99–100; social groups within
    society 89–96; traditional leaders 15, 65,
    89, 94, 99, 100–1, 111, 123; value of in
    explaining African politics 96–99
clientelism 54, 77, 109, 116, 119–20, 121,
    130, 139–40, 141, 142, 204, 216–7,
    218, 274–5; definition of 126; shrinking
    195–6, 206–7, 225, 226, 227, 263–4;
    in Côte d'Ivoire 124–5; in Zaire 233; in
    Zimbabwe 263–4, 265
client–patron networks *see* clientelism
coercion 118, 130–1, 253; state's diminishing
    powers of 245, in Zimbabwe 266
Cold War 154–161; British policy during
    158; Chinese policy during 155–6; Cuban
    policy during 155; French policy during
    158–9; impact of on African politics
    159–61; Somalia's external relations
    during 173–6; Soviet Union policy during
    154–5; United States policy during 156–8
colonialism 10–11; and bureaucratic
    authoritarianism 21, 26, 27, 273; and
    creation of state elite 15–16, 93, 101;
    emergence of 'tribes' during 60–3, 74–5;
    establishment of European rule 10–11;
    and forced labour 18, 90; formation of
    states during 11–12; and imposition
    of arbitrary boundaries 12–14, 23–4;
    reinforcing the non-hegemonic state
    14; underdevelopment during 16–19;
    and weak political institutions 20;
    underwriting weakness
    of links between state and society 14–15;
    see also decolonisation
commercial bourgeoisie 91–2
Communist Manifesto (Marx and Engels) 84, 105
Communauté Financiére Africaine (CFA)
    franc 159, 164
Comoros Islands 32, 283
comprador class 95–6, 101
conditions attached to foreign aid 163–4,
    172, 190–2, 196–201, 202, 246, 275,
    277, 281; *see also* structural adjustment
    programmes
Congo-Brazzaville 39, 168, 216, 254, 254

Congo-Kinshasa 3, 46, 47, 92, 116, 153, 229; *see also* Democratic Republic of Congo; Zaire
Convention People's Party (CPP), Ghana 110–11
corruption 26, 42, 93, 113, 191, 216–7, 251, 281; in Botswana 103; in Nigeria 77, 78, 79; response of military regimes to 76–7, 134, 135, 139, 142; and structural adjustment programmes 195; in Somalia 174; in Zaire 230–5; in Zambia 251
Côte d'Ivoire ; centralised state 122–5; economic policy and performance 43, 124, 187; ethnic balancing within 65; and France 19, 122, 158, 159, 164; independence of 122; one-party state in 111, 123–4; patron–client networks in 124–5; personal rule in 116–7, 122–126; rebellion (2002) 125–6, 280, 283, 169; return to multi-party politics 125–6, 249, 250; trade 19, 187, 204; *see also* Houphouët-Boigny, Félix
coups *see* military coups
courts: executive's domination of 111, 115, 124
CPP (Convention People's Party), Ghana 110–11
Crigler, T. Frank 177
crisis of accumulation 214–218, 219, 221, 222, 227, 244; definition of 237; in Zaire 230–33
crisis of governance 218–19; in Zaire 231–232
Cuba, relations with Africa 155, 162, 176

Darfur 169–70, 280; *also see* Sudan
Daloz, Jean-Pascal 217
de Gaulle, Charles 131, 158
De Beers 101
debt: British position on 166–7; crisis, origins of 188–90; Ghana and 189, 206, 207; Multilateral Debt Relief Initiative (MDRI) for Heavily Indebted Poor Countries (HIPC) 196–202, 207; relief of, international policies 166–7, 196–202, 278; relief of and political conditions 171–2, 209; Zambia's crisis of 189–90; Zaire and 232; Zimbabwe and 262
decolonisation 32–34; constitutional reforms immediately prior to 20, 25, 75, 114; nationalist campaigns bringing 16, 20, 25, 36, 93, 94, 101, 112, 123; legitimacy generated by 21; elections at the point of 20, 110, 112, 114; Zimbabwe's 259

democracy 51, 240–268; aid conditionality in support of 163–4, 245–6; in Angola 256; in Botswana 100–03, 260; and civil society–state relationship 258–9; development of in late 1980s and 1990s 240–2; in Côte d'Ivoire 125; and ethnic groups 66, 254; in the Gambia 138, 253, 255, 282; in Ghana 111, 207, 242; independence elections 20, 110, 112, 114; Islam and 70; in Kenya 26–7, 245; and military regimes 42, 140–1, 254–5; in Malawi 69, 247, 252, 253; nature of 242–3; need for credible opposition 249–50; need for strong civil society 250–1; need for suitable political culture 255–8; need for strong economy 251–2; need to separate state and ruling party 252–4; obstacles to consolidation of 248–57; and one-party state 112; reasons for emergence of multi-party 244–8; in Tanzania 54, 242–3, 253; in Uganda 253; in Zambia 247, 250, 252, 253; in Zimbabwe 264–6; *see also* centralisation of state
Democratic Republic of the Congo (DRC) 173; Mobutu ousted 235; regional conflict in 46, 153, 156, 168, 222, 224, 229–30, 235–6; *see also* Congo-Kinshasa; Zaire
Denise, Auguste 125
Denmark 167
dependency theorists *see* underdevelopment
diamonds: and Botswana's economy 100, 102; sustaining insurgent movements 224; and conflict in the Democratic Republic of Congo 236
disengagement: from the state 219–25, 227–9, 232–4, 275
Djibouti 32, 46, 159, 173, 248, 282, 283
Doe, Samuel 163
DRC *see* Democratic Republic of the Congo
Dumont, René 93

Economic Community of West African States (ECOWAS) 126, 153
Egypt 67, 70–1, 135, 248, 255, 282, 283; ancient 8; and Cold War patronage 154, 176; Islamist militants in 70
Eisenhower, Dwight 131
Eluki, Ahundu 231
emigration: disengagement through 219
Engels, Friedrich 38, 39, 84, 85
entrepreneurs 43, 91, 220, 221, informal sector 94–5

Equatorial Guinea 115, 118, 132, 168, 253–4
Eritrea 11, 46, 47, 222, 224, 280
Eritrean People's Liberation Front (EPLF)
  46, 47
Ethiopia 3, 11, 193, 222, 282; border
  clash with Eritrea; and China 168; and
  Christianity 11, 67; and Cuba 155;
  deposition of Selassie 136; Eritrea's
  secession from 45, 47; and feudalism 87;
  Marxist–Leninist 'revolution' 40–1, 136,
  141; Mengistu, fall of 47, 153–4; military
  coup (1974) 39, 141; and Soviet Union
  154, 155, 162, 175; war with Somalia 14,
  46, 173, 175–6, 178; and United States
  156, 175
Ethiopian People's Revolutionary
  Democratic Front 222
ethnicity 59–66, 273; as agent of political
  mobilisation 48, 75–77, 98; and colonial
  boundaries 14; creation of 'tribes' 60–3;
  definition 60; 'ethnic balancing' 64–6,
  140, 196, 216; instrumentalism as an
  explanation of 62–3; in Kenya 22; lineage
  10; and multi-party democracy 174, 254;
  and nationalism 36–7, 111; and Nigeria
  74–7; primordialism as an explanation of
  60–1; and state and civil society 73; in
  Tanzania 49
European Community 176
European Union (EU) 59, 152, 163, 164,
Executive Outcomes (EO) 227
exit strategies *see* disengagement

famine: in Sudan (1988) 2; in Somalia
  (1992) 177
Fanon, Frantz 123
Fatton, Robert 228, 256
FAZA (*Force Aérienne Zairoise* – Zairian air
  force) 234–5
feudalism 86, 87
Finer, S.E. 136–7
First, Ruth 136
FIS (*Front Islamique de Salut*), in Algeria 70, 165
food subsidies, removal of: in Ghana 204,
  206–7; removal of state 194–5, 196; in
  Zambia 189, 195; in Zimbabwe 262, 263
foreign investment 41, 43; and 'Africa
  Rising' phenomenon 277–8; Chinese 168;
  De Beers in Botswana 101; in Ghana 206;
  and NEPAD 280; and state capitalist
  regimes 43; and structural adjustment
  programmes 193, 206, in Zaire 230

Forrest, Joshua 225
FPI (*Front Populaire Ivoirien*) 250
France 11; Africa policy during Cold War 154,
  158–9; Africa policy during New World
  Order 126, 164–5; and Algeria 32; aid,
  provision of 159, 164; and colonisation
  of Africa 11; and decolonisation 32; and
  military coups 159; military intervention
  in Arica 71, 138, 165; military relations
  with Africa 71, 159; and Rwanda 71, 165;
  and Somalia 176; and Zaire 165
Franco-African summit (1982) 158
Freedom House 282
Frente Popular para la Liberacion de Saguia
  el Hamra y Rio de Oro (POLISARIO) 159
Front Islamique du Salut (FIS), Algeria 70, 165
Front Populaire Ivoirien (FPI) 250
Fulani-Hausa 76, 75
Fulbe 62–3

Gabon 43, 117, 138, 159, 167, 168, 246,
  252, 282
Gaddafi, Muammar 42, 167, 170, 280; *see
  also* Libya
Gambia, The 3, 13, 241, 282; election
  (1996) 253; military coup (1994) 138
Gbagbo, Laurent 126, 250, 280
George, Susan 190
Germany 36, 159, 161, 176, 247; and
  colonisation 11, 13; democracy and the
  Third Reich 251–2; loss of colonies 13
Ghana 62, 91, 154, 253, 278, 282; ancient 8;
  cocoa production 18, 136, 189, 203, 204,
  221; and debt 206, 207; defence spending
  140, 174; centralisation of state in 110–11;
  economic decline and reasons for 204–5;
  military coups in 134, 136, 140, 204;
  multi-party politics, return to (1990s) 140,
  207; and Peoples' Defence Committees
  (PDCs) 42; populist governance of 42;
  Rawlings regime 42, 204–7; smuggling
  of cocoa crop 189, 204; and structural
  adjustment 205–6; trade 19; and United
  Kingdom 166; and United States 172
Gitonga, Afrifa 252
Gleneagles Agreement 196, 207, 278
Glickman, Harvey 254
Great Britain *see* United Kingdom
guardian coups 135, 137, 140–1; definition
  of 148
guerrilla movements 32, 36, 39, 47, 48,
  219, 221–2, 224, in Zimbabwe 263–4

Guinea 32, 111, 168, 252, 283; decolonisation 32, 154; selling of coffee in parallel markets 221; and Soviet Union 154

Guinea-Bissau 11, 19, 30n, 32, 48, 153, 221, 280

Habré, Hissène 163
Hausa-Fulani 74–6
Health care: in Botswana 103; improvement under colonialism 19; decline in 1980s 218, 236; in Nigeria 79; and structural adjustment policies 206, 262–3, in Tanzania 52, 54; and United Kingdom policy 166; in Zaire 236, in Zambia 189; in Zimbabwe 262–3
Heavily Indebted Poor Countries (HIPC) *see* Multilateral Debt Relief Initiative (MDRI)
hegemonial exchange model 64–6, 77; definition of 81
HIPC (Heavily Indebted Poor Countries) *see* Multilateral Debt Relief Initiative (MDRI)
Hobbes, Thomas 137
Hobsbawm, Eric 220
Horowitz, Donald 46
Houphouët-Boigny, Félix 65, 116–7; at apex of patron–client network 124–5; architect of one-party state and state centralisation 111, 122–5; death of 125, 164; deputy in French parliament 158; and electoral campaign of 1990 125, 250; ostentatious spending 116–7; and personal rule 122–5; *see also* Côte d'Ivoire
hudud crimes 78–9; definition of 81
Huntington, Samuel: analysis of military coups 136, 137; assessment of democratic consolidation 249
Hurd, Douglas 164
Hutu 61
Hyden, Goran 53, 114

Ibo 74, 75, 76
IFIs (international financial institutions): and Ghana 207–8; and structural adjustment programmes 42, 190–6; and Tanzania 54; usurping sovereignty of African states 201; *see also* IMF; World Bank
IMF (International Monetary Fund) 190, 202, 263; Africa policy, China's challenge to 169; and food subsidies in Liberia

195; and Multilateral Debt Relief Initiative 167, 196; *see also* World Bank; international financial institutions
imperialism *see* colonialism
import substitution 188, 191, 193, 196, 203, 215, 217; in Ghana 203, 206; in Zaire 230; in Zambia 189
independence *see* decolonisation
informal sector entrepreneurs 94–5
Inga-Shaba power scheme 230
insurgency campaigns 32, 71, 78, 80, 147, 155, 165, 173, 175, 221–2, 224, 235, 256, 275
international bourgeoisie 95–6
international financial institutions (IFIs): and Ghana 207–8; and structural adjustment programmes 42, 190–6; and Tanzania 54; usurping sovereignty of African states 201; *see also* IMF; World Bank
International Labour Organisation 102
International Monetary Fund (IMF): 190, 202, 263; Africa policy, China's challenge to 169; and food subsidies in Liberia 195; and Multilateral Debt Relief Initiative 167, 196; *see also* World Bank; international financial institutions
inverted states 109, 225, 226, 227, 229, 244, 275
irredentism 14, 46, 153; *see also* Somalia
Islam 10–11, 62–3; *hudud* crimes 78–9; *jihad* 69; spread of 67; the *shari'a* 69–70
Islamic State 71
islamist politics: in Africa 69–71; in Algeria 70, 71–2; 135, 165; and the 'Arab Spring' 70–1; blended with populism in Libya 42; objectives of 70–1; in Mali 71, 72; in Nigeria 71, 78–80; in Somalia 70, 71; terrorist groups 70–1; *see also* Al-Qaeda; *Al-Qaïda au Maghreb Islamique*; Al-Shabab; Boko Haram
Italy 36, 230; colonisation 11; and Somalia 23, 173, 174, 176,

Jackson, Robert 116, 117, 118, 124, 172
Jammeh, Yara 253
Janowitz, Morris 136, 137
Japan 159
Jawara, Dawda 138
jihad 69, 70, 80
Jowitt, Kenneth 41
judiciary: executive's domination of 111, 115, 124

Kabaka Yekka party 143–4
Kabaka, of Buganda 143–4
Kabanga, Archbishop 231
Kabila, Laurent Désiré 235
Kaiser, Paul 52
KANU (Kenya African National Union):
and centralisation of state 25–6; internal
competition for candidate selection 113–4;
and multi-party democracy 26–7, 250
Kariuki, J.M. 114
Karl-i-Bond, Nguza 256
Katanga 46, 156, 229
Kaunda, Kenneth 37, 116, 242, 247, 250,
274; exclusion from election (1996) 252
Keita, Modibo 138
Kenya 14, 65, 135, 145, 167–8, 178, 190,
221, 253, 254, 278, 282, 283; aid and
suspension of (1990s) 164, 246; and Al-
Shabab 71; army mutinies (1964) 158;
British colonialism 23–4; centralisation
of state 26–7; colonial boundaries
23–4; and corruption 217; decolonisation
24–5; divided opposition in 1990s 250;
economy 24, 43, 216; electoral violence
(2007) 256–7; ethnic make-up 22;
historical inheritance 22–27; Mau Mau
uprisings 24–5; multi-party competition,
return to 27, 164; as one-party state 25–7,
113–4; as an overdeveloped state 216;
nationalist elite 25; nature of parliament
113–4, 242; relationship with Somalia
14, 23–4, 46, 173; victim of terrorism
70, 71, 163
Kenya African National Union (KANU):
and centralisation of state 25–7;
competition for candidate selection
113–4; and multi-party democracy 27
Kenya People's Union 26
Kenyatta, Jomo 25, 26, 65, 116–7; and
Kariuki 114
Kérékou, Lieutenant-Colonel Mathieu 39
Khama III Boikanyo 101
Khama, Seretse 101
Khomeini, (Ayatollah) Sayed Ruhollah
Mousavi 70
Kikuyu 22, 24
Kirdi 62–3
Kiir, Salva 281
kleptocratic state 219, 232
Kofele-Kale, Ndiva 93
Kolingba, André 246
Kufuor, John 207

Laakso, Liisa 249
labour 196; in Botswana 102, 103;
exploitation of by West 17–18, 24; in
Marxist theory 85, 90–1; migrant 90–1,
102, 103; 'peasantariat' 90–1, 102, 103;
role in multi-party democracy campaign
247, 264; *see also* trade unions
Lamb, David 19
Lancaster House agreement 259, 262, 264
League of Nations 11
Lefebvre, Jeffery 162
legal–rational legitimacy 108, 109, 115,
116, 117, 124, 137, 216, 217, 218, 226
legitimacy: and political authority 130–1;
charismatic 108–9, 118, colonial state
and 20–1; crisis of 137, 214–19, 233;
definition of 108; and hegemonial
exchange 64, 77; ideology and 31;
independence elections generating 21;
legal–rational 108, 109, 115, 116, 117,
124, 137, 216, 217, 218, 226; and
military regimes 42, 137, 219; neo-
patrimonialisation/client–patron networks
generating 54, 119–20, 121, 124–5, 232,
274–5; re-legitimisation of state 246–7,
275; traditional 108; Weber's sources of
108–9
Léopold of Belgium, King 11, 13, 38
Lesotho 3, 14, 172, 218, 282
Leys, Colin 90, 114
Liberia 11, 138, 153, 163, 196, 222, 224,
227, 244, 282
Libya 11, 32, 70, 153, 167, 248, 280, 282,
283; conflict with Chad over Aouzou
Strip 46, 159; populist regime 42; and
Zimbabwe 170
life expectancy 19, 185, 277
Lincoln, Abraham 242
lineage 10, 36, 62, 67, 74; and modes of
production 87–8; *see also* ethnicity
Lissouba, Pascal 254
local government 111, 114–15, 124, 218,
274
Lomé Convention 163
Luling, Virginia 220
Lumumba, Patrice 156
lumpenproletariat 95–6
Luxembourg 167

Masai 22
Machel, Samora 37, 41
Machiavelli, Niccoló 115

Madagascar: and China 168; and France 165; Marxist–Leninist regime 40; military and regime change (2009) 255

Magendo see parallel markets

Majetein Somali Salvation Democratic Front 177

Major, John 166

Malawi 37, 43, 116, 250, 252, 254; constitution, manipulation of 253; donor pressure 246; economy 186, 190; political influence of church 69, 247; and structural adjustment programmes 196

Mali 71, 250, 253, 282, 283; ancient 8; coup (1968) 138; coup (2013) 280; Islamist activity in 71, 72; relations with China 169, relations with France 165; relations with the Soviet Union 154

Maluku steel mill 230

Mandela, Nelson 94, 242, 247, 253

Marcel Dassault Preguet 217

marketing boards 39, 204, 215, 220, 230, 232

Marx, Karl 38, 39, 41, 51, 84, 88–9; on feudalism 87; and lumpenproletariat 94; on social class 85–6

Marxism 245–6; classical class analysis 85–6; and the African mode of production 87–8; neo-Marxist class analysis 88–9, 92–3; problems with using Marxist analysis in Africa 38, 39, 50–1, 86–7, 96–8, 99, 101

Marxism–Leninist regimes 39–42, 155, 174, 175

Mau Mau uprisings 24–5

Mauritania 46, 70, 159, 183, 248, 282

Mauritius 135, 190, 241, 281

M'ba, Léon 138, 159

Mbeki, Thabo 240, 280

Mboya, Tom 86–7

MDC (Movement for Democratic Change), Zimbabwe 264, 265, 266–7

MDRI (Multilateral Debt Relief Initiative) 202

Melilla 32

Mengistu, Haile Mariam 40–1, 47, 141, 162, 175

middle class 251, 278, 281, 283

military: as threat of to consolidation of democracy 254–5

military aid: during Cold War to Africa 154–5, 161, 162, 169, 170, 174–5, 175, 176

military coups 3, 26, 32, 98, 113, 116, 130–48; and the African Union 280; 'breakthrough' 136, 141, 142; categories of 135–6; and civil society–state relationship 140–1; and counter-coups 139, 140; definition 132; 'guardian' 135, 137, 140–1; foreign intervention, role of 138; nature of 132–5; reasons for 135–8; personal rule as a precipitant 117; and populist governments 42; Portuguese 32, 39; and regime change 132, 134, 135–6, 137, 255; Uganda case study 143–8; veto coups 135–6

military rule: outcomes of 140–1; problems facing 138–40

missionaries 11, 67; and Yoruba language 75

Mistry, Percy 193

Mitterrand, François 164

MMD (Movement for Multi-Party Democracy), Zambia 247, 250, 252

Mobutu Sese Seko (Joseph Désiré) 37, 116, 161, 165, 172, 274; corruption 231; downfall and ousting of 235, 246; leadership style of 118, 229–233; relationship with France 165; relationship with United States 156, 161, 163; *see also* Congo-Kinshasa; Zaire

modes of production: African 87–8; articulation of 90; classical Marxist definition of 85–6

Moi, Daniel arap 114, 116, 253, 274; accession to power 26; and corruption 217, 253; donor pressure on, to institute reforms 27, 164, 246; exploitation of divided opposition (1990s) 250; regime of 26–7; *see also* Kenya

Montesquieu, Baron de 115

Morocco 43, 70, 135; borders, rejection of colonial 45, 46; colonisation 11; independence 32; occupation of Western Sahara 46, 156; relations with United States 156, 245; religion and government in 67, 70

Moss, Todd 266

Movement for Multi-Party Democracy (MMD), Zambia 247, 250, 252

Movement for Democratic Change (MDC), Zimbabwe 267, 268, 269, 270

Movimento Popular de Libertação de Angola (MPLA) 39, 161, 162, 172, 222, 256

Mozambique 253, 283; colonisation 11; independence 32, 90; forced labour during colonial era 18, 90; and scientific socialism 39, 41; and Soviet Union 154–5; insurgency in 221–2

MPLA (Movimento Popular de Libertação de Angola) 39, 161, 162, 172, 222, 256
Mugabe, Robert 92, 117, 259; and China 170; centralisation of the state 261–2; corruption 217; and multi-party democracy 249; personal rule 263; relationship with IMF 263; strategy to retain power 260–7; *see also* Zimbabwe
Multilateral Debt Relief Initiative (MDRI) 202
multi-party elections *see* democracy
Munslow, Barry 41
Museveni, Yoweri 147, 224, 252; intimidation during electoral campaign (2006) 253; *see also* Uganda

Namibia 32, 40, 47, 153; borders 13; Caprivi Strip 13; consolidation of democracy in 249, 252, 253, 282; decolonisation 155, 162, 221–2; and Soviet Union 155, 162
Nasser, General Abdel 154
nation: definition 35
National Party, South Africa 162, 245
National Party of Nigeria (NPN) 77
National Resistance Army, Uganda 147, 222
National Resistance Movement (NRM), Uganda 147
nationalism: definition of 35–6
nationalism, African: definition and features of 36–7; ideological variations of 37–45; origins 16; precipitating decolonisation 34; and state and civil society relationship 45–48
NEPAD (New Partnership for Africa's Development) 280
neo-colonialism 5, 102–3, 186–8; charges of Chinese 168–9; Nkrumah's writing on 186; *see also* debt; structural adjustment programmes; underdevelopment; unequal exchange
neo-patrimonialism 116, 118–9, 120; definition of 127, 216, 218, 256; *see also* clientelism; patrimonialism; personal rule
New Partnership for Africa's Development (NEPAD) 280
New World Order 172, 278; cession of proxy wars during 162; British policy during 165–7; Bush announces 161–2; Chinese policy during 167–70; foreign policies towards Africa during 165–78; French policy during 164–5; political

conditionality during 163–4; strategically downgrading of Africa during 162–3; United States policy during 163, 172, 177–8
Ngouabi, Marien 39
Niger 13, 71, 80, 168, 247, 280, 283
Nigeria 3, 167–8, 226, 253, 255, 283; and Boko Haram 71, 79–80; and China 169; civil war 76; colonial origins 74; consolidation of 'tribes' in 74–5; corruption in Rural Electricity Board 217; economy 43, 169; First Republic 75–6; ethnicity and politics in 74–8; ethnic groups 74; execution of Saro-Wiwa 110; military coups 76, 77, 133–4, 135; military rule 76–7, 77–8, 140; military veto 255; peacekeeping forces 138, 163; religion and politics in 78–80; Second Republic 77; *shari'a* law in 78–9; Third Republic 78–9; Yoruba, origins of 75
Nkrumah, Kwame 136; advocacy of one-party state 110–11, 203; and neo-colonialism 186; subordination of judiciary 111; *see also* Ghana
Nkomo, Joshua 260–1
non-hegemonic states: pre-colonial 9–10; colonial 14; *see also* inverted states; quasi-states; warlord states
Norway 167
NPN (National Party of Nigeria) 77
NRM (National Resistance Movement), Uganda 147
Nyerere, Julius K. 87, 116, 161, 253; assessment of *ujamaa* 53; on multi-party democracy 111, 242–3; and nationalism 49; one-party state, advocacy of 37, 111; socialism, advocacy of 50–2, 112; *see also* Tanzania; *ujamaa*

OAU (Organisation of African Unity) 153, 280; agreement on boundaries 45–6, 47–8, 173
Obama, Barak 279
Obasanjo, Olusegun 77, 78, 79, 161, 253, 255; *see also* Nigeria
Obote, Milton 143–5; on ethnic balancing 65; *see also* Uganda
oil 13, 24, 207, 208, 214, 277, 278; China and 167–8, 169, 170; economic impact of price increase (1970s) 189; and Nigeria 74, 77, 78
Okoya, Pierino 145

one-party state 111–13, 273–4; flaws
   of 112–13; Ghana becomes 110–11;
   justifications for 111–12, Kenya and
   Tanzania, representation in 113–14,
   242–3; Nyerere on 111, 112, 242
OPEC (Organisation of Petroleum Exporting
   Countries) 189
Operation Turquoise 165
Opolot, Shaban 144
Organisation of African Unity (OAU) 153,
   280; agreement on boundaries 45–6,
   47–8, 173
Organisation of Petroleum Exporting
   Countries (OPEC) 189
Ossowski, Stanislaw 92

PAMSCAD (Programme of Action to
   Mitigate the Social Costs of Adjustment),
   Ghana 207
parallel markets 204–5, 220–1, state elites
   exploiting 226, 234–5, in Zaire 232,
   234–5; *see also* smuggling
parliament: loss of power to executives
   113–14; French 158, Kenyan 113–14,
   Zimbabwean 262
Parson, Jack 103
Parti Démocratique de la Côte d'Ivoire (PDCI)
   123, 124, 125
Patrick, Stewart 266
patrimonialism 115–6, 117; *see also*
   clientelism, personal rule; neo-
   patrimonialism
patronage *see* clientelism
patron–client relationship *see* clientelism
PDCI (*Parti Démocratique de la Côte d'Ivoire*)
   123, 124, 125
PDCs (Peoples' Defence Committees),
   Ghana 42
'peasantariat' 90–1, 102, 103
peasants 18, 25, 41, 49–50, 52–4, 87,
   89–91, 265; Botswana 102; definition of
   peasant 89; Tanzania 'uncaptured' 53
Peoples' Defence Committees (PDCs),
   Ghana 42
personal rule 115–18; characteristics of 116–
   18; in Côte d'Ivoire 122–5; Mobutu's
   118; *see also* clientelism
PNDC (Provisional National Defence
   Council), Ghana 204–5, 206–7
POLISARIO (Frente Popular para la
   Liberacion de Saguia el Hamra y Rio
   de Oro) 159

political culture: and consolidation of multi-
   party democracy 21, 112, 255–7, and
   military coups 136–7
populism 42–3
Portugal: colonisation of Africa 11; and
   decolonisation of Africa 32, 154–5, 222;
   military coup 3
Poulantzas, Nicos 92
privatisation 205–6; *see also* structural
   adjustment programmes
Programme of Action to Mitigate the
   Social Costs of Adjustment (PAMSCAD),
   Ghana 207
proletariat 38, 85–6, 91, 102
Provisional National Defence Council
   (PNDC), Ghana 204–5, 206–7
proxy wars 160–1; ending of 162
Putnam, Robert D. 31

'quasi-states' 172; *see also* non-hegemonic state

Rawlings, Jerry 42, 203, 204–7, 253
Ray, Olivier 276
Religion 41, 66–72; faiths practised on
   continent 66; as instrument of political
   mobilisation 71–2; and Nigerian politics
   78–80; strengthening civil society 66–9;
   see also churches; Islamist politics; mosques
Reno, William 226, 227
Reyntjens, Filip 235
Rhodesia 14, 32, 156, 158, 259; *see also*
   Zimbabwe
Rhodesia Front 260
riots 137, 196, 219; food 95, 246; religious
   in Nigeria 79
Robinson, Pearl 43
Rodney, Walter 186
Rosberg, Carl 116, 117, 118, 124
Rothchild, Donald 64, 77
RPF (Rwandan Patriotic Front) 165, 222
Rural Electricity Board of Nigeria 217
Russia 154; organised crime in 226; *see also*
   Soviet Union
Rwanda 14, 158, 166, 186; and France 165;
   genocide 61, 163; and regional conflict in
   central Africa 47, 153, 165, 235, 236
Rwandan Patriotic Front (RPF) 165, 222

SADC (Southern African Development
   Community) 153
Salisbury, Lord (Robert Cecil) 13
Sandbrook, Richard 118, 216, 248

Sankara, Captain Thomas 42
SAPs *see* structural adjustment programmes
Saro-Wiwa, Ken 110
Scandinavian countries 159, 164, 166, 167
scientific socialism 39–42; in Somalia 174
'Scramble for Africa' 11; Nyerere's second 161
second economy *see* parallel markets
Senegal 13, 159, 240, 282; religion and politics in 70
Senghor, Léopold: socialist thought of 37, 38, 87, 112
Severino, Jean-Michel 276
Seychelles 32, 253, 281
shadow economy *see* parallel markets
Shagari, Alhaji 77
Shanin, Teodor 89
Shari'a law 69–70; in Nigeria 78–9
Shari'a, the 70–1
Sierra Leone 153, 168, 195, 222, 253, 282; British intervention in (2000) 166; diamond sustained insurgency 166, warlord state 227
Simpson, Chris 229
Sklar, Richard 92
Slavery 9, 11, 17, 22, 62, 88
Smith, Ian 32, 158
smuggling 95, 204, 205, 221, 226, 227, 232, 241
social class *see* class, social
socialism: African 38–9; Marx on 85–6; Nyerere on 50–1; scientific 39–42; Soviet Union promotion of in Africa 154–5; and *ujamaa* 49–54
Somali National Movement 177
Somali Patriotic Movement 177
Somali people 173; politically fragmented 14, 23, 46
Somali Revolutionary Socialist Party 174
Somali Youth League 173
Somalia 283; and Al-Shabab 71; Barré's regime 174–77; and China 174, 175; colonial 173; and decolonisation 173; ethnicity within 173; hosting Islamist terrorist groups 70, 71; joins Arab League 175; military coup (1969) 174; pursuit of irredentism 14, 46, 175; multi-party democracy, failure of 174, 220, 224; rejects OAU principle of inviolable boundaries 45, 173; relationship with Kenya 23, 24, 178–9; relationship with Soviet Union 155, 174–5, 176; relationship with United States 156, 163,

174, 175–6, 178; and scientific socialism 39; state collapse 177; and United Nation's peacekeeping operation (1992) 177–8; relationship with Ethiopia 14, 70, 71, 153, 175, 183
Somaliland 14, 178
South Africa 3, 22, 92, 101, 122, 155, 169, 227, 253, 282; and Angola 155, 162; colonial 11, 14, 18; destabilising neighbours 46, 100, 153, 155, 222; liberation struggle 32, 35, 40, 153, 155, 162, 221–2; migrant labour in 18, 102; and multi-party elections 242, 245, 249; political influence of church 68, 247; and proletariat 86, 91; regional settlement (1989) 162; relationship with United States 158, 162; traditional leaders 94; *see also* African National Congress of South Africa
Southall, Aidan 62
Southern African Development Community (SADC) 153
South Sudan 45, 46, 47, 224, 254, 281, 283
South West Africa People's Organisation (SWAPO) 155
sovereignty: definition of 152; and international relations 152; *see also* inverted states; neo-colonialism; 'quasi-states'
Soviet Union 112, 245; and African scientific socialist regimes 41; and African socialist regimes 38, 39; and Angola 161, 162; Cold War relations with Africa 154–5; seeking military bases 155, 174; and Somali–Ethiopia dispute 46, 175, 176; and Somalia 174–7; supply of arms to Africa 155, 161, 176
Standard and Poor 208
state: centralisation of 39, 109–115, 274, 218–19; and crisis of legitimacy 214–224; civil society's disengagement from 219–222, 227–9, 232–3; collapse 222–4; definition 6; formation of as a result of colonialism 11–12; elites, colonial 15–16, 93, 101; inverted 109, 225, 226, 227, 229, 244, 275; marketing boards marketing boards 39, 204, 215, 220, 230, 232; need for separation from ruling party, as prerequisite for consolidation of democracy 252–4; non-hegemonic states 9–10, 14; one-party 111–14, 242–3, 273–4; pre-colonial 8–10; survival strategies 224–5; vampire 219; warlord 226–7; *see also* centralisation of the state

Stevens, Siaka 195

Straw, Jack 166

street traders 95, 220–1

structural adjustment programmes (SAPs) 54, 77, 190–6 , 275; agricultural policy under 191; basic principles of 190–2; economic impact 192–3; and Ghana 205–7; political impact 195–6, 202, 218, 243, 246; public sector reform under 191–2; social impact 79, 193–5; trade policy under 191–2; and Zimbabwe 262–3

subsidies, food 193, 204; removal of state 194–5, 196, 206–7; in Zambia 189, 194; in Zimbabwe 262, 263

SucDen 187

Sudan 47, 153, 222, 283; Alagiah's reporting of famine (1998) 2; and China 169–70; export of oil 13, 168; Darfur 169–70, 280; independence 32; religion 67, 70; South Sudan's secession 46, 47; Western concerns over harbouring Islamist terrorists 70, 163

Sudan People's Liberation Army 46

SWAPO (South West Africa People's Organisation), Namibia 155

Swaziland 14, 94

Sweden 167

Syndicat des Chefs Coutumiers, Côte d'Ivoire 123

Taliban 70, 71

Tandja, Mamadou 280

Tanganikan African National Union (TANU) 242

Tanganyika 45, 49, 158; *see also* Tanzania

TANU (Tanganikan African National Union) 242

Tanzania 135; and Arusha Declaration 51–2, 53; and China 155–6, 167; colonial border 23; ethnic groups within 14, 49; invasion of Uganda (1979) 46, 147; military spending 144–5; and multi-party competition 242–3, 253; nationalism, nature of 49–50; and one-party state 111, 112, 113; second economy 221; and structural adjustment 54, 190; TAZARA railway 155–6; *ujamaa* 50–4; union of Zanzibar and Tanganyika 45; United Kingdom aid 166; victim of terrorism 70, 163

Taylor, Ian 168

TAZARA railway 155–6

TNCs (trans-national corporations) 41, 78, 95, 152, 277–8; and Botswana 101–2;

and China 167–8, 170; failure to invest in structural adjustment era 193, 238; and Ghana 205–6; warlord states, cooperation with 226–7; and Zaire 234, 235

Togo, 252; and China 169; colonial 11; hosting French military base 159; suspension of French development aid 164;

Touré, Ahmed Sékou: socialist thought of 38, 87, 111, 154

trade unions 4, 37, 66, 86, 258; agent of multi-party democracy 91, 246, 247, 258; agent of decolonisation 25, 273; co-optation of 99, 110, 123; in Zambia 247; in Zimbabwe 264

traditional leaders 15, 65, 89, 94, 99, 100–1; Côte d'Ivoire 123; Ghana 111

transnational corporations (TNCs) 41, 78, 95, 152, 277–8; and Botswana 101–2; and China 167–8, 170; failure to invest in structural adjustment era 193, 238; and Ghana 205–6; warlord states, cooperation with 226–7; and Zaire 234, 235

Transparency International 281

'tribes' *see* ethnicity

Tshisekedi, Etienne 256

Tsvangirai, Morgan 264, 266, 267

Tunisia 32, 116, 248, 282

Tutsi 61, 235

Tutu, Desmond 247

Twain, Mark 224

Uganda 168, 222, 278, 282; and Al-Shabab 71; Amin's regime 115, 118, 144–7; border 23; and Buganda 143; centralisation of the state 143–4; colonisation 143; decolonisation 16, 143, 158; intervention in Central Africa 47, 236 invasion of by Tanzania (1979) 46, 147, 153; military coup (1971) 144; military coup (1985) 147; and resistance to multi-party democracy 147, 252, 253; NRM insurgency 147, 222, 224; Obote's regimes 65, 143–5, 147; Museveni's regime 42, 147, 224, 252, 253; second economy 221; UK assistance in ending army mutiny 158; UK aid 166

Uganda National Congress 16

Uganda People's Congress (UPC) 143–4

ujamaa 37, 50–4; assessment of 54; failure to capture peasantry 53–4; nature of 51–2; as a strain of African socialism 50–1; viligisation programme 52–3

underdevelopment 16–19, 273; critics of 19; export of surplus 18; failure to invest in human resources 19; and an international bourgeoisie 95–6; in Kenya 24; of labour 17–8; monocrop economies 18; nature of 16–17; one-party state, as a justification of 112; as precursor to neo-colonialism 185–6; *see also* neo-colonialism; structural adjustment programmes; unequal exchange
unequal exchange: and China 169–70, nature of 186–8, and structural adjustment 192–3, 203, 208
UNICEF 190
Union des Syndicats des Travailleurs du Niger (USTN) 247
Union of Soviet Socialist Republics (USSR) *see* Soviet Union
UNITA (União Nacional para a Independência Total de Angola) 155, 161, 162, 222; rejection of (1992) election result 256
United Arab Emirates 167
United National Independence Party (UNIP), Zambia 247, 252
United Nations 71, 126, 152, 165, 167, 187; Chinese veto 170; and Congo civil war (1960) 46, 229; Economic Commission on Africa 192; report on resource exploitation in DRC (2001) 236; and Somalia (1992) 163, 177–8
United Somali Congress 177
United Kingdom 3, 101, 152; aid allocation 166; colonial rule of 25, 74, 100; 143; colonisation of Africa 11, 23–4, 146, 173; and debt relief 166–7; and decolonisation 32, 143; foreign relations with Africa during Cold War 154, 158, 163, 176; foreign relations with Africa during New World Order 165–7; and Sierra Leone 166; and Zimbabwe 32, 259, 264
United States of America 34, 66, 59, 60, 61, 111, 113, 183, 189, 193, 279; arms shipments to Africa 161, 174, 175; foreign relations with Africa during Cold War 138, 154, 155, 156–8; foreign relations with Africa during New World Order 161, 162, 163, 164, 172, 245–6; and Somalia 163, 174, 175–6, 177–8
UPC (Uganda People's Congress) 143–4
USA *see* United States of America

USSR (Union of Soviet Socialist Republics) *see* Soviet Union
USTN (*Union des Syndicats des Travailleurs du Niger*) 247

vampire state 219, 226; Mobutu's 229–236
veto coup 135
Victoria, Queen 23

warlords 109, 147, 177, 178, 224, 226–7
warlord states 226–7, 244, 275
Warren, Bill 19
Washington, George 111
Weber, Max: on legal–rational institutions 5, 109, 115, 217; on legitimacy 109, 118, 130; on patrimonial rule 117; on the state and its monopoly of violence 4; on social class 89, 92; on sovereignty 233–4
Western Sahara 46, 156, 159
Western Somali Liberation Front 175
Wilhelm II, Kaiser 23
Wiseman, John 249, 250
Worker's Banner (Ghana) 42
Workers' Party of Ethiopia 41
World Bank 147, 168, 190, 193, 193, 195, 196, 205, 206, 262, 277, 278; Berg Report (1981) 191, 192; *see also* International Monetary Fund; international financial institutions

Young, Crawford 15, 43, 62
Yoruba 74, 75, 76; colonial consolidation of 75
Yusuf, Mohammed 80

Zaire 205, 260; agriculture policy 230–1; and Angola 153, 159; centralisation of the state 231–2; collapse of state 47, 235; corruption in 231; crisis of accumulation 230–1; crisis of governance 231–3; disengagement from state by citizens 232–3; and FAZA 234–5; foreign business in 94, 234; and France 158, 159, 164, 165, 169; import substitution policy 230; natural resources 229; relations with United States 156, 161, 163, 167, 245; second economy 232, 234–5; survival strategies of state elite 233–4; *see also* Congo-Kinshasa; Democratic Republic of the Congo; Mobutu Sese Seko
Zambia 18, 116, 254; and China 155–6, 167; corruption in 234, 251; debt crisis

189–90; economic decline 189–90; manipulation of constitution 252; and multi-party democracy 242, 247, 250, 252; removal of state subsidies 194, 195; and structural adjustment 190, 193–5; trade union activity 91, 247

Zambian Congress of Trade Unions (ZCTU) 247

ZANU-PF *see* Zimbabwe African National Union – Patriotic Front

Zanzibar 23, 45, 49, 49, 54; *see also* Tanzania

ZAPU (Zimbabwe African People's Union) 155, 259–61; *see also* Zimbabwe

ZCTU (Zambian Congress of Trade Unions) 247

Zimbabwe 19, 40, 283; and China 167, 168, 170; centralisation of the state 260–2; corruption in 217; economic collapse 262–3, 265; electoral violence

(2002–2008) 266; General Election (2013) 267; independence 32, 90, 155, 221–2; intervention in Central Africa 47, 153; land reform 92, 263–4; Matabeleland, violence in (1982–5) 261; opposition, lack of electoral in 1980s and 1990s 249; opposition, development of (after 1997) 264–7; power sharing agreement (2008) 266–7, 282; referendum (2006) 264–5; relations with other African states 153, 280; and structural adjustment 194, 262–3; subjugation of ZANU 260–1; war 'veterans' 263–4, 265; *see also* Rhodesia

Zimbabwe African National Union – Patriotic Front (ZANU-PF) 249, 259–267; *see also* Zimbabwe

Zimbabwe African People's Union (ZAPU) 155, 259–61; *see also* Zimbabwe

Zolberg, Aristide 38